The
XML
Handbook™

ISBN 0-13-081152-1

90000

9 780130 811523

The Charles F. Goldfarb Series on Open Information Management

"Open Information Management" (OIM) means managing information so that it is open to processing by any program, not just the program that created it. That extends even to application programs not conceived of at the time the information was created.

OIM is based on the principle of data independence: data should be stored in computers in non-proprietary, genuinely standardized representations. And that applies even when the data is the content of a document. Its representation should distinguish the innate information from the proprietary codes of document processing programs and the artifacts of particular presentation styles.

Business data bases—which rigorously separate the real data from the input forms and output reports—achieved data independence decades ago. But documents, unlike business data, have historically been created in the context of a particular output presentation style. So for document data, independence was largely unachievable until recently.

That is doubly unfortunate. It is unfortunate because documents are a far more significant repository of humanity's information. And documents can contain significantly richer information structures than data bases.

It is also unfortunate because the need for OIM of documents is greater now than ever. The demands of "repurposing" require that information be deliverable in multiple formats: paper-based, online, multimedia, hypermedia. And information must now be delivered through multiple channels: traditional bookstores and libraries, the World Wide Web, corporate intranets and extranets. In the latter modes, what starts as data base data may become a document for browsing, but then may need to be reused by the reader as data.

Fortunately, in the past ten years a technology has emerged that extends to documents the data base's capacity for data independence. And it does so without the data base's restrictions on structural freedom. That technology is the "Standard Generalized Markup Language" (SGML), an official International Standard (ISO 8879) that has been adopted by the world's largest producers of documents and by the World Wide Web.

With SGML, organizations in government, aerospace, airlines, automotive, electronics, computers, and publishing (to name a few) have freed their documents from hostage relationships to processing software. SGML coexists with graphics, multimedia and other data standards needed for OIM and acts as the framework that relates objects in the other formats to one another and to SGML documents.

The World Wide Web's HTML and XML are both based on SGML. HTML is a particular, though very general, application of SGML, like those for the above industries. There is a limited set of markup tags that can be used with HTML. XML, in contrast, is a simplified subset of SGML facilities that, like full SGML, can be used with any set of tags. You can literally create your own markup language with XML.

As the enabling standard for OIM of documents, the SGML family of standards necessarily plays a leading role in this series. We provide tutorials on SGML, XML, and other key standards and the techniques for applying them. Our books vary in technical intensity from programming techniques for software developers to the business justification of OIM for enterprise executives. We share the practical experience of organizations and individuals who have applied the techniques of OIM in environments ranging from immense industrial publishing projects to websites of all sizes.

Our authors are expert practitioners in their subject matter, not writers hired to cover a "hot" topic. They bring insight and understanding that can only come from real-world experience. Moreover, they practice what they preach about standardization. Their books share a common standards-based vocabulary. In this way, knowledge gained from one book in the series is directly applicable when reading another, or the standards themselves. This is just one of the ways in which we strive for the utmost technical accuracy and consistency with the OIM standards.

And we also strive for a sense of excitement and fun. After all, the challenge of OIM—preserving information from the ravages of technology while exploiting its benefits—is one of the great intellectual adventures of our age. I'm sure you'll find this series to be a knowledgable and reliable guide on that adventure.

About the Series Editor

Dr. Charles F. Goldfarb invented the SGML language in 1974 and later led the team that developed it into the International Standard on which both HTML and XML are based. He serves as editor of the Standard (ISO 8879) and as a consultant to developers of SGML and XML applications and products. He is based in Saratoga, CA.

About the Series Logo

The rebus is an ancient literary tradition, dating from 16th century Picardy, and is especially appropriate to a series involving fine distinctions between things and the words that describe them. For the logo, Andrew Goldfarb incorporated a rebus of the series name within a stylized SGML/XML comment declaration.

The Charles F. Goldfarb Series on Open Information Management

As XML is a subset of SGML, the Series List is categorized to show the degree to which a title applies to XML. "XML Titles" are those that discuss XML explicitly and may also cover full SGML. "SGML Titles" do not mention XML per se, but the principles covered may apply to XML.

XML Titles

Goldfarb, Pepper, and Ensign
■ SGML Buyer's Guide™: Choosing the Right XML and SGML Products and Services

Megginson
■ Structuring XML Documents

Leventhal, Lewis, and Fuchs
■ Designing XML Internet Applications

Goldfarb and Prescod
■ The XML Handbook™

Jelliffe
■ The XML and SGML Cookbook: Recipes for Structured Information

SGML Titles

Turner, Douglass, and Turner
■ ReadMe.1st: SGML for Writers and Editors

Donovan
■ Industrial-Strength SGML: An Introduction to Enterprise Publishing

Ensign
■ SGML: The Billion Dollar Secret

Rubinsky and Maloney
■ SGML on the Web: Small Steps Beyond HTML

McGrath
■ ParseMe.1st: SGML for Software Developers

DuCharme
■ SGML CD

The XML Handbook™

- Charles F. Goldfarb
- Paul Prescod

Prentice Hall PTR, Upper Saddle River, NJ 07458
http://www.phptr.com

Library of Congress Cataloging-in-Publication Data

```
Goldfarb, Charles F.
    XML handbook / Charles F. Goldfarb, Paul Prescod.
      p. cm. -- (Charles F. Goldfarb series on open information
  management)
    Includes index.
    ISBN 0-13-081152-1 (pbk. : alk. paper)
    1. XML (Document markup language)  I. Prescod, Paul.  II. Title.
  III. Series.
  QA76.76.H92G65  1998
  005.7'2--dc21                                98-16708
                                              CIP
```

Editorial/Production Supervision: *Patti Guerrieri*
Acquisitions Editor: *Mark L. Taub*
Editorial Assistant: *Audri Bazlan*
Marketing Manager: *Dan Rush*
Manufacturing Manager: *Alexis R. Heydt*
Cover Design: *Anthony Gemmellaro*
Cover Design Direction: *Jerry Votta*
Series Design: *Gail Cocker-Bogusz*

 © 1998 Prentice Hall PTR
Prentice-Hall, Inc.
A Simon & Schuster Company
Upper Saddle River, NJ 07458

Prentice Hall books are widely used by corporations and government agencies for training, marketing, and resale.

The publisher offers discounts on this book when ordered in bulk quantities. For more information, contact: Corporate Sales Department, Phone: 800-382-3419; Fax: 201-236-7141; E-mail: corpsales@prenhall.com; or write: Prentice Hall PTR, Corp. Sales Dept., One Lake Street, Upper Saddle River, NJ 07458.

Printed in the United States of America

10 9 8 7 6 5 4 3 2

ISBN 0-13-081152-1

Prentice-Hall International (UK) Limited, London
Prentice-Hall of Australia Pty. Limited, Sydney
Prentice-Hall Canada Inc., Toronto
Prentice-Hall Hispanoamericana, S.A., Mexico
Prentice-Hall of India Private Limited, New Delhi
Prentice-Hall of Japan, Inc., Tokyo
Simon & Schuster Asia Pte. Ltd., Singapore
Editora Prentice-Hall do Brasil, Ltda., Rio de Janeiro

To Linda – With love, awe, and gratitude.

Charles F. Goldfarb

For Lilia – Your support makes it possible and
your love makes it worthwhile.

Paul Prescod

Contents

▌Part Five   The Technology of XML   423

Chapter 31 **XML basics**   424

Foreword

XML Everywhere

When HTML came onto the scene it sparked a publishing phenomenon. Ordinary people everywhere began to publish documents on the Web. Presentation on the Web became a topic of conversation not just within the computer industry, but within coffeehouses. Overnight, it seemed as though everyone had a Web page.

I see the same phenomenon happening today with XML. Where data was once a mysterious binary blob, it has now become something ordinary people can read and author because it's text. With XML, ordinary people have the ability to craft their own data, the ability to shape and control data. The significance of this shift is difficult to overstate, for not only does it mean that more people can access data, but that there will undoubtedly be more data to access. We are on the verge of a data explosion. One ignited by XML.

By infusing the Web with data, XML makes the Web a better place for people to interact, to do business. XML allows us to do more precise searches, deliver software components, describe such things as collections of Web pages and electronic commerce transactions, and much more. XML is changing not only the way we think about data, but the way we think about the Web.

And by doing so, it's changing the way we think about the traditional desktop application. I have already witnessed the impact of XML on all types of applications from word processors and spreadsheets to database managers and email. More and more, such applications are reaching out to the Web, tapping into the power of the Web, and it is XML that is enabling them to do so. Gone are the days of the isolated, incompatible application. Here are the days of universal access and shared data.

I joined Microsoft in the summer of 1996 with great faith in the Standard Generalized Markup Language (SGML) and a dream that its potential might one day be realized. As soon as I arrived at Microsoft, Jon Bosak of Sun Microsystems and I began discussing the possibility of creating an XML standard. Jon shared my enthusiasm for a markup language such as XML, understanding what it could mean to Web communication.

My goal in designing an XML standard was to produce a very simple markup language with as few abstractions as possible. Microsoft's success is due in no small part to its ability to develop products with mass-market appeal. It is this mass-market appeal that I wanted to bring to XML. Together with Jon and other long-time friends from the SGML world, C.M. Sperberg-McQueen, James Clark, Tim Bray, Steve DeRose, Eve Maler, Eliot Kimber, Dave Hollander, Makoto Murata, and Peter Sharpe, I co-designed the XML specification at the World Wide Web Consortium (W3C). This specification, I believe, reflects my original goals.

It was truly an exciting time. For years, we had all been part of a maverick band of text markup enthusiasts, singing its praises every chance we had, and before us was an opportunity to bring XML into the mainstream, maybe even into the operating system. At last, we were getting our chance to tell the World of the thing we had been so crazy about for all this time.

By the fall of 1996, many groups inside Microsoft, including Office, the Site Server Electronic Commerce Edition, the Data Access Group, to cite a few, were searching for an open format to enable interoperability on the Web. It was then that I began working with the managers of Internet Explorer 4, with the passionate Adam Bosworth, with Andrew Layman, with Thomas Reardon, to define the Channel Definition Format (CDF). CDF, the first major application of XML on the Web, became an immediate and incredible success, and XML started catching on like wildfire across the Web.

I remember those weeks and months that followed as a time where it seemed that everyday another new group within Microsoft began coding applications using XML. Developers, left and right, were turning on to XML. They frenetically began to develop applications using XML, because XML gave them what they wanted: an easy-to-parse syntax for representing data. This flurry of activity was so great that by October of 1997, almost a year after my arrival at Microsoft, Chairman Bill Gates announced XML as "a breakthrough technology." Since that time we've never looked back.

This book is an excellent starting point where you can learn and experiment with XML. As the inventor of SGML, Dr. Charles F. Goldfarb is one of the most respected authorities on structured information. Charles has had a very direct influence on XML, as XML is a true subset of SGML, and he clearly understands the impact that XML will have on the world of data-driven, Web-based applications.

Charles and I share a common vision, that the most valuable asset for the user or for a corporation, namely the data, can be openly represented in a simple, flexible, and human-readable form. That it can easily travel from server to server, from server to client, and from application to application, fostering universal communication with anyone, anywhere. This vision can now be realized through XML.

Enjoy the book!

Redmond, April 24, 1988

Jean Paoli

Product Unit Manager, XML Technologies

Microsoft Corporation

Co-editor of the XML Specification

Preface

The World Wide Web is undergoing a radical change that will introduce wonderful services for users and amazing new opportunities for Web site developers and businesses.

HTML – the HyperText Markup Language – made the Web the world's library. Now its sibling, XML – the Extensible Markup Language – has begun to make the Web the world's commercial and financial hub. XML has just been approved as a W3C Recommendation, and already there are millions of XML files out there, with more coming online every day.

You can see why by comparing XML and HTML. Both are based on SGML – the International Standard for structured information – but look at the difference:

In HTML:

```
<p>P200 Laptop
<br>Friendly Computer Shop
<br>$1438
```

In XML:

```
<product>
<model>P200 Laptop</model>
<dealer>Friendly Computer Shop</dealer>
<price>$1438</price>
</product>
```

Both of these may appear the same in your browser, but the XML data is *smart* data. HTML tells how the data should *look*, but XML tells you what it *means*.

With XML, your browser knows there is a product, and it knows the model, dealer, and price. From a group of these it can show you the cheapest product or closest dealer without going back to the server.

Unlike HTML, with XML you create your own tags, so they describe exactly what you need to know. Because of that, your client-side applications can access data sources anywhere on the Web, in any format. New "middle-tier" servers sit between the data sources and the client, translating everything into your own task-specific XML.

But XML data isn't just smart data, it's also a smart document. That means when you display the information, the model name can be a different font from the dealer name, and the lowest price can be highlighted in green. Unlike HTML, where text is just text to be rendered in a uniform way, with XML text is smart, so it can control the rendition.

And you don't have to decide whether your information is data or documents; in XML, it is always both at once. You can do data processing or document processing or both at the same time.

With that kind of flexibility, it's no wonder that we're starting to see a Brave New Web of smart, structured information. Your broker sends your account data to Quicken using XML. Your "push" technology channel definitions are in XML. Everything from math to multimedia, chemistry to CommerceNet, is using XML or is preparing to start.

You should be too!

Welcome to the Brave New XML Web.

What about SGML?

This book is about XML. You won't find feature comparisons to SGML, or footnotes with nerdy observations like "the XML empty-element tag does not contradict the rule that every element has a start-tag and an end-tag because, in SGML terms, it is actually a start-tag followed immediately by a null end-tag".[1]

Nevertheless, for readers who use SGML, it is worth addressing the question of how XML and SGML relate. There has been a lot of speculation about this.

---

1. Well, yes, I did just make that nerdy observation, but it wasn't a footnote, was it?

Some claim that XML will replace SGML because there will be so much free and low-cost software. Others assert that XML users, like HTML users before them, will discover that they need more of SGML and will eventually migrate to the full standard.

Both assertions are nonsense ... XML and SGML don't even compete.

XML is a simplified subset of SGML. The subsetting was optimized for the Web environment, which implies data-processing-oriented (rather than publishing-oriented), short life-span (in fact, usually dynamically-generated) information. The vast majority of XML documents will be created by computer programs and processed by other programs, then destroyed. Humans will never see them.

Eliot Kimber, a member of both the XML and SGML standards committees, says:

> There are certain use domains for which XML is simply not sufficient and where you need the additional features of SGML. These applications tend to be very large scale and of long term; e.g., aircraft maintenance information, government regulations, power plant documentation, etc.

> Any one of them might involve a larger volume of information than the entire use of XML on the Web. A single model of commercial aircraft, for example, requires some four million unique pages of documentation that must be revised and republished quarterly. Multiply that by the number of models produced by companies like Airbus and Boeing and you get a feel for the scale involved.

I invented SGML, I'm proud of it, and I'm awed that such a staggering volume of the world's mission-critical information is represented in it.

I'm also proud of XML. I'm proud of my friend Jon Bosak who made it happen, and I'm excited that the World Wide Web is becoming XML-based.

If you are new to XML, don't worry about any of this. All you need to know is that the XML subset of SGML has been in use for a decade or more, so you can trust it.

I am writing this the day after a meeting of the ISO committee that develops the SGML standard. We had the largest attendance in our 20-year history at that meeting. Interest in SGML has never been higher.

You should share that interest if you produce documents on the scale of an Airbus or Boeing. For the rest of us, there's XML.

About our sponsors

With all the buzz surrounding a hot technology like XML, it can be tough for a newcomer to distinguish the solid projects and realistic applications from the fluff and the fantasies. Our solution was to seek out companies with real products and realistic applications and tell their stories in sufficient detail that readers can see for themselves what is believable.

The application chapters are about what can be done with XML, extrapolating from actual experience with one or more users or prototype implementations. The case studies describe the XML experiences of specific named enterprises.

Some applications and case studies were done with full SGML before XML had a formal existence, but are within XML's capabilities. These are described as having been done with XML. Part of the proof of XML's viability is that people have used its core functions for over a decade.

The primary purpose of the tool chapters is to provide the vicarious experience of using a variety of XML tools without the effort of obtaining evaluation copies and installing them. They also provide useful information about uses and benefits of XML in general, which supplements the application-oriented discussions in the earlier parts of the book.

There are also two sponsored chapters on new XML-related technologies.

All sponsored chapters are identified with the name of the sponsor, and sometimes with the names of the experts who prepared the original text. All of the chapters were edited by me, sometimes extensively, in order to integrate them into the book. The editing objectives were to establish consistency of terminology and style, and to eliminate unnecessary duplication among the chapters. I believe the result was faithful to the intentions of the expert preparers with regard to bringing out the important characteristics of their applications and products.

The sponsorship program was organized by Linda Burman, the president of L. A. Burman Associates, a consulting company that provides marketing and business development services to the XML and SGML industries.

We are grateful to our sponsors just as we are grateful to you, our readers. Both of you together make it possible for the *XML Handbook* to exist. In the interests of everyone, we make our own editorial decisions and we don't recommend or endorse any product or service offerings over any others.

Our fourteen sponsors are:

- Adobe Systems Incorporated, http://www.adobe.com
- ArborText, Inc., http://www.arbortext.com
- Chrystal Software, http://www.chrystal.com
- Frank Russell Company Advanced Technology Labs, http://www.russell.com
- Inso Corporation, http://www.inso.com
- Interleaf, Inc., http://www.interleaf.com
- ISOGEN International, http://www.isogen.com
- Junglee Corporation, http://www.junglee.com
- Microsoft Corporation, http://www.microsoft.com
- Microstar Software Ltd., http://www.microstar.com
- POET Corporation, http://www.poet.com
- SoftQuad Inc., http://www.sq.com
- Texcel International, http://www.texcel.com
- webMethods, http://www.webmethods.com

Acknowledgments

The principal acknowledgment in a book of this nature has to be to the people who created the subject matter. In this case, I take special pleasure in the fact that all of them are friends and colleagues of long standing in the SGML community.

Tim Bray and C. Michael Sperberg-McQueen were the original editors of the XML specification, later joined by Jean Paoli. Dan Connolly put the project on the W3C "todo list" and shepherded it through the approval process.

But all of them agree that, if a single person is to be thanked for XML, it is Jon Bosak. Jon not only sparked the original ideas and recruited the team, but organized and chairs the W3C XML Working Group.

As Tim put it: "Without Jon, XML wouldn't have happened. He was the prime mover."

Regarding the content of the book, Paul and I would like to thank Jean Paoli, Eliot Kimber, David Siegel, Andy Goldfarb, Lars Marius Garshol, and Steve Newcomb for contributing great material; Bryan Bell, inventor of MIDI and document system architect extraordinaire, for his advice and support; Steve Pepper and Bob DuCharme for talent-spotting and Richard Lander for his insights into XSL.

We also thank Lilia Prescod, Thea Prescod, and Linda Goldfarb for serving as our useability test laboratory. That means they read lots of chapters and complained until we made them clear enough.

Prentice Hall PTR uses Adobe FrameMaker to compose the books in my series. We thank Lani Hajagos of Adobe for providing Paul and me with copies.

Paul and I designed, and Paul implemented, an SGML-based production system for the book. It uses James Clark's Jade DSSSL processor, FrameMaker+SGML, and some ingenious FrameMaker plug-ins designed and implemented by Doug Yagaloff of Caxton, Inc. We thank Doug, and also Randy Kelley, for their wizard-level FrameMaker consulting advice.

But a great production system is nothing without a great Production Editor. We were fortunate to have Patti Guerrieri, who epitomizes grace – and skill – under fire. She coped with an untested system and a book that doubled in size, and still met the deadline.

This was my second project in which Linda Burman served as marketing consultant. I thank her – again – for her sage counsel and always cheerful encouragement.

My personal thanks, also, to Mark Taub, now an Editor-in-Chief at Prentice Hall PTR, for his help, encouragement, and management of the project.

As the senior author, I gave myself the preface to write. I'm senior because Paul's folks were conceiving him about the same time that I was conceiving SGML. (In return, Paul got to write the history chapter, because for him it really is history.)

This gives me the opportunity to thank Paul publicly for the tremendous reservoir of talent, energy, and good humor that he brought to the project. The book benefitted not just from his XML knowledge and fine writing skills, but from his expertise in SGML, Jade, and FrameMaker that enabled us to automate the production of the book (with the previously acknowledged help from our friends).

Thanks, Paul.

Charles F. Goldfarb
Saratoga, CA
May 15, 1998

Part One

- The Brave New Web
- Data and documents
- Structured information
- XML concepts
- XML in the real world

The Who, What, and Why of XML

Why XML?

Many of the most influential companies in the software industry are promoting XML as the next step in the Web's evolution. How can they be so confident about something so new? More important: how can *you* be sure that your time invested in learning and using XML will be profitable?

We can all safely bet on XML because the central ideas in this new technology are in fact very old and have been proven correct across several decades and thousands of projects. The easiest way to understand these ideas is to go back to their source, the *Standard Generalized Markup Language* (SGML).

XML is, in fact, a streamlined subset of SGML, so SGML's track record is XML's as well.

And if your interest is in moving data from Web sites to a browser or a spreadsheet, stay with us. All of this is interconnected and extremely relevant. For the amazing truth about XML is that with it, data processing and document processing are the same thing! If you understand where it all comes from, you'll understand where it – and the Web – are going.

1.1 | Text formatters and SGML

XML comes from a rich history of text processing systems. *Text processing* is the subdiscipline of *computer science* dedicated to creating computer systems that can automate parts of the document creation and publishing process. Text processing software includes simple word processors, advanced news item databases, hypertext document presentation systems and other publishing tools.

The first wave of automated text processing was computer typesetting. Authors would type in a document and describe how they would like it to be formatted. The computer would print out a document with the described text and formatting.

We call the file format that contained the mix of the actual data of the document, plus the description of the desired format, a *rendition*. Some well-known rendition notations include *troff*, *Rich Text Format* (*RTF*), and *LaTeX*.

The system would convert the rendition into something physically perceivable to a human being – a *presentation*. The presentation medium was historically paper, but eventually electronic display.

Typesetting systems sped up the process of publishing documents and evolved into what we now know as desktop publishing. Newer programs like *Microsoft Word* and *Adobe Pagemaker* still work with renditions, but they give authors a nicer interface to manipulate them. The user interface to the rendition (the file with formatting codes in it) is designed to look like the presentation (the finished paper product). We call this *What You See Is What You Get* (*WYSIWYG*) publishing. Since a rendition merely describes a presentation, it makes sense for the user interface to reflect the end-product.

1.1.1 *Formatting markup*

The form of typesetting notation that predates WYSIWYG (and is still in use today) is called *formatting markup*. Consider an analogy: you might submit a manuscript to a human typesetter for publication. Imagine it had no formatting, not even paragraphs or different fonts, but rather was a single continuous paragraph that was "marked up" with written instructions for how it should be formatted. You could write very precise instructions for layout: "Move this word over two inches. Bold it. Move the next work beside it. Move the next word underneath it. Bold it. Start a new line here." and so forth.

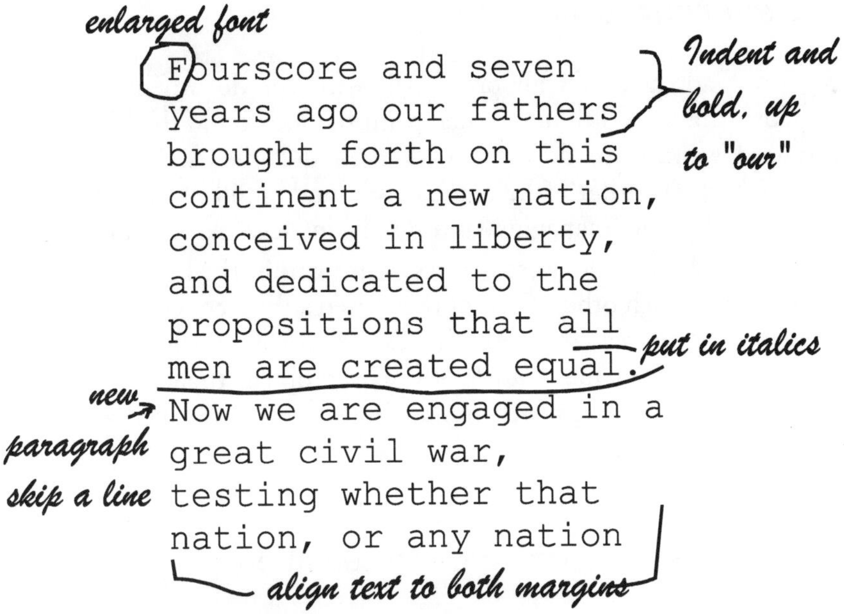

enlarged font

> Fourscore and seven years ago our fathers brought forth on this continent a new nation, conceived in liberty, and dedicated to the propositions that all men are created equal. Now we are engaged in a great civil war, testing whether that nation, or any nation

Indent and bold, up to "our"

put in italics

new paragraph

skip a line

align text to both margins

Figure 1-1   A manuscript "marked up" by hand

Formatting markup is very much the same. We "circle" text with instructions called *tags* or *codes* (depending on the particular formatting markup language). Here is an example of markup in one popular formatting markup language called LaTeX.

Example 1-1. A document with formatting markup

This is a marked up document. It contains words that are {\it italicized}, {\bf bold faced}, {\small small} and {\large large}.

In this markup language, the curly braces describe the extent of the formatting. So the italics started with the "\it" command extend until the end of the word "italicized". Because the markup uses only ordinary characters on typical keyboards, it can be created using existing text editors instead of special word processors (those came later).

1.1.2 *Generalized markup*

This process is adequate if your only goal is to type documents into the computer, describe a rendition and then print them. Around the late sixties, people started wanting to do more with their documents. In particular, IBM asked Charles Goldfarb (the name may sound familiar) to build a system for storing, finding, managing, and publishing legal documents.

Goldfarb found that there were many systems within IBM that could not communicate with each other. Each of them used a different command language. They could not read each other's files, just as you may have had trouble loading WordPerfect files into Word. The problem then, as now, was that they all had a different *representation* (sometimes also called a *file format*) for the information.

1.1.2.1 Common document representation

In the late sixties, Goldfarb and two other IBM researchers, Ed Mosher and Ray Lorie, set out to solve this problem. The team recognized three important facts. First, the programs needed to support a common document representation.

That part is easy to understand. Tools cannot work together if they do not speak the same language. As an analogy, consider the popularity of Latin terms in describing chemical and legal concepts and categories. To a certain extent, chemists and lawyers have chosen Latin as a common language for their fields. It made sense in the text processing context that the common language should be some form of markup language, because markup was well understood and very compatible with existing text editors and operating systems.

1.1.2.2 Customized document types

Second, the three realized that the common format should be *specific* to legal documents.

This is a little more subtle to grasp, but vital to understanding XML. The team could have invented a simple language, perhaps similar to the representation of a standard word processor, but that representation would not have allowed the sophisticated processing that was required. Lawyers and scientists both use Latin, but they do not use the same terminology. Rather they use Latin words as building blocks to create domain specific vocabularies (e.g. "habeas corpus", "ferruginous"). These domain specific vocabularies are even more important when we are describing documents to computers.

Computers are dumb

Usually we take for granted that computers are not very good at working with text and documents. We would never, for instance, ask a computer to search our hard disk and return a document that was a "letter" document, that was to "Martha" and that was about "John Smith's will". Even though this example seems much simpler than something a lawyer or chemist would run into, the fundamental problems are the same.

Most people recognize that the computer is completely incapable of understanding the concepts of "letter", "Martha" or "a will". Instead we might tell it to search for those words, and hope that we had included them all in the document. But what would happen if the system that we wanted to search was massive? It might turn up hundreds of unrelated documents. It might return documents that contained strings like "Martha, will you please write me a letter and tell me how John is doing?"

The fundamental problem is that the computer does not in any way understand the text. The solution is to teach the computer as much about the document as possible. Of course the computer will not understand the text in any real sense, but it can pretend to, in the same way that it pretends to understand simple data or decimal numbers[1]. We can make this possible by reducing the complexity of the document to a few structural *elements* chosen from a common vocabulary.

But computers can be trained

Once we "teach" computers about documents, we can also program them to do things they would not have been able to otherwise. Using their new

---

1. We hope we haven't disillusioned anyone here. Computers may seem to know everything about math, but it is all a ruse. As far as they are concerned, they are only manipulating zeros and ones.

"understanding" they can help us to navigate through large documents, organize them, and automatically format the documents for publication in many different media, such as hypertext, print or tape.

In other words, we can get them to process text for us! The range of things we can get them to do with the documents is much wider than what we would get with WYSIWYG word processors or formatting markup.

Let us go back to the analogy of the typesetter working with a document marked up with a pen on paper to see why this is so powerful.

Imagine if we called her back the next day and told her to "change the formatting of the second chapter". She would have a lot of trouble mentally translating the codes for presentation back into high level constructs like sections and paragraphs.

To her, a title would only look like a line of text with a circle around it and instructions to make it italicized and 18 point. Making changes would be painful because recognizing the different logical constructs would be difficult. She probably could eventually accomplish the task by applying her human intuition and by reading the actual text. But computers do not have intuition, and cannot understand the text. That means that they cannot reliably recognize logical structure based totally on formatting. For instance they cannot reliably distinguish an italicized, 18 point title from an italicized, 18 point warning paragraph.

Even if human beings were consistent in formatting different types of documents (which we are not) computers would still have trouble. Even in a single document, the same formatting can mean two different things: italics could represent any kind of emphasis, foreign words, certain kinds of citations or other conventions.

Abstractions and renditions

Computers are not as smart as we are. If we want the computer to consider a piece of text to be written in a foreign language (for instance for spell checking purposes) then we must label it explicitly `foreign-language` and not just put it in italics! We call "foreign language" the *abstraction* that we are trying to represent, and we call the italics a particular rendition of the abstraction.

Formatting information has other problems. It is specific to a particular use of the information. Search engines cannot do very interesting searching on italics because they do not know what they mean. In contrast, the search engine could do something very interesting with citation elements: it could return a list of what documents are cited by other documents.

Italics are a form of markup specific to a particular application: formatting or printing. In contrast, the citation element is markup that can be used by a variety of applications. That is why we call this form of structural markup *generalized markup*. Generalized markup is the alternative to either formatting markup or WYSIWYG (lampooned by XML users as What You See is *All* You Get). Generalized markup is about getting more.

Because of the ambiguity of formatting, XML users typically do not bother to encode the document's presentational features at all, though XML would allow it. We are not interested, for instance, in fonts, page breaks and bullets. This formatting information would merely clutter up our abstract document's representation. Although typographic conventions allow the computer to print out or display the document properly, we want our markup to do more than that.

Stylesheets

Of course we must still be able to generate high quality print and online renditions of the document. Your readers do not want to read XML text directly. Instead of directly inserting the formatting commands in the XML document, we usually tell the computer how to generate formatted renditions *from* the XML abstraction.

For example in a print presentation, we can make the content of TITLE elements bold and large, insert page breaks before the beginning of chapters, and turn emphasis, citations and foreign words into italics. These rules are specified in a file called a *stylesheet*. The stylesheet is where human designers can express their creativity and understanding of formatting conventions. The stylesheet allows the computer to automatically convert the document from the abstraction to a formatted rendition.

We could use two different stylesheets to generate online and print renditions of the document. In the online rendition, there would be no page breaks, but cross-references would be represented as clickable hypertext links. Generalized markup allows us to easily produce high-quality print and online renditions of the same document.

This may well turn out to be the feature of XML that will save organizations and individuals the most money in the near future. We can even use two different stylesheets in the same medium. For instance, the computer could format the same document into several different styles (e.g. "New

York Times" style vs. "Wired Magazine") depending on the expressed preferences of a Web surfer, or even based on what Internet Service Provider they use.

We can also go beyond just print and online formatting and have our document be automatically rendered into braille or onto a text-to-speech machine. Generalized markup is highly endorsed by those who promote the *accessibility* of information to the visually impaired. XML should be similarly useful to those who want to widen the use of the Web.

Generalized markup documents are also "future-proof". They will not have to be redone to take advantage of future technologies. Instead, new stylesheets can be created to render existing documents in new ways.

Future renditions of documents might include three-dimensional virtual reality worlds where books are rendered as buildings, chapters as rooms and the text as wallpaper! Once again, the most important point is that these many different renditions will be possible without re-encoding the document. There are millions of SGML documents that predate the Web, but many of them are now published on it.

Typically, they were republished in HTML without changing a single character of the SGML source's markup or data, or editing a single character of the generated HTML. The same will be true of the relationship between XML and all future representations.

The key is abstraction. SGML and XML can represent abstractions, and from abstractions you can easily create any number of renditions. This is a fact well-known to the world's database programmers, who constantly generate new renditions – reports and forms – from the same abstract data.

Element types

Enough hype about generalized markup! You probably want to know what it looks like. To mark up a letter, we could identify the components of the letter like this:

Example 1-2. A simple memo

```
<to>Charles Goldfarb</to>
<from>Paul Prescod</from>
<re>John Smith's will</re>

<p>John Smith wants to update his will. Another wife left him.</p>
```

This text would be part of an XML document. The markup identifies components, called elements, of the document in ways that the computer can understand. The start-tag "<to>" marks the beginning of an element and the end-tag "</to>" marks the end of the element. Each element is an instance of an *element type*, such as "to", "from", "re" and "p".

If you use an XML-aware, you may never work with markup at the textual tag level, but you would still annotate sections of the document in this way (using whatever graphical interface the word processor provides).

Instead of each element type describing a formatting construct, each one instead describes the logical role of its elements – the *abstraction* it represents. The goal is for the abstraction to be descriptive enough and suitably chosen so that particular uses of the document (such as printing, searching and so forth) can be completely automated as computer processes acting on the elements.

For instance, we can search for a document that is "to" Martha, about ("re") John Smith's will. Of course the computer still does not understand the human interaction and concepts of sender and receiver, but it does know enough about the document to be able to tell me that in a "to" element of this particular document, the word "Martha" appears. If we expanded the letter a little to include addresses and so forth, we could also use an appropriate stylesheet to print it as a standard business letter.

Documents and databases

We can make our letter example even more precise and specific:

Example 1-3. Another letter

```
<to>Martha</to>
<from>Paul</to>
<re><customer-name>John Smith</customer-name>
    <customer-number>802-31348-5749</customer-number>
    <document-type-request>will</document-type-request>
</re>

<p>John Smith wants to update his will. Another wife left him.</p>
```

If you are familiar with databases, you might recognize that this looks database-ish in the sense that the customer number could be stored in a special index and you could easily search and sort this document based on customer numbers, document type requests and so forth.

But you can only do this sort of thing if your letter processing system understands your company's concepts of customer-numbers and your documents consistently provide the information. In other words, you must define your own set of element types just as the IBM team did.

In fact, many people have noticed that XML documents resemble traditional relational and object database data in many ways. Once you have a language for rigorously representing documents, those documents can be treated more like other forms of data.

But the converse is also true. As we have described, structured documents have many features in common with databases. They can preserve the abstract data and prevent it from being mingled with rendition information.

Furthermore, you can actually use this structured markup to represent data that is not what we would traditionally think of as documents, but too complex to be handled in conventional databases. In this brave new world, DNA patterns are data, and so are molecular diagrams and virtual reality worlds. In other words, generalized markup allows us to blow the doors off the word "document" and integrate diverse types of data. This database-ization of documents and document-ization of data is one of the major drivers of the XML excitement. Prior to XML, the Web had no standard data interchange format for even moderately complex data.

It may not have been obvious to its early, publishing-oriented adapters, that SGML would change the entire world of databases and electronic data interchange (EDI). But SGML's unique usefulness as a data interchange representation was a direct consequence of this second decision – to make SGML extensible through a customized vocabulary (set of element types).

1.1.2.3   Rule-based markup

The IBM team's third realization was that if computer systems were to work with these documents reliably, the documents would have to follow certain rules.

For instance a courtroom transcript might be required to have the name of the judge, defendant, both attorneys and (optionally) the names of members of the jury (if there is one). Since humans are prone to make mistakes, the computer would have to enforce the rules for us.

In other words the legal markup language should be specified in some formal way that would restrict elements appropriately. If the court stenographer tried to submit a transcript to the system without these elements being properly filled in, the system would check its *validity* and complain that it was *invalid*.

Of course, court transcripts have a different structure from wills, which in turn have a different structure from memos. So you would need to rigorously define what it means for each type of document to be valid. In SGML terminology, each of these is a *document type* and the formal definition that describes each type is called a *document type definition* (DTD).

Once again we can see why it is so important that the language provide us with the flexibility to choose our own vocabulary (our own set of element types). After all, the constraints that we apply must be described in terms of those element types. We use the word *document type* to refer both to a vocabulary and the constraints on its use.

Once again, this concept is very common in the database world. Database people typically have several layers of checking to guarantee that improper data cannot appear in their databases. For instance syntactic checks guarantee that phone numbers are composed of digits and that people's names are not. Semantic checks ensure that business rules are followed (such as "purchase order numbers must be unique"). The database world calls the set of constraints on the database structure a *schema*. In their terminology, DTDs are schemas for documents.

Once you have a document type worked out, you can describe for the computer how to print or display documents that conform to it with a *stylesheet*. So you might say that the address line in memos would be bolded, or that there should be two lines between speeches in a court transcript. These processes can work reliably because documents are constrained by the document type definition.

For instance, a letter cannot have a postscript ("P.S.") at the beginning of the document nor an address at the end. Because there is no convention for formatting such a letter, a stylesheet would not typically do a good job with it. In fact, it might crash, as some word processors do when they try to load corrupted documents. The document type definition protects us from this.[1]

In 1969, the IBM team developed a language that could implement their vision of markup that was not specific to a particular system. They called it the *Generalized Markup Language* (which, not coincidentally, has the same initials as the names Goldfarb, Mosher and Lorie).

---

1. Of course, computer programmers will always invent new excuses for crashing software.

However, it wasn't until 1974 that Goldfarb proved the concept of a "validating parser", one that could read a document type definition and check the accuracy of markup, without going to the expense of actually processing a document. As he recalls it: "At that point SGML was born – although it still had a lot of growing up to do."

Between 1978 and 1986, Goldfarb acted as technical leader of a team of users, programmers and academics that developed his nascent invention into the robust International Standard (ISO 8879) they called the *Standard Generalized Markup Language*.

That team, with many of the same players still involved, is now JTC1/WG4, which continues to develop SGML and related standards. Two of the most important are *HyTime*, which standardizes the representation of hyperlinking features, and DSSSL, which standardizes the creation of stylesheets.[1]

The SGML standard took a long time to develop, but arguably it was still ahead of the market when it was created. Over those years, the basic concepts of GML were broadened to support a very wide range of applications. Although GML was always extensible and generalized, the SGML standard added many features and options, many intended for niche markets. But the niches had to be catered for: some of the niche users have document collections that rival the Web in size!

By the time it was standardized in 1986, SGML had become large, intricate and powerful. In addition to being an official International Standard, SGML is the defacto standard for the interchange of large, complex documents and has been used in domains as diverse as programming language design and airplane maintenance.

1.2 | HTML and the Web

In 1989, a researcher named Tim Berners-Lee proposed that information could be shared within the CERN European Nuclear Research Facility using hyperlinked text documents. He was advised to use an SGML-ish

---

1. Knowing the full names probably won't help much, but just in case, HyTime is short for "Hypermedia/Time-based Structuring Language" and DSSSL (pronounced "dis-sal") is short for "Document Style Semantics and Specification Language". We warned you that it wouldn't help much.

syntax by a colleague named Anders Berglund, an early adopter of the new SGML standard. They started from a simple example document type in the SGML standard[1] and developed a hypertext version called the *Hypertext Markup Language* (HTML).

Relative to the 20 year evolution of SGML, HTML was developed in a hurry, but it did the job. Tim called his hypertext system the *World Wide Web* and today it is the most diverse, popular hypertext information system in existence. Its simplicity is widely believed to be an important part of its success. The simplicity of HTML and the other Web specifications allowed programmers around the world to quickly build systems and tools to work with the Web.

HTML inherited some important strengths from SGML. With a few exceptions, its element types were generalized and descriptive, not formatting constructs as in languages like TeX and Microsoft Word. This meant that HTML documents could be displayed on text screens, under graphical user interfaces, and even projected through speakers for the sight impaired.

HTML documents used SGML's simple angle bracket convention for markup. That meant that authors could create HTML documents in almost any text editor or word processor. The documents are also compatible with almost every computer system in existence.

On the other hand, HTML only uses a fixed set of element types. As we discussed before, no one document type can serve all purposes, so HTML only adopted the first of GML's revelations, that document representations must be standardized. It is not extensible and therefore cannot be tailored for particular document types, and it was not very rigorously defined until years after its invention. By the time HTML was given a formal DTD, there were already thousands of Web pages with erroneous HTML.[2]

---

1. That DTD was based on the very first published DTD, from a 1978 IBM manual written by Goldfarb, derived in turn from work that he and Mosher had done in the early 70's.
2. Today there are tens of thousands with misleading or downright erroneous informational content, so perhaps bad HTML is not that big a problem in practice.

1.2.1 *HTML gets extended – unofficially!*

As the Web grew in popularity many people started to chafe under HTML's fixed document type. Browser vendors saw an opportunity to gain market share by making incompatible extensions to HTML. Most of the extensions were formatting commands and thus damaged the Web's interoperability. The first golden rule, standardization was in serious danger.

For instance Netscape's popular CENTER element cannot be "pronounced" in a text to speech converter. A BLINK element cannot be rendered on some computers. Still, this was a fairly understandable reaction to HTML's limitations.

One argument for implementing formatting constructs instead of abstractions is that there are a fixed number of formatting constructs in wide use, but an ever growing number of abstractions. Let's say that next year biologists invent a new formatting notation for discussing a particular type of DNA. They might use italics to represent one kind of DNA construct and bold to represent another. In other words, as new abstractions are invented, we usually use existing formatting features to represent them. We have been doing this for thousands of years, and prior to computerization, it was essentially the only way.

We human readers can read a textual description of the meanings of the features ("in this book, we will use Roman text to represent...") and we can differentiate them from others using our reasoning and understanding of the text. But this system leaves computers more or less out of the loop.

For instance superscripts can be used for trademarks, footnotes and various mathematical constructs. Italics can be used for references to book titles, for emphasis and to represent foreign languages. Without generalized markup to differentiate, computers cannot do anything useful with that information. It would be impossible for them to translate foreign languages, convert emphasis to a louder voice for text to speech conversion, or do calculations on the mathematical formulae.

1.2.2 *The World Wide Web reacts*

As the interoperability and scalability of the Web became more and more endangered by proprietary formatting markup, the World Wide Web Consortium (headed by the same Tim Berners-Lee) decided to act. They attacked the problem in three ways. First, they decided to adopt the SGML convention for attaching formatting to documents, the stylesheet.

They invented a simple HTML-specific stylesheet language called *Cascading Style Sheets* (CSS) that allowed people to attach formatting to HTML documents without filling the HTML itself with proprietary, rendition-oriented markup.

Second, they invented a simple mechanism for adding abstractions to HTML. We will not look at that mechanism here, because XML makes it obsolete. It allowed new abstractions to be invented but provided no mechanism for constraining their occurrence. In other words it addressed two of GML's revelations: it brought HTML back to being a single standard, more or less equally supported by the major vendors, and it allowed people to define arbitrary extensions (with many limitations).

But they knew that their stool would not stand long on two of its three legs. The (weakly) extensible HTML and CSS are only stopgaps. For the Web to move to a new level, it had to incorporate the third of SGML's important ideas, that document types should be formally defined so that documents can be checked for validity against them.

Therefore, the World Wide Web Consortium decided to develop a subset of SGML that would retain SGML's major virtues but also embrace the Web ethic of minimalist simplicity. They decided to give the new language the catchy name Extensible Markup Language (XML). They also decided to make related standards for advanced hyperlinking and stylesheets.

The first, called the Extensible Linking Language (XLink), is inspired by HyTime, the ISO standard for linking SGML documents, and by the Text Encoding Initiative, the academic community's guidelines for applying SGML to scholarly applications.

The second, called the Extensible Style Language is a combination of ideas from the Web's Cascading Style Sheets and ISO's DSSSL standard.[1]

---

1. This description necessarily presented as linear, straightforward, and obvious a process that was actually messy and at times confusing. It is fair to say that there were many people outside the World Wide Web Consortium who had a better grasp on the need for XML than many within it, and that various member corporations "caught on" to the importance of XML at different rates.

1.3 | Conclusion

Now we've seen the origins of XML, and some of its key ideas. Unlike lots of other "next great things" of the high-tech world, XML has solid roots and a proven track record. You can have confidence in XML because the particular subset of SGML that is XML has been in use for a dozen years.

Where is XML going?

- HTML++
- Database publishing
- Electronic commerce
- Metadata
- Science on the Web

The XML effort is new ground in many senses. The Web has never before had access to the new features that XML offers. It will take a while for the Web culture to understand the strengths (and weaknesses) of the new language and learn how to properly deploy it. Still, XML is already becoming a building block for the next generation of Web applications and specifications.

2.1 | Beyond HTML

XML was originally conceived as a big brother to HTML. As its name implies, XML can be used to extend HTML or even define whole new languages completely unlike HTML. At first, the thousands of authors accustomed to HTML will probably use it as a mere HTML extension and slowly grow into its more powerful abilities.

For instance, a company might want to offer technical manuals on the Web. Many manuals have a formatting for tables (e.g., a table listing a software product's supported languages) and repeat the formatting on several tables in the manual (perhaps once per program in a package). The format-ting of these tables can be very intricate.

For instance the rows may be broken into categories with borders between them. The title of each column and row might be in a particular font and color. The width of the columns might be very precisely described. The final row ("the bottom line") might be colored. HTML could provide the formatting markup that the layout would require, but it would require a lot of duplication. In fact, it would be such a hassle that most companies would choose to use a graphic or an *Adobe Portable Document Format* (PDF) file instead.

To demonstrate how XML can help, we will use an example table from the specification for HTML tables. We will simplify the example some-what, but the XML solution will still be shorter (in characters) and easier to read.

```
A graphic of a table
            CODE-PAGE SUPPORT IN MICROSOFT WINDOWS
==================================================================
Code-Page | Name                        | Windows Windows Windows
   ID     |                             | NT 3.1 NT 3.51    95
==================================================================
    1200  | Unicode (BMP of ISO 10646)  |    X        X
    1250  | Windows 3.1 Eastern European|    X        X        X
    1251  | Windows 3.1 Cyrillic        |    X        X        X
    1252  | Windows 3.1 US (ANSI)       |    X        X        X
    1253  | Windows 3.1 Greek           |    X        X        X
    1254  | Windows 3.1 Turkish         |    X        X        X
    1255  | Hebrew                      |                      X
    1256  | Arabic                      |                      X
    1257  | Baltic                      |                      X
    1361  | Korean (Johab)              |                      X
==================================================================
```

Figure 2-1   A Formatted Table (based on an example in the HTML 4.0 Recommendation)

If there are many of these tables the cumulative effort of doing this man-ual work can add up to a large burden, especially since it must be main-tained as products change. Even with an HTML authoring tool, you will probably have to do the layout manually, over and over again. As if this internal expense was not disturbing enough, every person who reads the annual report over the Web must download the same formatting informa-

Example 2-1. The HTML Markup to Implement the Table (based on an example in the HTML 4.0 Recommendation)

```
<TABLE border="2" frame="hsides" rules="groups">
<CAPTION>CODE-PAGE SUPPORT IN MICROSOFT WINDOWS</CAPTION>
<COLGROUP align="center">
<COLGROUP align="left">
<COLGROUP align="center" span="2">
<COLGROUP align="center" span="3">
<THEAD valign="top"><TR><TH>Code-Page<br>ID<TH>Name
<TH>Windows<br>NT 3.1<TH>Windows<br>NT 3.51<TH>Windows<br>95
<TBODY>
<TR><TD>1200<TD>Unicode (BMP of ISO/IEC-10646)<TD>X<TD>X<TD>
<TR><TD>1250<TD>Windows 3.1 Eastern European<TD>X<TD>X<TD>X
<TR><TD>1251<TD>Windows 3.1 Cyrillic<TD>X<TD>X<TD>X
<TR><TD>1252<TD>Windows 3.1 US (ANSI)<TD>X<TD>X<TD>X
<TR><TD>1253<TD>Windows 3.1 Greek<TD>X<TD>X<TD>X
<TR><TD>1254<TD>Windows 3.1 Turkish<TD>X<TD>X<TD>X
<TR><TD>1255<TD>Hebrew<TD><TD><TD>X
<TR><TD>1256<TD>Arabic<TD><TD><TD>X
<TR><TD>1257<TD>Baltic<TD><TD><TD>X
<TR><TD>1361<TD>Korean (Johab)<TD><TD><TD>X</TABLE>
```

tion row after row, column after column, table after table, year after year. Right thinking Web page authors will understand that this situation is not good. The repetition leads to longer download times, congested servers, dissatisfied customers and perhaps irate managers.

The XML solution would be to invent a simple extension to HTML that is customized to the needs of the manual. It would have table elements that would only require data that varies from table to table. None of the redundant formatting information would be included. We would then use a sophisticated stylesheet to add that information back in. The beauty of the stylesheet solution is that the formatting information is expressed only in one place. Surfers only have to download that once. Also, if your company decides to change the style of the tables, all of them can be changed at once merely by changing the stylesheet. Here is what that might look like:

The difference between this XML version and the HTML version is not as dramatic as in some examples, but the XML version is clearer, has fewer lines and characters and is easier to maintain. More important, the stylesheet can choose to format this in many different ways as time goes by and tastes change. All the XML version represents is the actual information about Windows code pages, not the tabular format of a particular presentation of it.

Example 2-2. XML Version of the Table

```
<CODE-PAGE-TABLE>
<CP NUM="1200" NAME="Unicode (BMP of ISO/IEC-10646)"
   PLATFORMS="NT3.1 NT3.51"/>
<CP NUM="1250" NAME="Windows 3.1 Eastern European"
   PLATFORMS="NT3.1 NT3.51 WIN95"/>
<CP NUM="1251" NAME="Windows 3.1 Cyrillic"
   PLATFORMS="NT3.1 NT3.51 WIN95"/>
<CP NUM="1252" NAME="Windows 3.1 US (ANSI)"
   PLATFORMS="NT3.1 NT3.51 WIN95"/>
<CP NUM="1253" NAME="Windows 3.1 Greek"
   PLATFORMS="NT3.1 NT3.51 WIN95"/>
<CP NUM="1254" NAME="Windows 3.1 Turkish"
   PLATFORMS="NT3.1 NT3.51 WIN95"/>
<CP NUM="1255" NAME="Hebrew"
   PLATFORMS="WIN95"/>
<CP NUM="1256" NAME="Arabic"
   PLATFORMS="WIN95"/>
<CP NUM="1257" NAME="Baltic"
   PLATFORMS="WIN95"/>
<CP NUM="1261" NAME="Korean (Johab)"
   PLATFORMS="NT3.1 NT3.51 WIN95"/>
```

One thing to note is that the extra download of a stylesheet does take time. It makes the most sense to move formatting into a stylesheet when that formatting will be used on many pages or in many parts of the same page. The goal is to amortize the cost of the download over a body of text. A similar caveat applies to the time it takes to make the stylesheet and design the table elements. Doing so for a single table would probably not be cost effective. Our example above basically shifts the complexity from the document to the stylesheet, on the presumption that there will probably be many documents (or at least many tables) for every stylesheet. In general, XML is about short term investment in long term productivity.

Once you have made that investment you can sometimes realize more radical productivity gains than you first intended. Imagine that you use XML tables to publish the financial information in your company's annual report. Your accountants may be able to use their software's report writing feature to directly transfer accounting information into the XML table. This can save one more opportunity for typos between the accountants' printout and the Web author's keyboard. There might also be opportunities for automation at the other end of the spectrum. Other software might transform the XML table directly into a format required for submission to some government agency.

2.2 | Database publishing

The last example hints at the way XML can interact with systems that are not typically associated with documentation. As documents become more structured they can become integrated with the other structured data in an organization. Some of the same techniques can be used to create them (such as report writing software or custom graphical user interfaces) and some of the same software will be able to read them (such as spreadsheets and database software). One particularly popular application of XML will surely be the publishing of databases to the Web.

Consider for instance a product database, used by the internal ordering system of a toy manufacturer. The manufacturer might want the database to be available on the Web so that potential clients would know what was available and at what price. Rather than having someone in the Web design department mark up the data again, they could build a connection between their Web server and their database using the features typically built into Web servers that allow those sorts of data pipes. The designers could then make the products list beautiful using a stylesheet. Pictures of the toys could be supplied by the database. In essence, the Web site would be merely a view on the data in the database. As toys get added and removed from the database, they will appear and disappear from the view on the Website. This mechanism also gives the Website maintainer the freedom to update the "look and feel" of the Website without dealing with the database or the plumbing that connects it to the Web server!

XML is also expected to become an important tool for interchange of database information. Databases have typically interchanged information using simple file formats like one-record per line with semi-colons between the fields. This is not sufficient for the new object-oriented information being produced by databases. Objects must have internal structure and links between them. XML can represent this using elements and attributes to provide a common format for transferring database records between databases. You can imagine that one database might produce an XML document representing all of the toys the manufacturer produces and that document could be directly loaded into another database either within the company or at a customer's site. This is a very interesting way of thinking about documents, because in many cases human beings will never see them. They are documents produced by and for computer software.

Example 2-3. A products database in XML

```
<TOYS>
<ITEM>
<TITLE>GI John</TITLE>
<MANUFACTURER>War Toys Inc.</MANUFACTURER>
<PRICE>50.95</PRICE>
<IN-STOCK>3000</IN-STOCK>
</ITEM>
<ITEM>
<TITLE>Leggo!</TITLE>
<MANUFACTURER>Grips R US</MANUFACTURER>
<PRICE>64.95</PRICE>
<IN-STOCK>2000</IN-STOCK>
</ITEM>
<ITEM>
<TITLE>Hell On Wheels</TITLE>
<MANUFACTURER>Li'l Road Warriors</MANUFACTURER>
<PRICE>150.95</PRICE>
<IN-STOCK>3200</IN-STOCK>
</ITEM>
</TOYS>
```

2.3 | Electronic commerce

Presume that a retailer decides that it wants to start selling a line of toys from the database. They might contact the manufacturer to organize the sale. The two could agree on an XML-based product-request message format and formalize it in an XML document type. In fact, there might already be an industry standard XML document type appropriate for the task. Once that has been chosen, orders for the part can be sent automatically from the purchaser's computer to the supplier's. This sort of electronic commerce has been possible for years, but XML allows it to be easily standardized, highly extensible and wired into the backbone technologies of the Internet. The easy availability of the software and standards will allow much smaller organizations to use electronic commerce.

2.4 | Metadata

There is a special type of data that interests the larger Web publishers. It is called metadata: information about information. XML is the basis for

Example 2-4. An order for a Toy

```
<Toy-Order>
<Order-No>967634</Order-No>
<Message-Date>19961002</Message-Date>
<Buyer-EAN>5412345000176</Buyer-EAN>
<Toy><Number>523953-432</Number><Quantity>18</Quantity></Toy>
<Toy><Number>438312-716</Number><Quantity>13</Quantity></Toy>
<Toy><Number>232332-136</Number><Quantity>23</Quantity></Toy>
</Toy-Order>
```

metadata standards such as Microsoft's Channel Definition Format (CDF) for describing "Web Push Channels", Netscape's Meta Content Framework (MCF) for tracking information about Web sites and the *Platform for Internet Content Selection* which allows the filtering of inappropriate material from computer screens based on external descriptions of content. These applications are called metadata because they are used to describe other information resources. The "violent content" label on a video tape is a perfect example of metadata. The data provided, "violent content" describes the contents of the tape – it is data about data.

CDF describes things like about Web channels, such as their schedules and logos and can carry a description of the channel. This may sound familiar to you. If you think about it, you will notice that even TV Guide is metadata! Some future online version might use XML. Netscape's MCF can describe things like who is in charge of a Web page, what other pages are related to it, how they are related and so forth.

Example 2-5. Channel Description Format

```
<?XML version="1.0"?>
<CHANNEL HREF="http://www.rocktv.com/channels">
<ABSTRACT>
RockTV is your 24-hour rock station! Nothing but geology,
geography and rock collecting. All day! All night!
</ABSTRACT>
</CHANNEL>
```

XML is convenient for these tasks for several reasons. It can be edited in standard text editors and specialized XML word processors. XML's syntax will be familiar to the millions of Web maintainers who must eventually learn to apply metadata. XML expresses the hierarchy and links of these documents nicely. It is also well suited to encoding the textual portions of specifications. For instance every channel will have a textual description hoping to convince you to subscribe. XML can allow these descriptions to use its hypermedia features to create very compelling displays.

The next step in the evolution of metadata on the Web is a standardized layer on top of XML called *Resource Description Framework* (RDF). RDF is still under development, but when it is finished, it will be an XML document type for metadata that will be extensible at the metadata level as XML is at the document level. What that means is that RDF documents will be able to describe new relationships between documents, images and other Web resources. This will allow new relational vocabularies to be developed just as XML document types allow new markup vocabularies. Older metadata standards like PICS and CDF will eventually be revamped in terms of XML and RDF. In one sense, this sounds very complicated: PICS is based on RDF which is based on XML. But on the other hand, it will not be so complicated in practice. PICS and CDF will have a set of element types that you must learn to apply according to the XML syntax described in this book. RDF, the middle layer, will only be visible to the wizards who invent new ways of cataloging, describing and organizing information – the librarians of the future.[1]

Example 2-6. Describing the owner of a document in RDF

```
<RDF:assertions href="http://www.bar.com/some.doc>
    <bib:author>
  <RDF:resource>
    <bib:name>John Smith</bib:name>
  <bib:email>john@smith.com</bib:email>
  <bib:phone>+1 (555) 123-4567</bib:phone>
      </RDF:resource>
  </bib:author>
</RDF:assertions>
```

2.5 | Science on the Web

Although the Web was originally invented in a physics laboratory for communication among physicists, it never developed into a great system for

---

1. Luckily, the librarians of the present are very much involved in these standardization efforts.

communicating mathematical formulae. Markup for mathematics is more complex than it seems at first to non-mathematicians, and the mathematicians have not yet agreed exactly how they want to do it.

Suffice to say that there are some attempts to do math on the Web that attempt to do too much and others that do not do enough. The World Wide Web Consortium is working on a new XML-based language called *MathML*. Hopefully MathML will strike a good middle ground. MathML markup is demonstrated in Example 2-7 and a rendered formula is in Figure 2-2.

Example 2-7. MathML Markup for a Formula

```
<mrow>
  <mrow>
    <msup>
      <mi>x</mi>
      <mn>2</mn>
    </msup>
    <mo>+</mo>
    <mrow>
      <mn>4</mn>
      <mo>&invisibletimes;</mo>
      <mi>x</mi>
    </mrow>
    <mo>+</mo>
    <mn>4</mn>
  </mrow>
  <mo>=</mo>
  <mn>0</mn>
</mrow>
```

$$x^2 + 4x + 4 = 0$$

Figure 2-2   MathML Formula Rendered

The *Chemical Markup Language* (CML) is an XML-based language for describing the management of molecular information on computer networks. Using a Java viewer that is under development, users can view and manipulate molecules in 2 and 3 dimensions. *Bioinformatic Sequence*

Markup Language is a standard for encoding DNA, RNA and protein sequence information.

The specs for both of these applications are available on the CD-ROM that accompanies this book.

As you can see, XML is branching out into a wide variety of problem domains. Whatever your discipline, you should consider if there is some part of your workflow that could be made more efficient with standardization based on XML. In subsequent parts of this book, we will explore in detail a wide array of applications of the kinds we have been describing.

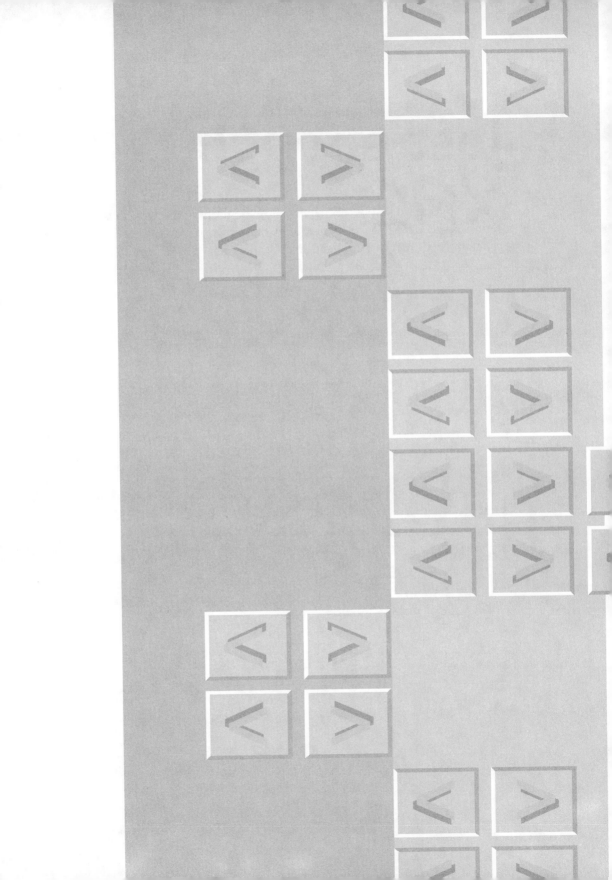

Just enough XML

- Elements
- Character set
- Entities
- Markup
- Document types

In this chapter we will explore the fundamental concepts of XML documents and XML systems. If XML were a great work of literature then this chapter would be the Cliff notes. The chapter will introduce the ideas that define the language but will avoid the nitty gritty details (the *syntax*) behind the constructs. As a result, some concepts may remain slightly fuzzy because you will not be able to work with them "hands on". Later chapters will provide that opportunity.

This early presentation of these ideas will allow you to see XML's "big picture". We will do this by walking through the design process for an XML-like language. Hopefully by the end of the process, you will understand each of the design decisions and XML's overall architecture.

Our objective is to equip you with "just enough" XML to appreciate the application scenarios and tool descriptions in the following parts of the book, but being over-achievers we may go a little too far. Feel free to leave at any time to read about XML in the real world.

3.1 | The goal

First we should summarize what we are trying to achieve. In short, "What is XML used for?" XML is for the *digital representation* of documents. You probably have an intuitive feel for what a document is. We will work from your intuition.

Documents can be large and small (). Both a multi-volume encyclopedia and a memo can be viewed as documents. A particular volume of the encyclopedia can also be called a document. XML allows you to think of the encyclopedia whichever way will allow you to get your job done most efficiently. You'll notice that XML will give you these sorts of options in many places. XML also allows us to think of an email message as a document. XML can even represent the message from a police department's server to a police officer's handheld computer that reports that you have unpaid parking tickets.[1]

When we say that we want to *digitally represent* documents we mean that we want to put them in some kind of computer-readable code so that a computer can help us store, process, search, transmit, display and print them. In order for a computer to do useful things with a document, we are going to have to tell it about the structure of the document. This is our simple goal: to put the documents in a code that the computer can "understand" in-so-far as computers can understand anything.

XML documents can include pictures, movies and other multimedia, but we will not actually represent the multimedia components as XML. If you think of representation as a translation process, similar to language translation, then the multimedia components are the parts that we will leave in their "native language" because they have no simple translation into the "target language" (XML). We will just include them in their native formats as you might include a French or Latin phrase in an English text without explicit translation. Most pictures on the Web are files in formats called GIF or JPEG and most movies are in a format called MPEG. An XML document would just refer to those files in their native GIF, JPEG or MPEG formats. If you were transcribing an existing print document into XML, you would most likely represent the character-text parts as XML and the graphical parts in these other formats.

---

1. Sorry about that.

3.2 | Elements: The logical structure

Before we can describe exactly how we are going to represent documents, we must have a model in our heads of how a document is structured. Most documents (for example books and magazines) can be broken down into components (chapters and articles). These can also be broken down into components (titles, paragraphs, figures and so forth). It turns out that just about every document can be viewed this way.

In XML, these components are called *elements*. Each element represents a logical component of a document. Elements can contain other elements and can also contain the words and sentences that you would usually think of as the text of the document. XML calls this text the document's *character data*. This hierarchical view of XML documents is demonstrated in Figure 3-1.

Markup professionals call this the *tree structure* of the document. The element that contains all of the others (e.g. `book`, `report` or `memo` is known as the *root element*. This name captures the fact that it is the only element that does not "hang" off of some other element.

The elements that are contained in the root are called its *sub-elements*. They may contain sub-elements themselves. If they do, we will call them *branches*. If they do not, we will call them *leaves*.

Thus, the `chapter` and `article` elements are branches (because they have sub-elements), but the `paragraph` and `title` elements are leaves (because they only contain character data).[1] The root element is also referred to as the *document element* because it holds the entire logical document within it. The terms *root element* and *document element* are interchangeable.

Elements can also have extra information attached to them called *attributes*. Attributes describe properties of elements. For instance a `CIA-record` element might have a security attribute that gives the security rating for that element. A CIA database might only release certain records to certain people depending on their security rating. It will not always be clear which aspects of a document should be represented with elements and which should be represented with attributes, but we will give some guidelines in Chapter 32, "Creating a document type definition", on page 448.

---

1. You can see from this terminology that markup experts tend to have an environmentalist bent. The latest word sweeping the markup world is "grove", a term that recognizes that a single document may have multiple trees, for attributes (see below) as well as elements.

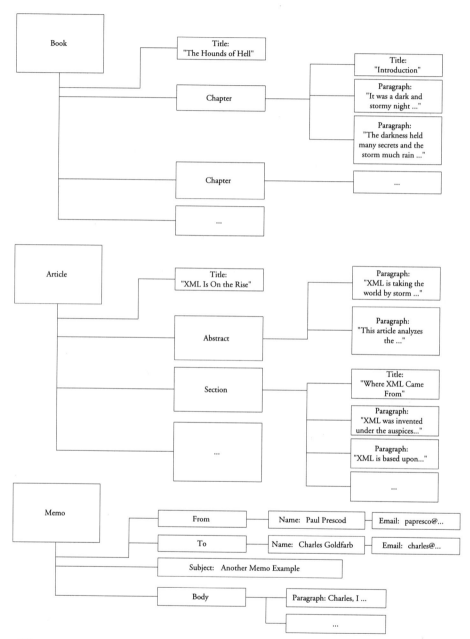

Figure 3-1   Hierarchical views of documents

Real-world documents do not always fit this *tree* model perfectly. They often have non-hierarchical features such as cross-references or hypertext links from one section of the tree to another. XML can represent these structures too. In fact, XML goes beyond the powerful links provided by HTML. More on this in 3.8, "Hyperlinking and Addressing", on page 45

3.3 | Unicode: The character set

Texts are made up of characters. If we are going to represent texts, then we must represent the characters that comprise them. So we must decide how we are going to represent characters at the bits and bytes level. This is called the *character encoding*. We must also decide what characters we are going to allow in our documents. This is the *character set*. A particularly restrictive character set might allow only upper-case characters. A very large character set might allow Eastern ideographs and Arabic characters.

If you are a native English speaker you may only need the fifty-two upper- and lower-case characters, some punctuation and a few accented characters. The pervasive *7 bit ASCII character set* caters to this market. It has just enough characters (128) for all of the letters, symbols, some accented characters and some other oddments. ASCII is both a character set *and* a character encoding. It defines what set of characters are available and how they are to be encoded in terms of bits and bytes.

XML's character set is Unicode, a sort of ASCII on steroids. Unicode includes thousands of useful characters from languages around the world.[1] However the first 128 characters of Unicode are compatible with ASCII and there is a character encoding of Unicode, *UTF-8* that is compatible with 7 bit ASCII. This means that at the bits and bytes level, the first 128 characters of UTF-8 Unicode and 7 bit ASCII are the same. This feature of *Unicode* allows authors to use standard plain-text editors to create XML immediately.

---

1. It also includes some not-so-useful characters – there is an entire section dedicated to "dingbats" and there is a proposal to include "Klingon", the artificial language from *Star Trek*™.

3.4 | Entities: The physical structure

An XML document is defined as a series of characters. An XML processor starts at the beginning and works to the end. XML provides a mechanism for allowing text to be organized non-linearly and potentially in multiple pieces. The parser reorganizes it into the linear structure.

The "piece-of-text" construct is called an *entity*. An entity could be as small as a single character or as large as all the characters of a book.

Entities have *names*. Somewhere in your document, you insert an *entity reference* to make use of an entity. The processor replaces the entity reference with the entity itself, which is called the *replacement text*. It works somewhat like a wordprocessor macro.

For instance an entity named "sigma", might contain the name of a Greek character. You would use a reference to the entity whenever you wanted to insert the sigma character. An entity could also be called "introduction-chapter" and be a chapter in a book. You would refer to the entity at the point where you wanted the chapter to appear.

One of the ideas that excited Ted Nelson, the man who coined the word *hypertext*, was the idea that text could be reused in many different contexts automatically. An update in one place would propagate across all uses of the text. The feature of XML that allows this is called the external entity. External entities are often referred to merely as entities, but the meaning is usually clear from context. An XML document can be broken up into many files on a hard disk or objects in a database and each of them is called an entity in XML terminology. Entities could even be spread across the Internet. Whereas XML elements describe the document's logical structure, entities keep track of the location of the chunks of bytes that make up an XML document. We call this the physical structure of the document.

 Note   *The unit of XML text that we will typically talk about is the entity. You may be accustomed to thinking about files, but entities do not have to be stored as files.*

For instance, entities could be stored in databases or generated on the fly by a computer program. Some file formats (e.g. a *zip* file) even allow multiple entities to reside in the same file at once. The term that covers all of these possibilities is entity, *not* file. Still, on most Web sites each entity will reside in a single file so in those cases external entities and files will functionally be the same. This setup is simple and efficient, but will not be sufficient for very large sites.

Entities' bread and butter occupation is less sexy than reusing bits of text across the Internet. But it is just as important: entities help to break up large files to make them editable, searchable, downloadable and otherwise usable on the ordinary computer systems that real people use. Entities allow authors to break their documents into workable chunks that can fit into memory for editing, can be downloaded across a slow modem and so forth.

Without entities, authors would have to break their documents unnaturally into smaller documents with only weak links between them (as is commonly done with HTML). This complicates document management and maintenance. If you have ever tried to print out one of these HTML documents broken into a hundred HTML files then you know the problem. Entities allow documents to be broken up into chunks without forgetting that they actually represent a single coherent document that can be printed, edited and searched as a unit when that makes sense.

Non-XML objects are referenced in much the same way and are called *unparsed entities*. We think of them as "data entities" because there is no XML markup in them that will be noticed. Data entities include graphics, movies, audio, raw text, PDF and anything else you can think of that is not XML (including HTML and other forms of SGML).[1] Each data entity has an associated *notation* that is simply a statement declaring whether the entity is a GIF, JPEG, MPEG, PDF and so forth.

Entities are described in all of their glorious (occasionally gory) detail in Chapter 33, "Entities: Breaking up is easy to do", on page 476

3.5 | Markup

We have discussed XML's conceptual model, the tree of elements, its strategy for encoding characters, Unicode, and its mechanism for managing the size and complexity of documents, entities. We have not yet discussed how

---

1. Actually, a data entity could even contain XML, but it wouldn't be treated as part of the main XML document.

to represent the logical structure of the document and link together all of the physical entities.

Although there are XML word processors, one of the design goals of XML was that it should be possible to create XML documents in standard text editors. Some people are not comfortable with word processors and even those who are may depend on text editors to "debug" their document if the word processor makes a mistake, or allows the user to make a mistake. The only way to allow authors convenient access to both the structure and data of the document in standard text editors is to put the two right beside each other, "cheek to cheek".

As we discussed in the introduction, the stuff that represents the logical structure and connects the entities is called markup. An XML document is made up exclusively of markup and character data. Both are in Unicode. Both are termed *XML text*. This last point is important! No matter how intuitive it might seem, we do not use the word "text" to mean character data.

 Caution   The term XML text refers to the combination of character data and markup, not character data alone. Character data + markup = text.

Markup is differentiated from character data by special characters called *delimiters*. Informally, text between a less-than ("<") and a greater-than (">") character or between an ampersand ("&") and a semicolon (";") character is markup. Those four characters are the most common delimiters. This rule will become more concrete in later chapters. In the meantime, here is an example of a small document to give you a taste of XML markup.

The markup between the less-than and greater-than is called a *tag*.

You may be familiar with other languages that use similar syntax. These include HTML and other SGML-based languages.

3.6 | Document types

The concept of a document type is fairly intuitive. You are well aware that letters, novels and telephone books are quite different, and you are probably comfortable recognizing documents that conform to one of these categories. No matter what its title or binding, you would call a book that listed

Example 3-1. A small XML document

```
<?xml version="1.0"?>
<!DOCTYPE Q-AND-A SYSTEM "http://www.q.and.a.com/faq.dtd">
<Q-AND-A>
<QUESTION>I'm having trouble loading a WurdWriter 2.0 file into
WurdPurformertWriter 7.0. Any suggestions?</QUESTION>

<ANSWER>Why don't you use XML?</ANSWER>

<QUESTION>What's XML?</QUESTION>

<ANSWER>It's a long story, but there is a book I can
recommend...</ANSWER>
</Q-AND-A>
```

names and phone numbers a phone book. So, a document type is defined by its elements. If two documents have radically different elements or allow elements to be combined in very different ways then they probably do not conform to the same document type.

This notion of a document type can be formalized in XML. A *document type definition* (or *DTD*) is a series of definitions for element types, attributes, entities and notations. It declares which of these are legal within the document and in what places they are legal. A document can claim to conform to a particular DTD in its *document type declaration*.[1]

DTDs are powerful tools for organizational standardization in much the same way that forms, templates and style-guides are. A very rigid DTD that only allows one element type in a particular place is like a form: "Just fill in the blanks!". A more flexible DTD is like a style-guide in that it can, for instance, require every list to have two or more items, every report to have an abstract and could restrict footnotes from appearing within footnotes.

DTDs are critical for organizational standardization, but they are just as important for allowing robust processing of documents by software. For example, a letter document with a chapter in the middle of it would be most unexpected and unlikely to be very useful. Letter printing software would not reliably be able to print such a document because it is not well defined what a chapter in a letter looks like. Even worse is a situation where a document is missing an element expected by the software that processes

---

1. The document type declaration is usually abbreviated "DOCTYPE", because the obvious abbreviation would be the same as that for document type definition!

it. If your mail program used XML as its storage format, you might expect it to be able to search all of the incoming email addresses for a particular person's address. Let us presume that each message stores this address in a `from` element. What do we do about letters without `from` elements when we are searching them? Programmers could write special code to "work around" the problem, but these kinds of workarounds make code difficult to write.

HTML serves as a useful cautionary tale. It actually has a fairly rigorous structure, defined in SGML, and available from the World Wide Web Consortium. But everybody tends to treat the rules as if they actually came from the World Wrestling Federation – they ignore them.

The programmers that maintain HTML browsers spend a huge amount of time incorporating support for all of the incorrect ways people combine the HTML elements in their documents. Although HTML has an SGML DTD, very few people use it, and the browser vendors have unofficially sanctioned the practice of ignoring it. Programming workarounds is expensive, time consuming, boring and frustrating, but the worst problem is that there is no good definition of what these illegal constructs mean. Some incorrect constructs will actually make HTML browsers crash, but others will merely make them display confusing or random results.

In HTML, the `title` element is used to display the document's name at the top of the browser window (on the title bar). But what should a browser do if there are two titles? Use the first? Use the last? Use both? Pick one at random? Since the HTML standard does not allow this construct it certainly does not specify a behavior. Believe it or not, an early version of Netscape's browser showed each title sequentially over time, creating a primitive sort of text animation. That behavior disappeared quickly when Netscape realized that authors were actually creating invalid HTML specifically to get this effect! Since authors cannot depend on non-sensical documents to work across browsers, or even across browser versions, there must be a formal definition of a valid, reasonable document of a particular type. In XML, the DTD provides a formal definition of the element types, attributes and entities allowed in a document of a specified type.

There is also a more subtle, related issue. If you do not stop and think carefully about the structure of your documents, you may accidently slip back into specifying them in terms of their formatting rather than their abstract structure. We are accustomed to thinking of documents in terms of their rendition. That is because, prior to GML, there was no practical way to create a document without creating a rendition. The process of creating a

DTD gives us an opportunity to rethink our documents in terms of their structure, as abstractions.

Here are examples of some of the declarations that are used to express a DTD:

Caution *A DTD is a concept; markup declarations are the means of expressing it. The distinction is important because other means of expressing DTDs are being proposed (see Chapter 39, "XML-Data", on page 570). However, most people, even ourselves, don't make the distinction in normal parlance. We just talk about the declarations as though they are the DTD that they describe.*

Example 3-2. Markup declarations

```
<!ELEMENT Q-AND-A (QUESTION,ANSWER)+>
<!-- This allows: question, answer, question, answer ... -->

<!ELEMENT QUESTION (#PCDATA)+>
<!-- Questions are just made up of text -->

<!ELEMENT ANSWER (#PCDATA)+>
<!-- Answers are just made up of text -->
```

Some XML documents do not have a document type declaration. That does not mean that they do not conform to a document type. It merely means that they do not claim to conform to some formally defined document type definition.

If the document is to be useful as an XML document, it must still have some structure, expressed through elements, attributes and so forth. When you create a stylesheet for a document you will depend on it having certain elements, on the element type names having certain meanings, and on the elements appearing in certain places. However it manifests itself, that set of things that you depend on is the document type.

You can formalize that structure in a DTD. In addition to or instead of a formal computer-readable DTD, you can also write out a prose description. You might consider the many HTML books in existence to be prose definitions of HTML. Finally, you can just keep the document type in your head and maintain conformance through careful discipline. If you can achieve this for large, complex documents, your powers of concentration are astounding! Which is our way of saying: we do not advise it. We will discuss DTDs more in Chapter 32, "Creating a document type definition", on page 448.

3.7 | Well-formedness and validity

Every language has rules about what is or is not valid in the language. In human languages that takes many forms: words have a particular correct pronunciation (or range of pronunciations) and they can be combined in certain ways to make valid sentences (grammar). Similarly XML has two different notions of "correct". The first is merely that the markup is intelligible: the XML equivalent of "getting the pronunciation right". A document with intelligible markup is called a *well-formed* document. One important goal of XML was that these basic rules should be simple so that they could be strictly adhered to.

The experience of the HTML market provided a cautionary tale that guided the development of XML. Much of the HTML on the Web does *not* conform to even the simplest rules in the HTML specifications. This makes automated processing of HTML quite difficult.

Because Web browsers will display ill-formed documents, authors continue to create them. In designing XML, we decided that XML processors should actually be prohibited from trying to recover from a *well-formedness* error in an XML document. This was a controversial decision because there were many who felt that it was inappropriate to restrict XML implementors from deciding the best error recovery policy for their application.

The XML equivalent of "using the right words in the right place" is called *validity* and is related to the notion of document types. A document is *valid* if it declares conformance to a DTD in a document type declaration and actually conforms to the DTD.

Documents that do not have a document type declaration are not really *invalid* – they do not violate their DTD – but they are not valid either, because they cannot be validated against a DTD.

If HTML documents with multiple titles were changed over to use XML syntax, they would be *well-formed* and invalid (presuming the HTML DTD was also converted to XML syntax). If we remove the document type declaration, so that they no longer claim to conform to the HTML DTD, then they would become merely well-formed but neither valid nor invalid.

Caution   *For most of us, the word "invalid" means something that breaks the rules. It is an easy jump from there to concluding that an XML document that does not conform to a DTD is free to break any rules at all. So for clarity, we may sometimes say "type-valid" and "non-type-valid", rather than "valid" and "invalid".*

You should think carefully before you decide to make a document that is well-formed but not valid. If the document is one-of-a-kind and is small, then making it well-formed is probably sufficient. But if it is to be part of any kind of information system (even a small one) or if it is a large document, then you should write a DTD for it and validate your document regularly. When you decide to build or extend your information system, the fact that the document is guaranteed to be consistent will make your programming or stylesheet writing many times easier and your results much more reliable.

3.8 | Hyperlinking and Addressing

If you have used the Web, then you probably do not need to be convinced of the importance of hyperlinking. One thing you might not know, however, is that the Web's notions of hyperlink are fairly tame compared to what is available in the best academic and commercial hypertext systems. XML alone does not correct this, but it has an associated standard called XLink that goes a long way towards making the Web a more advanced hypertext environment.

The first deficiency of today's Web links is that there are no standardized mechanisms for making links that are external to the documents that they are linking from. Let's imagine, for example that you stumble upon a Web page for your favorite music group. You read it, enjoy it and move on. Imagine next week you stumble upon a Web page with all of the lyrics for all of their songs (with appropriate copyrights, of course!). You think: there should be a link between these two pages. Someone visiting one might want to know about the other and vice versa.

What you want to do is make an *external link*. You want to make a link on your computer that appears on both of the other computers. But of course you do not have the ability to edit those two documents. XLink will allow this external linking. It provides a representation for external links, but it does not provide the technology to automatically publish those links to the world. That would take some kind of *link database* that would track all of the links from people around the world. Needless to say this is a big job and though there are prototypes, there is no standardized system yet.

You may wonder how all of these links will be displayed, how readers will select link sheets and annotations, how browsers will talk to databases and so forth. The simple answer is: "nobody knows yet."[1]

Before the first Web browser was developed there was no way to know that we would develop a convention of using colored, underlined text to represent links (and even today some browsers use other conventions). There was also no way to know that browsers would typically have "back" buttons and "history lists". These are just conventions that arose and browser features that became popular.

This same process will now occur with external links. Some user interface (perhaps a menu) will be provided to apply external link sheets, and there will probably be some mechanism for searching for link sheets related to a document on the Web. Eventually these will stabilize into standards that will be ubiquitous and transparent (we hope!). In the meantime, things are confused, but that is the price for living on the cutting edge. XLink moves us a notch further ahead by providing a notation for representing the links.

Another interesting feature of XML extended links is that they can point to more than one resource. For instance instead of making a link from a word to its definition, you might choose to link to definitions in several different dictionaries. The browser might represent this as a popup menu, a tiny window with the choices listed, or might even open one window for each. The same disclaimer applies: the XML Link specification does not tell browsers exactly what they must do. Each is free to try to make the most intuitive, powerful user interface for links. XML brings many interesting hypertext ideas from university research labs and high tech companies "to the masses." We still have to work out exactly how that will look and who will use them for what. We live in interesting times!

---

1. But we've got some ideas. See Chapter 13, "Extended linking", on page 176.

3.9 | Stylesheets

To a certain extent, the concerns described above are endemic to generalized markup. Because it describes structure, and not formatting, it allows variations in display and processing that can sometimes disturb people.

However, as the Web has evolved, people have become less and less tolerant of having browser vendors control the "look and feel" of their documents. An important part of all communication, but especially modern business communication, is the idea of style. Stylesheets allow us to attach our own visual style to documents without destroying the virtue of generalized markup. Because the style is described in a separate entity, the stylesheet, software that is not interested in style can ignore it.

For instance most search engines would not care if your corporate color is blue or green, so they will just ignore those declarations in the stylesheet. Similarly, software that reads documents aloud to the sight-impaired would ignore font sizes and colors and concentrate on the abstractions – paragraphs, sections, titles and so forth.

The Web has a very simple stylesheet language called *Cascading Style Sheets* (CSS), which arose out of the early battles between formatting and generalized markup in HTML. Like any other specification, CSS is a product of its environment, and so is not powerful enough to describe the formatting of documents types that are radically different in structure from HTML.

Because CSS is not sufficient, the World Wide Web Consortium is working on a complementary alternative called the Extensible Stylesheet Language (XSL). XSL will have many features from CSS, but will also borrow some major ideas from ISO's DSSSL stylesheet language. XSL will be extensible, just as XML is, so that it will be appropriate for all document types and not just for HTML. Like the linking specification, XSL is still under development so its exact shape is not known. Nevertheless, there is a proposal for a general design that we will review later on.

3.10 | Conclusion

There are a lot of new ideas here to absorb, but we'll be repeating and reemphasizing them as we move along. At this point, though, we're ready to look in-depth at the ways that XML is being used in the real world.

XML in the real world

- Real-world concepts
- Application scenarios
- Case studies
- XML tools
- Jargon demystified

pplications are the reason for using technology, so it makes sense to get a good idea of what XML is used for before digging into the details of the language.

And since XML may be somewhat different from the technologies that you are accustomed to using, it is also helpful to see how people actually work with it; how the tools are used.

We're going to cover those subjects at length in the next three parts of the book. In preparation, we need to examine some often elusive – but vital – concepts relating to real-world use of XML.

4.1 | Is XML for documents or for data?

What is a document?

My dictionary says:

"Something written, inscribed, engraved, etc., which provides evidence or information or serves as a record".

Documents come in all shapes and sizes and media, as you can see in Figure 4-1. Here are some you may have encountered:

- Long documents: books, manuals, product specifications
- Broadsides: catalog sheets, posters, notices
- Forms: registration, application, etc.
- Letters: email, memos
- Records: "Acme Co., Part# 732, reverse widget, $32.50, 5323 in stock"
- Messages: "job complete", "update accepted"

An e-commerce transaction, such as a purchase, might involve several of these. A buyer could start by sending several documents to a vendor:

- Covering note: a letter
- Purchase order: a form
- Attached product specification: a long document

The vendor might respond with several more documents:

- Formal acknowledgment: a message
- Thank you note: a letter
- Invoice: a form

The beauty of XML is that the same software can process all of this diversity. Whatever you can do with one kind of document you can do with all the others. The only time you need additional tools is when you want to do different kinds of things – not when you want to work with different kinds of documents.

And there are lots of things that you can do.

4.2 | Endless spectrum of application opportunities

Sorry about that, we've been reading too many marketing brochures. But it's true, nevertheless.

Figure 4-1 Documents come in all shapes and sizes.

At one end of the spectrum we have the grand old man of generalized markup, *POP* – Presentation-Oriented Publishing. You can see him in Figure 4-2.

At the other end of the spectrum is that darling of the data processors, *MOM* – Message-Oriented Middleware. She smiles radiantly from Figure 4-3.

Let's take a closer look at both of them.

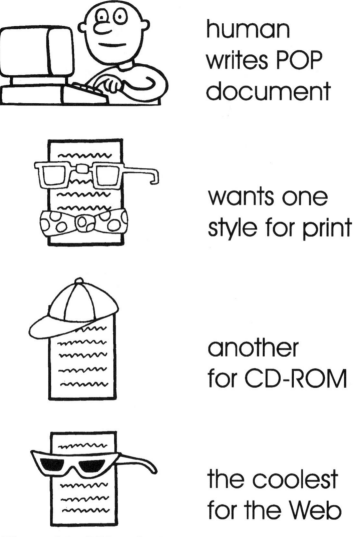

human
writes POP
document

wants one
style for print

another
for CD-ROM

the coolest
for the Web

Figure 4-2 POP application.

4.2.1 *Presentation-oriented publishing*

POP was the original killer app for SGML, XML's parent, because it saves so much money for enterprises with Web-sized document collections.

POP documents are chiefly written by humans for other humans to read.

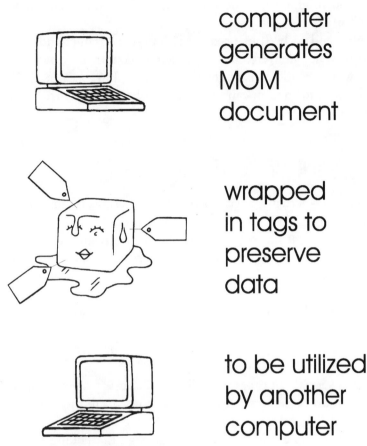

computer
generates
MOM
document

wrapped
in tags to
preserve
data

to be utilized
by another
computer

Figure 4-3   MOM application.

Instead of creating formatted renditions, as in word processors or desktop publishing programs, XML POP users create unformatted abstractions. That means the document file captures what is *in* the document, but not how it is supposed to look.

To get the desired look, the POP user creates a stylesheet, a set of commands that tell a program how to format (and/or otherwise process) the document. The power of XML in this regard is that you don't need to choose just one look – you can have a separate stylesheet for every purpose.[1]

---

1. We know that all office suites have some degree of stylesheet support today, but XML (well, GML) did it first, and still is the only way to do it cleanly.

At a minimum, you might want one for print, one for CD-ROM, and another for a Web site.

POP documents tend to be (but needn't be) long-lived, large, and with complex structures. When delivered in electronic media, they may be interactive. How they will be rendered is of great importance, but, because XML is used, the rendition information can be – and is – kept distinct from the abstract data.

4.2.2 *Message-oriented middleware*

MOM is the killer app – actually, a technology that drives lots of killer apps – for XML on the Web.

Middleware, as you might suspect from the name, is software that comes between two other programs. It acts like your interpreter/guide might if you were to visit someplace where you couldn't speak the language and had no idea of the local customs. It talks in the native tongue, using the native customs, and translates the native replies – the messages – into your language.

MOM documents are chiefly generated by programs for other programs to read.

Instead of writing specialized programs (clients) to access particular databases or other data sources (servers), XML MOM users break the old two-tier client/server model. They introduce a third tier, the "middle tier", that acts as a data integrator. The middle-tier server does all the talking to the data sources and sends their messages in XML to the client.

That means the client can read data from anywhere, but only has to understand data that is in XML documents. The XML markup provides information about the data (i.e., metadata) that was in the original data source schema, like the database table name and field names (also called "cell" or "column" names).

The MOM user typically doesn't care much about rendition. He does care, though, about extracting the original data accurately and making some use of the metadata. His client software, instead of having a specialized module for each data source, has a single "XML parser" module. The parser is the program that separates the markup from the data, just as it does in POP applications.

And just like POP applications, there can be a stylesheet, a set of commands that tell a program how to process the document. It may not look much like a POP stylesheet – it might look more like a script or program – but it performs the same function. And, as with POP stylesheets, there can be different MOM stylesheets for different document types, or to do different things with message documents of a single document type.

There is an extra benefit to XML three-tier MOM applications in a networked environment. For many applications, the middle-tier server can collect all of the relevant data at once and send it in a single document to the client. Further querying, sorting, and other processing can then take place solely on the client system. That not only cuts down Web traffic and overhead, but it vastly improves the end-user's perceived performance and his satisfaction with the experience.

MOM documents tend to be (but needn't be) short-lived, non-interactive, small, and with simple structures.

4.2.3 *Opposites are attracted*

To XML, that is!

How is it that XML can be optimal for two such apparently extreme opposites as MOM and POP? The answer is, the two are not really different where it counts.

In both cases, we start with abstract information. For POP, it comes from a human author's head. For MOM, it comes from a database. But either way, the abstract data is marked up with tags and becomes a document.

Here is a terminally cute mnemonic for this very important relationship:

Data + Markup = DocuMent

Aren't you sorry you read it? Now you'll never forget it.

But XML "DocuMents" are special. An application can do three kinds of processing with one:

- *Parse it*, in order to extract the original data. This can be done without information loss because XML represents both metadata and data, and it lets you keep the abstractions distinct from rendition information.
- *Render it*, so it can be presented in a physical medium that a human can perceive. It can be rendered in many different ways, for delivery in multiple media such as screen displays, print, Braille, spoken word, and so on.

- *Hack it*, meaning "process it as plain text without parsing". Hacking might involve cutting and pasting into other XML documents, or scanning the markup to get some information from it without doing a real parse.

The real revelation here is that data and documents aren't opposites. Far from it – they are actually two states of the same information.

The real difference between the two is that when data is in a database, the metadata about its structure and meaning (the schema) is stored according to the proprietary architecture of the database. When the data becomes a document, the metadata is stored as markup.

A mixture of markup and data must be governed by the rules of some *notation*. XML and SGML are notations, as are RTF and Word file format. The rules of the notation determine how a parser will interpret the document text to separate the data from the markup.

Notations are not just for complete documents. There are also data object notations, such as GIF, TIFF, and EPS, that are used to represent such things as graphics, video (e.g., MPEG), and audio (e.g., AVI). Document notations usually allow their documents to contain data objects, such as pictures, that are in the objects' own data object notations.

Data object notations are usually (not always) in *binary*; that is, they are built-up from low-level ones and zeros. Document notations, however, are frequently *character-based*. XML is character-based, which is why it can be hacked.

In fact, a design objective of XML was to support the "desperate Perl hacker" – someone who needs to write a program in a hurry, using a scripting language like Perl, and who doesn't use a real XML parser. Instead, his program scans the XML document as though it were plain text. The program might search for markup strings, but can also search for data.

A hacker[1] often uses cues that have special meaning to him, like giving special treatment to a tag that occurs at the start of a line, even though those cues have no meaning to a parser. That's why serious hackers do their XML editing with programs that can preserve a document's source and

---

1. As used here, and by most knowledgeable computer people, "hacker" has none of the "cracker" stigma given the term in the popular press. The only security compromised by a desperate Perl hacker is his job security, for leaving things to the last minute!

reproduce it character-for-character. They don't let the software decide which characters are important enough to preserve.

Since databases and documents are really the same, and MOM and POP applications both use XML documents, there are lots of opportunities for synergy.

4.2.4 *MOM and POP – They're so great together!*

Classically, MOM and POP were radically different kinds of applications, each doing things its own way with different technologies and mental models. But POP applications frequently need to include database data in their document content – think of an automotive maintenance manual that has to get the accurate part numbers from a database.

Similarly, MOM applications need to include human-written components. When the dealer asks for price and availability of the automotive parts you need, the display might include a description as well.

With the advent of generalized markup, the barriers to doing MOM-like things in POP applications began to disappear. Some of the POP-like applications you'll read about in the next part of the book appear to have invented the middle tier on their own. And now, with the advent of XML, MOM applications can easily incorporate POP functionality as well.

In fact, we'd go so far as to say there is no longer a difference in kind between the two, only a difference in degree. There really is "an endless spectrum of application opportunities". It is a multi-dimensional spectrum where applications need not be implemented differently just because they process different document types. The real differentiators are other document characteristics, like persistency, size, interactivity, structural complexity, percentage of human-written content, and the importance of eventual presentation to humans.

At the extremes, some applications may call for specialized (or optimized) techniques, but the broad central universe of applications can all be implemented similarly. Much of the knowledge that POP application developers have acquired over the years is now applicable to MOM applications, and vice versa. Keep that in mind as you read the application descriptions and case studies.

That cross-fertilization is true of products and their underlying technologies as well. All of the product descriptions in this book should be of interest, whether you think of your applications as chiefly being MOM or being POP. It is the differences in functionality and design that should cause you to choose one product over another, not their marketing thrust or apparent orientation. We've included detailed usage examples for leading tools in each category so you can look beyond the labels.

4.3 | XML tools

Our coverage of tools falls into three broad categories.

Editing and composition

These are the classic tools of POP applications, but now with applicability to the MOM world as well. Editors are used for creating and revising documents. Composition tools produce renditions, but composition functionality is sometimes included in editors.

Content management

A major benefit of XML is the ability to store and work with components of documents, rather than only being able to deal with the document as a whole. These tools use databases to store information components so they can be controlled, managed, and assembled into end-products in the same way as components of automobiles, aircraft, or other complex devices. Think of them as the MOM and POP store (Figure 4-4).[1]

Middle-tier tools

These are the vital MOM application tools for creating middle-tier servers. They integrate data sources and allow applications to interoperate.

---

1. Generations ago the Mom and Pop store (grocery, convenience, etc.) was the achievement of the entrepreneurial couple who'd lifted themselves out of the working class. Today they'd have an Internet start-up and be striving for a successful IPO!

Figure 4-4   Content management: The MOM and POP store.

In each category, we cover a number of products with detailed usage examples. Although there is often functional overlap among them, each has unique strengths that are targeted towards a particular kind of use. We've tried to emphasize those differences in order to discuss different tool characteristics in each chapter.

There is also a survey of tools that are available for free, in categories such as XML parsers, XSL engines, converters, and viewers. Some 55 of them are on the CD-ROM accompanying this book.

Tool capabilities are also discussed in the application scenarios and case studies.

4.4 | XML jargon demystifier

One of the problems in learning a new technology like XML is getting used to the jargon. A good book will hold you by the hand, introduce terms gradually, and use them precisely and consistently.

Out in the real word, though, people use imprecise terminology that often makes it hard to understand things, let alone compare products. And, unlike authors,[1] they sometimes just plain get things wrong.

---

1. We should be so lucky!

For example, you may see statements like "XML documents are either well-formed or valid." As you've learned from this book, that simply isn't true. All XML documents are well-formed; some of them are also valid.[1]

In this book, we've taken pains to edit the application and tool chapters to use consistent and accurate terminology. However, for product literature and other documents you read, the mileage may vary. So we've prepared a handy guide to the important XML jargon, both right and wrong. Think of it as a MOM application for XML knowledge.

4.4.1 *Structured vs. unstructured*

XML documents are frequently referred to as *structured* while other text, such as rendition notations like RTF, are called *unstructured*.

In fact, renditions can have a rich structure, composed of elements like pages, columns, and blocks. The real distinction being made is between "abstract" and "rendered". Keep that in mind when you read about "structured" and "unstructured", even in this book

4.4.2 *Tag vs. element*

Tags aren't the same thing as elements. Tags describe elements.

In Figure 4-5 the package, metaphorically speaking, is an element. The contents of the package is the content of an element. The tag describes the element. It contains two names:

- the *element type name* ("Wristwatch"), which says what type of element it is, and
- a *unique identifier*, or ID ("WW42-3729"), which says which particular element it is.

A tag could also include attributes describing other properties of the element, such as *Manufacturer="Hy TimePiece Company"*.

When people talk about a *tag name*:

---

1. So does that mean a merely well-formed document is "invalid"? No, an invalid document is one that isn't well-formed; it breaks the rules of the XML notation. Hey, we didn't promise to justify XML jargon, just to explain it.

1. They are referring to the element type name.

2. They are making an error, because tags aren't named.

Figure 4-5   What's in a tag?

4.4.3 *Document type, DTD, and markup declarations*

A *document type* is a class of similar documents, like telephone books, technical manuals, or (when they are marked up as XML) inventory records.

A *document type definition* (*DTD*) is the set of rules for using XML to represent documents of a particular type. These rules might exist only in your mind as you create a document, or they may be written out.

Markup declarations, such as those in Example 4-1, are XML's way of writing out DTDs.

Example 4-1. Markup declarations in the file `greeting.dtd.`

```
<!ELEMENT greeting  (salutation, addressee) >
<!ELEMENT salutation (#PCDATA) >
<!ELEMENT addressee  (#PCDATA) >
```

It is easy to mix up these three constructs: a document type, XML's markup rules for documents of that type (the DTD), and the expression of those rules (the markup declarations). It is necessary to keep the constructs separate if you are dealing with two or more of them at the same time, as when discussing alternative ways to express a DTD. But most of the time, even in this book, "DTD" will suffice for referring to any of the three.

4.4.4 *Document, XML document, and document instance*

The term *document* has two distinct meanings in XML.

Consider a really short XML document that might be rendered as:

Hello World

In one sense, the abstract message you get in your mind when you read the rendition is the *real document*. Communicating that abstraction is the reason for using XML in the first place.

In a formal, syntactic sense, though, the complete text (markup + data, remember) of Example 4-2, is the *XML document*. Perhaps surprisingly, that includes the markup declarations for its DTD in Example 4-1. The XML document, in other words, is a character string that *represents* the real document.

In this example, much of that string consists of the markup declarations, which express the greeting DTD. Only the last four lines describe the real document, which is an instance of a greeting. Those lines are called the *document instance*.

Example 4-2. A greeting document.

```
<?xml version="1.0"?>
<!DOCTYPE greeting SYSTEM "file://greeting.dtd">
<greeting>
<salutation>Hello</salutation>
<addressee>World</addressee>
</greeting>
```

4.4.5 *Coding, encoding, and markup*

People refer to computer programs as *code*, and to the act of programming as *coding*.

There is also the word *encoding*, which refers to the way that characters are represented as ones and zeros in computer storage. XML has a declaration for specifying an encoding.

You'll often see (in places other than this book) phrases like "XML-encoded data", "coded in HTML", or "XML coding".

But using XML isn't coding. Not in the sense of programming, and not in the sense of character encoding. What those phrases mean are "XML document", "marked-up in HTML", and "XML markup".[1]

4.5 | Conclusion

We've covered the key concepts of XML itself, and of the ways in which it is used in the real world. Now we are ready to examine those real-world uses in depth, with application scenarios, case studies of actual users, and detailed descriptions of the tools of the tag trade.

---

1. Although dynamic HTML pages contain so much scripting that the phrase "HTML coding" is almost warranted.

Part Two

- Three-tier Web applications
- Multi-platform electronic publishing
- Electronic commerce/EDI

What You Can Do with XML

Personalized frequent-flyer Web site

- Three-tier XML Web application
- What makes Web sites "hot"
- Client/server Web model is changing
- Website personalization

"If the current frequent-flyer Web site model is
the ultimate in doing business on the Web, I predict
that business on the Web will never really take off".
So says high-flying XML consultant Dianne Kennedy
of XMLXperts Ltd., `http://www.xmlxperts.com`,
who prepared this chapter. It is sponsored by
SoftQuad Inc., `http://www.sq.com`.

I f you surf the Web as well as travel by air, you have probably
stopped by your favorite airline frequent-flyer Web site. How
would you rate that experience?

5.1 | Today's frequent-flyer sites

It might have been fun to find the site and to see all the last minute "bar-
gains" offered for frequent flyers. Perhaps those specials were initially
enough to motivate you to return to the site, if only to dream of taking a
vacation in the middle of your biggest project!

Beyond viewing the posted specials, perhaps you interacted with the site
in a limited way, by entering your frequent flyer number to see your current
point balance. But during heavy traffic hours on the Web, such interactions
can take quite a long time.

And once you know how many points you've accumulated, what about
the whole series of new questions it stimulates for which the Web site can't
provide an answer. At that point, you must resort to calling the "1-800"

number to learn more about your award options and eventually book a flight.

Bottom line: once the novelty wears off, this Web experience, like countless others, is less than satisfying.

5.2 | What's wrong with today's Web model?

Today's Web model is a "client/server" model. In this model, any personalized interaction takes place on the Web server you have contacted. As a result, there is little of it.

Typical Web pages today are static brochures rendered in HTML to provide eye-appealing display. In fact, the Web sites that are rated the "hottest" in today's market are those that provide multi-media sizzle – heavy on graphics, animation, and sound. Personalized content, while a consideration, has not yet become the primary distinguishing characteristic of a "hot" Web site. But as the shift takes place from simply providing entertainment value to facilitating business transactions, personalized content will become "hot".

In today's airline frequent-flyer Web sites, there is a great deal of HTML information that the customer can view. If this information and its associated links changes daily, the Web site becomes more interesting and is more likely to generate return visits. Likewise, interactivity generates more site traffic.

But currently interactivity requires lengthy periods where the customer must be "connected" to remote servers. Queries from the customer go to the server, and resulting responses are shipped back to the customer for viewing in HTML. Unfortunately, a Web server can handle only a limited number of connections at one time.

Every time a new piece of information is requested, a transaction between the client's Web browser and remote Web servers is required. Sooner or later the number of transactions slows the server and the customer experiences lengthy time-outs when queries are processed and data is transferred back to the browser.

5.3 | A better model for doing business on the Web

Today, XML has enabled a new breed of Web server software, one that allows the Web developer to add a new "middle tier" server to the Web model. One example of such software is *HoTMetaL Application Server*, described in Chapter 28, "HoTMetaL Application Server", on page 378. It is used in Figure 5-1 to illustrate the new three-tier Web architecture.

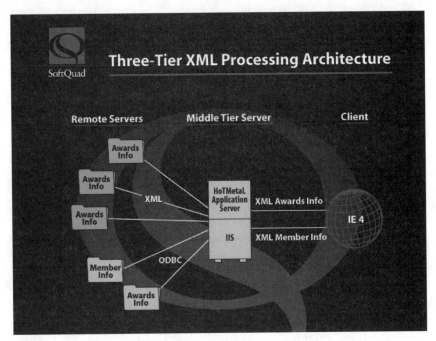

Figure 5-1   Three-tier architecture with *HoTMetaL Application Server.*

Remember, in the old Web model, the customer using a browser such as *Internet Explorer* or *Netscape* on the client interacted directly with data sources on remote servers. The client maintained its connection throughout the interactive session. Each query was sent a response in HTML which could be directly viewed by the client browser. Maintaining the connection between the client and server was critical.

In the new three-tier Web model, the information that fits the profile of the customer is retrieved at once from remote databases by software on the middle tier, either as XML documents or through an ODBC or similar database connection. From that point, continued interaction with the remote databases is no longer required. The connection to the remote servers can be, and is, terminated.

Once all information that fits the customer profile has been assembled by software on the middle tier, it is sent in XML to the client. Now the requirement for further interaction between the client and the middle tier server is eliminated as well.

Rich XML data, directly usable by client applications and scripting languages like *JavaScript*, has been delivered to the client. The connection between the client and middle tier server can now be terminated. At this point, all computing becomes client-based, resulting in a much more efficient use of the Web and a much more satisfying customer experience.

To understand the new three-tier Web model better, one must understand the role XML plays as an enabling technology. One must also understand how efficient delivery of structured data to the client makes all the difference.

5.4 | An XML-enabled frequent-flyer Web site

Initially, differences between the Softland Air XML-enabled frequent-flyer Web site shown in Figure 5-2 and existing frequent-flyer sites may not be apparent. Both provide a pleasing HTML-rendered site brochure. Both enable you to select the services you wish to use. But here the similarities end. New business functions, not possible with today's non-XML sites, quickly become apparent.

From the initial *Softland Air* screen you can select the "frequent flyer" option. This option will cause the frequent-flyer page in Figure 5-3 to be displayed, by traversing a simple hyperlink. When the frequent-flyer page is displayed, it asks you to enter your membership identification number.

Once you have entered your membership number, a personalized, interactive Web experience begins. The next screen that is displayed (Figure 5-4) not only returns your number of frequent flyer points, but shows you destinations for which you have already qualified for awards. This screen will

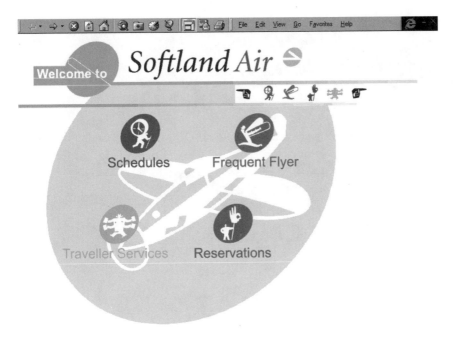

Figure 5-2   "Welcome to *Softland Air*"

vary from member to member, based upon the points a member has in the frequent-flyer database and other personal information the database holds, such as point of origin.

In addition to showing you the awards you have already earned, the *Softland Air* Web site enables you to select destinations of interest. You can see that you have 46,000 points and are qualified to go anywhere in North America in economy through first class. You can also go to Hawaii or the Caribbean by economy class. You do not qualify to go to Europe, but you can see that you nearly have enough points for a European trip.

Suppose you are interested in going to Europe. To learn more about options to get there, you would select a destination on the "Awards Specials" part of the screen. This destination information is added to your profile, along with your point of origin and the number of points you currently have. It will be used to personalize the ongoing transactions.

Once you have selected a destination, the Web page shows you awards, both on *Softland Air* and on partner airlines, that fit the destination you have selected. From this screen you can see what destinations in Europe

Figure 5-3 "Members, sign in here"

most nearly "fit" with the number of award points you hold. As you do not currently qualify for a trip to Europe, you can use the "Planned Trips" portion of the screen to determine what trips you can take by this summer in order to qualify for the award you want.

Using the screen in Figure 5-4, you can plan trips and even book tickets. In this way you can put enough miles in the bank to be able to earn the award to Europe.

Notice how the entire transaction is personalized for the client interacting with the Web site. It is also important to note that aside from logging on to enter your membership number and select the frequent-flyer transaction, all other transactions occurred on the PC in your home or office. Because the middle-tier server can aggregate data from remote sources, package it as XML documents, and send it to the client, a continuous connection to the servers was not required.

This is quite a different model from what we have today on the Web. And XML, working with programs like SoftQuad's HoTMetaL Application Server in the middle tier, is the reason.

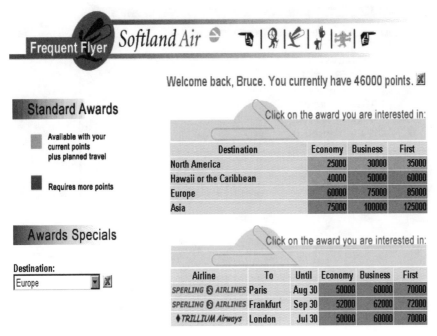

Figure 5-4   Personalized frequent-flyer information

5.5 | Understanding the *Softland Air* scenario

When you connect to the *Softland Air* Web site you first sign in with your membership ID. Your membership number is used to extract your name, the number of award points you have earned, and your point of origin from the "member information" database. This information is sent from remote databases to the middle tier server, which combines it into an XML document (see Figure 5-5). Once the data is in XML, the member name, point of origin, and number of award points can be addressed and used by middle-tier and client applications.

At this point, the middle-tier software knows who signed on. It can request all relevant awards information from both its own awards database and the remote databases maintained by its partner airlines. Figure 5-6 shows the XML data for award specials items from remote awards databases. Note that because this data is in XML, we can easily see the number

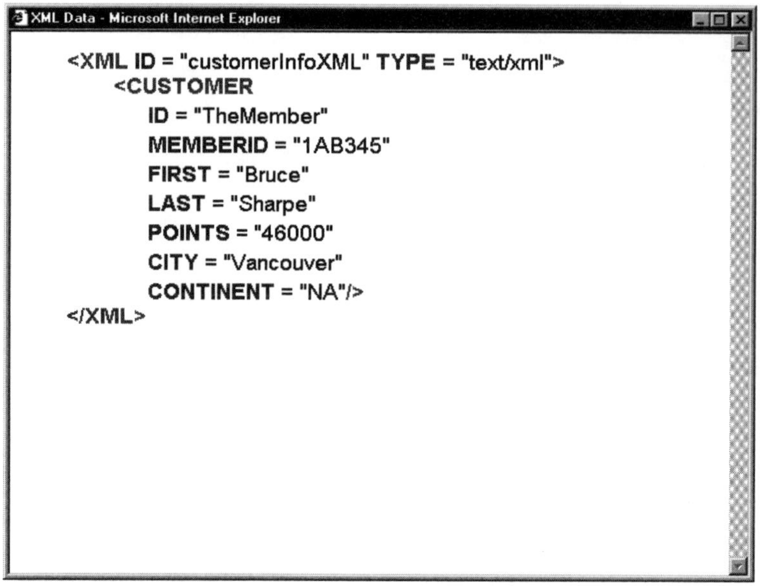

```
XML Data - Microsoft Internet Explorer                    _ □ ×

    <XML ID = "customerInfoXML" TYPE = "text/xml">
        <CUSTOMER
            ID = "TheMember"
            MEMBERID = "1AB345"
            FIRST = "Bruce"
            LAST = "Sharpe"
            POINTS = "46000"
            CITY = "Vancouver"
            CONTINENT = "NA"/>
    </XML>
```

Figure 5-5 XML document generated from member information database

of points required for each award, the partner airline name, the point of origin, the destination, and the dates the special runs. Again, this information is available for use by both middle-tier and client-side processing based on member queries.

The middle-tier server can also request all flight point earnings information from all remote flight information databases, as shown in Figure 5-7. We can easily see the number of points that would be earned from each flight, the partner airline name, the point of origin, the destination, and the date of flight and class of service. This information is available for use by middle-tier and client-side processing.

The information that is sent to the middle tier is compact, personalized, and precise. It differs from HTML because it contains the actual abstract data, not the look of the screen. Middle-tier software, like the *HoTMetaL Application Server*, acts to assemble and deliver the right information at the right time, minimizing Web traffic and providing a higher degree of user interaction and satisfaction.

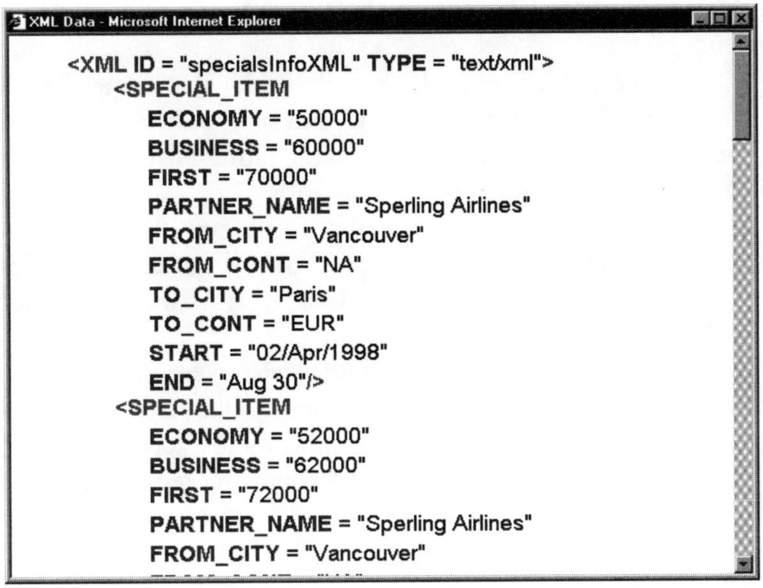

```
XML Data - Microsoft Internet Explorer

<XML ID = "specialsInfoXML" TYPE = "text/xml">
    <SPECIAL_ITEM
        ECONOMY = "50000"
        BUSINESS = "60000"
        FIRST = "70000"
        PARTNER_NAME = "Sperling Airlines"
        FROM_CITY = "Vancouver"
        FROM_CONT = "NA"
        TO_CITY = "Paris"
        TO_CONT = "EUR"
        START = "02/Apr/1998"
        END = "Aug 30"/>
    <SPECIAL_ITEM
        ECONOMY = "52000"
        BUSINESS = "62000"
        FIRST = "72000"
        PARTNER_NAME = "Sperling Airlines"
        FROM_CITY = "Vancouver"
```

Figure 5-6 XML document generated from award specials database

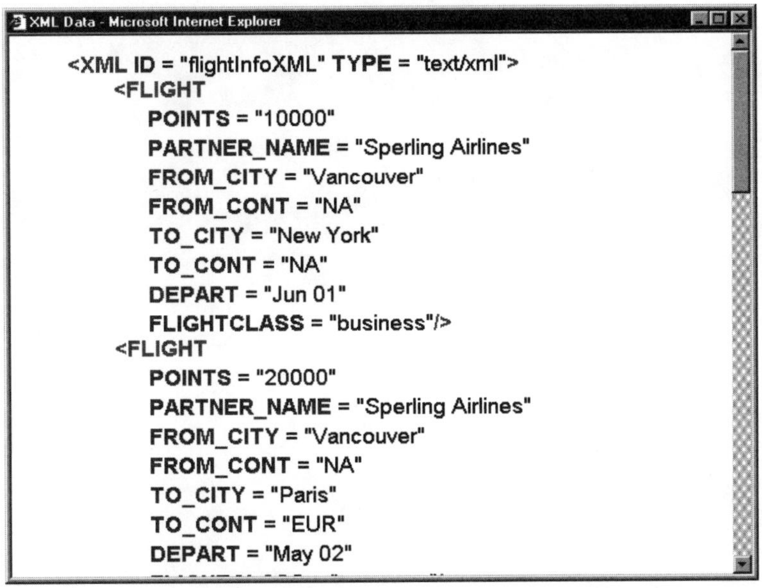

```
XML Data - Microsoft Internet Explorer

<XML ID = "flightInfoXML" TYPE = "text/xml">
    <FLIGHT
        POINTS = "10000"
        PARTNER_NAME = "Sperling Airlines"
        FROM_CITY = "Vancouver"
        FROM_CONT = "NA"
        TO_CITY = "New York"
        TO_CONT = "NA"
        DEPART = "Jun 01"
        FLIGHTCLASS = "business"/>
    <FLIGHT
        POINTS = "20000"
        PARTNER_NAME = "Sperling Airlines"
        FROM_CITY = "Vancouver"
        FROM_CONT = "NA"
        TO_CITY = "Paris"
        TO_CONT = "EUR"
        DEPART = "May 02"
```

Figure 5-7 XML document with flight point earnings

5.6 | Towards the Brave New Web

The World Wide Web continues to evolve rapidly. Today the "hottest" Web sites are those that provide multimedia sizzle. But as the shift takes place from simply providing entertainment value to facilitating business transactions, dynamic personalized content will become "hot".

Products like SoftQuad's HoTMetaL Application Server allow the Web site developer to add a new middle tier server to the Web model. It is this middle tier that enables business transactions in a way that was simply not possible before XML.

The *Softland Air* scenario shows how a middle-tier server, using XML as a structured information interchange representation, enables personalized data aggregation and organization from multiple remote databases, and interactive delivery to client browsers based upon end-user requirements.

Building an online auction Web site

- Three-tier Web application
- Dynamic generation of XML documents
- Extracting data from XML documents
- Creating a user interface

6

An online auction is the epitome of a complex real-time interactive application, so the Microsoft Web Applications Team built a realistic *Auction Demo* to show how simply one can be implemented as an XML three-tier Web application. This chapter is sponsored by Microsoft Corporation, `http://www.microsoft.com`, and was prepared by Charles Heinemann.

The *Auction Demo* is a three-tier Web application that simulates an online auction using technologies that are available in *Internet Explorer 4.0* (IE 4.0). It allows you to view the items available for auction, place bids on those items, and monitor the bids placed by fellow bidders.

Like other three-tier Web applications, the Auction Demo has data sources on the back end, a user interface on the client, and a Web server in the middle. We'll see how it was developed, using just three permanent Web pages:

userInterface.htm

This page uses *Dynamic HTML* (DHTML) to allow the Web browser to present the auction information to the user. It contains scripts that collect or update data on the middle tier by requesting *Active Server Pages* (ASP).

auction.asp

This page is an ASP file. When userInterface.htm requests this page, the scripts in it are executed on the server. The scripts generate auction.xml, an XML document that contains the latest auction data, which is delivered to the client.

makebid.asp

This page is requested by userInterface.htm when the user wants to make a bid. It is executed on the middle tier, causing the data source to be updated with the new bid information.

The user interface (UI) for the *Auction Demo* is shown in Figure 6-1. It is the rendition of the userInterface.htm *Dynamic HTML* page, which is downloaded to the client when the user clicks on a link to the auction.

That page has scripts within it that handle all the client-side activity. That includes requesting data from the middle tier in order to display the most current values of the items and bids. We'll see later how the UI page does its thing, but first let's look at how the middle tier collects and transmits the data. It does so by packaging the data as XML documents.

6.1 | Getting data from the middle tier

The role of the middle tier in a Web application is to gather information from data sources and deliver it in a consistent manner to clients. In the Auction Demo we start with a single data source, an ODBC-compliant database. (Later we'll see how multiple data sources of different kinds can be accessed.)

The "Auction" database used for the *Auction Demo* is a relational database with two tables, an "Item" table and a "Bids" table. The "Item" table contains data about each of the items up for auction. It is shown in Figure 6-2.

For the sake of clarity, we'll just cover the "Item" table in this chapter (the "Bids" are handled similarly). You can see the full demo at http:// www.microsoft.com/xml. We want to deliver the data in that table in the form of an XML document, so the client's user interface page won't have to know anything about the actual data source.

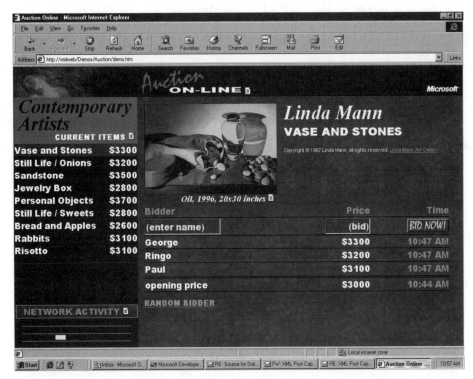

Figure 6-1   The *Auction Demo* user interface.

Title	Artist	Dimensions	Materials	Year
Vase and Stones	Linda Mann	20x30 inches	Oil	1996
Still Life / Onions	Linda Mann	20x30 inches	Oil	1997
Sandstone	Linda Mann	20x30 inches	Oil	1995
Jewelry Box	Linda Mann	20x30 inches	Oil	1994
Personal Objects	Linda Mann	20x30 inches	Oil	1995
Still Life / Sweets	Linda Mann	20x30 inches	Oil	1994
Bread and Apples	Linda Mann	20x30 inches	Oil	1995
Rabbits	Linda Mann	20x30 inches	Oil	1996
Risotto	Linda Mann	20x30 inches	Oil	1995

Figure 6-2   The *Auction Demo* item table.

6.1.1 Defining the XML document structure

The key to creating useful XML documents is the proper structuring of the data. For the *Auction Demo*, that means deciding how a record in the "Item" table will be represented as an ITEM element in XML. There is a straightforward mapping, shown in the following data-less element:

Example 6-1. Template for an ITEM element.

```
<ITEM>
  <TITLE></TITLE>
  <ARTIST></ARTIST>
  <DIMENSIONS></DIMENSIONS>
  <MATERIALS></MATERIALS>
  <YEAR></YEAR>
</ITEM>
```

For each field in the "Item" table, there is a corresponding subelement of the ITEM element.

To generate XML documents with these ITEM elements, the *Auction Demo* uses ASP files.

6.1.2 Using ASP files to generate XML documents

XML can be generated on the middle tier using *Active Server Pages*. ASP offers an environment in which Web authors can create documents dynamically by intermixing markup languages with in-line scripts. The scripts can be written in a variety of scripting languages, including *JScript* and *VBScript*, and can invoke server-side components to access databases, execute applications, and process information.

When a browser requests an ASP file, it is first processed by the server, which delivers a generated Web page containing standard markup.

In an ASP file, commands and scripts are delimited by "<%" and "%>". Everything not so delimited is markup or data that will appear in the generated page. For example, consider the following trivial ASP file:

The file, after establishing that the scripting language is *VBScript*, creates the variable "Total" with the value "2". The following line generates an

Example 6-2. Sample ASP file.

```
<%@ LANGUAGE = VBScript%>
<%DIM Total = 2%>
<AMOUNT><%=Total%></AMOUNT>
```

XML "AMOUNT" element whose content is generated by executing the small script, which in this case retrieves the value of "Total".

When the browser requests this file, it will actually receive the XML document that is generated from the file, as shown in Example 6-3:

Example 6-3. XML document generated by sample ASP file.

```
<AMOUNT>2</AMOUNT>
```

Note that the ASP syntax (<% . . . %>) does not cause an XML parsing error. That is because the ASP file is not itself an XML document. The ASP file is processed on the server and only the generated XML document is returned to the client.

In the case of the *Auction Demo*, the file auction.asp is used to access the "Auction" database and generate XML containing the data within the "Item" and "Bids" tables. The ability to generate XML on the middle tier makes it possible to provide the Web application with content that can be manipulated on the client and refreshed without having to refresh the entire user interface.

In Example 6-4, auction.asp begins like the ASP file in Example 6-2, by declaring the scripting language. The next two lines are the XML declaration and the start-tag of the root element (AUCTIONBLOCK) of the XML document to be generated, which we will call "auction.xml".

Example 6-4. Start of auction.asp.

```
<%@ LANGUAGE = VBScript %>
<?XML VERSION="1.0"?>
<AUCTIONBLOCK>
```

Next, a connection to the "Auction" database is established and that connection is opened:

Example 6-5. Connecting to the database.

```
<%
Set Conn = Server.CreateObject("ADODB.Connection")
Conn.Open "Auction","Auction","Auction"
%>
```

A "record set" variable (ItemRS) is now established to contain each record of the "Item" table as it is accessed, and a "Do While" loop is begun to perform the access.

Example 6-6. Preparing to access the "Item" records.

```
<%
Set ItemRS = Conn.Execute("select * from item")
Do While Not ItemRS.EOF
%>
```

Next, the template in Example 6-1 is used to create the XML ITEM element that will be generated. Just as in Example 6-2, a small script is inserted as the content of each subelement of ITEM within auction.asp. In this case, the script extracts the corresponding field's data from the record set.

Example 6-7. Markup and scripts to generate an ITEM element.

```
<ITEM>
  <TITLE><%=ItemRS("Title")%></TITLE>
  <ARTIST><%=ItemRS("Artist")%></ARTIST>
  <DIMENSIONS><%=ItemRS("Dimensions")%></DIMENSIONS>
  <MATERIALS><%=ItemRS("Materials")%></MATERIALS>
  <YEAR><%=ItemRS("Year")%></YEAR>
</ITEM>
```

After an ITEM element is generated, the script moves to the next record in the record set. The loop is then repeated. Once all of the records have been run through, the root element is ended.

The complete auction.asp file is in Example 6-9.

Example 6-10 is an abridged version of the XML document (auction.xml) generated by the auction.asp file in Example 6-9.

Example 6-8. Repeating the loop and ending the document.

```
<%
ItemRS.MoveNext
Loop
%>
</AUCTIONBLOCK>
```

Example 6-9. The complete auction.asp file.

```
<%@ LANGUAGE = VBScript %>
<?XML VERSION="1.0"?>
<AUCTIONBLOCK>
<%
Set Conn = Server.CreateObject("ADODB.Connection")
Conn.Open "Auction","Auction","Auction"
Set ItemRS = Conn.Execute("select * from item")
Do While Not ItemRS.EOF
%>
  <ITEM>
    <TITLE><%=ItemRS("Title")%></TITLE>
    <ARTIST><%=ItemRS("Artist")%></ARTIST>
    <DIMENSIONS><%=ItemRS("Dimensions")%></DIMENSIONS>
    <MATERIALS><%=ItemRS("Materials")%></MATERIALS>
    <YEAR><%=ItemRS("Year")%></YEAR>
  </ITEM>
  <%
  ItemRS.MoveNext
  Loop
  %>
</AUCTIONBLOCK>
```

Example 6-10. Abridged auction.xml document generated by auction.asp.

```
<?XML VERSION="1.0"?>
<AUCTIONBLOCK>
  <ITEM>
    <TITLE>Vase and Stones</TITLE>
    <ARTIST>Linda Mann</ARTIST>
    <DIMENSIONS>20 X 30 inches<DIMENSIONS>
    <MATERIALS>Oil</MATERIALS>
    <YEAR>1996</YEAR>
  </ITEM>
  <ITEM>
  . . .
  </ITEM>
  . . .
</AUCTIONBLOCK>
```

6.1.3 *Generating XML from multiple databases*

One powerful reason to generate XML documents on the middle tier is that they can contain data that is sourced from multiple independent databases. The technique is similar to what we've already seen. The only difference is that multiple database connections are made instead of one.

The ASP file in Example 6-11 does just this, generating a single XML document with data from the databases "Gallery1" and "Gallery2".

The XML generated by the ASP file in Example 6-11 looks structurally just like Example 6-10, an AUCTIONBLOCK element with multiple ITEM children. However, the data content originates from two different data sources.

Also notice that, for the DIMENSIONS, MATERIALS, and YEAR elements, the source fields in the "Gallery2" database are actually labeled differently from the corresponding fields in "Gallery1." One benefit of consolidating the data on the middle tier is that the semantics can be identified consistently, and therefore made more easily accessible.

6.1.4 *Generating XML from both databases and XML data sources*

The middle tier can source data of different kinds, not just databases. In Example 6-11, the ASP file, as in previous examples, first accesses data from "Gallery 1", an ODBC compliant database. However, it then adds data from "Gallery 3", a source of XML documents.

The Gallery3 XML document is processed by the MSXML parser (details below), which allows access to the document's data content. Note that there is no way – and no need – to tell whether Gallery3 is a persistent document, or was generated by another middle-tier application.

Also, look at the YEAR element. Just as with the Gallery2 database in the previous example, the original semantic label – in this case the DATE generic identifier – is changed on the middle tier to ensure consistency.

Example 6-11. Generating one XML document from two databases.

```
<%@ LANGUAGE = VBScript %>
<?XML VERSION="1.0"?>
<AUCTIONBLOCK>
<%
'The connection to the Gallery1 data source is made
Set Conn = Server.CreateObject("ADODB.Connection")
Conn.Open "Gallery1","Gallery1","Gallery1"
Set ItemRS = Conn.Execute("select * from item")
Do While Not ItemRS.EOF
%>
  <ITEM>
    <TITLE><%=ItemRS("Title")%></TITLE>
    <ARTIST><%=ItemRS("Artist")%></ARTIST>
    <DIMENSIONS><%=ItemRS("Dimensions")%></DIMENSIONS>
    <MATERIALS><%=ItemRS("Materials")%></MATERIALS>
    <YEAR><%=ItemRS("Year")%></YEAR>
  </ITEM>
  <%
  ItemRS.MoveNext
  Loop
  %>
<%
'The connection to the Gallery2 data source is made
Set Conn = Server.CreateObject("ADODB.Connection")
Conn.Open "Gallery2","Gallery2","Gallery2"
Set ItemRS = Conn.Execute("select * from item")
Do While Not ItemRS.EOF
%>
  <ITEM>
    <TITLE><%=ItemRS("Title")%></TITLE>
    <ARTIST><%=ItemRS("Artist")%></ARTIST>
    <DIMENSIONS><%=ItemRS("Size")%></DIMENSIONS>
    <MATERIALS><%=ItemRS("Medium")%></MATERIALS>
    <YEAR><%=ItemRS("Date")%></YEAR>
  </ITEM>
  <%
  ItemRS.MoveNext
  Loop
  %>
</AUCTIONBLOCK>
```

Example 6-12. Generating one XML document from a database and another XML document.

```
<%@ LANGUAGE = VBScript %>
<?XML VERSION="1.0"?>
<AUCTIONBLOCK>
<%
Set Conn = Server.CreateObject("ADODB.Connection")
Conn.Open "Gallery1","Gallery1","Gallery1"
Set ItemRS = Conn.Execute("select * from item")
Do While Not ItemRS.EOF
%>
  <ITEM>
    <TITLE><%=ItemRS("Title")%></TITLE>
    <ARTIST><%=ItemRS("Artist")%></ARTIST>
    <DIMENSIONS><%=ItemRS("Dimensions")%></DIMENSIONS>
    <MATERIALS><%=ItemRS("Materials")%></MATERIALS>
    <YEAR><%=ItemRS("Year")%></YEAR>
  </ITEM>
  <%
  ItemRS.MoveNext
  Loop
  %>
<%
'Here the connection to the Gallery3 data is made
Set XML = Server.CreateObject("msxml")
XML.URL = "http://datasource3/Gallery3.xml"
Set Items = XML.root.children
For I = 0 to Items.length - 1
%>
  <ITEM>
    <TITLE><%=Items.item(I).children.item("TITLE").text%>
    </TITLE>
    <ARTIST><%=Items.item(I).children.item("ARTIST").text%>
    </ARTIST>
    <DIMENSIONS><%=Items.item(I).children.item("DIMENSIONS").text%>
    </DIMENSIONS>
    <MATERIALS><%=Items.item(I).children.item("MATERIALS").text%>
    </MATERIALS>
    <YEAR><%=Items.item(I).children.item("DATE").text%>
    </YEAR>
  </ITEM>
<%Next%>
</AUCTIONBLOCK>
```

6.2 | Building the user interface

The user interface is critical to the success of any application. It must allow the user to interact with the application in an efficient and straightforward manner. The user interface for the *Auction Demo* was built using DHTML.

DHTML is a set of features in *Internet Explorer 4.0* for creating interactive and visually interesting Web pages. It is based on existing HTML standards and is designed to work well with applications, *ActiveX* controls, and other embedded objects.

With DHTML a developer can create a robust and efficient UI without additional support from applications or embedded controls, or even return trips to the server. A *Dynamic HTML* page is self-contained, using styles and scripts to process user input and directly manipulate the HTML markup and other text within the page.

Let's see how userInterface.htm creates the Auction Demo interface by using scripts and the *IE 4.0 Document Object Model*. Two basic techniques are employed: procedural scripts and descriptive binding.

6.2.1 *Using procedural scripts*

Internet Explorer 4.0 includes the *MSXML* parser, which exposes the parsed XML document as a *document object model*.[1] Once exposed, scripts can access the data content of the XML elements and dynamically insert the data into the user interface.

The userInterface.htm code in Example 6-13 applies *MSXML* to auction.xml, the XML document generated by auction.asp. That creates an *ActiveX* object representing the parsed document.

Example 6-13. Creating the auction document object.

```
var auction = new ActiveXObject("msxml");
auction.URL = "http://Webserver/auction.asp";
```

---

1. The W3C is currently developing a common document object model for XML and HTML. There is a working draft on the CD-ROM. The *IE 4.0 Document Object Model* attempts to maintain compliance with the W3C draft as it evolves.

In Example 6-14, the script next retrieves the root element. It then navigates the tree until it locates the TITLE element within the first ITEM element of auction.xml. The innerText property is used to insert the data content of TITLE into the user interface as the value of the "item_title" attribute, which appears on a DIV element.

Example 6-14. Extracting data from the auction document object.

```
var root = auction.root;
var item0 = root.children.item("ITEM",0)
var title = item0.children.item("TITLE").text;
document.all("item_title").innerText = title;
<DIV ID="item_title"></DIV>
```

One of the benefits of using procedural scripts to display XML documents is that you can manipulate the data content of an XML element before you display it. For example, if you wanted to display the dimensions of each painting using the metric system, rather than feet and inches, your script could simply convert the content of the DIMENSIONS element from inches to centimeters.

6.2.2 *Using descriptive data binding*

The *IE 4.0 XML Data Source Object* (XML DSO) is a declarative alternative to the procedural scripts described in the last section. The XML DSO is an applet (see Example 6-15) that enables the data of XML elements to be bound as the content of HTML elements.

Example 6-15. The *IE 4.0 XML Data Source Object* applet.

```
<APPLET ID=auction CODE=com.ms.xml.dso.XMLDSO.class MAYSCRIPT
       WIDTH=0 HEIGHT=0>
    <PARAM NAME="url" VALUE="auction.asp">
</APPLET>
```

In Example 6-15, the "url" parameter points the XML DSO to auction.asp, which causes auction.xml to be generated on the middle tier. A persistent XML source could also have been used.

In Example 6-16, data binding is used to populate the part of the user interface that shows the painting and the caption beneath it.

Example 6-16. Data binding with the XML DSO.

```
<TD>
  <DIV STYLE="margin-left:16px;
margin-top:16px;margin-right:16px">
    <DIV ID=pict></DIV>
      <DIV CLASS="details">
        <SPAN DATASRC=#auction DATAFLD=MATERIALS></SPAN>,
        <SPAN DATASRC=#auction DATAFLD=YEAR></SPAN>,
        <SPAN DATASRC=#auction DATAFLD=DIMENSIONS></SPAN>
      </DIV>
    </DIV>
  </DIV>
</TD>
```

With the XML DSO applet embedded in the Web page, no scripting is required to bind the data content of XML elements to HTML elements. Instead, the name of the document object (ID of the APPLET in Example 6-15) is specified as the value of the DATASRC attribute, and the generic identifier of the XML element is specified for the DATAFLD attribute.

One advantage of displaying XML with the XML DSO is that the XML document is processed asynchronously to the rendering of the page. Therefore, if the inventory of paintings were very large, the initial elements of the XML document could be displayed even before the last elements were processed.

6.3 | Updating the data source from the client

We have seen how userInterface.htm on the client obtained data to display to the user by invoking auction.asp on the middle tier. It can also enable the user to make his own bid by invoking another middle tier page, make-bid.asp.

In the *Auction Demo*, the user bids by overwriting the price and bidder name in the first row of the bid table. A bid therefore consists of the "title" of the item currently displayed, the "price" of the new bid, and the name of the new "bidder".

These data items must be passed as parameters to makebid.asp, which executes a script to process them and update the database. The script returns to the client a "return message" XML document: a single element containing information about the status of the processing.

The script in userInterface.htm (see Example 6-17) begins by assigning the title of the current item up for auction to the "title" variable, the value of the "price" text box to the "price" variable, and the value of the "bidder" text box to the "bidder" variable.

It then creates the return message document object, which will state whether makebid.asp successfully updated the database. The three variables are passed as parameters to the ASP file when it is invoked.

Example 6-17. Sending a new bid to makebid.asp.

```
var title = current_item.children.item("TITLE").text;
var price = price.value;
var bidder = bidder.value;
var returnMsg = new ActiveXObject("msxml");
returnMsg.URL = "http://auction/makebid.asp?title=" +
  title + "&price=" + price + "&bidder=" + bidder;
```

In Example 6-18, makebid.asp (called by userInterface.htm in Example 6-17) assigns the values of the parameters "title", "price", and "bidder" to variables with the same names.

The "BidRS" record set object is then created and a connection to the "Auction" database is made. Note that the connection is made for both reading and writing. The "Bids" table is then opened and the new information is added to the record set, after which the connection is closed. The process is much the same as it was for auction.asp, except that the database is written to instead of just being read.

Finally, makebid.asp generates the return message document with the status of the update.

Example 6-18. The makebid.asp file updates the database.

```
<%@ LANGUAGE = VBScript %>
<%
  title = Request.QueryString("title")
  price = Request.QueryString("price")
  bidder = Request.QueryString("bidder")

  Set BidRS = Server.CreateObject("ADODB.RecordSet")
  connect = "data source=Auction;user id=sa;password=;"
  BidRS.CursorType = 2
  BidRS.LockType = 3   ' read/write
  BidRS.Open "Bids", connect

  BidRS.AddNew
  BidRS("item") = title
  BidRS("price") = price
  BidRS("bidder") = bidder
  BidRS.Update
  BidRS.Close
%>
<STATUS>OK</STATUS>
```

6.4 | Conclusion

The entire *Auction Demo* was built using the methods described above. You can get a head start on building a similar Web application by modifying these scripts to suit your particular requirements.

XML enables Web applications by providing dynamic, accessible content that can be navigated and manipulated on the client. In addition, it enables the updating of content without having to refresh the entire user interface. This ability saves time by reducing round trips to the server for information that already exists on the client.

With XML, users can manage data over the Internet just as they presently do on their local machines. As a result, the Web is made a more interactive and interoperable medium. As the information superhighway is transformed into the data superhighway, Web applications similar to the

Auction Demo will allow for better utilization of the vast resources made available by the Web.

 ***Analysis***   The Auction Demo clearly illustrates the architecture of a three-tier application. It uses the middle tier as a transient data aggregator and normalizer. In other chapters you'll see different approaches to the middle tier, including persistent storage of metadata and the use of object paradigms rather than data paradigms.

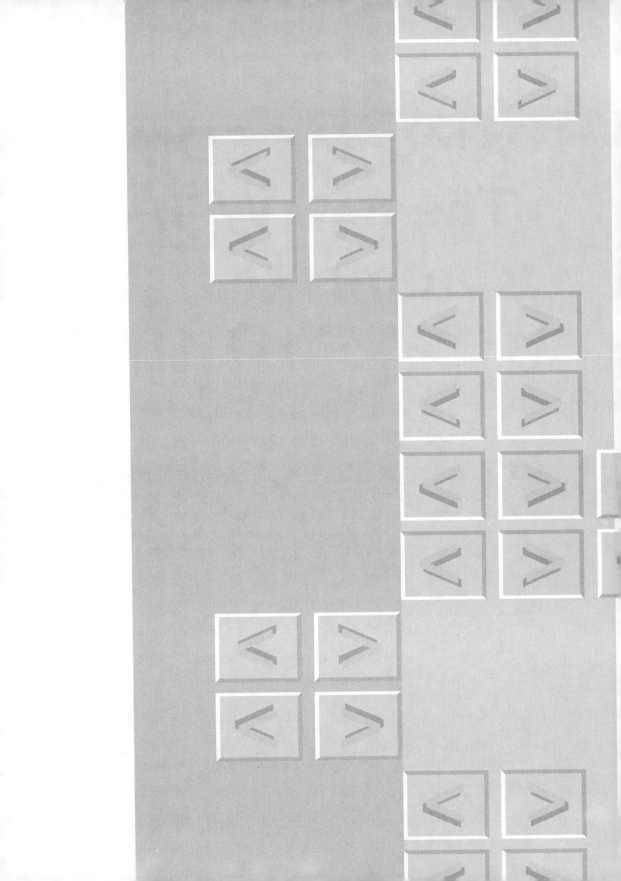

XML and EDI: The new Web commerce

- Traditional EDI: Built on outdated principles
- Ubiquitous EDI: A quantum leap forward
- The New EDI: Leveraging XML and the Internet

XML and the Internet will dramatically reshape the Electronic Data Interchange (EDI) landscape. By driving down costs and complexity, EDI will become a truly ubiquitous technology that will reshape business as we know it. This introduction to EDI is sponsored by POET Software Corporation, http://www.poet.com, developers of object-oriented software for XML-based information systems. It was prepared by Mike Hogan.

Over the past several decades, corporations have invested trillions of dollars in automating their internal processes. While this investment has yielded significant improvements in efficiency, that efficiency has not been extended to external processes.

In effect, companies have created islands of automation that are isolated from their vendors and customers – their trading partners. The interaction among companies and their trading partners remains slow and inefficient because it is still based on manual processes.

7.1 | What is EDI?

Electronic Data Interchange (EDI) has been heralded as the solution to this problem. *EDI* is defined as the exchange of data between heterogeneous systems to support transactions.

EDI is not simply the exportation of data from one system to another, but actual interaction between systems. For example, Company B is a supplier to Company A. Instead of sending purchase orders, bills and checks in hard copy form, the two might connect their systems to exchange this same data electronically.

In the process they could benefit in many other ways, including faster turnaround on orders, better inventory control, reduced financial float, complete real-time information about orders and inventory for improved decision-making, reduced costs for manual data input, and more. Companies that have implemented EDI rave about the various benefits.

In fact, these benefits can be expanded to a chain of suppliers. For example, Company C might be a supplier to Company B above. If companies B and C implement EDI, then Company A gains the additional benefits of superior integration with their entire *supply chain* of suppliers.

7.1.1   *Extranets can't hack it*

There is a significant gap between the business benefits described above and the actual implementation of EDI. This is because the actual implementation of "traditional EDI" is fundamentally flawed. It is difficult and costly to implement and, even worse, it requires a unique solution for each pair of trading partners. This situation is analogous to requiring a unique telephone line to be wired to each person to whom you wish to speak.

Many people falsely proclaimed the Internet as the solution to this problem. By implementing EDI over a single network, our problems would be solved. This "solution" was so exciting it was even given its own name, the extranet. Unfortunately, a network with a common protocol is still only a partial solution.

This is because the systems implemented in each company are based on different platforms, applications, data formats (notations), protocols, schemas, business rules, and more. Simply "connecting" these systems over the Internet does not, by itself, solve the problem. To use the phone system analogy again, this is analogous to wiring each business into the global phone network, only to realize that each company's phone system is unique, and incompatible with every other phone system.

And given the trillions of dollars companies have invested in automation, they are not simply going to replace these systems with new "compatible" solutions, assuming such things existed.

7.1.2 *XML can!*

The eXtensible Markup Language (XML) provides a solution for EDI over the Internet. XML is a universal notation (data format) that allows computers to store and transfer data that can be understood by any other computer system. XML maintains the content and structure, but separates the business rules from the data. As a result, each trading partner can apply its own business rules. This flexibility is critical to creating a complete solution for EDI.

There are additional technologies which are also part of the complete solution. Security, for example, is critical to EDI. Transactional integrity, connection stability, authentication and other services are also critical to implementing a complete solution. These requirements are addressed by technologies that are layered on top of the Internet. We refer to them generically as *Internet-based services*.

The final piece of the EDI solution is data storage. XML introduces a unique set of requirements for hierarchical naming and structure. It also requires rich relationships and complex linking. XML's use in EDI adds further requirements for metadata and versioning. These requirements levy heavy demands on database technology.

7.1.3 *The new EDI*

By combining XML, the Internet, Internet-based services and database connectivity, we have a complete solution for *New EDI*. Together, these technologies will not only change EDI, they will change our entire business landscape. EDI will metamorphose from a handful of unique interconnections, defined by the supply chain, into a "supply web". The supply web is an intelligent common fabric of commerce over the Internet.

According to Metcalfe's Law[1], the value of a network is roughly proportional to the number of users squared. Imagine what this means when your EDI "network" expands from a one-to-one proposition, to a true network that encompasses practically every company in the world. Suddenly, the trillions of dollars companies have invested in internal automation increase in value by several factors. By the same token, this information can also be

---

1. Robert Metcalfe is the creator of Ethernet.

extended to customers, adding significant value to the vendor-customer relationship, thereby enhancing customer loyalty.

This is a pivotal time in the history of technology. With the emergence of XML, all of the pieces are available to create a universal mechanism for EDI. The Internet provides the transport. XML provides the flexible, extensible, structured message format. Various Internet-based services provide solutions for security, transactional integrity, authentication, connection stability, network fail-over and more.

Add to this sophisticated data storage and you have all of the pieces necessary to unite corporate islands of automation into a single coherent fabric of electronic commerce. This will result in dramatic improvements in efficiency, cost-savings, superior access to real-time data for analysis and decision-making, superior inventory management, and more.

Let's examine these propositions in detail, and the technology that makes them possible. The new EDI is already emerging as the driving force behind the use of XML on the Web.

7.1.4 *Ubiquitous EDI: A quantum leap forward*

Ubiquitous EDI will have a profound impact on business-to-business and business-to-consumer relationships. The many problems with current implementations of EDI have relegated it to large enterprises and selected industries. However, the combination of the Internet, Internet-based technologies, and XML will open up EDI not only to small-to-medium enterprises (*SMEs*), but also to individuals (Example 7-1).

Through deployment of these technologies, EDI will experience growth and market penetration that will rival the e-mail market. Electronic commerce will finally blossom on the Web and become an everyday part of our lives. In short, EDI will usher in a new era in computing. The Internet will metamorphose from a transport for Web pages into a ubiquitous and seamless foundation for every imaginable transaction. In the future, EDI will touch every aspect of computing.

Various forms of "data interchange" have been implemented with various degrees of success. Examples include OLE and DDE for sharing data among heterogeneous applications on the same computer. CORBA, Java RMI, COM and COM+ are generalized technologies for data interchange

Example 7-1. The value of data interchange.

Mike opens his company expense report, and in the microsecond it takes to launch, he reminisces about the old days when he had to fill out these things himself. Now the computer does it for him. Mike recently took a trip to Utah to close a major deal. In the process he purchased a plane ticket, a rental car and various meals. In the old days, he used to enter all of these charges manually into an expense program...not any more.

Mike uses a corporate American Express card for these purchases. When he opens the expense report, it automatically connects to American Express, via EDI, and presents a list of new charges. Mike selects the charges that are appropriate for this expense report.

American Express sends this data to Mike's computer, which automatically formats the data into his expense report. Mike then clicks the send button and the expense report is sent to his manager to approve. Then the company's bank instantly wires the money to Mike's bank account.

Behind the scenes, all these companies are establishing connections, as needed, to share information in a secure and reliable manner using XML and the Internet. But Mike doesn't concern himself with what goes on behind the scenes, he's off to close another big deal in Washington.

among systems. Then there is the traditional EDI market for the "Electronic exchange of data to support business transactions".[1]

In focusing on the traditional EDI market, the seminal questions are: "What is the real value of EDI?" and "Why should I care?"

7.1.5 *The value of EDI*

While traditional EDI is very costly and difficult to implement, the potential benefits are very significant. Companies that have implemented EDI rave about benefits like improved efficiency, vendor management, cost savings, superior access to information for decision making, tighter inventory control, customer responsiveness, and its a competitive advantage that can be marketed to attract new customers.

---

1. *European Workshop on Open Systems Technical Guide on Electronic Commerce (EWOS ETG 066)*

EDI was initially implemented to improve efficiency by enabling companies to eliminate costly and slow manual methodologies, like the processing of purchase orders and bills. It was thought that by allowing the computers of two or more companies to share this information, they could achieve dramatic improvements in efficiency.

However, the largest savings are derived from a complete shift to EDI that allows companies to completely eliminate their hardcopy processes. The traditional 80/20 rule applies in reverse to EDI, meaning that it is the last 20% of your trading partners to convert to EDI who account for 80% of the potential savings.

This is because even with 80% of your trading partners using EDI, you must still maintain the same manual processes for the remaining 20% who don't. While most companies have not been able to completely convert from hardcopy processes to EDI, the 20% savings companies have realized have still been very significant. With ubiquitous EDI enabling companies to completely eliminate their manual processes, the savings will improve dramatically.

With EDI, companies are also able to manage their supply chains much more efficiently. Through EDI, companies have been able to reduce the average time from issuance of an order to receipt of goods from several weeks, to a matter of days. By improving inventory control, companies are able to minimize their investment in costly inventory, while still being able to address spikes in business. For industries where inventory costs are a significant part of their business, like manufacturing, this represents a significant cost savings.

EDI also reduces the financial float by eliminating the typical order generation, delivery and processing, by 5-7 days. By combining EDI with Electronic Funds Transfer (EFT) companies can also reduce the financial float by 8-10+ days. Based on the amount of money[1] involved, this can represent a significant savings.

EDI also provides companies with superior real-time information upon which to base decisions. Everyone recalls stories of companies who simply didn't have the data to realize how bad things were, until it was too late. With EDI, companies have access to complete data in real-time. The ability

---

1. *Electronic Commerce/Electronic Data Interchange and Electronic Funds Transfer (EC/EDI/EFT)*, http://www.dfas.mil/dir_init/ec_edi/ index.htm

to collect, manipulate and measure information about your relationships with vendors and customers can be critical to your company's success.

Customer responsiveness is becoming increasingly important. Many companies have leveraged technology to dramatically improve customer responsiveness. A good example of this is Federal Express, which has created a Web site where customers can track the status of their packages.

This is only accomplished through FedEx's end-to-end dedication to EDI. By capturing information about the package status at each step in the process, and making this information accessible to customers, they have made themselves leaders in customer support. This is critical to building and growing businesses, especially in the Internet-age.

Some companies who have implemented EDI with one supplier, have gone on to market this capability to other potential customers, as a unique selling point. This has enabled them to grow their business. As EDI becomes more ubiquitous, the tide could shift to the point where companies will not accept vendors who are not EDI-capable. This refers back to the dramatic savings that can be achieved by a complete conversion to EDI.

7.2 | Traditional EDI: Built on outdated principles

"Traditional" EDI is based on outdated principles that will cause it to fade into technological obscurity, as it becomes embraced and replaced by the "New" EDI. Traditional EDI refers to the use of rigid transaction sets with business rules embedded in them. This model simply does not work in today's rapidly changing business environment.

This problem is compounded by the fact that companies have chosen to interpret these transaction set standards in ways that suit their unique business requirements. As a result, vendors who engage in EDI with multiple customers typically must create a unique solution to handle the transaction sets from each company. This makes the implementation of EDI far too expensive, especially for SMEs.

These and other problems have hindered the growth of EDI. However, by solving the problems of traditional EDI, we will usher in a new era, where EDI is as common as an Internet account is today.

7.2.1   *The history of EDI*

EDI is a process for exchanging data in electronic format between heterogeneous applications and/or platforms in a manner that can be processed without manual intervention.

EDI dates back to the 1970s, when it was introduced by the Transportation Data Coordinating Committee (TDCC). The TDCC created transaction sets for vendors to [1] follow in order to enable electronic processing of purchase orders and bills.

At the time, the technology landscape was very different from what it is today. Lacking ubiquitous powerful CPUs, a common transport, and a file format that allows for flexibility, they defined strict transaction sets. These transaction sets addressed the needs for data content, structure and the process for handling the data. In other words, the business rules were embedded into the transaction set.

The incorporation of business rules into the definition of the transaction set causes many problems, because:

1.   Business rules vary from company to company;
2.   Business rules for one size company may be completely inappropriate for companies of another size;
3.   Business rules are subject to change over time according to changes in market dynamics.

In short, the use of fixed and rigid transaction sets, while necessary at the time, have limited the value of EDI, and therefore stunted its growth.

7.2.2   *EDI technology basics*

Traditional EDI is based on fixed transaction sets. These transaction sets are defined by standards bodies such as the United Nations Standard Messages Directory for Electronic Data Interchange for Administration, Commerce and Transport (EDIFACT), and the American National Standards Institute's (ANSI) Accredited Standards Committee X12 sub-group.

---

1. *The Mythical Value of EDI Standards* by Alan Chute, http://www.filex.com/filex/edimyth.htm

Transaction sets define the fields, the order of these fields, and the length of the fields. Along with these transaction sets are business rules, which in the lexicon of the EDI folks are referred to as "implementation guidelines".

To actually implement EDI, the trading partners would follow these steps:

1. Trading partners enter into an agreement, called a trading arrangement.

2. They select a Value Added Network (VAN).

3. The trading partners typically either contract for, or build themselves, custom software that maps between the two data set formats used by these trading partners.

4. Each time a new trading partner is added, new software would have to be written to translate the sender's data set for the recipient. In other words, you start from scratch with each new trading partner.

Transaction sets are typically transmitted over expensive proprietary network service providers called VANs, which generally base charges on a mixture of fixed fees and message lengths. These fees can become quite substantial, but they are typically overshadowed by the cost to build and maintain the translation software. The VANs provide value-added services such as:

1. Data validation (compliance) and conversion

2. Logging for audit trails

3. Customer support

4. A secure and stable network

5. Accountability

6. Transaction roll-back to support uncommitted transactions

It is important to note that EDI is not simply the exportation of data from one system to another, but a bi-directional mechanism for interaction between systems. Because these disparate systems typically employ different file formats (data notations), schemas, data exchange protocols, etc., the process of exchanging data is very difficult.

7.2.3 *The problems of traditional EDI*

Traditional EDI suffers from many problems that have limited its growth. One of the most significant problems is the fact that it is based on the transfer of fixed transaction sets. This rigidity makes it extremely difficult to deal with the normal evolution necessary for companies to introduce new products and services, or evolve or replace their computer systems.

In addition, these transaction sets include strict processes for handling the data. These processes are not universally acceptable to companies in various industries and of various sizes. This problem is compounded by a standardization process that is too slow to accommodate the accelerating pace of business today.

In addition, the high fixed costs of implementation have been too much to justify for SMEs. In short, there are a host of problems which, despite the benefits of EDI, have prevented its universal adoption.

7.2.3.1 Fixed transaction sets

EDI is currently built on transaction sets that are fixed in nature. For example, a contact field might include the individual's name, title, company, company address and phone number. However, the company does not have the flexibility to add or subtract fields.

Why is this important?

Companies cannot be frozen in time by a fixed transaction set. This prevents them from evolving by adding new services or products, changing their computer systems and improving business processes. This inflexibility inherent in the current custom solutions required to map data between each trading partner pair is untenable, despite the significant benefits of EDI (Example 7-2).

7.2.3.2 Slow standards evolution

EDI standards are defined by standards bodies that are structurally ill-equipped to keep up with the rapid pace of change in the various business environments they impact, as illustrated by Example 7-2.

These standards accommodate many companies with very different needs. They also encompass not just the ontology, but the associated busi-

Example 7-2. Problems of traditional EDI: Healthcare

The transaction sets created for the healthcare system were defined for the traditional indemnity model, where the insurance company pays the doctor on a per visit basis. However, the movement toward managed care was not foreseen in this transaction set. Since managed care pays the doctor a set fee per patient, but does not reimburse on a per visit basis, the standard transaction set simply doesn't work.

The typical doctor sees a mixture of patients, some having managed care insurance and others with indemnity insurance. In order to accommodate this scenario, the doctor is forced to create a false "per visit" fee for managed care patients. This false fee, which is required in order to "complete" the transaction set, creates havoc with the doctor's other billing systems, which EDI was supposed to help.

Rigid transaction sets that enforce process as well as content are simply not flexible enough to address the ever-changing business environment.

ness processes. As a result, it is very slow and difficult, if not impossible, to develop one-size-fits-all solutions.

The current process for defining standards for transaction sets can take years. This simply will not work in today's business environment, which is characterized by accelerated change and increased competition. However, in an effort to jump-start the creation of industry ontologies in the form of DTDs for XML, the work of the traditional EDI standards bodies could be enormously valuable.

Historically, technology standards that are defined and managed in a top-down fashion, like EDI standards, have been replaced by bottom-up standards that allow for independent and distributed development. In other words, technologies like XML, that support greater flexibility and diversity, while providing compatibility between implementations, typically replace inflexible managed solutions like fixed transaction sets. The XML standardization process is managed by the World Wide Web Consortium (W3C).

7.2.3.3 Non-standard standards

Despite the perception of standardization, there remains some flexibility in the interpretation of these standards. The simple fact of the matter is that companies have unique needs, and these needs must be translated into the information they share with their trading partners.

In practical terms, the customer is at a significant economic advantage in defining these "standards", vis-a-vis the supplier. As a result, suppliers are forced to implement one-off solutions for each trading partner. In many of the industries where EDI is more prevalent, the suppliers also tend to be the smaller of the two partners, which makes the financial proposition even worse (see 7.2.3.4, "High fixed costs", on page 108).

Because of the various informational needs of companies, it is impractical to expect that EDI standards can be a one-size-fits-all proposition. The variables of company size, focus, industry, systems, etc. will continue to create needs that are unique to each company. As evidence, consider the amounts companies spend on custom development and customization of packaged applications.

7.2.3.4   High fixed costs

While large companies tout the financial and operational benefits of EDI, these same benefits have eluded the SMEs. That is because of the high fixed costs of implementation, which must be balanced against savings that are variable.

Depending on the level of automation, implementing EDI for a large enterprise is not substantially more expensive than it is for SMEs. In fact, it can be more expensive for the SMEs. Larger companies can often implement a single EDI standard, while the SMEs must accommodate the various standards of their larger partners. This can be very expensive.

Yet, ironically, the benefits are variable. So, if savings are 2% of processing costs, this might not be a substantial number for the manufacturer of car seat springs, but it can be a huge number for GM, Ford or Chrysler. SMEs simply do not have the scale to compensate for the high fixed costs of traditional EDI.

Because of this some of the SMEs that claim to implement EDI are actually printing a hardcopy of the data feeds and re-typing them in their systems. The reason they implemented this faux-EDI is to meet customer requirements, but they simply do not have the transactional scale to justify the investment. Something must be done to bring down these costs (Example 7-3).

Example 7-3. Problems of traditional EDI: Retail

One large retailer requires its vendors to implement EDI in order to qualify as a vendor. However, like all traditional EDI implementations, the data set is unique to the retailer.

For small companies, implementing this system can be quite an investment. Retail is a very fast-paced industry, because it is forced to cater to ever-changing customer demands. As a result, some suppliers to this retailer have implemented this costly technology, only to later lose their contract with the retailer. In fact, because of the significant investment in technology these companies were forced to make, they have sued the retailer.

If this technology were universally applicable, the vendor's investment in a single customer would be eliminated, as would the retailer's legal liability.

7.2.3.5   Fixed business rules

Business rules are encapsulated in the definition of the transaction sets as implementation guidelines. However, business rules are not something that can be legislated, nor can they be rigid.

Business rules that are applicable for a large enterprise, may be completely inappropriate for an SME. To make matters worse, business rules for a medium-sized enterprise may be wholly inappropriate for a small enterprise.

These business rules will also vary between industries. Even companies that are in the same industry, and the same size will implement different business rules. What's more, business rules change over time. The earlier healthcare example demonstrates this point.

Traditional EDI focuses too much on process as an integral part of the transaction set. This is a fatal flaw. New technologies, like XML, support the separation of process, or business rules, from the content and structure of the data. Achieving this separation is critical to widespread adoption of EDI.

The linkage between transaction sets and business rules creates additional problems. The real-life implementation of EDI typically requires custom solutions for each trading partner pair. This creates havoc when trying to implement or modify global business rules.

For example, if your company changed business policy to begin accepting purchase orders, which you had refused to accommodate in the past, you would have to manually change the individual software for each trading partner. You could not make these changes on a global basis using traditional EDI.

This problem also impacts your ability to upgrade or replace your internal systems, since they are uniquely woven into the EDI software in place. In essence, you can become locked into systems that may become obsolete by the time you actually implement the total solution.

7.2.3.6   Limited penetration

EDI penetration has been very limited, when compared to the penetration rates of other automation technologies. Yet the majority of the value of EDI is derived by complete elimination of the hard-copy processes EDI is meant to replace.

As mentioned above, EDI benefits do not follow the 80/20 rule, because converting the first 80% of your vendors to EDI results in only 20% of the potential cost savings. The remaining 80% of the costs remain, since the company is forced to maintain all of the old manual process in tandem with the electronic processes. The most significant savings come only from completely replacing all manual processes with EDI.

The real value of any network is in its adoption by users. Remember Metcalfe's Law: The value of any network is roughly proportional to the number of users squared.

But EDI, in its current state, is *not* a single interlinked network. On the contrary it is a series of one-to-one chains of data flow. As a result, it is vulnerable to alternative "networked" solutions like those enabled by XML, the Internet, Internet-based services, and database connectivity.

7.3 | The new EDI: Leveraging XML and the Internet

Now that we've established the tremendous benefits of EDI, and the structural problems of traditional EDI, the obvious question is: "How can we fix the problems?"

Fortunately, new technologies are coming together to completely reshape the EDI landscape. Today, EDI is currently implemented in a 1-to-1 manner between trading partners. These partnerships can then be extended through tiers to create a supply chain.

This is all changing!

The new paradigm is the *supply web*. The supply web is based on utilization of XML, the Internet, Internet-based services and database connectivity to create a network, or "web", of trading partners.

Implementation and operational costs will plummet, trading partners will implement one-size-fits-all solutions, and adoption will skyrocket And the benefits will not be limited to the trading partners, they will be driven down to end-users as well. EDI will become as commonplace as e-mail.

In short, EDI will dramatically alter the business computing landscape, moving the world forward from our current islands of automation toward a single fabric of commerce tying together businesses and end-users.

Traditional EDI is based on the technologies that existed in the 1970s. Now it is time to build a new EDI architecture on current technologies like XML, the Internet, Internet-based services and database connectivity.

- XML provides the ability to separate the data and structure from the processes.
- The Internet provides the ubiquitous connectivity upon which a Web of interconnected trading partners can flourish.
- Internet technologies provide a layer of security, authentication, transactional support and more, to support the needs of EDI.
- Database connectivity means that XML data, and the business rules that interact with that data, can be communicated among disparate systems by means of middle-tier data filters and aggregators.

Together, these technologies will remove the barriers to widespread adoption of EDI. By leveraging these technologies, EDI will become more flexible, more powerful, less expensive and ultimately ubiquitous.

7.3.1 *XML*

XML is closely related to HyperText Markup Language (HTML), the original document representation of the World Wide Web, as both are based on SGML. While HTML enables the creation of Web pages that can be viewed on any browser, XML adds tags to data so that it can be processed by any application. These tags describe, in a standardized syntax, what the data is, so that the applications can understand its meaning and how to process it Example 7-4.

For example, in HTML a product name and a price might be somewhere in the text. But the computer only knows that there is a collection of characters and numbers. It cannot discern that this data represents a product name and price. As a result, little can be done with the data.

With XML, however, the product name is tagged (e.g. product_name), as is the product price (e.g. product_price). More importantly, there is an association between the product price and the product name.

This information results in significant additional value. For example, a user can now search for the best price on a specific product.

Example 7-4. XML insulates applications from diversity: Customer record

The following example demonstrates one of the values of XML. Below are three different types of message documents from three different companies (A,B and C). Each describes its respective company's customer data:

Company A:
```
<Person name="Mike Hogan" phone="6502864640"
                    E-mail="mph@poet.com" />
```
Company B:
```
<Person name="Mike Hogan" street address="999 Baker Way"
       city="San Mateo" zip="94404" phone="6502864640"/>
```
Company C:
```
<Person name="Mike Hogan" phone="6502864640"/>
```

The XML parser parses, or disassembles, the messages to show the "person" element, which has associated attributes ("name", "phone", etc.). These attributes, as you can see, differ in content and organization.

However, if your application was written to extract a person's name and phone number, it could work equally well with each of these document types without modification. In fact, if these companies evolve their data to include additional information, your application continues to function without modification. This flexibility is one of the benefits of XML.

XML documents must be "well-formed", which means that most document-type information – grammar and hierarchy – can be embedded in the tags that "mark up" the individual document. There can also be an associated *document type definition* (DTD), containing additional meta-information that describes the data.

In either case, XML is self-describing. As a result, applications can be very flexible in their ability to receive, parse and process very diverse sets of information. This enables companies to write a single application that will work with diverse sets of customers. In fact, such a system is even capable of processing information from new trading partners in an ad hoc fashion. This capability completely changes the dynamics of EDI.

Using XML, companies can separate the business rules from the content and structure of the data. By focusing on exchanging data content and structure, the trading partners are free to implement their own business rules, which can be quite distinct from one another. Yet, using templates, companies can work with legacy EDI, non-XML datatypes as well.[1]

7.3.2 *The Internet*

Many companies heralded the cost savings and ubiquity of the Internet as the death knell for VANs. However, this future has not come to pass...yet.

The boldest of these claims was based on the notion that the extranet would redefine the new computing paradigm. What these pundits failed to realize was that the Internet alone does not address the needs of the EDI community.

The EDI community is generally limited to the largest enterprises. EDI is mission critical, and requires a dependable network. It also requires a level of security that couldn't find on the Internet. To put it simply, the savings were not sufficient to justify the switch.

Furthermore, connectivity is only a small part of the problem, the largest issue is the exchange of data in a universal fashion.

All these issues have now been addressed.

- Technology is now available to provide dial-up services to support the Internet in addressing up-time and throughput for mission critical information.
- Security has improved dramatically.

---

1. *Introducing XML/EDI,* http://www.geocities.com/WallStreet/Floor/5815/start.htm

■ The use of XML will broaden the EDI customer base to include SMEs and individuals. This new group of customers is much more price sensitive, so they are inclined to seek an Internet-based solution.

■ The ability to exchange data in a more democratic and ad hoc manner will cause an explosion in the average number of EDI connections.

The current average number of EDI trading partners, for those companies who utilize EDI at all, is two. Building EDI solutions based on XML, and operating this over the Internet, which offers a low-cost ubiquitous transport, will dramatically expand the value of EDI, according to Metcalfe's Law.

7.3.3 *Internet technologies*

Internet technologies have improved, and continue to improve dramatically, now providing a critical mass of technologies that is capable of replacing the services of VANs. Consider the following list of VAN services, each followed by the Internet-based alternatives that offer greater functionality and flexibility:

Data validation and conversion

XML DTDs, XML validation, templates, and structure-based data feed interpretation.

Intermediary-based logging for audit trails

Ubiquitous XML-savvy repositories employed by all trading partners enables rich logging for audit trails. Combining these with electronic signatures ensures system and company identification.

Consulting, customer service and customer support

This function could be handled by VANs capable of making the transition to Internet technologies, or by the other legions of consultants.

Security and accountability

Public key cryptography, certificate authorities, digital signatures can assure secure transactions.

Connection reliability, stability

New technologies in bandwidth allocation, general improvement in the stability of the Internet and alternative fail-over solutions like dial-up continue to move the Internet toward supporting critical real-time data flow. (Remember, it was originally designed to withstand nuclear attack!)

Trading partner negotiation

Directories (X.500, LDAP, NDS, Active Directory), certificate authorities, digital signatures, e-mail, Internet versions of the Better Business Bureau, etc., can support this function.

Transactional support (roll-back, etc.)

The improvements in remote messaging systems and transaction processing monitors provide a layer of transaction support that is capable of adding transactional integrity even on unstable networks.

Because of the knowledge and experience of the VAN community, and because of the anticipated growth of the entire EDI market, the VAN community is well positioned to transition into consulting or systems integrator roles, helping companies implement these new technologies.

7.3.4 *XML data storage*

In other technological transitions, data storage has been a moot point, since the data could be mapped more-or-less directly into relational tables or file systems. More recently, object-oriented database management systems became available for this purpose.

XML data, however, is composed of self-describing information elements that are richly linked, and that utilize a hierarchical structure and naming mechanism. These qualities enable new data-access capabilities based on the tree structure, such as context-sensitive queries, navigation, and traversal.

"Native" XML-based support for these new capabilities can be provided by a value-added content management layer above the DBMS. *POET CMS* is an example of an object-oriented data storage solution that was designed for this type of use.

7.3.5 *Data filtering*

The source of the vast majority of EDI-related information is currently in mainframes and relational databases. This data will be marked-up on the fly with XML tags. XML data will also come from data sources such as:

- XML content management systems
- Various Internet resources
- EDI-XML documents, both full documents like purchase orders and short inter-process messages
- Result sets from applications, also in XML

These diverse sources must be communicated with by a middle-tier "data filter" that can speak to each source in a manner that the source will recognize. The data must then be filtered in source-dependent ways, based on one's confidence in the data, application of consistent business logic, resolution of the various element-type name ontologies, response mechanisms, security, caching for performance, etc. Only then can the application address the data in a consistent manner and receive consistent responses from the middle tier.

The role of a data filter is shown in Figure 7-1. Products such as *POET Object Server* and *POET CMS* can be used to build one.

The middle tier could maintain valuable meta-information that would add structure and context to the data stream. Such information could include:

- Routing for the query, response, etc.
- Source of the information (to indicate credibility, etc.)
- Time stamps
- Data, DTD, and tag normalization
- Context and navigation aids

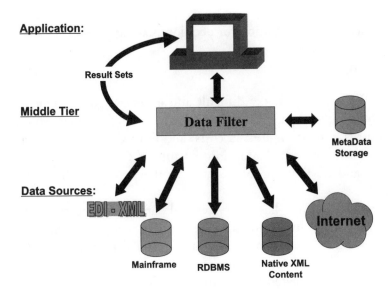

Figure 7-1 Data filter in an XML-based EDI system

Further details on XML content management and the use of object-oriented storage systems in the management of XML data can be found in Chapter 27, "POET Content Management Suite", on page 364.

7.4 | Conclusion

After decades of investment in corporate data centers, we have created islands of automation inside companies. Their isolation from trading partners limits the value companies can recognize from these systems.

EDI offers the ability to change all of this. EDI offers benefits like:

- improved efficiency
- supply chain management
- real-time data and metrics
- better planning
- superior execution
- control systems
- resource management

- cost savings
- superior access to information for decision making
- customer responsiveness
- ... and more.

However, traditional EDI is very difficult and expensive to implement. Because of problems like rigid transaction sets that embed business rules, slow standards development, high fixed costs, and limited market penetration, EDI has not achieved broad adoption. Fortunately, new technology is now available to address these problems and, in the process, reshape the EDI industry.

XML, the Internet, Internet-based services and database connectivity are combining to create a revolution in EDI. Instead of forcing companies to adapt their systems and business processes to the EDI data, this data will dynamically adapt to the companies' existing systems.

EDI will no longer be isolated to certain industries or the largest enterprises, it will become as ubiquitous as e-mail. EDI will transition from a one-to-one supply chain to a richly interconnected web of trading partners forming the supply web. Proprietary networks will become extinct, over time, and VANs will evolve or evaporate.

This supply web will result in dramatic improvements in efficiency. Companies will slash costs, while improving access to critical information. This information will be pushed all the way to the end-user, providing superior customer support as well.

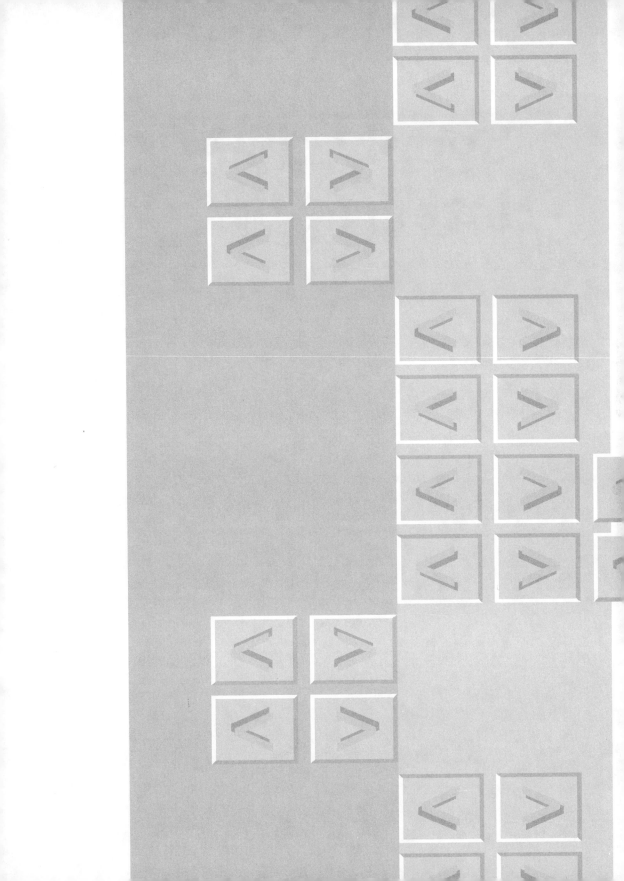

Supply chain integration

- Middle-tier Web application
- Web Interface Definition Language (WIDL)
- XML Remote Procedure Call (RPC)

Supply chain management is tricky business for suppliers and manufacturers. Ideally, they should have real-time access to one another's inventory and schedule planning systems, but that is expensive to achieve with traditional EDI. webMethods, `http://www.webmethods.com`, who sponsor this chapter, and Joe Lapp, who prepared it, believe there is a better means of business-to-business communication.

M anaging a manufacturing business is in some ways a lot like feeding a family. The home is the factory and grocery stores are the suppliers. Parents manufacture meals for themselves and for their children.

But before they can make a meal they must be sure the refrigerator is stocked with the right foods in the necessary quantities. As they serve dinners, the food levels diminish, so they have to time their shopping to be sure that they always have enough food for the next meal. Sometimes the family must scale up to feed unexpected in-laws, and sometimes the family must scale back when little Billy's big belly is staying at Grandma's.

8.1 | Linking up a supply chain

Manufacturers and suppliers struggle with these issues all the time. Suppliers are caught up in the challenge, as they must feed parts to multiple manufacturers. They must be sure that manufacturers have parts when they're needed, but they have to be careful not to overstock their products when manufacturer demand is not high enough to sell them. The supplier may itself be a manufacturer and have its own suppliers.

A series of businesses that feed parts to one another in sequence is known as a *supply chain*.

Suppose Manufacturer X decides to maximize the efficiency of its link in a supply chain. It wants to integrate its Manufacturer Resource Planning (MRP) system with the planning systems of its suppliers, thereby providing each side with rich inventory information in real-time.

The manufacturer benefits by having access to up-to-date availability information of supplier parts, including parts delivery schedules. The supplier benefits by having access to the manufacturer's current parts inventory levels and to the manufacturer's expected rates of depleting the inventory.

8.2 | Supply chain integration requirements

Manufacturer X does not want to lose an arm or a leg or a bevy of shareholders in the process of implementing the solution. It requires an inexpensive solution that it could put together in a period of weeks, rather than in a period of months or years. This rules out traditional Electronic Data Interchange (EDI).

In an earlier time, EDI might have won hearts and ears and pocketbooks, but now the Internet and XML offer better ways to do things. Manufacturer X is aware of what is currently possibly with technology and imposed the following general requirements:

- The system must integrate with Manufacturer X's existing MRP system.
- Manufacturer X must communicate with its suppliers over the Internet. Private network solutions are too costly.
- Access to manufacturer data must be secure. Only registered suppliers may access the data. Suppliers may not access the data of other suppliers. Data must remain secure in transit over the Internet.
- The effort and expense required of both Manufacturer X and its suppliers must be minimized.

The problem can be solved by employing a tool that allows disparate applications to interoperate over the Web. Let's take a look at one.

8.3 | The *B2B Integration Server*

The webMethods *Business-to-Business Integration Server* (B2B) sits between applications to enable them to communicate despite differences between them. The applications need only agree in an abstract sense on the nature of the services they offer, and on the data to be exchanged between these services.

The server employs *WIDL* (Web Interface Definition Language) technology for expressing these abstractions. Once the abstractions have been established, any two applications can communicate, regardless of their programming languages, whether they accept and/or receive XML messages, and regardless of the DTDs to which the XML messages conform.

In other words, B2B makes applications accessible to one another over the Web, and it makes existing Web data accessible to applications. It provides the communications infrastructure needed to do the job, including security, passage through firewalls, and access to proxies. It also translates between message representations, such as URIs, CGI query data, and differing XML message document types.

Let's see how these capabilities can be applied to integrate a supply chain.

8.4 | Overview of the system

A somewhat generalized version of the system architecture is depicted in Figure 8-1.

The generalization allows us to demonstrate the applicability of the solution to supply chains in general. Here, the B2B server sits on the manufacturer's site and mediates all exchanges between suppliers and the manufacturer. B2B assumes responsibility for hiding network, protocol, and security issues from the supplier and manufacturer systems, and hiding differences in how the systems are interfaced.

Supplier systems access the manufacturer's MRP system to obtain part inventory levels, and communication between the systems is completely

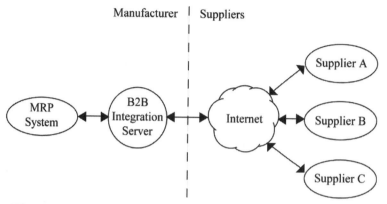

Figure 8-1   Supply chain integration architecture.

automated. The suppliers issue requests to the B2B integration server in the form of XML messages, sending the requests via the standard POST method of HTTP.

B2B translates these requests into calls to the MRP system. It then translates responses from the MRP system into XML reply messages that it sends back to the supplier. This request/reply mechanism for accessing services is called *Remote Procedure Call* (RPC).

The MRP system must also access supplier data. In order to minimize the impact on the suppliers, B2B uses standard URIs and CGI queries for the requests and allows both HTML and XML to be used in the responses. (See Chapter 38, "WIDL and XML RPC", on page 554 for more information on these technologies.)

Upon receiving a response, the B2B server uses WIDL to convert the HTML or XML into a data representation that is suitable for the MRP system to consume. It then passes the converted data to the system, completing the request/response circuit.

8.5 | The manufacturer services

The manufacturer services comprise half of the complete integration solution. These services give suppliers access to inventory level information found in the manufacturer's MRP system.

Figure 8-2 shows how the manufacturer provides services to its suppliers. A supplier issues a request to the B2B server, which in turn calls upon a piece of software known as a "plug-in." The plug-in acts on the MRP system to perform the request and returns data back to B2B. B2B translates the data into the appropriate form for delivery to the supplier.

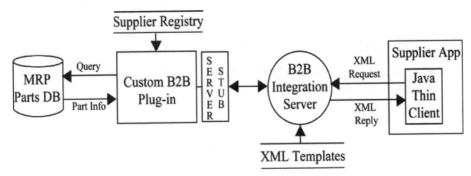

Figure 8-2 Providing suppliers with manufacturer services.

Several pieces shown in Figure 8-2 are key to the solution and merit some discussion.

8.5.1 *B2B plug-in*

The plug-in is code that Manufacturer X wrote to communicate with its MRP system. It is written in Java and exposes an interface to the B2B server. The most important "method" (or program function) of this interface is one that retrieves part information from the MRP system when the method is called. The method inputs a part number and outputs information about the part.

The plug-in will only return part information to the suppliers that provide the parts; suppliers cannot acquire information about the parts that other suppliers provide. The plug-in accomplishes this by looking up the supplier's user name in the supplier registry to fetch the associated supplier ID. The retrieved ID must match the supplier ID that the MRP database associates with the part.

8.5.2 *Server stub*

A server stub is a portion of code that links into the plug-in and that allows the B2B server to invoke an API that the plug-in exposes. Server stubs enable the B2B server to communicate with plug-ins written in any programming language. They also benefit the server by hiding the details of the plug-in's method signatures (that is, its name and parameter definitions).

When a supplier requests B2B to invoke a manufacturer service, B2B hands the input parameters to the server stub, telling the stub which Java method to invoke on the plug-in. The stub invokes the method and then provides B2B with the method's output parameters, which B2B returns to the supplier.

8.5.3 *XML requests and replies*

B2B communicates with the supplier via XML. It receives XML requests from the supplier and it sends XML replies back to the supplier. When B2B receives a request it translates the XML into set of input parameters and hands these parameters to the server stub. When the stub returns output parameters, it translates the output parameters into an XML reply.

Manufacturer X chose to represent these XML request and reply messages using a "generic" message DTD. A generic DTD is capable of representing any set of input or output parameters, thereby allowing all message exchanges to use the same DTD. For efficiency, the solution uses an encoder/decoder module to translate XML into input parameters and to translate output parameters into XML.

8.5.4 *Java thin client*

The Java thin client is a piece of software that Manufacturer X developed and distributed to all of its suppliers. It contains the webMethods thin client, which allows the client to submit and receive XML messages. However, the supplier could choose to use any XML-aware client.

The thin client provides suppliers with default behavior to jump-start their integration efforts with software that understands the generic XML DTD. To use the manufacturer services, the thin client must first establish a secure SSL session and log in to the server with a user name and a password that Manufacturer X provided.

8.5.5 *Manufacturer interface specification*

The solution requires that we define the set of services that the stub offers, and it requires that we state the data inputs and outputs for each service. We accomplish this by using WIDL 3.0 to define an interface specification.

Example 8-1 shows a portion of the interface specification that does the job. A supplier invokes the "getInventory" method to retrieve inventory information as a function of a part number.

Example 8-1. WIDL interface specification for the manufacturer services.

```
<WIDL NAME="com.Manufact-X.PartsInventory" VERSION="3.0">
  <RECORD NAME="PartHandle">
    <VALUE NAME="partNumber"/>
  </RECORD>
  <RECORD NAME="PartInventory">
    <VALUE NAME="inventoryLevel" TYPE="i4"/>
    <VALUE NAME="targetLevel" TYPE="i4"/>
    ...
  </RECORD>
  ...
  <METHOD NAME="getInventory" INPUT="PartHandle"
      OUTPUT="PartInventory"/>
  ...
</WIDL>
```

The developer uses the B2B release of the *webMethods Automation Toolkit* to generate the server stub from this interface specification. The toolkit includes GUI-based tools for designing the interface specification and for generating the source code for the stubs, so that the developer does not need to be familiar with either WIDL or XML.

8.6 | The supplier services

The supplier services comprise the second half of the complete integration solution. These services give the manufacturer access to supplier inventory levels and delivery schedules.

Figure 8-3 portrays how the manufacturer utilizes the services of the supplier. Suppliers make their information available from Web servers in the form of HTML or XML pages.

8.6.1 *Client stub*

The client stub provides APIs that the plug-in calls to access the information found on these pages. The plug-in runs a background thread that periodically invokes these APIs to retrieve supplier part information. The thread updates the MRP system with the part information that the APIs return.

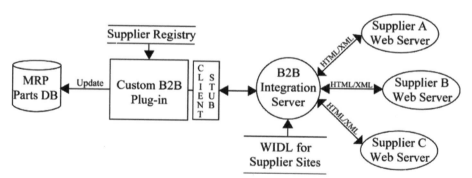

Figure 8-3   Providing the manufacturer with supplier services.

The B2B server uses Web automation to make the supplier Web sites available to the plug-in. B2B can provide Web automation services to any application, not just plug-ins, but Manufacturer X wanted to centralize the entire integration solution within the plug-in.

Web automation *wraps a Web site* so that it looks like a set of APIs (functions). As shown in Figure 8-3, there is no need to put Web automation technology on any of the wrapped web-sites themselves. The B2B server merely sits between the Web site and the client (in this case, the plug-in) and makes the web-site accessible to the client through the APIs of a client stub.

8.6.2 *Supplier interface specification*

A developer generates the client stub by first designing a WIDL 3.0 interface specification for the supplier services. Example 8-2 shows a portion of this specification.

The interface specification defines the APIs that the stub will expose, including the input and output parameters of each API. Since the plug-in is written in Java, the stub implements the APIs as Java methods. The developer links the client stub into the plug-in so that the plug-in can call these methods. The stub methods in turn use the services of the B2B server.

Example 8-2. WIDL interface specification for the supplier services.

```
<WIDL NAME="com.Supplier.PartAvailability" VERSION="3.0">
  <RECORD NAME="LoginProfile">
    <VALUE NAME="username"/>
    <VALUE NAME="password"/>
  </RECORD>
  <RECORD NAME="Availability">
    <VALUE NAME="dateRefreshed"/>
    <RECORDREF NAME="parts" DIM="1" RECORD="Part"/>
  </RECORD>
  <RECORD NAME="Part">
    <VALUE NAME="partNumber"/>
    <VALUE NAME="availableInventory" TYPE="i4"/>
    <VALUE NAME="quantityInTransit" TYPE="i4"/>
    ...
  </RECORD>
  ...
  <METHOD NAME="login" INPUT="LoginProfile"/>
  <METHOD NAME="getAvailability" OUTPUT="Availability"/>
  ...
</WIDL>
```

Next the developer uses WIDL to wrap the supplier Web sites so that each site conforms to the interface specification. The Toolkit does this through direct interaction with a Web site, and again the developer need not have any knowledge of WIDL. Once the WIDL files have been created, one configures the B2B server to wrap the Web sites by dropping the files into a directory.

Each supplier site then has the same interface, consisting of the set of methods that the client stub exposes. The input parameters of a method fill out a form on a supplier Web site. The output parameters of the method contain data extracted from the pages that the site returns upon submitting the form parameters.

This approach allows the suppliers to return the information in any form – HTML pages using any presentation or XML messages using any DTD. The supplier can even have a B2B Integration Server receive the form parameters and reply with XML messages, allowing the supplier to have tight integration with other manufacturers as well. The manufacturer's B2B server makes the form of the supplier data transparent to the plug-in.

Once per day, the plug-in iterates over the suppliers listed in the supplier registry. For each supplier it retrieves a supplier ID, a URI, a user name, and a password. The URI specifies the location of the supplier site. The user name and password are items that the supplier provided to the manufacturer; they allow the manufacturer to log in to the supplier site.

For each supplier in the registry, the plug-in invokes methods on the client stub. It first invokes "login" to authenticate with the supplier's site and then invokes "getAvailability" to acquire the part availability data. Finally, the plug-in writes the part availability data to the manufacturer's MRP database, keeping the database accurate to within a day.

8.7 | Conclusion

The B2B Integration Server allows Manufacturer X to integrate tightly with its suppliers. It allows the manufacturer's MRP system to communicate with the supplier planning systems without requiring the MRP system to have any knowledge of the Internet, of XML, or of the supplier system interfaces.

These facilities enabled Manufacturer X to implement the solution in only two weeks. Had Manufacturer X gone with a CORBA solution or with a solution involving traditional EDI, it would still be negotiating the platform and protocol details with the suppliers. The *B2B Integration Server* provided Manufacturer X with a significantly simpler, faster, and less expensive way to get the job done.

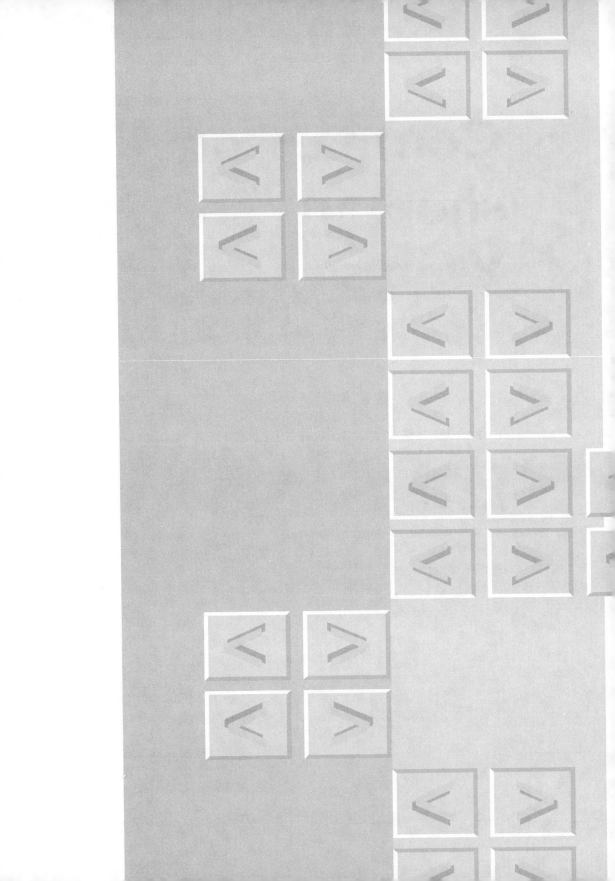

Comparison shopping service Web site

- Middle-tier Web application

- Virtual Database technology (VDB)

- Dynamic merchant Web site aggregation

9

Comparison shopping is a universal pastime, and it has never been easier than on the World Wide Web. Junglee Corporation, http://www.junglee.com, sponsors of this chapter, have created a technology that makes it easier still, and a working Web site to prove it. The chapter was prepared by Anand Rajaraman, STS Prasad, and Debra Knodel.

Despite the fears of some publishers that the Web would dry up the market for books, so far the reverse has been true. Not only are people buying books about the Web and its technologies, but book selling over the Web is widely regarded as proof of the viability of electronic commerce.

9.1 | Shopping online for books

But there is plenty of room for improvement in the process. Consider what the experience is like today.

A shopper seeking the best price for the best books on a given topic doesn't have an easy time of it today. The shopper must view several Web sites, initiate a search on each site for the desired product, and interpret the results of each search.

Unfortunately, every Web site has a separate structure and vocabulary for search and results presentation, making it awkward for the shopper to quickly evaluate the results. Figure 9-1, for example, shows the difference between the search and result pages of two online bookstores, Amazon.com and Powells.com.

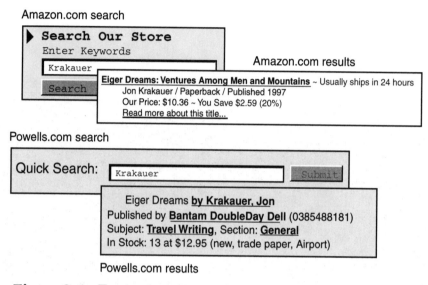

Figure 9-1   Two bookstores, two views.

It would certainly be more convenient if all bookstores could be searched with a single query, and all the results could be presented together. There is now a Web service that does just that.

9.2 | The *Junglee Shopping Guide*

The *Junglee Shopping Guide* is a configurable comparison shopping service that uses *Virtual Database* (VDB) technology to aggregate dozens of merchant Web sites across a wide range of product categories, consolidating them into a single shopping guide.

A customer enters specific attributes about a desired item, such as brand name, price range, author (for books) or category (for gifts). The *Shopping Guide* does the rest, automatically searching through thousands of products from a variety of merchants.

The results are displayed in a single table. From it the customer can make informed purchase decisions, comparing product features, availability, and price.

The *Shopping Guide* leverages the power of XML to deliver results in a form that can be manipulated by the browser without round trips to the Web server. For example, XML allows browser-side sorting and filtering of data, and presentation of the data to suit specific user preferences based on stylesheets.

VDB technology makes this possible by transforming the Internet into a database. Data is collected from Web sites based on a user query, and structured into a standard representation for each category. The search results are delivered in XML, using a uniform document type definition (DTD) for all sites, regardless of the original form of the data (typically HTML).

Figure 9-2 shows a sample result from book shopping.

```
<?XML version"1.0"?>
<!DOCTYPE booklist SYSTEM "book.dtd">
<booklist>
<Book>
  <Merchant>Amazon.com </Merchant>
  <Title> Eiger Dreams </title>
  <Author> Krakauer, Jon </Author>
  <Format> Paperback </Format>
  <Price> $10.36 </Price>
  <Availability> Ships in</Availability>
</book>
</booklist>
```

Figure 9-2 Sample books document.

Let's look at the underlying technology.

9.3 | How the *Shopping Guide* works

Figure 9-3 shows how the VDB manages this process using wrappers.

A *wrapper* is a Java program designed to extract data from Web sites. The wrapper may in turn use *extractors* (not shown) to extract attributes from unstructured (non-XML) text. Data transformations and data validations are applied to determine data integrity.

A wrapper is created for each Web site, while an extractor is typically created for an entire collection of Web sites with similar information. An extractor consists of extraction rules and dictionaries to provide sophisticated linguistic processing for unstructured text

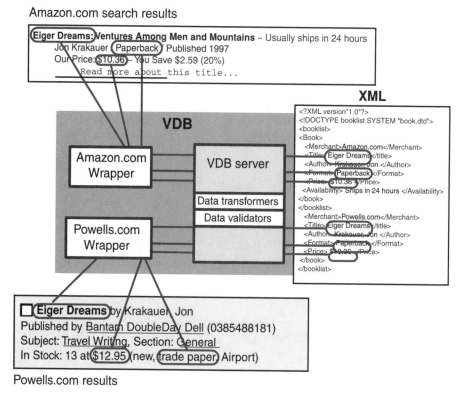

Figure 9-3   How the VDB works.

Once the data is gathered and transformed, it can be presented in response to a query in a combined form, such as the one shown in Figure 9-4. The results are displayed using the XML DSO in *Internet Explorer 4.0.*[1]

Dynamic HTML and data binding are used to create a compelling user experience. The Web shopper can choose between multiple views and can manipulate the data from the browser without the need for round trips to the server.

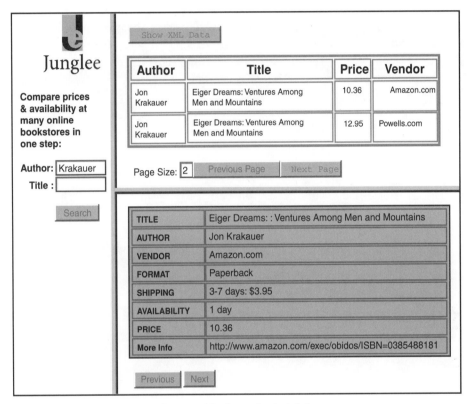

Figure 9-4   *Shopping Guide* unified results in XML.

9.4 | Conclusion

VDB technology transforms the Internet into a database enabling powerful structured searches, while XML provides an efficient mechanism for deliv-

---

1. A *Netscape* version is being developed.

ering structured data to browsers. You can learn more about VDB in Chapter 29, "Junglee Virtual DBMS", on page 386.

The XML version of the Junglee *Shopping Guide* is a working prototype that illustrates the power of XML and VDB technology. It provides access to hundreds of merchants and millions of products.

 **Tip**   You can experience the XML Junglee Shopping Guide in *action at* `http://www.junglee.com/tech/xml_demo.html`. *Until browser support for XML is ubiquitous, a version that presents its results in HTML is available at* `http://www.junglee.com/shop/index.html`

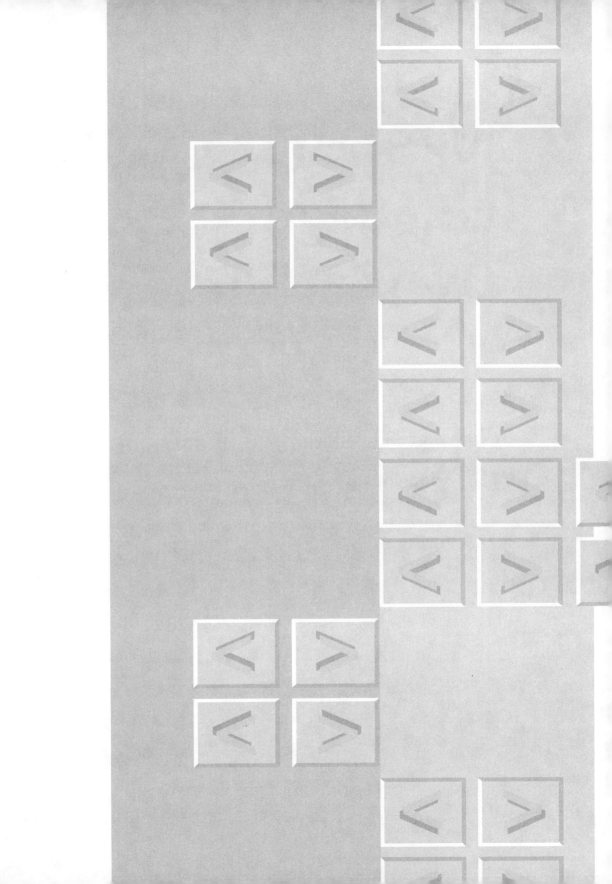

Natural language translation

- Content management
- New directions in translation
- Versioning
- Reuse

10

Translating documents can be a real challenge in today's global market, but content management can improve the process dramatically. Chrystal Software, a Xerox New Enterprise company, `http://www.chrystal.com`, sponsored this chapter to show you how. It was prepared by Robin Gellerman, Steve Kiser, and Simon Nicholson.

Companies have tremendous opportunities to reach new customers in today's global market. Improved global communications allow companies to be known instantly around the world. Modernized manufacturing practices make it possible to create a diverse set of products brought to market faster than ever before. Fewer trade barriers allow products to be sold and distributed globally.

10.1 | Mistakes can be costly

In the rush to new markets, some make careless mistakes that can be costly. Here are a few examples from the Marketing Hall of Shame:

- Parker Pen planned to introduce the ball-point pen in a new country with the slogan: *"It won't leak in your pocket and embarrass you"*. The company introduced its product with the mistranslated slogan: *"It won't leak in your pocket and make you pregnant"*. This was not the message that Parker Pen originally conceived.

- The sales figures for the Chevy Nova in several Spanish speaking countries were far below expectations. After some analysis, GM found a tremendous problem. It wasn't in the car itself, but in the name. Nova means "no go" in Spanish – not a characteristic many of us hope for when buying a car.

- After repeated requests from their biggest customers in five countries, a telecommunications manufacturer quickly added a security menu option to a new model of cellular phone. Although the new menu item was a trivial engineering change and was implemented within a day, the documentation could not keep pace. The change to the English, French, German, and Spanish versions of the documentation took six weeks - thirty times longer than the product change.

These examples, whether truth or urban myth, illustrate the importance of accurate and timely language translation in today's global marketplace. These companies experienced short-term embarrassment for their mistakes. Other mistakes could be far more costly. What if the process of translation was so complicated that it slowed the introduction of your product to a new market by a year? What if a mistranslation introduced a safety issue for the consumer?

10.2 | It's a small world

Products are coming to market faster, compressing product delivery times. At the same time, expansion into new markets increases the need for more languages. In response to these pressures, companies must accelerate time tables, streamline processes, and manage document creation and translation concurrently. This is not a luxury – it is a requirement.

Opening of global markets is not the sole reason for this increased need for multilingual documents. Other factors are at play. The creation of international organizations through partnerships and mergers such as Rover and BMW, Ford and Mazda, and the European Union are increasing the demand. Employees are more mobile and more geographically dispersed. More source document content is written in languages other than English.

Although English is recognized as the international language of business, there remain several compelling reasons for delivering information in the native language of the consumer. First, it allows you to more effectively communicate information and ideas to the target audience. Second, in some cases, documentation in the local language is not just a good idea-it is the law. Companies may not be able to carry on business unless they provide localized documentation. And for many, translation is required just to keep up with the competition.

The more companies recognize the strategic benefits of concurrent product development and document delivery, the more serious the need for solutions becomes. XML and content management are providing those solutions today. And, as a result, making the world a much smaller marketplace.

This chapter outlines the process used to translate technical information, describes the challenges and areas for improvement, and explains how XML and content management help companies control costs and make production more efficient.

10.3 | Business challenges

10.3.1 Cost containment

In the technical documentation market, companies spend millions of dollars annually on translation. An IBM study in 1995 estimated $50 billion was spent for translation worldwide with an estimated annual growth rate of 15%. And the cost is growing, driven by the desire for simultaneous worldwide launch of new products and the need to support new languages and markets.

In some cases the development of documents in a different language variant can be as high as 10% of the cost of the development of the source. With global translation spending forecast to grow at 15% per annum, businesses need to implement new solutions now.

Translation is expensive, costing 15 to 25 cents per word including revisions. It is also time-consuming: Translation and proofreading with one review cycle takes many hours per page or chapter. Additional revisions cost even more time and money.

10.3.2 *Fast-paced product development*

In most industries, product development schedules are now a fraction of what they were a decade ago. Also, products in many industries demand a frequent "technology refresh" to stay competitive, increasing the frequency of product versions. With as little as six weeks to deliver a product, these companies cannot afford to double that time to revise and translate documentation. These compressed schedules force companies to establish concurrent processes.

Rapid product development also allows companies to manufacture more makes and models of their products. This increases complexity of multiple document variations that must all be released simultaneously. Managing the slight variations between products and their supporting documentation is the key to streamlining the translation process.

10.3.3 *Diverse documents*

The diversity of documents that must be developed, delivered, and maintained is growing. Figure 10-1 shows an example.

An automotive manufacturer makes a design change to a part that is used in five different car models. All of the accompanying documentation, including the workshop manuals and owners guide must be modified to reflect the change.

Even if that change results in modifying only two paragraphs of text, each medium used to distribute information, such as print, CD-ROM and the World Wide Web, must be updated. Now multiply that by the number of languages needed in each country where the cars are sold. It is apparent that this is a sizable problem.

10.4 | Translations today

The greatest productivity improvements to be realized in the translation process are not in the translation itself, but in making the entire process more efficient. Although technology exists for automatic machine translation, it is not perfect. Machine translation lacks the subtlety and error

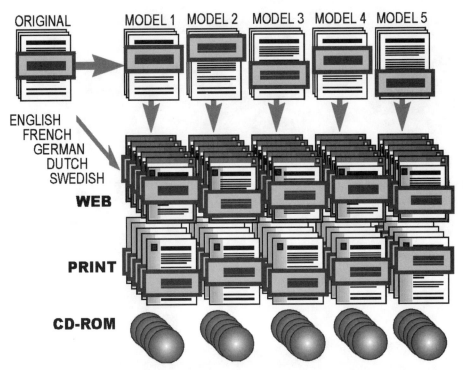

Figure 10-1 Complexity is multiple products, languages, and media.

checking provided by a human translator. Translation remains an art, not an exact science.

Here is how a typical document gets revised and translated today (Figure 10-2). Generally, the work begins on the source language document. A variety of people including photographers, authors, technicians, marketing and legal, create and review the text and graphics. After identifying the changes and redundant content, the material is sent out for translation. This manual process reduces unnecessary translation and allows the translator to avoid re-translating content that has not changed. The newly translated material is returned and integrated into a document called a "variant", a document containing the translated content for a single language. Since most companies require multiple languages, there will be multiple variants that must be kept in sync with the source.

As changes occur to the source document, incremental revisions are sent out for translation. During this stage, translators may need to directly inter-

Figure 10-2   The process of translating documents.

act with the original author to resolve ambiguities in meaning which are bound to exist.

Things really heat up when product development is complete. The final content, often including changes to previously submitted content, is sent out for translation. The final set of translations are then integrated into the variant documents. After translation to the target languages is completed, a final check ensures all changes are complete, and reflected in the translations and inserted in the proper places.

Translation is a specialized service, so most companies contract with experts to perform this task. The most accurate translators are native speakers, often requiring pieces of the document to be sent all over the world. This increases the complexity of communication and causes synchronization nightmares when a last-minute engineering change occurs. And you thought it was hard to communicate with your documentation department down the hall!

Last minute changes can put on-time delivery at risk, leaving you three choices to meet the delivery date: Increase the translation staff, extend the delivery date, or ship the product without appropriate documentation. Given the huge cost, both monetarily and in customer satisfaction, which would you choose?

10.5 | New directions

The biggest challenge in the management of today's language translation is to manually keep track of content - what is new, reused, revised, translated, reviewed, and approved. With the combination of XML and content management, companies can automate this critical function to simplify processes, shorten time-to-market, reduce rework, and control costs.

10.5.1 *Components*

The key to making the translation process more efficient is to work with smaller parts. XML breaks up the information into smaller information components (Figure 10-3). The smaller and more specific the component is, the more addressable and reusable it is. With smaller information units, it is easier to pinpoint changes, translate only new information, and automatically update information reused throughout the document. Similar to advanced technologies and methods used in engineering and manufacturing of items such as cellular phones, new cars, and software, components simplify complexity and increase flexibility for adapting to change.

A component is a piece of information that can be used independently, such as a paragraph, chapter, instructional procedure, warning note, part number, order quantity, graphic, side-bar story, video clip, or one of an infinite variety of additional information types.[1] For the translation process, components have a positive and profound impact.

When managed by a content management system, these components can be controlled, revised, reused, and assembled into new documents.

---

1. For more information about components, see Chapter 26, "Astoria: Flexible content management", on page 352.

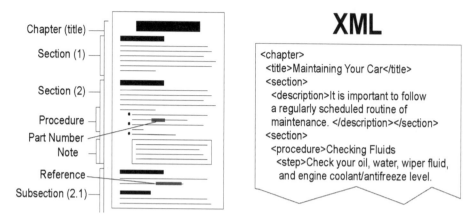

Chapter (title)
Section (1)
Section (2)
Procedure
Part Number
Note
Reference
Subsection (2.1)

XML

```
<chapter>
  <title>Maintaining Your Car</title>
  <section>
    <description>It is important to follow
    a regularly scheduled routine of
    maintenance. </description></section>
  <section>
    <procedure>Checking Fluids
      <step>Check your oil, water, wiper fluid,
      and engine coolant/antifreeze level.
```

Figure 10-3   Document components described with XML.

10.5.2 *Reduce reinvention with reuse*

The ability to reuse components within documents has an important impact on the translation process. Reuse can be as simple as locating a component from one document and linking it into a new document. This method of linked reuse instead of copying makes updates more efficient. When components stored in a content management system change, the information is revised only one time. All of the documents containing that component are automatically updated.

Reuse is helpful even before translation. Using a content management system, the original technical writer can create a standard glossary containing translated terms and phrases (Figure 10-5). With assistance from the content management system from inside the authoring tool, the writer is prompted with approved terms, phrases, and other content.

The writer can easily reuse components or create new terms. This allows for greater control over document content and terminology reducing ambiguities, inconsistencies, and unneeded rework. One example of a controlled language is Simplified English, used in the aerospace industry.

The type of automated reuse shown in Figure 10-4 will also help in the translation process. The glossary can be translated once into the target languages. The glossary terms will be automatically inserted into the language prototype before being passed to the translator. This reduces the volume of work by reducing the amount of new material.

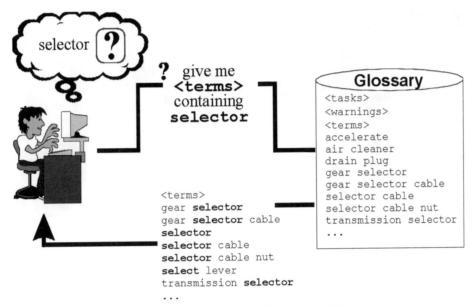

Figure 10-4 Reuse of glossary terms reduces rework.

When a standard term in the glossary needs to change, the update is made once. All the documents using the term are automatically updated. Reuse makes it simpler to identify changes and reduces rework. This approach can reduce total translation time by 50% and reduce costs by 15%.

10.5.3 Identify changes with versioning

When components are maintained in a content management system, changes can be automatically recorded and tracked (Figure 10-5). Without burdening the author, the system automatically collects revision information and identifies what changed. Instead of sending the entire document, only modified components need to be extracted and sent for translation. This streamlines the process because it reduces the volume of data being sent out and relieves the translator from manually identifying the changes from previous versions.

Another benefit of components is that they can be translated as they become available rather than waiting for a complete document. This makes it possible to manage concurrent translation along with product development.

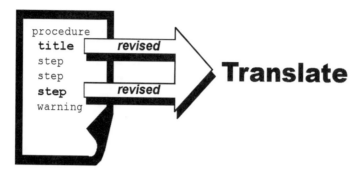

Figure 10-5   Component versioning saves time by identifying only pieces that change.

10.5.4 *Alignment enables concurrent authoring and translation*

When stored in the content management system, the source and target language of the document are guaranteed to be aligned with identical structures (Figure 10-6). For instance, if the source contains a <procedure> element with a unique attribute of "123," the language variants will also contain this element with this attribute.

Figure 10-6   Source and target language documents have identical structures.

This alignment has several immediate advantages. First, when a source language component is ready for translation, its language variants are also identified. These components can be clearly identified, locked, and submitted to the translator. After translation, the components are correctly versioned, providing a full life-cycle history of all components including the language variants. Since the structures are identical, it is also easy to identify and distribute changes to end-users, regardless of language used.

10.6 | In the real world

A major automotive manufacturer produces all the documentation required to deliver a fully serviceable automobile to buyers. This documentation includes in-car handbooks, workshop manuals, customer representative training guides and reference material. The documentation is translated into a variety of languages for the company's global markets. Currently, these guides are delivered in a hard copy format as well as in multimedia such as CD-ROMs.

After installing Chrystal Software's Astoria content management solution and implementing concepts described in this chapter, composition time for each language version went from about three weeks to less than 2 days. With the time saved, the company can better manage the translation process. They now review documents in-house and control updates and versions within the content management system, reducing the dependency on translation suppliers for review. As a result, overall production time for updates was cut by 50%.

By using XML and content management for managing the creation, translation, and revision of multiple document sets, companies can:

- Reduce initial translation costs by reusing common content across documents.

- Improve document consistency through controlled vocabulary authoring.

- Improve re-translation by pinpointing re-translation units.

- Shorten time to market by overlapping authoring and translation processes and minimizing volume of translation.

Securities regulation filings

- EDGAR: The U.S. Securities and Exchange Commission quarterly reporting system

- Document creation and revision under rigid conformance requirements

- Software visualization assistance for authors

Filing documents to conform to government regulations is a necessity in enterprises throughout the world. Although knowing that the misery is shared won't make the task any easier, the information in this chapter can. The chapter is sponsored by Interleaf, Inc., `http://www.interleaf.com`.

Government documents tend to be rigid in their requirements and must be completed with extreme care. The penalties for error can be large. Many enterprises have seized on XML (and its parent, SGML) as a solution. An XML DTD and validating parser can enforce many of the requirements for completing a government filing.

Indeed, many government agencies use XML themselves and some allow or even require their filings to be XML documents. However, even if XML use isn't a filing requirement, there are plenty of benefits from using XML to prepare your filings, as we'll see in this chapter.

But creating XML in the raw can be intimidating to the non-programmer business analysts or other content experts who must prepare the filings. These professionals could take charge of their own XML documents if they had the right sort of visual tools.

11.1 | Visualizing an XML document

The following examples illustrate the difference between writing XML element type declarations and generating them with a visual tool. Figure 11-1 shows a DTD in the standardized plain-text form that is processed by XML software. To create this, the actual XML element type declarations must be typed out, completely and correctly.

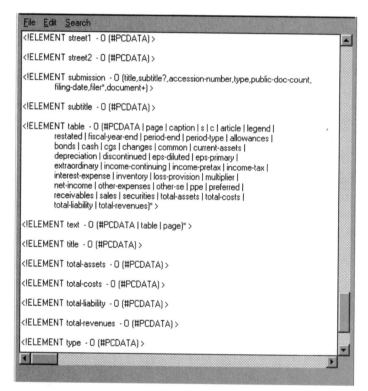

Figure 11-1   Standard plain-text XML DTD.

Alternatively, a DTD could be assembled using a visual tool (see Figure 11-2). The user need only point and click the mouse on the appropriate element type (in this case, business-address was selected), and the tool automatically generates the opening and closing tags. The tool also shows all the element types that are subordinate to business-address, such as street1 and street2. Additionally, when defining the DTD for business-address, the content developer can indicate which related element types are mandatory, thereby ensuring that all the necessary elements are completed.

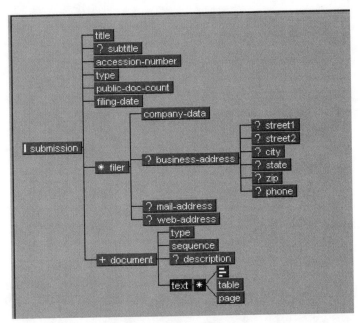

Figure 11-2 Visual DTD modeling.

In Figure 11-3, a document is being created for the U.S. Securities and Exchange Commission (SEC). It is a quarterly report known, for some reason, as *EDGAR*.

The data and markup are entered manually in a plain-text programmer's editor. There are no built-in validation checks to ensure that the markup is correct, with the correct spelling, syntax, and closing tags (although some of those could be validated externally). And there are no simple means for aligning columns when editing tables.

Figure 11-4 shows what is possible with a visual tool. In the screen shot, the items on the left strip (outside the document margins) identify the XML elements on each line. And the user can insert the XML tags graphically into the document to improve the appearance and the alignment of the table columns.

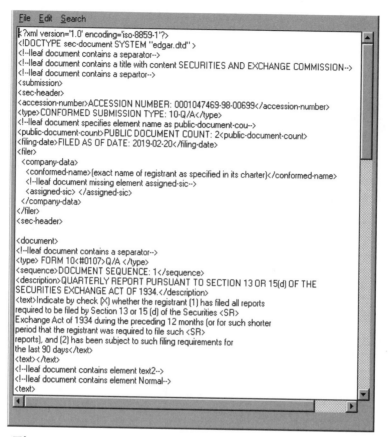

File Edit Search

```
<?xml version='1.0' encoding='iso-8859-1'?>
<!DOCTYPE sec-document SYSTEM "edgar.dtd" >
<!--lleaf document contains a separator-->
<!--lleaf document contains a title with content SECURITIES AND EXCHANGE COMMISSION-->
<!--lleaf document contains a separator-->
<submission>
<sec-header>
<accession-number>ACCESSION NUMBER: 0001047469-98-00699</accession-number>
<type>CONFORMED SUBMISSION TYPE: 10-Q/A</type>
<!--lleaf document specifies element name as public-document-cou-->
<public-document-count>PUBLIC DOCUMENT COUNT: 2<public-document-count>
<filing-date>FILED AS OF DATE: 2019-02-20</filing-date>
<filer>
  <company-data>
    <conformed-name>[exact name of registrant as specified in its charter]</conformed-name>
    <!--lleaf document missing element assigned-sic-->
    <assigned-sic> </assigned-sic>
  </company-data>
</filer>
<sec-header>

<document>
<!--lleaf document contains a separator-->
<type> FORM 10<#0107>Q/A </type>
<sequence>DOCUMENT SEQUENCE: 1</sequence>
<description>QUARTERLY REPORT PURSUANT TO SECTION 13 OR 15(d) OF THE
SECURITIES EXCHANGE ACT OF 1934.</description>
<text>Indicate by check (X) whether the registrant (1) has filed all reports
required to be filed by Section 13 or 15 (d) of the Securities <SR>
Exchange Act of 1934 during the preceding 12 months (or for such shorter
period that the registrant was required to file such <SR>
reports), and (2) has been subject to such filing requirements for
the last 90 days</text>
<text></text>
<!--lleaf document contains element text2-->
<!--lleaf document contains element Normal-->
<text>
```

Figure 11-3   Standard plain-text XML document instance.

An XML visual editing and publishing tool could make a difference in a government filing application. Let's see how.

11.2 | An EDGAR Submission with XML

It is the beginning of your company's new fiscal quarter. As are all public companies in the U.S., your company is required to make an EDGAR submission to the SEC. You are responsible for generating the EDGAR sub-

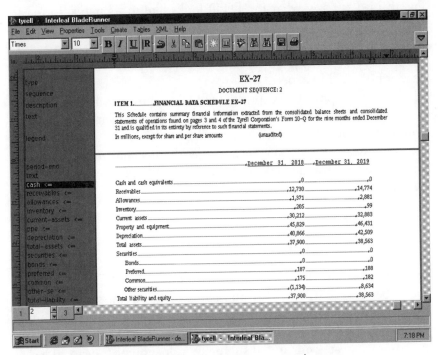

Figure 11-4   WYSIWYG XML document creation.

mission from information provided to you by the legal and financial departments.

Also, you have been asked to generate an HTML version of the EDGAR submission for your company's Web Site. However, some content from the formal SEC submission should not be include in the HTML version. The publishing challenge you face now is how do you quickly and easily generate multiple versions of the EDGAR submission with full or partial content?

11.2.1 *Reviewing the EDGAR DTD*

The SEC published the EDGAR DTD for public use. The DTD is available from the SEC Web Site. The DTD defines the required contents for an EDGAR submission and how that content must be organized. So, you obtain a copy of the DTD file. What do you do with it? How do you easily read and understand it?

In Figure 11-1 we saw what the DTD looks like in its native form. To many, the content is not user-friendly! Someone who knows how to read a DTD can use it to gain an understanding of the document structure requirements. However, in your position at your company, you are neither a programmer nor a DTD expert.

An alternative, graphical view of the DTD was shown in Figure 11-2, as presented by a visual modeling tool. With this view, the relationship of one section of an EDGAR submission to another is obvious. The optional sections are identified with question marks. With this information you are more easily able to formulate a submission that will conform to the SEC's regulatory requirements.

11.2.2 *Creating an instance of the DTD*

With an understanding of the content and structure of an EDGAR submission, you begin constructing your company's submission. Interleaf BladeRunner simplifies the task of creating an initial submission containing the minimal required sections. With a copy of the EDGAR DTD on your desktop, you can create your initial submission document (i.e. an EDGAR DTD instance) with a single click of the mouse.

Now you can begin entering the content that you obtain from the Legal and Finance departments. As you author the submission document, how can you be assured that it will conform to the SEC regulations?

11.2.3 *Checking your EDGAR instance for conformance*

As you continue to add to the EDGAR document, it is very important that the organization of your information adheres to the structure rules as defined in the DTD. Interleaf *BladeRunner* provides two modes of operation:

- "Normal mode" allows you to enter text freely into your submission document. This mode will be useful after you have become familiar with the requirements of the DTD;
- "Conformance checking" mode prevents you from creating a document that does not conform to the rules as defined by the DTD.

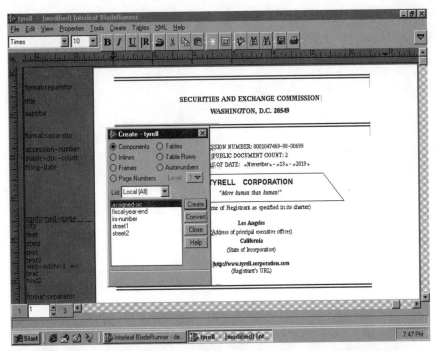

Figure 11-5   Enforcing the DTD in conformance checking mode.

As you become more experienced in creating an EDGAR document, you may find yourself switching between these two modes. Therefore, after you have created the submission document, it is important to be able to *validate* it for conformance.

As shown in Figure 11-5, *BladeRunner* provides a non-conformance error report that identifies various types of structure errors you may have created while using the normal mode of operation.

11.2.4 *Repairing non-conforming elements*

If your submission document contains structural errors, you obviously must fix those before submitting it to the SEC. *BladeRunner* includes "repair tools" for repairing structure errors. Figure 11-6

For example, one of the elements of an EDGAR submission document is "submission date". Since you are new to the EDGAR submission document type, you instinctively enter the date as follows:

```
April 5, 1998
```

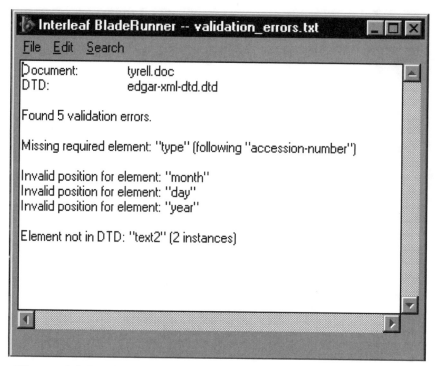

Figure 11-6   Conformance checking error report.

Figure 11-6 shows that this presentation of the submission date is "non-conforming" according to the EDGAR DTD. The submission is correctly presented as follows:

```
1998 April 5
```

Another example is the accession number, which is a required piece of information for the EDGAR document. There is a structure flow rule in the EDGAR DTD which requires that the accession number paragraph in the document must be followed by the type of document. However, being unfamiliar with the document structure, when you created the document you forgot to enter the "type" paragraph following the "accession number" paragraph.

These are examples of two non-conforming document structures which *BladeRunner* provides a utility to repair. For the first example above, you are able to use the "fix element order" utility to correctly sequence a non-conforming organization of information. For the second example, you are able to use the "insert missing element" utility to insert some or all missing elements within the EDGAR document.

11.2.5 *Generating your EDGAR submission*

Now you have a complete and conforming submission document. The next step is to publish the document in two electronic forms: in XML for submission to the SEC, and in HTML to place on your Web site for viewing by any Web browser. Recall that for the Web site you must also remove some of the document content and reorganize the information.

11.2.6 *Publishing for the SEC*

BladeRunner includes a "Publish" feature that allows you to transform documents into different representations. You can also conditionally publish a document according to user-defined rules and specifications, according to the content of the document, and/or according to rules embedded within the document's DTD.

You publish the formal submission as an XML instance and route it to Legal for review. It can be accompanied by an XSL stylesheet that specifies the formatting and presentation rules.

11.2.7 *Repurposing for your Web site*

To produce the Web site version, you first apply conditional publishing rules to the document. In this case, the conditional rules would specify that:

1. The overview section of the EDGAR document should appear in the Web version ahead of the financial data table. In the formal SEC submission, the overview section appears at the end.

2. Information that appears ahead of the financial data table in the formal SEC submission should not appear in the Web version.

3. Information that appears following the financial data table in the formal SEC submission should not appear in the Web version.

Next you position the EDGAR document (the same document that was used to create the formal SEC submission) adjacent to the *BladeRunner* Catalog for Web delivery.

You can now use the same "Publish" feature that you used to generate the SEC submission, except this time you specify that HTML should be produced.

11.3 | Conclusion

Several business process improvements result when government filings such as EDGAR are prepared with XML and a visual document production tool like Interleaf *BladeRunner*.

1. Making the EDGAR submission in a timely fashion with assurance that the submission is complete.
2. Making company information available to the general public immediately following your formal submission to the SEC.
3. Publishing multiple presentations of the company's financial information without having to create and manage different documents for each.
4. Lowering the overhead cost of producing an EDGAR submission.

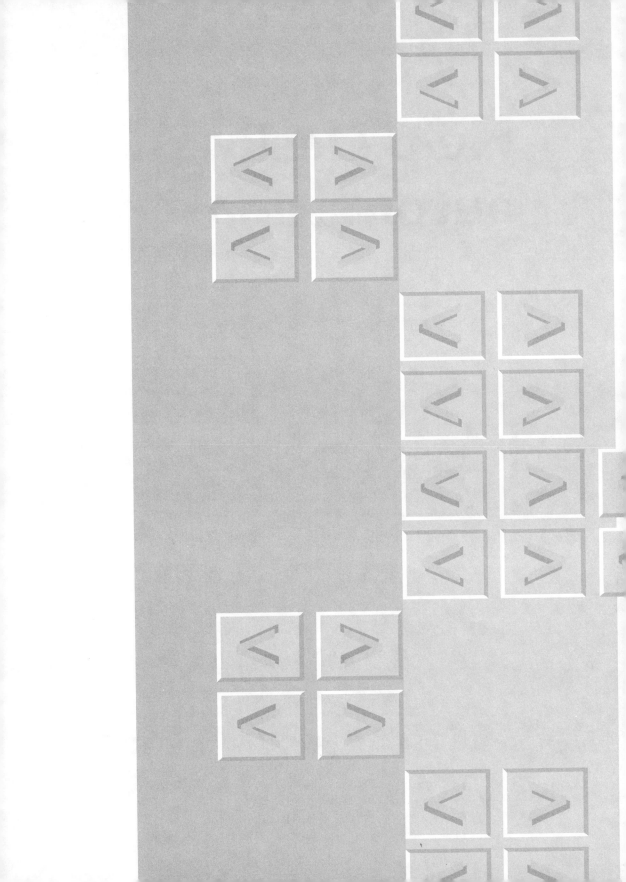

Help Desk automation

- Content management application
- Technical support knowledge base
- Web-based extranet system

12

This chapter describes an XML-based technical support application that ties the Help Desk function to a dynamic repository of product information. It is sponsored by Texcel International, http://www.texcel.com, and was prepared by Jeremy Pollock, Derek Yoo, and Amy Krane.

Technical support is the bane of many high-tech enterprises. Yet, as products get more complicated, the Help Desk increasingly becomes the front line in the battle for customer satisfaction. But as this application demonstrates, the Help Desk might need help itself.

12.1 | The hapless Help Desk

Consider the plight of the Help Desk at a manufacturer of sophisticated, highly customized equipment that includes software-controlled electronic and mechanical components.

12.1.1 The old way

When our story began, the solutions provided by Support Engineers at the Help Desk varied with regard to accuracy, completeness, and applicability to the particular problem the customer faced. In addition, they were in many different file formats, so engineers in different locations might not be able to view a solution.

The speed with which a Support Engineer could obtain a solution also varied widely. Technical fixes and workarounds were stored as whole documents on the file system, making the data in them difficult to maintain, update, and retrieve. A solution document authored by a Support Engineer could cover any number of distinct topics, but was categorized as a single file pertaining to only one topic.

Further, there was no automated way to verify the integrity of the source material and to update all instances of the same information that might occur in separate documents. Nor was it easy to share the information among Help Desk personnel, as the authoring tool was not integrated with the solution repository.

In other words, there was no way to ensure that the customer was getting the most up-to-date, correct, and personalized solution to his problem. This resulted in poor customer satisfaction and high support costs.

12.1.2 *What needed to be done?*

With the advent of ever faster and more comprehensive communications – and the Web as a strategic delivery platform – customers have come to expect fast, highly specific information. The success of the company depended on satisfied customers and functioning equipment.

To meet that need, the company realized, the Help Desk had to be linked into a knowledge repository containing the installation, maintenance, and reference documentation for the products, as well as the custom solutions developed by the Support Engineers in the course of assisting Field Engineers and customers.

Ideally, solutions should be generated that are accurate and personalized for each customer. Therefore, in this application, the Support Engineers must be provided with a tool for authoring custom solution documents, as well as the means to search for and retrieve relevant information from the knowledge base. Moreover, it is desirable to maximize the Help Desk investment by provided a controlled means to add these solutions to the knowledge repository for use by others.

Additional requirements were the ability to share and reuse information gathered in the field into the knowledge repository, providing accessible, usable feedback for the product documentation cycle. At the same time, the organization wanted to gain portable, modular information that could be shared with its business partners and OEMs.

To show how an organization could accomplish these goals, an XML-based *Help Desk Solution System* prototype was developed. The prototype uses *Texcel Information Manager*, a content management system that is tuned to manage XML data content, element structure, metadata, and links. The product combines a dynamic document repository built on object database technology with applications for collaborative authoring, such as workflow and electronic review and commenting. Customized Java applets and integration with an existing call-tracking system comprise the balance of the prototype.

12.1.3 *Helping the Help Desk*

Consider a scenario with the prototype system in use.

In this scenario a field engineer experiences a problem with a piece of equipment installed at a customer site. He visits the manufacturer's technical support Web site, and attempts to solve his problem by searching for published technical solution information. No relevant published information is found, so the call is automatically routed to a Support Engineer at corporate headquarters who is using the Help Desk Solution System.

The Support Engineer calls up customer information from the customer tracking system, which is integrated with the Solution System, to determine the appropriate model number and other customer usage characteristics. Then he searches for applicable technical information in the dynamic knowledge repository, which consists of both published and in-process technical and maintenance documents, technical notes, training materials, and workarounds and customer solution documents submitted by other support personnel.

Although useful, the information already available and published does not specifically address the customer's problem. So the Support Engineer generates a new, custom XML solution document that combines information gained on the call, customer data, and information in the repository.

The new solution is checked into the repository, and automated system-supplied metadata is generated. Once in the repository, the solution document is available to other Support Engineers, although still in draft form.

The document is then automatically routed for review and approval via an integrated workflow system, part of the standard *Texcel Information*

Manager product. Subject matter experts and technical editors comment on the document, using the browser-based review and commenting tool component of the product.

In addition, references to source material indicated by the Support Engineer are turned into cross-repository links to maintenance information. The new XML solution document is now available in final form for search and retrieval by other Support Engineers.

12.2 | How the *Solution System* works

12.2.1 *Information flow*

Support Engineers interact with the *Solution System* through a Java applet run from a standard Web browser. The back-end knowledge repository built using *Texcel Information Manager* contains maintenance and reference information marked up in XML.

The repository also contains other material contributed by subject matter experts in popular file formats such as *Word* and *PowerPoint*, and various graphics formats. XML metadata is associated with all objects managed in the repository. A customer support call-tracking system, running on an SQL database, also supplies data to the *Solution System*.

Support Engineers create custom, personalized solution documents using an embedded XML editing tool. The solution documents incorporate the correct product model numbers and other details from the customer records in the SQL call tracking system, which is automatically integrated into fields within the solution editor.

Once authored and approved, the solutions are categorized and stored in the repository in a way that facilitates economical querying. Each element within a solution document instance is decomposed into a unique object in the repository. A solution document instance or any element contained therein can be retrieved on demand.

12.2.2 *Architecture*

The XML *Help Desk Solution System* consists of several client, server, and database components, as shown in Figure 12-1. The clients are a Java applet for solution research and authoring, and the *Texcel Work Queue* (an automatically generated to-do list).

The Java applet provides a GUI interface for querying the repository, and a query results display, as well as an integrated solution editor, a help Function, and a research and discovery function. The *Work Queue* delivers tasks to the user according to his role in the review and approval cycle.

The Java server application connects to multiple Java applet clients, interfaces with the document repository as well as the SQL database (through JDBC), and handles the workflow initiation and routing.

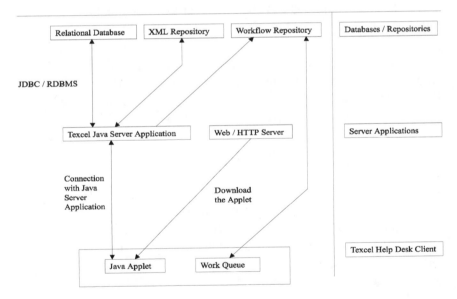

Figure 12-1 The XML *Help Desk Solution System.*

12.3 | Using the *Help Desk Solution System*

Now let's step through the application scenario and discuss the tools and technology – including the role of XML – in use at each step. We start at the Support Engineer's desk, where he is researching a solution to a problem reported by a Field Engineer on behalf of a customer.

12.3.1   *Make the query*

The Support Engineer queries the repository for solution documents that match the problem reported by the Field Engineer (Figure 12-2).

The *Help Desk Solution System* Java applet is running in a standard Web browser.

SQL queries are run against the customer call tracking system, incorporating the appropriate product name and type into the correct fields in the applet.

The search process uses the Texcel query language, which is specifically designed and optimized to query XML (and full SGML) data. The search can find information contained in any element or piece of metadata, based on any combination of element types, metadata, and data content. Searches can be run on material that is not yet released, such as solutions and reference material that is in draft form; this status information is stored as metadata.

The search tool GUI shields the user from the complexity of the query language, while generating well-formed queries and usable results.

The results of the search are presented in a tabular format in the *Solution System* applet. When an item is selected, it is converted on the fly from XML to HTML, using standard functionality of the *Texcel Information Manager* Web Application module.

12.3.2   *Research product information*

The Support Engineer researches background information in the product information repository using the *Texcel Information Manager* Explorer interface (Figure 12-3).

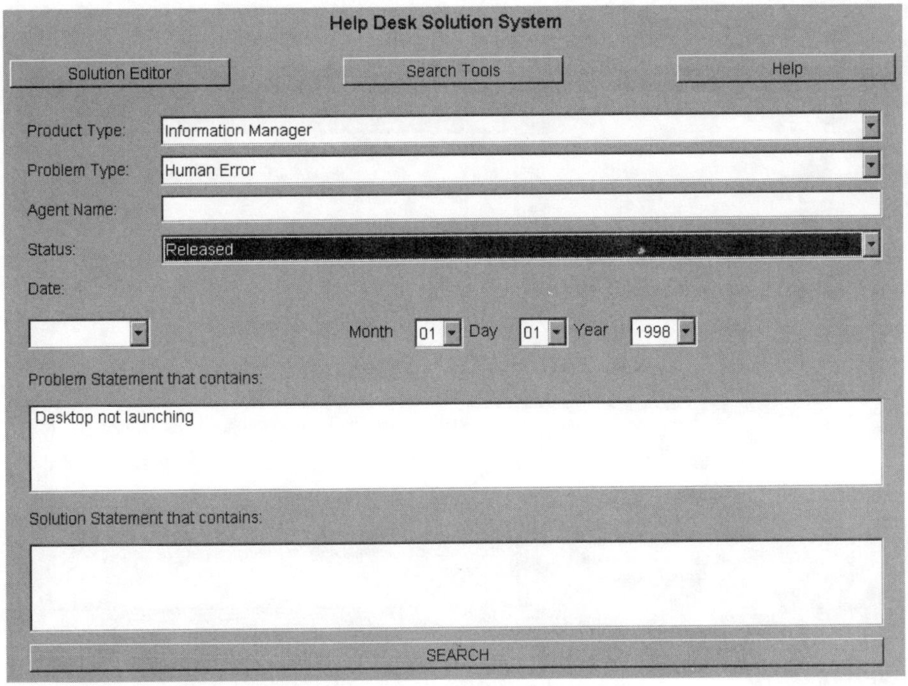

Figure 12-2   Search panel of client applet

Use of XML provides both tagged elements and metadata. The element structure can be seen in the repository browser and used for various functions. For example, a user can select a single element for updating.

A logical structure has been created for the repository, much like the folders and subfolders used in file system organization, making navigation straightforward.

12.3.3 *Write a solution*

The Support Engineer develops a new solution to the specific problem, based on interaction with the Field Engineer as well as research into the knowledge repository (Figure 12-4).

An XML document type is used that has been designed for the *Solution System* application.

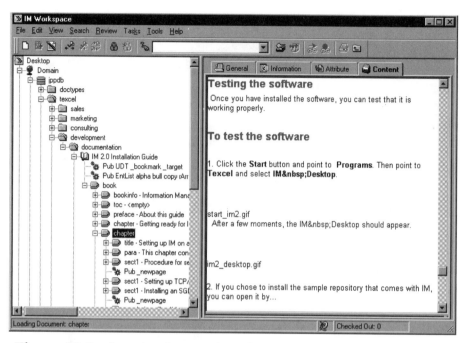

Figure 12-3   Browsing the repository for research and discovery.

Tags are not visible to the end user. Instead, the Support Engineer is able to use standard word processing functions, such as creating bulleted lists and specifying fonts.

The new document automatically includes the customer ID number and the part number of the machine that was malfunctioning, which has been extracted from the SQL database through a JDBC interface to the relational database. This information is inserted into the document and tagged with XML, as shown in Example 12-1.

12.3.4 *Update the repository*

The document is completed and submitted to the repository.

The solution document is composed and an XML parser runs to check the solution document for well-formedness.

The user selects the priority level of the document, which is used to determine which review process is used.

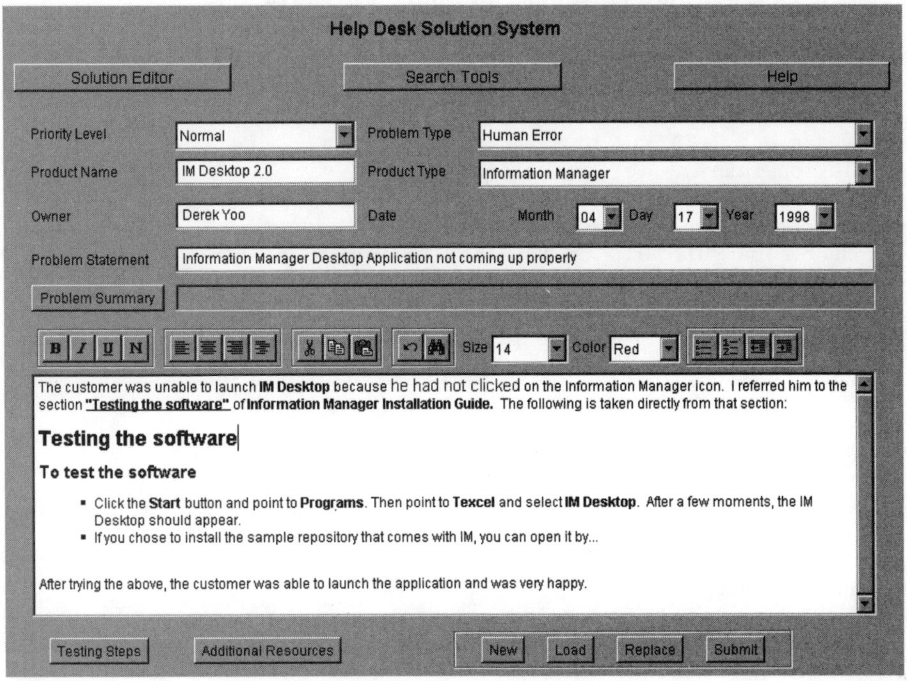

Figure 12-4 XML Solution Editor running within a Java client.

The solution document is now available to all users although still in draft or unapproved form.

12.3.5 *Route for approval*

Because the Support Engineer has authored new information, the solution document is automatically routed for approval. The routing is managed through the work queue shown in Figure 12-5.

The solution document is submitted to the Java server application, which communicates with the Texcel workflow repository.

A "case" or process is selected and the document is automatically routed to the correct people, such as the technical editors and engineers, for review and approval.

Example 12-1. **Solution document marked up in XML.**

```
<?XML version="1.0"?>
<solution id="solution-1000">
<solution-info>
<owner>Derek Yoo</owner>
<date>Sat Jan 31 22:30:50  1998</date>
</solution-info>
<product-grp>
<product-type>SST</product-type>
<product-name>Self Service Terminal 100A</product-name>
</product-grp>
<problem-grp>
<problem-statement> Terminal 100A will not recover from a power
failure. Screen remains blank after power is restored.
</problem-statement>
</problem-grp>
<solution-grp>
<solution-statement>
<para>The solution is to simply turn the main power switch for the
terminal off and then on again.</para>
</solution-statement>
<testing-steps>
<step></step>
</testing-steps>
</solution-grp>
</solution>
```

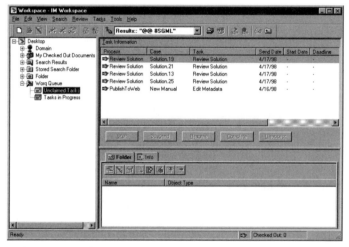

Figure 12-5   Work queue component of *Solution System.*

12.3.6 *Check in document to knowledge base*

The solution document is checked into the knowledge base and shredded into XML objects.

The check-in process parses the document and labels each element with a unique repository identifier, which can be used for retrieval and linking purposes. In addition, individual elements can be called out of the repository and reused in new solution documents as either copies of, or links to, the original information. These capabilities are part of Texcel Information Manager's support for XML.

Analysis   At first glance, this application appears to have many of the characteristics of the "large tech manual" publishing applications, perhaps because tech manuals are part of the information base. But other aspects of the application are more like classic database systems, with an emphasis on capturing bits of data, "cleaning" them, combining them with other data, and presenting them together in reports.

XML, of course, works both ends of this street quite well, and this app demonstrates that the ends are really connected; that XML document processing and XML data processing are only different in degree, not in kind.

Extended linking

- Extended linking defined
- XLink applications
- XPointers
- Strong link typing

Extended linking and strong link typing will let the Web traverse to locations where it has never been. Those concepts are explained simply and clearly in this chapter sponsored by ISOGEN International, `http://www.isogen.com`. It was prepared by Steven R. Newcomb of TechnoTeacher, Inc., `http://www.techno.com`, co-editor of the HyTime International Standard (ISO/IEC 10744).

uture generations of Web browsers and editors will reduce the effort required to keep our personal affairs organized and our corporate memories up to the minute. The productivity of many kinds of work will be enhanced, and in many ways. It's all going to happen basically because of two simple enhancements to the Web paradigm.

The W3C's draft XLink "extended link" facility proposes to give all of us the ability to annotate documents, and to share those annotations with others, even when we cannot alter the documents we are annotating. In other words, we won't have to change a document in order to supply it with our own annotations – annotations that a browser can make appear as though they were written right into the annotated document.

13.1 | The Shop notes application

As an example, consider a technician's set of online maintenance manuals. These are electronic books that the technician is not (and should not be) authorized to change. With the Web's existing HTML hyperlinks, the technician cannot write a note in a manual that can take future readers of that manual, including himself, to his annotations. Nor can the technician's annotations be displayed in their proper context – the parts of the manual that they are about.

13.1.1 *What is extended linking?*

By using *extended linking*, when the technician makes an annotation, he does so purely by authoring his own document; no change is made to the read-only manual document that he is annotating.

The big difference between "extended" linking and present-day HTML linking is this. With an HTML (or "simple") link, traversal can only begin at the place where the link is; traversal cannot begin at the other end. With an "extended" link, however, you can click on any of the link's anchors, and traverse to any other anchor, regardless of where the link happens to be.

Tip   Extended linking allows the starting anchor of a link to be different from the link itself. Instead of HTML's "A" tagged element that is linked to one other element, you can have (say) an "L" tag that links two or more other elements to one another.

A simple link (top of Figure 13-1) is always embedded ("inline") in (for example) the InstallLog text from which it provides traversal; the link cannot be traversed by starting at the target anchor (for example, the Installation procedure document).

An extended link (bottom of Figure 13-1) can appear in a separate document, and provide traversal between the corresponding parts of two other documents: for example, the technician's shop notes document ("TechLog") and the read-only installation manual. Because the location of this particular link is not the same as any of its anchors, it is said to be "out-of-line" (not embedded).

In our example, an annotation takes the form of just such an extended link element.

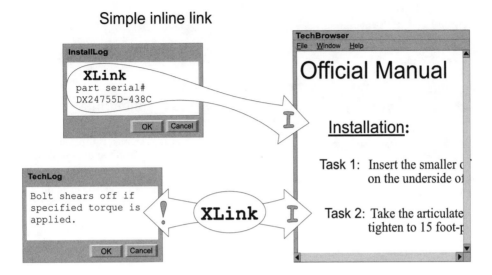

Simple inline link

Extended, out-of-line link

Figure 13-1   Simple vs. extended linking.

13.1.2 *Displaying extended links*

One way to realize the benefits of extended links is to display an icon at each anchor that indicates something about the other anchor. (The mechanism that supports this is discussed in greater detail under "Strong link typing", below.)

For example, as shown in Figure 13-2, a reader of the installation manual on the right will know that, if he clicks on the exclamation point displayed near Task 2, he will see a shop note about that task. If he clicks on the pound sign, he will be shown the serial number of a part that was installed according to the procedure, recorded in an "InstallLog" document.

Similarly, a reader of the annotation in the shop notes document ("TechLog") will know that clicking on the "I" icon will bring him to the installation instruction that the annotation discusses.

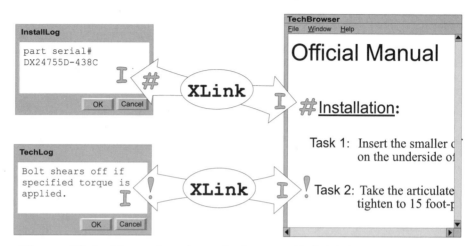

Figure 13-2   The exclamation point icon near Task 2 indicates that a shop note is available.

13.1.3   *Notes survive to new versions of manuals*

The technician's annotations – his "shop notes" – accumulate over time, and they represent a valuable asset that must be maintained. If the technician were to write shop notes inside each manual, when a new version of a manual is received it would be a chore to copy annotations from the old manual to the new manual.

With extended linking, however, the annotations are not in the old version; they are in a separate document. Therefore, the shop notes don't disappear when an annotated manual is replaced by a newer version.

That is because each link is equipped with "pointers" – pieces of information that can tell a browser where (for example) clickable icons should be rendered that indicate the availability of an annotation. Each such "XPointer" (as it is called) can point at anything in any XML document.

In our technician's shop, when a manual is replaced by a new version, the XPointers keep on working, even with the new manual, so the new manual is instantly and automatically equipped with the old manual's annotations.

In most cases, the XPointers don't have to be changed, because they continue to point at the right things, even in the new manual. If, because of differences between the old and new versions of the manual, some XPointers in the shop notes don't still point at the right things (or perhaps have nothing to point at any more), certain techniques can be used to detect each such situation. By dealing with these problem spots, the maintainers of the shop notes can minimize their efforts.

Moreover, XPointers and extended links enhance the potential for achieving high levels of quality and consistency, even when there are voluminous shop notes that annotate many manuals.

13.1.4 *Vendors can use the notes*

Some shop notes may also have value to the vendors of the manuals they annotate; they may beneficially influence subsequent versions of the manual. An editor of the manual can load (i.e., make his browser aware of) all the shop notes of many repair shops; this has the effect of populating the manual with icons representing the annotations of all the shops. The most common trouble spots in the manual will be made obvious by the crowds of annotation icons that they appear to have accumulated (Figure 13-3).

The fact that the shop notes take the form of interchangeable XML documents that use standardized extended links makes the task of sharing internal shop notes with manual vendors as easy as sending them any other kind of file. There is no need to extract them from some other resource, or to format them in such a way that they can be understood by their recipients. They are ready to work just as they are, in the tradition of SGML, HyTime, HTML, and now XML.

13.2 | Other applications of extended linking

The above "shop notes" example is just a sample of the kinds of enhancements that extended linking will bring to our interactions with information resources. Some of the broader implications are a bit more startling.

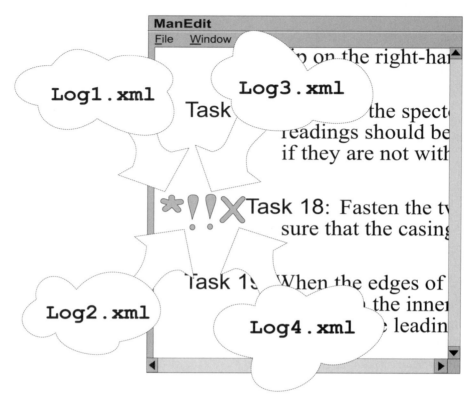

Figure 13-3   Task 18 evidently prompted three kinds of annotations in four different shop logs.

13.2.1 *Public resource communities of interest*

For example, many web sites today contain HTML links to public resources. One is the U.S. Government's online service for translating any U.S. postal code into its corresponding Congressional district and the name of its current incumbent Representative (`http://www.house.gov/zip/ZIP2Rep.html`).

However, if those HTML links were to become XLink extended links, an XLink-enabled browser could render this U.S. government Web page in such a way as to add to it a catalog of the activists and lobbying organizations who refer readers of their websites to this particular U.S. government resource. The "marketplace of ideas" represented by the aggregate of such organizations is thus revealed in a new and interesting way.

13.2.2 *Guidance documents*

Another startling possibility is the association of browser-controlling metadata with any and all Web resources.

In this scenario, a document of annotations (or a set of such documents) can be a user's companion during excursions on the Web. These annotations might make suggestions to users as to where to find more recent material, or they might even take control of the browser's link traversal ability in order to protect children from disturbing material.

While the latter XLink-enabled possibility may sound inimical to the freedom of speech, in fact it enhances liberty. It provides a new public medium for free speech: documents that censor the Web and/or otherwise provide guidance to Web travelers in the form of annotations that appear only in their designated contexts.

Of course, no adult is required to use any such guidance document, just as no one is required to read any particular book, but it's easy to predict that many will pay for the privilege of using many kinds of such "guidance documents."

More importantly, everyone will have the tools to write such guidance documents, so the technical ability to provide guidance (and, yes, even to provide censorship services) will be widely distributed, rather than being dangerously concentrated in a few generalized rating services. The creation and maintenance of guidance documents may well become a thriving cottage industry. Anyone can be a critic.

In the case of electronic commerce, it's easy to imagine that vendors will attempt to provide guidance documents designed to annotate the online sales catalogs of their competitors. In response, some providers of online sales catalogs will take steps to render the pointers in these kinds of guidance documents invalid and unmaintainable.

Regardless of all this, the overall impact on electronic commerce will certainly be positive; increasing the meaningful interconnectedness of the Web will help more people find exactly what they're looking for.

And it may turn out to be a mistake, in many cases, for catalog owners to attempt to render the pointers used to annotate their catalogs invalid, because similar pointers could be used, for example, by impartial consumer testing organizations to attach "best buy" recommendations to certain products. The guidance documents of consumer testing organizations will probably be quite popular, and well worth the cost of using them.

13.2.3　*Computer-augmented memory*

Extended linking has the potential to make radical improvements in our ability to keep track of what we are doing. Someday, we can expect to automatically annotate each piece of information we work with in such a way that, in effect, it refers future readers to the work we did with respect to it.

In other words, practically everything we do can be usefully seen as an annotation of one or more other pieces of work. If everything we do is, in some sense, an annotation of one or more other things, everything we do can all be found far more easily, starting from any piece of work anywhere in the "chain" (or, more likely, "tree" or "graph") of relevant information.

This is because extended linking allows all links to be bidirectional. (Or, rather, "n-directional", to account for extended links with more than two ends.) All of the connections among our affairs can then be tracked more or less automatically, so that each of us can enjoy a radical reduction in filing, cross-indexing, and other organizational chores, and with vastly increased ability to find what we're looking for quickly and easily.

Obviously, this same idea is even more significant in the realm of corporate memory. Even with today's behemoth enterprise integration technologies, it's still too hard to figure out what has happened, who is doing what, how various plans and projects are going to integrate, and where the relevant paperwork can be found.

Going a step further, there is an ISO standardization activity (ISO CD 13250) seeking ways to exploit extended linking in such a way as to create living, easily explored and maintained "maps" of all of the information resources available to an organization (see "Topic Navigation Maps", http://www.hightext.com/tnm). This goal sounds almost insanely ambitious, but extended linking, in combination with strong link typing (see below), could make it practical and achievable.

13.2.4 *Intellectual property management*

The advent of extended linking also offers interesting new possibilities for the management and exploitation of intellectual property.

For example, metadata regarding the licensing policies of owners of Web resources could be associated with those resources by means of extended links. Such metadata could be changed when the resources are sold or licensed, without requiring any changes to the assets themselves.

This method greatly reduces the likelihood of inadvertent damage to the assets, and greatly increases the ease with which ownership and/or management policies can change. There is already an official, internationally-ratified ISO standard for using extended linking for exactly this purpose (see `http://www.ornl.gov/sgml/wg8/document/n1920/html/clause-6.7.html#clause-6.7.3`).

Such activity policies, and the means by which they are associated with online assets, could well become a source of private law that will strongly influence the development of intelligent agents (see `http://www.hytime.org/papers/higgins1.html`).

13.3 | Strong link typing

With the XLink extended link facility, there is no limit to the number of links that can be traversed from a single point in a single document. Many different documents can contain links to the very same anchor, with the result that, theoretically, at least, an unlimited number of traversals are possible, starting from a single point. In addition, there are no limits on the kinds of annotations that can be made, nor on the purposes to which such annotations may be put.

Therefore, it makes sense to provide some easy way to sort the annotations (i.e., the links) into categories. For example, some kinds of annotations will be made in order to provide "metadata" about the document, and these will often take effect in some way other than by rendering an icon on the display screen. Some kinds of annotations are interesting only for specialized purposes.

13.3.1 *Hiding the installation log*

Going back to our earlier example, the technician can create an annotation that indicates the serial number of a new part that he installed in accordance with a particular maintenance procedure. The fact that such an annotation is available would be of interest only to someone who was auditing the installation of parts; it probably wouldn't appear even to the technician, despite the fact that it was he who created the annotation.

The technician's installation log annotation can be hidden from most people because it is "strongly typed": it has been clearly and unambiguously labeled as to its intended meaning and purpose, so all browsers can see what kind of link it is. In effect, the link says, "I am a Part-Installation-Log-Entry." People who aren't interested in part installation records can arrange for their browsers to hide them.

13.3.2 *Why do we need strong link typing?*

People may still choose to be made aware of other kinds of annotations made by our technician. For example, other technicians may wish to read our technician's accounts of any special situations that he has experienced when attempting to follow a particular instruction, or about successful and unsuccessful experiments with substitute parts.

The notion of "strong link typing" is virtually absent from HTML links. Basically, in HTML, the browser software knows where the user can go, but not why the author of the document being browsed thought the user might like to go there. The human reader can usually divine something from the context about the material that will be shown if the "anchor" hyperlink is traversed, but the browser itself is basically unable to help the user decide whether to click or not to click, so it can't hide any available traversals.

To be able to hide the availability of unwanted kinds of links can save a lot of time and effort. So the draft W3C XLink recommendation also provides for the addition of strong typing features, not only to extended links, but also to the "simple" links that closely resemble the familiar HTML "anchor" (<a>) element. Thus, browsers can start supporting strong link typing promptly, even before they can handle extended linking.

13.3.3 *Anchor role identification*

The notion of strong link typing includes the notion of "anchor role" designation.

For example, the simple link at the top of Figure 13-1 characterizes its target anchor as an installation instruction; in the diagram, this is indicated by the "I" icon in the arrowhead. Similarly, the extended link at the bottom of Figure 13-1 characterizes one of its anchors as a shop note (the exclamation point) and the other anchor as an installation instruction (another "I" arrowhead).

Thus, a link can do more than just identify itself by saying, for example, "I am a Part Installation Log Entry." It can also specify which of its anchors fulfill which roles in the relationship it expresses.

For example, our Part Installation Log Entry link can say, in effect, "I signify that part [pointer to entry in parts catalog or inventory record] was installed in [pointer to information that identifies the unit being maintained] in accordance with maintenance directive [XPointer to instruction in manual]."

In other words, the log entry link is a three-ended link whose anchor roles might be named "replacement-part" (indicated with a "#" icon), "maintained-unit" ("@" icon), and "maintenance-directive" ("I" icon) (Figure 13-4).

The fact that an anchor plays some specific role in a relationship often determines whether the relationship is interesting or even relevant in a given application context.

13.4 | Conclusion

It is easy to see that the impact of extended linking will be significant, and that technical workers and electronic commerce will be early beneficiaries. Extended linking will enhance the helpfulness and usefulness of the Web environment. The burden of many kinds of paperwork will be very substantially mitigated.

On the horizon, there appears to be serious potential for significant improvements in the availability of all kinds of knowledge, due to the possibility of creating and interchanging Topic Navigation Maps. Intellectual

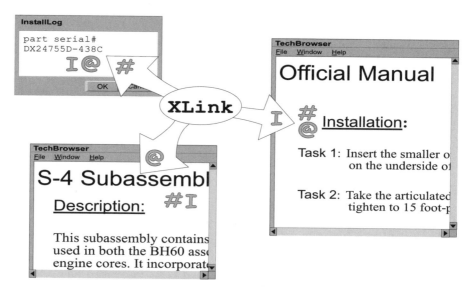

Figure 13-4   Link with two traversal possibilities at each anchor, distinguishable because of anchor role identification.

property management, and the Web-based utilization of intellectual property, will become easier and more orderly.

All of these benefits, and probably many more, emanate from two very simple enhancements of the Web paradigm in the draft XLink and XPointers recommendations of the World Wide Web Consortium:

- Allowing the starting anchor of a link to be different from the link itself; and
- Strong link typing, in which links plainly exhibit the kind of relationship they represent, and the roles their anchors play in that relationship.

Tip   For more on XLink and XPointers, see Chapter 34, "Extensible Linking Language (XLink)", on page 498. The text of the XLink and XPointer drafts are on the CD-ROM.

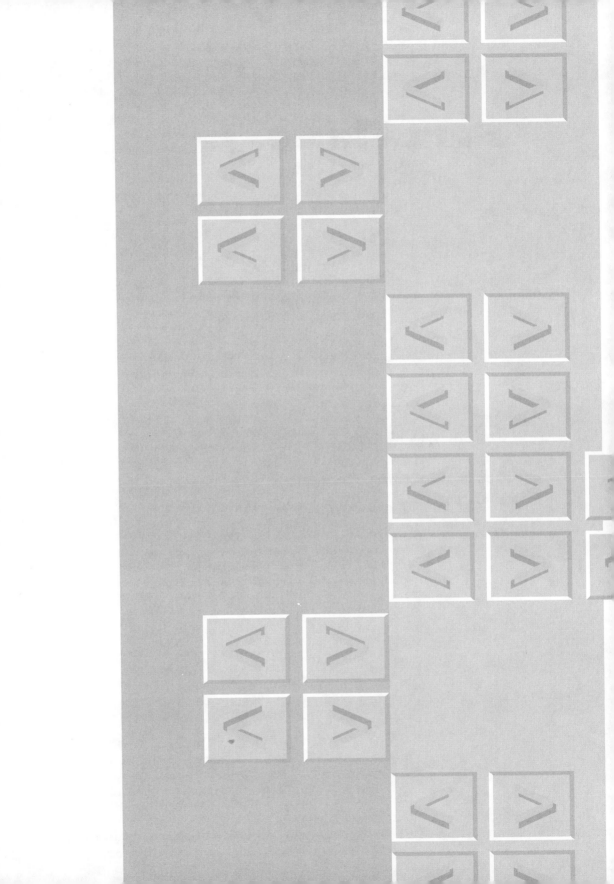

Part Three

- Real-world case studies
- Doing business on the Web
- Preparing for XML

What's Being Done with XML

Hitachi Semiconductor

- Semiconductor industry
- Product data sheets
- Automating transformations
- Web-based searching

14

Distributing the right document to the right customer at the right time presents a formidable challenge for a semiconductor manufacturer. This chapter is sponsored by Adobe Systems Incorporated, http://www.adobe.com, and was prepared by Lani Hajagos.

Hitachi Semiconductor (America), Inc. maintains nearly 1,000 data sheets comprising a total of 70,000 pages, and each must be made available to prospective customers, primarily design engineers, on the Web, CD-ROM, and on paper. The publishing function is mission-critical because the data sheets provide the chips' performance characteristics and interface specifications. Without them, Hitachi Semiconductor's customers cannot use the chip in their designs. Therefore, the chip cannot be released to market without the data sheet.

14.1 | Introduction

The company urgently needed a way to simplify version control and publish on all media from a single, manageable source file. "In the fast-paced semiconductor industry, we revise our documents an average of four times a year, so version control is challenging enough with 970 publications," says Bob Tabone, program manager for marketing communications. "With 970 times three versions-Web, CD-ROM, and paper-it would be nightmarish."

HM511664C Series

---

2. $\overline{CAS}$ = V$_{IH}$ to disable Dout.

AC Characteristics (Ta = 0 to +70°C, V$_{CC}$ = 5 V ±10%, V$_{SS}$ = 0 V)[1], [14], [15], [17], [18]

Test Conditions

- Input rise and fall time : 5 ns
- Input levels: V$_{IL}$ = 0 V, V$_{IH}$ = 3.0 V
- Input timing reference levels : 0.8 V, 2.4 V
- Output load : 1 TTL gate + C$_L$ (50 pF) (Including scope and jig)

Read, Write, Read-Modify-Write and Refresh Cycles (Common parameters)

| Parameter | Symbol | HM511664C | | | | | | Unit | Notes |
| | | -6 | | -7 | | -8 | | | |
		Min	Max	Min	Max	Min	Max		
Random read or write cycle time	t$_{RC}$	105	—	125	—	145	—	ns	
$\overline{RAS}$ precharge time	t$_{RP}$	40	—	50	—	60	—	ns	
$\overline{RAS}$ pulse width	t$_{RAS}$	60	10000	70	10000	80	10000	ns	23
$\overline{CAS}$ pulse width	t$_{CAS}$	15	10000	20	10000	20	10000	ns	22, 24
Row address setup time	t$_{ASR}$	0	—	0	—	0	—	ns	
Row address hold time	t$_{RAH}$	10	—	10	—	10	—	ns	
Column address setup time	t$_{ASC}$	0	—	0	—	0	—	ns	
Column address hold time	t$_{CAH}$	15	—	15	—	15	—	ns	
$\overline{RAS}$ to $\overline{CAS}$ delay time	t$_{RCD}$	20	45	20	50	20	60	ns	8
$\overline{RAS}$ to column address delay time	t$_{RAD}$	15	30	15	35	15	40	ns	9
$\overline{RAS}$ hold time	t$_{RSH}$	15	—	20	—	20	—	ns	
$\overline{CAS}$ hold time	t$_{CSH}$	60	—	70	—	80	—	ns	25
$\overline{CAS}$ to $\overline{RAS}$ precharge time	t$_{CRP}$	10	—	10	—	10	—	ns	
$\overline{OE}$ to Din delay time	t$_{ODD}$	15	—	15	—	15	—	ns	

Figure 14-1   Original process: Printed data sheet.

Hitachi Semiconductor solved its challenge using Adobe's FrameMaker+SGML software, an integrated SGML authoring and publishing tool that shields the end user from the technicalities of SGML (see Chapter 21, "FrameMaker+ SGML: Editing+ composition", on page 278). In phase one of the solution, the company adopted the product to create a single source file for multiple output formats, including SGML, HTML, PDF, and RTF. In phase two, the company added XML.

14.2 | The business case

The company's product data sheets are authored in Japan by 200 design engineers who use a word processing application and save as RTF files. The documents, ranging from 3 to 1,000 pages, are complex: typically 40 percent tables, 40 percent graphics, and 20 percent free text (see Figure 14-1). Structure is crucial for semiconductor documentation, so detailed style sheets help the authors comply. The files reference external graphics in EPS format, created by Adobe Illustrator.

Publishing occurs at Hitachi Semiconductor's headquarters in Brisbane, California. The RTF and EPS files are checked into a document management system, which stores all the text and graphics files related to a publication as a single compound document.

The publishers convert the RTF files to SGML and the EPS files into GIF files. After this conversion, the company publishes its documents in hardcopy and three electronic formats for the Web and CD-ROM: HTML for browsing, PDF for printing, and SGML for downloading – for example, for inclusion in the customer's design automation tool.

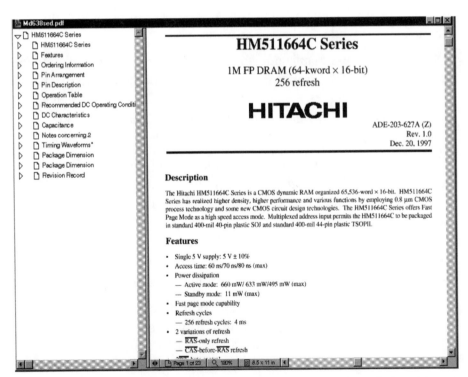

Figure 14-2   Revised process: PDF rendition of a datasheet displayed in *Adobe Acrobat.*

14.3 | Phase 1: Creating a single source file

The main drawback of the original process was that Hitachi Semiconductor could not render PDF files from the SGML source, and had to render them from the RTF file instead. "Without a single source file, we could not have a high confidence level that we were producing PDF files from the same version as the SGML file," says Tabone. "That was unacceptable from a quality standpoint."

In addition, the company had to manually add bookmarks and links to the PDF files that were created from RTF, a process that required an average of five hours per document. At 40 documents per month, this meant the company spent 200 person-hours recreating information that already existed in another format. Long publishing lead times left the company with out-of-date documents: approximately 30 percent of published pieces became obsolete while on the company's shelves.

When Hitachi Semiconductor adopted the use of Adobe FrameMaker+SGML software in late 1996, the company became able to maintain a single source file and to shorten lead times. The product has since become one of the most important tools in Hitachi Semiconductor's publishing suite.

Hitachi Semiconductor can now produce PDF files from the SGML source, simply by choosing the "Save As PDF" command (see Figure 14-2). By saving the hyperlinks from the SGML file and automatically creating bookmarks, *FrameMaker+SGML* eliminates a labor-intensive process. Hitachi Semiconductor is able to provide print vendors with production-ready files because *FrameMaker+SGML* handles composition and pagination of the data sheets and automatically generates indexes and tables of contents.

Hitachi Semiconductor wrote a Perl script to automate the check-in process into the document management system. The script validates the SGML files, notifying their creators if any errors are present, and converts EPS files to GIF files. This automated process gives the company confidence it is using the correct source file and also dramatically reduces the time required for editing, proofing, and publishing (see Figure 14-3).

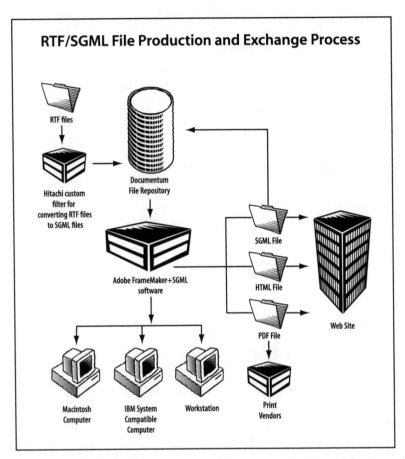

Figure 14-3 Workflow currently employed by Hitachi Semiconductor.

14.4 | Phase 2: Automating transformations with XML

While *FrameMaker+SGML* solved the initial challenge – creating a single source file for multiple delivery mechanisms – SGML still imposed certain limitations for Hitachi. Its wide range of options and specialized features were overkill for the Web environment.

"In addition", says Tabone, "no Web tools are available to allow customers to take advantage of an SGML document's rich data format. For example, there is nothing today that will enable our customers to search our document set for all chips with performance in a certain range." The answer to these problems came in the form of XML.

"XML provides the structure of SGML without its complexity," says Tabone. An added benefit for the company, whose authors are in Japan, is that XML accepts only integrated double-byte character support.

14.5 | "Publishing on steroids"

When the eXtensible Style Language (XSL) specification (see Chapter 35, "Extensible Style Language (XSL)", on page 516) is complete, Hitachi Semiconductor will use it to automate data transformations – for example, specifying the location and appearance of an element of type "author."

"XSL will enable us to specify the production process as well as the content – in the same markup language," says Tabone. "We'll acquire a sure, solid methodology for automating the processes throughout the production environment, from input to delivery. No longer will we need special filters and dedicated people to run the transformations. It's publishing on steroids". (See Figure 14-4.)

Adobe recently added the capability to save *FrameMaker+SGML* files as XML. Prior to this availability, Hitachi set up a process, using commercially-available parsers, to adapt its SGML documents for use with XML. Around 80 percent of the parsing happens without any manual intervention, so Hitachi expects that the adaptation process will take four months or less.

14.6 | Facilitation of Web-based searching

XML not only improves the production process, it also will benefit Web site visitors by enabling them to search for products by type and significant characteristics. Hitachi Semiconductor will tag the searchable characteristics during the RTF-to-SGML conversion process. The tags will retained when the file is exported as XML. As soon as developers introduce the appropriate tools, Hitachi Semiconductor plans to add the tags automati-

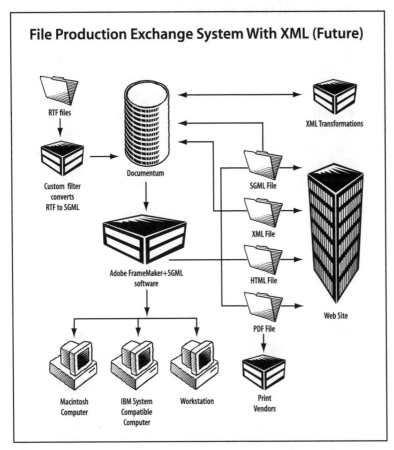

File Production Exchange System With XML (Future)

RTF files

Custom filter
converts
RTF to SGML

Documentum

Adobe FrameMaker+SGML
software

SGML File

XML File

HTML File

PDF File

XML Transformations

Web Site

Macintosh
Computer

IBM System
Compatible
Computer

Workstation

Print
Vendors

Figure 14-4   Future workflow incorporating XML.

cally to an index data file, and customers will be able to perform queries and searches against the index file.

By publishing XML documents on the Web, Hitachi Semiconductor will combine the accessibility of HTML with much of the richness of SGML. Customers who previously downloaded SGML will be able to download the XML instead. Those who need styles will be able to separately download the XLS style sheet. Customers who do not have XML-enabled browsers will be able to view HTML, which a Web-based application will create from XML on the fly.

14.7 | Quantifiable savings

When Hitachi Semiconductor began using FrameMaker+SGML and gained the ability to create PDF files directly from the SGML source documents, the company reduced print costs 40 percent and reduced its print cycle 66 percent-from three months to one month. "With shrinking product design cycles, faster time-to-market is not just a nice benefit for our customers, it's a business imperative," says Tabone. Customers download an average of 19,000 product data sheets as PDF files each month, saving the company $19,000 in postage costs.

Tabone expects that XML will augment those gains. He calculates that XML will reduce printing costs another 15 percent, and shave another two weeks from lead time for a 50 percent gain.

Hitachi Semiconductor also benefits from the ability to create all its deliverables – paper, PDF, and XML – from a single source. That is, the company can manage a larger volume of information more reliably and accurately. The publication process is more automated, freeing employees with high-level publishing skills to apply their talents to other projects.

14.8 | Conclusion: A new dimension of automation

Tabone views XML as an important publishing technology for the next decade. "Three things will matter in the 21st century: information, information, and information. If you can't deliver information on time, correctly, reliably, and in the format the customer wants, you're out of business. By providing structure and rich information about the document, XML lets companies better serve their consumers' information requirements."

The use of XML also positions Hitachi Semiconductor to meet anticipated recommendations from the Electronic Component Information Exchange (ECIX) Project, an association of eight leading semiconductor manufacturers, including Hitachi Semiconductor, seeking to standardize the way semiconductor product information is presented to consumers.

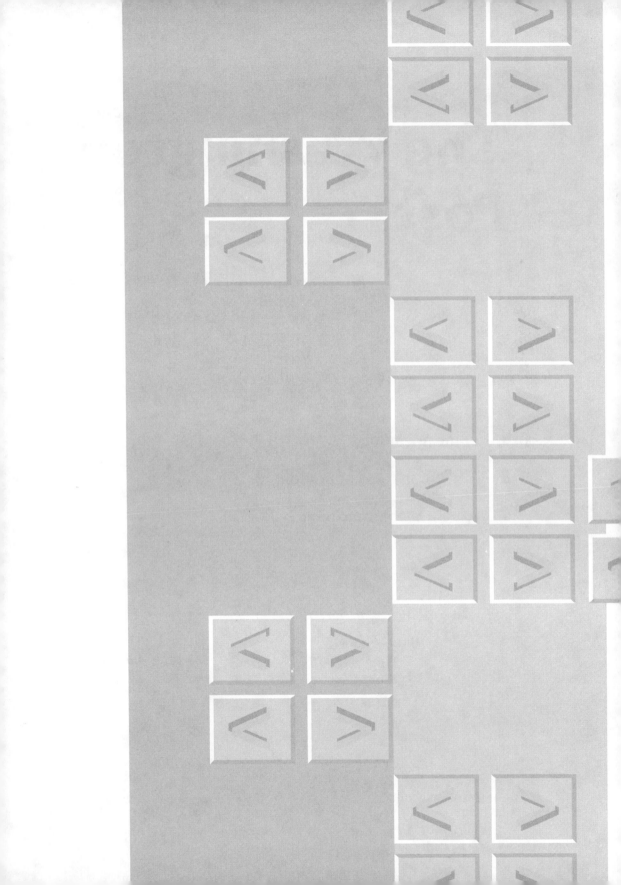

The Washington Post

- Online recruiting
- Middle-tier Web application
- Virtual Database technology (VDB)

Chapter 15

Classified job recruitment ads have moved online, along with direct recruitment Web sites from employers. Now there is technology to integrate them all. This chapter is sponsored by Junglee Corporation, http://www.junglee.com, and was prepared by Peter Norvig and Debra Knodel.

Newspaper classified ads have traditionally been the major resource for job seekers. Now the classifieds, like much time-sensitive data, are moving online. And the newspapers, anxious to preserve their franchises, are among those taking them there.

15.1 | The *Post* Web site

The Washington Post's Web site, www.washingtonpost.com, includes a job listings area in its CareerPost employment section. When the section first opened, it offered 6,000 job listings. They were all obtained from one source, the Post's classified ads from its print edition publishing system.

CareerPost subsequently began to utilize Junglee Corporation's JobCanopy™ at the site. In just six weeks, the *Post* was able to integrate the job listings of 50 employer Web sites. Doing so more than doubled the number of listings, to greater than 15,000.

By April, 1998, the *Washington Post* site had grown to list over 25,000 jobs from more than 150 employers.

15.2 | Job searching online

JobCanopy enables the *Post* to access job listings from any type of data source, including newspaper feeds, employer Web sites, text files, a variety of databases, and publishing systems. The listings from these diverse sources are integrated into relational database tables that can be accessed through the supplied user interface. Job seekers can then conduct highly targeted queries into a rich database of job information.

For the job seeker, the system provides a one-stop search interface, with powerful, tightly-targeted search options, and a uniform, easy-to-compare result format.

For the employer, it offers "do nothing" access to a large pool of qualified candidates. Without having to submit or re-format job listings in any way, the employer's jobs can be seen in high-traffic destination sites like (Career-Post) by job candidates who have narrowed down their searches.

The value of online recruiting through this technology becomes even more apparent when we examine how you would go about searching for a job at two individual employer sites in the absence of an aggregated database.

Consider two sites, Andersen Consulting and CACI International. The search method differs slightly, and there are specific limitations for each site.

15.2.1 *Andersen Consulting*

Figure 15-1 shows the Andersen Consulting site.

The Andersen site operates on link-based navigation. To search you must select an alphabetical range based on the job title you are looking for. Through a subsequent series of links you arrive at a detailed job summary. Since link-based navigation sites do not allow keyword searches, you need to know the exact job title for best results from this site.

15.2.2 *CACI International*

Figure 15-2 shows the CACI International search site.

This is a form-based site that allows keyword searches in three available categories: Region, Job Title, or Description. Your search is limited to a word in either a job title or a description.

This type of search errs on the side of recall rather than precision. For instance, if you enter "MS" in the description field you may get jobs with masters degree requirements, or "Microsoft", or "Mississippi".

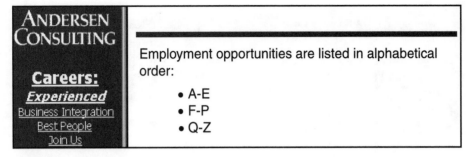

Figure 15-1   Andersen Consulting recruitment site.

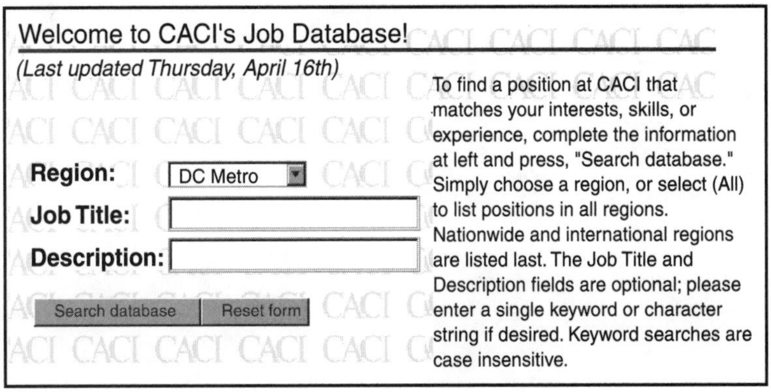

Figure 15-2   CACI International job listing site.

15.2.3   *CareerPost*

The *CareerPost* site is shown in Figure 15-3.

At this site you can customize your search by selecting from eight criteria. (The underlying *JobCanopy* technology actually supports 31 criteria.)

A search provides a uniform result list of available positions, as shown in Figure 15-4.

If you click one of these job titles, such as the CACI entry, a detailed page is presented. It includes a summary of the job attributes and, in this case, the full text from CACI's home site (see Figure 15-5).

Powered By Junglee
CareerPost Main Page
Resume Connection
Job View
Featured Employers
What Color Is Your Parachute?
Career Path
International Herald Tribune
Frequently Asked Questions
How to Place an Ad
Advanced Search
To search more than 25,000 job listings, including jobs from the previous two Sunday editions of the Washington Post, select one or more criteria below, then click the search button.
JOB FAIRS & SPECIAL EVENTS
Open House: April 29th
ORBCOMM
Job Category
All
Accounting
Activism
Administrative Supp
Advertising
Aerospace
Featured Employers
All
AC&E Ltd.
ACI
AETEA Info Tech Inc.
ALEX-Alternative Experts, Inc.
ARINC
Job Location
All
Alexandria, VA
Arlington, VA
Anne Arundel, MD
Balitmore, MD
The Disrict
Fairfax, VA
To select more than one criteria per box, hold down the command key (Mac) or the control key (Win) while selecting.
Job Categoryy
All
Education
Disregard
Years of Experience
Disregard
Date Posted
All
Keyword
Enter one or more keywords using AND, OR, or a 'phrase in single quotes.'

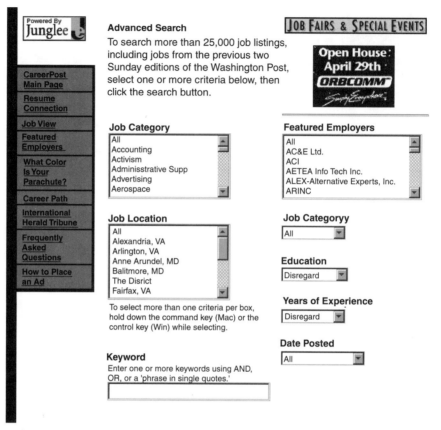

Figure 15-3 The *CareerPost* job search site.

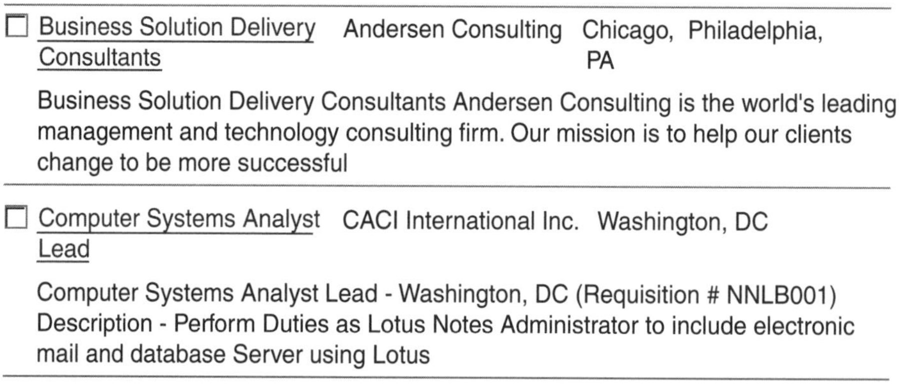

Business Solution Delivery Consultants
Andersen Consulting
Chicago, Philadelphia, PA
Business Solution Delivery Consultants Andersen Consulting is the world's leading management and technology consulting firm. Our mission is to help our clients change to be more successful
Computer Systems Analyst Lead
CACI International Inc.
Washington, DC
Computer Systems Analyst Lead - Washington, DC (Requisition # NNLB001) Description - Perform Duties as Lotus Notes Administrator to include electronic mail and database Server using Lotus

Figure 15-4 Results of *CareerPost* search.

Summary

Company Name: CACI International Inc.

Job Title: Computer Systems Analyst Lead

Job Status: Full-time

Job Code: NNLB001

Job Category: computers

Education: Bachelors

Contact E-Mail: job62@careers.caci.com

Contact Fax: (703) 841-8887

Contact Address: 1100 North Gleve Rd. / Attn: Recruiters / Arlington, VA 22201

Date Posted: 04/18/98

Listing Source: http://www.caci.com/Employment/job posts.html

The Full Text

Computer Systems Analyst Lead, Washington, DC (Requisition # NNLB001)

Description - Perform Duties as Lotus Notes Administrator to include electronic mail and database Server using Lotus Domino Server 4.6. Act as Webmaster in maintaining and developing the HFPA website. Prepare HTML pages and scripts using Netscape Enterprise Server. Perform Microsoft NT server administration. Provide end user support for Microsoft Win 95, NT workstation and NT server Version 4.x.

Required - Bachelors Degree in Computer Science, Information Systems, Engineering or Business. Experience implementing an enterprise wide Lotus notes environment using Lotus Domino Server. Excellent Written and Oral Communications skills. Knowledge of Network applications and architectures including Novell NetWare and M.S. Windows NT. Familiar with RDBMSs. Lotus Notes Administrator Experience. LAN/WAN operations and administration. Web Development Requires a Lotus Notes 4.5 Applications Development Certificate.

Desired - Web Development, Knowledge of Lotus Domino Server, Netscape Enterprise Server, Powerbuilder and Java.

Figure 15-5   Job title summary

15.3 | How *JobCanopy* works

JobCanopy is based on Junglee's Virtual Database (VDB) technology. VDB uses a combination of wrappers and extractors to extract multiple forms of data from employer Web sites.

Note   VDB is discussed in Chapter 9, "Comparison shopping service Web site", on page 132 and in Chapter 29, "Junglee Virtual DBMS", on page 386.

Figure 15-5 illustrates the extractor functionality. The attributes that appear in the summary fields were all pulled from unstructured text at the CACI home site. If the original site is marked up with XML using the Junglee Jobs DTD, then extraction of data will be even easier and error-free. However, even sites that are not in XML can be converted to XML by *Job-Canopy*, as shown in Example 15-1.

Example 15-1. Converted "jobs" document.

```
<jobs>
 <h2><category val="computer">Computer-Related careers</category>
 </h2>
 <job>
 <h3><jobtitle>Programmer</jobtitle></h3>
 Need a C++ programmer. <degree>BSEE or BSCS</degree>
 required. Reply by
 <expires>
     <month>12</month>/<day>14</day>/<year>1998</year>
 </expires>.
 </job>
```

The results of any query to the "Jobs" VDB can be presented as relational tables or as XML or HTML documents.

15.4 | Summary

The *Washington Post* job listing site demonstrates the practical use of XML-based middle-tier data aggregation to serve thousands of job seekers each day. It relies on VDB technology, which presents the Internet to its client applications seamlessly as a single virtual database.

Frank Russell Company

∎ Extranet XML financial publishing

∎ Business and technical requirements identification

∎ Structure-driven style

16

This chapter is the chronicle of an extraordinary project: demanding requirements, ambitious goals, leading-edge technology, business school management techniques, and – did I mention "mission-critical"? – a trillion dollars riding on the outcome. And XML figures in it as well. The chapter is sponsored by Frank Russell Company Advanced Technology Labs, http://www.russell.com, and was prepared by Bryan Bell and Randy Kelley.

As a leading investment management and asset consulting firm, Frank Russell Company improves the financial security of people throughout the world. Russell provides investment solutions for institutions and individuals, guiding the investment of more than $1 trillion for clients in more than 25 countries.

16.1 | Background

During the eighties, Russell pioneered the use of "color" presentations and "high touch" relationship management with its group of clients. Recently, Russell has experienced explosive growth in the investment management division, marketing private mutual fund products to the institutional marketplace, and retail funds through a group of selected distribution partners.

Immediately you can visualize the tension between high quality/high touch and explosive growth. There needed to be a strategy to address the increasing production volume demands without sacrificing quality or profit margins. This led to a requirement for automation.

Russell traditionally viewed its printed "client books" as products. This project was the first to begin to stress that the importance of the book is really Russell's content, and that the book itself is merely a rendition.

Russell had been using the "print, then distribute" metaphor for decades. But as the newer digital technologies and communication processes were taking hold, and the World Wide Web's popularity became undeniable, the Russell Advanced Technology Lab began an effort to evangelize, design, produce and deliver a new metaphor: "distribute, then print".

Along with this shift in metaphors come real quality control issues, especially revolving around color printing. Not only were the traditional problems of re-purposing content for different media (i.e. for paper, CD-ROM, electronic, FAX, and email) an issue, but also an entirely new set of workflow and authoring issues was recognized with respect to the re-use of component objects from within the created documents.

Also, the trend to customizing the content product – moving from generic content to a specialized product for an individual information consumer, a "market of one" – was extremely interesting to Russell.

This chapter chronicles both the team's journey and the Russell solution that is currently in production.

16.2 | Project strategy considerations

Russell has steadily been increasing its own awareness that it truly is a large publishing concern, producing millions of pages of color and black and white output for its clients every year. And as a major financial intellectual property publisher, it is also realizing that printing and electronic delivery systems play a very strategic role in its continued growth and success.

There were five principle strategic considerations for the conduct of the project:

- Proceeding from a theoretical abstraction to practical applications.
- Phasing deliverables with measurable return on investment.
- Continuing research in parallel with focused development projects.
- Alignment with overall corporate strategies.
- Executive sponsorship.

16.2.1 *Proceeding from a theoretical abstraction to practical applications*

The project team, though capable of grasping both the short- and long-term objectives for the enterprise, required a methodology to manage scope creep. We chose to divide the task into two clear groups:

- the theoretical research and related effort towards general solutions; and
- day-to-day development.

We were always able to have discussions from the abstract down to the practical by mapping them onto the architecture and life cycle models. When new technologies or vendor products came onto the radar, we were able to discuss them in the context of both the theory and practical project impact using a systematic method.

16.2.2 *Phasing deliverables with measurable return on investment*

This concept may sound similar to the concept of milestones, but is really quite different. This method assumes that there is *no* other project beyond the goals of this one.

It also assumes that this project must justify its own return on investment and bear management review based on its own merits.

Another key element is the "openness" of each phase's architecture, so that later phases can be "bolted on" seamlessly with very little trauma to users or developers.

16.2.3 *Continuing research in parallel with focused development projects*

Scope creep is an ever-present danger in technology. Change is a constant. Managing new inputs from press, rumors, research, and outside influence is a constant pressure on fixed milestones and deliverables.

We have chosen "discretion as the better part of valor" by separating the tasks of research and development into two distinct activities. The development tasks have clearly documented milestones, schedules, and budgets, with methodology in place to monitor their success weekly.

The research tasks are managed more loosely, with overall topics of interest. They use annual funding, rather than project-based funding, and measure deliverables by the published output from the team.

We believe that this separation keeps developers on the hook for "cleaner" deliverables and return on investment, while still allowing us to respond to the crucial happenings that are a day-to-day part of the technology world.

16.2.4 *Alignment with overall corporate strategies*

Any technology project can be fraught with risk. Any technology project can solve a specific technical application and add value if properly executed. It is our experience that the real "grand slam winner" projects are the ones that support the overall mission, culture, vision, and business objectives of an enterprise.

In theory every part of an enterprise is supposed to be working on things that contribute to the goals of the entire enterprise. Straying too far from this principle increases risk and confuses observers, whereas following this principle makes a project's justification much easier to defend and publicize.

16.2.5 *Executive sponsorship*

For several reasons, this is the most powerful thing you can do to enhance a project's chance for success:

- Executives are generally seasoned professionals who have earned a place of authority by knowing how to exploit strengths and manage around weaknesses.
- Executives are generally the best funded portion of an enterprise.

- Executives generally have a clear understanding of the long-term objectives of the enterprise.
- Executives generally have a feeling for the short-term pressures on operations.

These executive qualities enhance a group's ability to make sure their work is done with the support and point-of-view of the senior management and shareholders.

16.3 | Identifying the needs

Russell began to realize the extremely high importance of publishing to the company when it found out the cost. A study determined that almost 1/3 of every expense dollar worldwide was attributable to documents and their production, printing and distribution.

16.3.1 *Business requirements*

The question then became: "How to distribute financial services publications better to a geographically diverse audience, while maintaining "premium" typographical quality, data integrity, security and compliance?"

16.3.1.1 Compliance

Russell operates in a heavily regulated environment. There is a legal requirement to reproduce documents related to a customer from many years in the past.

16.3.1.2 Premium typographic quality

Russell customers typically evaluate large amounts of financial information in a limited time. Russell adds tremendous value for their customers by simplifying and clarifying these numbers through the use of text, graphics, charts, and color.

16.3.1.3 Data integrity

It is extremely important that the document received by our customers is identical to the one that we sent them.

16.3.1.4 Security

Because of the confidential nature of financial information, it is imperative that only the appropriate people can view these files.

16.3.2 Technical requirements

There were significant technical requirements to be met in addition to the business requirements.

16.3.2.1 Scalability

At Russell, a *Quarterly Investment Review* (QIR) runs from 20-125 pages, averaging around 50 pages. There are hundreds of clients who each get a customized QIR each quarter. Multiple authoring, editing, assembly, and compliance steps are required throughout the process.

16.3.2.2 Low licensing impact for reader software

The problem with end-user licensing of software is that it penalizes a business for the success of a document.

16.3.2.3 Ease of use

To us, the lab team, ease of use is the single most important factor in the true success of a product.

16.3.2.4   Cross-platform

Russell cannot control the platforms that our customers use. We have to provide our information in an easily accessible form on virtually every platform available.

16.3.2.5   Multilingual capability

Russell has offices in London, New York, Winston-Salem, Paris, Hong Kong, Toronto, Tokyo, Sydney, and Auckland. Russell has clients in 25 countries.

16.4 | Create an abstract architecture

Russell's Advanced Technology Lab team set off to learn about the state of the art in publishing systems, SGML, PDF, and document delivery systems.

Russell had been a pioneer of Postscript assembly and color graphics in the financial services industry. Now the Lab team desired to modernize Russell's publication capabilities to support "lower than page" granularity and the "distribute then print" metaphor. The team felt that this type of system could meet Russell's business objectives.

The team, working with consultants, created a "Request For Information and Statement of Direction" for a system to purchase (Figure 16-1).

The team also performed research on document life cycles and included the "life cycle requirements" shown in Figure 16-2.

Russell searched the SGML community for a publishing solution to meet its requirements and found no single commercial product in the marketplace. We then asked the big question: "Why isn't there one already"? The team felt that there were many companies and institutions with document problems similar to, if not more complex than, Russell's.

So we spent several more months analyzing vendor capabilities and mapping them onto the life cycle graphic until we finally found what we felt was a possible reason. Namely, that the authoring, consuming, and archiving stages of a document's life require different system capabilities and orientations: component management, document management, and records management, respectively (Figure 16-3).

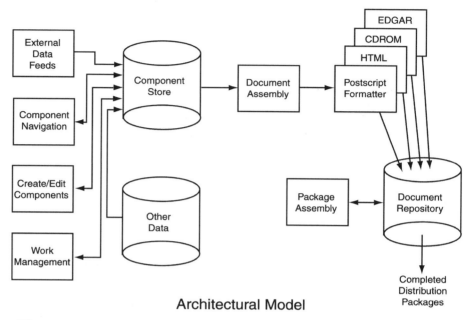

Architectural Model

Figure 16-1   Architectural model of desired system.

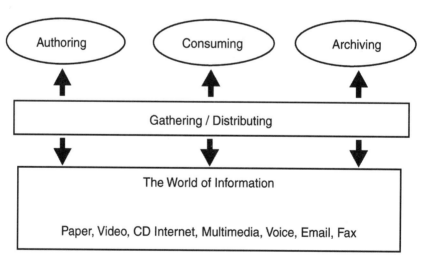

Figure 16-2   Document life cycle requirements.

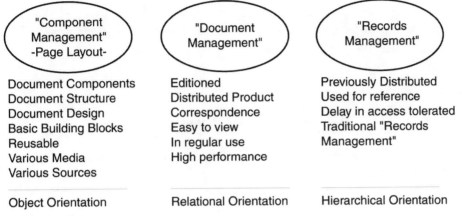

Figure 16-3   Document system orientations.

Armed with this insight, we developed the "knowledge management model" shown in Figure 16-4.

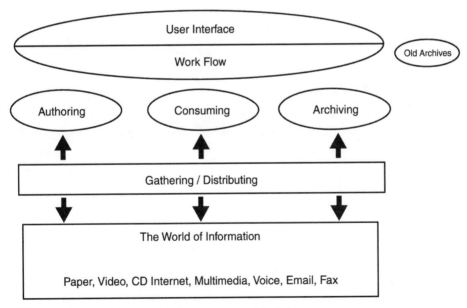

Figure 16-4   Knowledge Management Model

Russell's management and the Lab team then decided to build and integrate a solution out of commercially available off-the-shelf (COTS) products. The team decided to break the deliverables into different phases that would be integrated upon completion.

16.5 | Implement applications

Our initial choice for an application was the *Quarterly Investment Review*. The QIR is representative of many of our publications because it consists of a combination of generic, proprietary, customer-specific, and reusable components.

16.5.1 *Real-world design issues*

In order to apply the theoretical architecture to specific application designs for the QIR publications, we had to come to grips with real-world issues of internetworking and document representation (file formats) standards, to name a few.

16.5.1.1   Internetworking

The WWW family of technologies was chosen for its popularity. Its open-standard nature met our basic technical requirements for global electronic delivery, easy access, cheap per-seat licensing costs, cross-platform availability, and security.

The extranet model best served our clients in this application. That is, WWW technologies connected, via public and/or private networks, to a restricted Web site.

16.5.2 *Document representation*

Our team is very firmly attached to the notion that document representation is the key to an organization's success with knowledge management. In the SGML Buyers Guide (1998), the authors clearly express this point:

"Don't let the software you buy determine the representation. Let the representation you need determine the software you buy".

In our case, we needed to choose document representations for all three stages of the document life cycle.

During the authoring stage, documents are most useful in an "abstract" unrendered representation, in which the data can easily be reused and reprocessed. During the consumption and archiving stages, however, the document must be in a rendered form so that it can be presented and displayed quickly and consistently.

16.5.2.1   Abstract document representation

At the time our work began, SGML was the only document representation that preserved the abstract data and had the "industrial strength" for Russell's requirements. So we used it.

XML, as a streamlined subset of SGML, is by definition, not as feature-rich. However, like its parent it preserves the abstraction, and it seems to be more than adequate for Russell's purposes. XML's capabilities, along with its new-found popularity, promise to bring great momentum to the entire document industry.

16.5.2.2   Rendered document representation

Portable Document Format (PDF) was chosen for the rendered document representation. The archiving requirement, that it must be readable for a minimum of ten years time, was the dominant deciding criterion.

Large document collections have been faced with this need for some time; for example, those of the Library of Congress and Department of Defense in the U.S. At Russell and many other enterprises, the final formatted image of a document must be retrievable to meet business needs for compliance and reference. Our strong desire to use electronic documents to meet our goals was dependent upon a satisfactory decision in this single topic.

We first considered using SGML to meet our archiving requirements. It has successfully been used for simple partial renditions (e.g., HTML), but fully rendered final-form and graphics are outside its design objectives. Although it is undeniably the best representation for long-term preservation of text, that is not what we mean by archiving. To be compliant, from our archive we must be able to retrieve exactly what the client printed originally.

We made the choice to use PDF because it met the rendered image requirement for both text and graphics, was widely used across many platforms, had a publicly specified format, and supported a large set of the world's languages. We were also attracted to its usability in for email distribution and on-screen display.

PDF supports full text search, linking, and page by page loading. It has a development kit available, a compressed file size, interactive forms, cheap seats, and also prints extremely well.

16.5.3 *Phased implementation plan*

We also did some parallel processing, with secondary teams doing research and advanced studies on upcoming phases. The implementation teams, however, focused on the deliverables.

One team was assigned to create archiving requirements for the corporation. Another team worked on object databases and SGML abstractions.

A third team worked on graphical design. Its goal was to constrain the number of presentation layouts in order to optimize for batch processing. Finally, a fourth team had the task of tracking and understanding key standards like SGML, XML, Hytime, and various related W3C activities.

16.5.3.1   Phase I: Records management business study

The technical work on this phase was deferred. Our main candidate for an archiving product was in the middle of an acquisition, which created an unacceptable business risk.

However, Russell did conduct a two-year study on document archiving requirements for its Investment Management Business. Once the business case for records management was made, Russell hired a full-time professional archivist to champion the deployment of the technology.

16.5.3.2 Phase II: Document management of PDF files

Russell's corporate Information Technology department had previously deployed a document management system. We used it in the interests of corporate harmony and worked with its vendor's R&D department on the beta version of an application to make documents available over the Web.

This product allows you to build a query on a Web-based form (Figure 16-5), which can be tailored to meet application requirements.

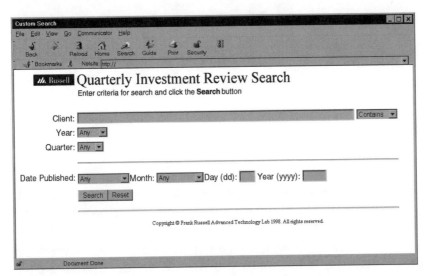

Figure 16-5   Document management search screen.

The query results are delivered as an HTML frame (Figure 16-6), the form of which can also be customized. Our users found that it made the interface to the product's library services, particularly document check-out, much more appealing than it had been.

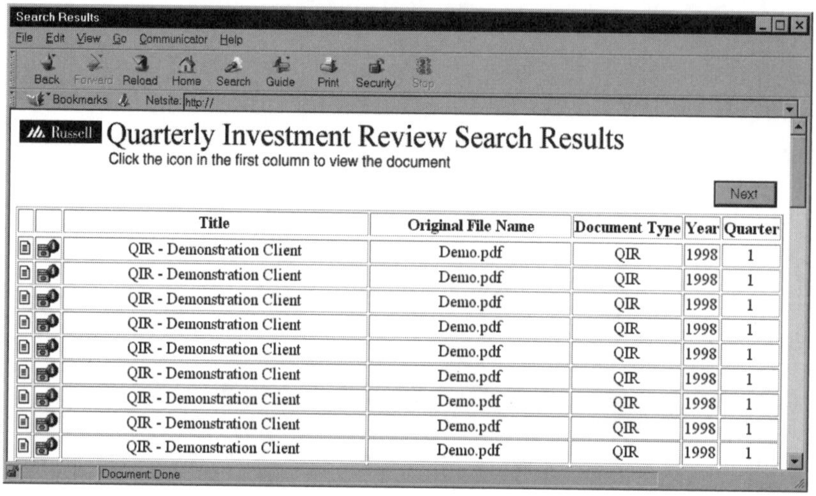

Figure 16-6   Document management search results.

16.5.3.3   Phase III: Document assembly and formatting

The objective of this phase was to create structured documents in SGML that could be auto-assembled, and to implement "auto-check-in" to the document management system.

As the assembly and formatting phase of the project began, the team focused on the issues of: How much structure do we need?, What are the quality levels required for the publication in its final form? What should the user interface experience be like for editing sections, book assembly and releasing books to the document management system?

We decided to purchase a product that supported integrated structured editing, layout, and typographic control.

The users for this phase are a small group of document editors who compile and author the QIR documents for clients at Russell. Their typical quarterly work cycle involves revising the previous quarter's document files, graphics, and tables, and launching a new composite book for each client. New document pages are created approximately 10% of the time.

The users are trained in popular word processors, spreadsheet, and graphics packages, but have no experience in SGML. They are accustomed to setting the indents, font style, size of a page, and common typography settings. They are often under the spotlight to make a production deadline in hours and therefore must be able to make edits quickly with minimal amount of new steps. They are only interested in software that makes their life easier.

The team quickly found that the system must make the SGML transparent to the user, that the layout must be WYSIWYG, and that the application should assist in the creation of a consistent layout throughout the book.

How we used structure

The approach taken was to replace the use of paragraph style codes with meaningful SGML element-type names. The document was then formatted in real time, based on the element types, thereby giving the users their customary WYSIWYG effect.

A welcome side-effect was that the list of element-type choices was much smaller than the full list of paragraph styles typically presented by a WYSIWYG editor, because of the context enforced by the DTD. In addition, the product has a "guided authoring" feature, which automatically inserts required elements. It allowed us to layout a typical page easily, and still allowed deviations by making choices permitted by the DTD.

One area of improvement to the overall professionalism of the book was in the consistency of format and layout. In the old system, each page was laid out individually and it often deviated slightly as editing continued over several quarters of revisions.

In the new system, we used a series of matched templates created by a professional typographer, and we used structure to drive the formatting of the text. The resultant books were consistent, and compliant with corporate guidelines. This achievement was a significant win since "document police" (people trying to enforce style quality control issues from a corporate perspective) are not often welcome.

Document editing

With all of these facilities available, we found that we needed to simplify the application menus. Doing so would limit access to designer pallets and provide users with a simpler interface to this complex and powerful tool.

Simplifying was done by using the application's custom user interface feature. It required no programming, although some developer expertise is required.

Training the users on the new system consisted of five sessions of one day in length, including hands on lab sessions. The authoring tool took 50% of the training time, with the remaining time being spread on a general introduction, graphics, book building, and lab sessions. The users quickly grasped the system's capabilities and found it to be a huge improvement over the previous system.

How much structure do we need?

Once Russell made the decision to use a structured representation of its publications, the challenge became to decide how much structure was appropriate and for what reasons. The team approached this from two viewpoints: long-term and short-term.

The long-term objectives of using structure were to add value to the intellectual property and aid with repurposing, navigation, automation and archiving.

The short-term goals were to enforce consistency in the typography, assure better quality control, and facilitate the aggregation of disparate content sources into single publications with a high degree of automation. Other short-term goals were to facilitate document assembly with automation, and to improve the user's experience.

Final-form quality requirements

Russell's output quality requirements are extremely high (Figure 16-7). When we looked at the commercially available database-driven publishing systems and dynamic Web page assemblers, none were capable of presenting publications as well as Russell's legacy systems. Also, although the Web publishing systems were great for producing pages from the current state of the database, they were not capable of satisfying our compliance requirements.

Book assembly

The team wanted to make the user experience during book building as straightforward as possible by presenting only immediately relevant information. We built a simple windowing scheme, based on a customer database, that presented the bookbuilding experience on two screens (Figure 16-8 and Figure 16-9).

Along with the customer name and the component "bill of materials" list selections, the book building interface also gathers the metadata required

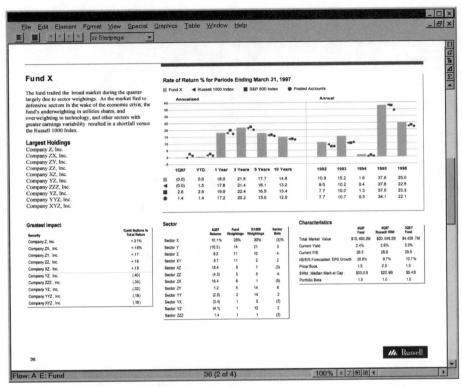

Figure 16-7   Fund page example in editing system.

for check-in to the document management system and stores it for later use. This may seem trivial, but it completely removes the user pain from the document management check-in process.

Releasing books to the document management system

Final preparation of a book for review and release is invoked by a single custom menu item, "Publish", on the File menu. The "Publish" command creates a PostScript file of the book, which is then distilled into a PDF file. During this process, the PDF file is updated with the document management system check-in metadata that was gathered during the book building.

The "Publish" command eliminates a large number of print and configuration item choices for the user and controls the way PDF files are created.

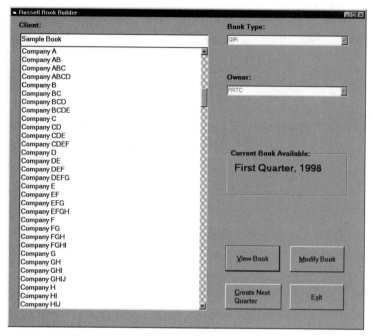

Figure 16-8   Russell BookBuilder (1 of 2)

This plug-in also automatically generates bookmark hyperlinks for the PDF table of contents from the SGML structural element hierarchy. Figure 16-10

16.5.3.4   Phase IV: XML and the future

In 1995 we began a pure research project into the notion of "Knowledge Management Systems". These are automated systems that would be the next logical extension for publishing, collaborative authoring, and electronic delivery.

At Russell we believe that XML systems are the beginning of an entirely new age of documents. In the same way that ASCII allowed people to interchange bits in the past, adoption of XML as "the data representation" will allow people to exchange "bits with meaning" in the future.

That was the original promise of SGML, but we feel the SGML community, for whatever reasons, fell short on realizing that promise to its fullest commercial degree. One might even say that XML is SGML done right for

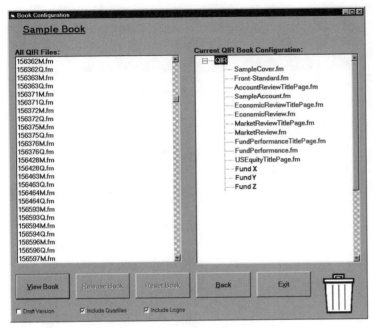

Figure 16-9   Russell BookBuilder (2 of 2)

the masses, which still leaves SGML there for those for whom XML falls short.

We believe the marriage of XML, databases, WWW, EDI, and publishing technologies is going to be the cornerstone of extremely significant developments over the next decade. Areas most likely to be affected will include content aggregation, simplified database connectivity, document distribution, and electronic commerce.

We also feel there is great danger in "almost open" or "almost standard" representations and technologies. The power and future of information technologies is determined by the degree of vendor and platform independence that they offer for the long term.

For the long term – not one version or two versions, but years and decades later. At Russell, we never lose sight of that goal. It is our company's information, stored in an open representation, that we expect to bring us true value in the future.

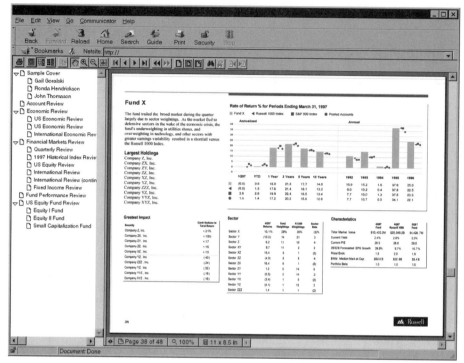

Figure 16-10   Fund page example in PDF book.

16.6 | Conclusion

In the past internetworking of systems was complex. Now, with the World Wide Web and TCP/IP, internetworking is routine and affordable. The next frontier is content interoperability.

Interoperability has always been a challenge. We at Russell Advanced Technology Labs believe that XML is the interchange/interface language of the future, and that it will do for content interoperability what the WWW and TCP/IP did for internetworking.

We built an SGML application three years ago because it was the right thing to do. We have now converted it to XML because it is the right thing to do. The SGML to XML conversion took one developer three days.

While others discuss the potential values of XML, Russell is already enjoying the benefits of a production extranet XML publishing system.

Welcome to the future.

Agent Discovery

- Media industry
- Middle-tier Web application
- Image search and procurement
- Web automation

Here's an application interesting enough to be the subject of one of the Discovery Channel's own programs: How they implemented Web searching for images and automated procurement in just eight days! This chapter is sponsored by webMethods, Inc., `http://www.webmethods.com`, and was prepared by Charles A. Allen.

E
lectronic commerce on the Web takes many forms. Browser-based purchasing is one form that has proliferated at a healthy pace as businesses large and small have begun deploying electronic storefronts enabling customers to buy direct over the Web.

Aggregating purchasing functions across disparate browser-based purchasing systems is one of the first places where so-called *agent technologies* have begun to establish a foothold.

A next-generation electronic commerce application called *Agent Discovery* illustrates how Web-based procurement can be automated using XML-based technologies. It demonstrates a number of integration principles that will become increasingly important as XML itself proliferates on the Internet.

17.1 | *Agent Discovery*

Agent Discovery automates the procurement of images across the electronic commerce Web sites of numerous photo agencies. The idea for *Agent Discovery* was conceived by Discovery Communications, Inc. (DCI), operators of the Discovery Channel, and AnswerThink Consulting Group (ACG).

Web Automation technology from webMethods was employed to deliver a solution that enables Agent Discovery to exchange data automatically and simultaneously with different photo agencies' Web sites.

Before Agent Discovery, the company's worldwide design group had no alternative but browser-based manually intensive online searches.

Using webMethods' Web Automation Server and the Web Interface Definition Language (WIDL), a working system was built in only eight days. It immediately enabled DCI to realize huge savings in the amount of time designers spend searching for and purchasing images over the Web.

Here are the basic steps that were taken to build the image search and procurement functionality of *Agent Discovery*:

1. The target photo agencies' Web sites were identified.
2. The functionality of target Web sites was cataloged.
3. A matrix of functions provided by all photo agencies was created.
4. An aggregate interface of all *Agent Discovery* functions was defined in WIDL.
5. A separate WIDL was developed for each Web site, implementing functions provided by each site and defining conditions for successful invocation.
6. A Java servlet was developed to dynamically invoke the services defined in each WIDL implementing the *Agent Discovery* interface.

Now picture yourself as a designer who might need these functions. Figure 17-1

17.2 | Picture this

Imagine you're a designer of a Web site, magazine, or corporate branding campaign, tasked with procuring a large number of compelling images to convey messages of "efficiency" and "innovation". Thanks to the Web, you are able to access the image databases of dozens of on-line photo agencies, retrieving images that match your search criteria.

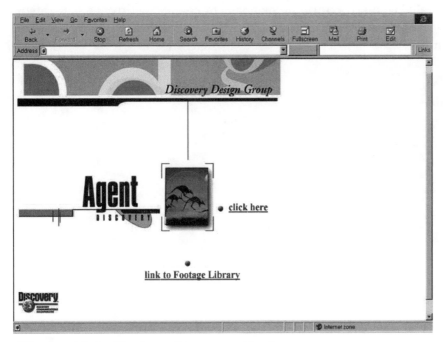

Figure 17-1   The *Agent Discovery* application.

Unfortunately, you have to log into each system separately, submit the search criteria repeatedly, and switch back and forth between multiple browser instances to compare images from each agency.

When you are finally ready to purchase the images you've selected from a number of agencies, there are various mechanisms for payment and delivery. Most commonly, you must right-click and save images to your local disk, losing both the captions that allowed you to find the images in the first place, as well as the rights information associated with each image.

17.2.1 *Access vs. integration*

The Web has provided you with an amazing degree of access, but it has also placed on your shoulders an incredible burden of integration.

You are now responsible for navigating through numerous systems, each with a slightly different usage model. The information, though delivered through a common medium, has no common form. You spend hours of your valuable time performing manually intensive repetitive tasks that have been learned only through hard-won experience in the trenches of the Web. Figure 17-2

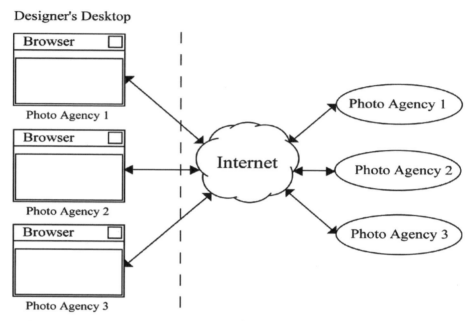

Figure 17-2   Separate browser windows for each photo agency.

This is not the job you signed up for. You're stuck shuffling bits rather than selecting images that fill your needs. There must be a better way. But how do you go about convincing each of the photo agencies to agree on and implement common interfaces and formats? Even if you could convince them that this is, in principle, a good idea, how would you agree on a technology platform?

17.2.2 *The solution: Web automation*

For *Agent Discovery*, photo agencies had already made the investment in Web-based electronic commerce applications; all the necessary functionality was accessible. The shortest path to integration was to leverage the systems that had already been put in place by the various photo agencies, sidestepping the need to achieve consensus among a large number of competing companies.

With this approach, the speed of development was compelling. More impressive still was the immediacy of the return on investment.

Finding the right images quickly and efficiently is a key requirement for any media company, particularly DCI, whose brand is known for compelling images. Designers at DCI were faced with the dilemma outlined in this image procurement scenario. Web automation removed the repetitive tasks from the process of procuring images without impacting the services of the photo agencies. Figure 17-3

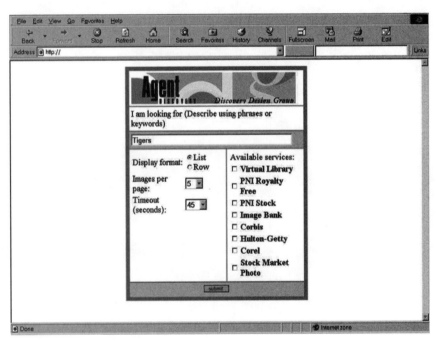

Figure 17-3   Designers can select photo agencies to search.

17.3 | What is Web automation?

Imagine everything a browser can do: sign-on to a secure Web-site; navigate through pages; submit queries; retrieve the results. Now imagine that business applications can do the same thing, automatically, without human intervention and without using a browser. This is the power of *Web automation.*

Interactions normally performed manually in a browser, such as HTTP authentication, entering information into a form, submitting the form, and retrieving HTML or XML documents, are automated. This is done by capturing details such as input parameters, service URLs, and data mapping methods for output parameters. Mechanisms for conditional processing are provided to enable robust error handling.

In essence, the *Web Automation Server* makes the Web look like one large application server. It is a middle-tier component that provides an abstraction layer between business applications and the remote functionality that lives behind Web servers.

The *Web Automation Server* and WIDL transform the Web from an *access medium* into an *integration platform,* providing a practical and cost-effective infrastructure for business-to-business electronic commerce over the Web. Figure 17-4

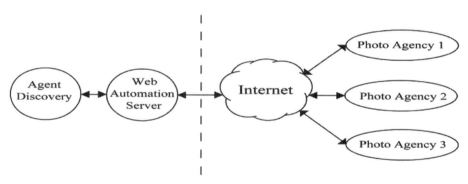

Figure 17-4   The *Web Automation Server* aggregates services.

17.4 | Discovering common ground

In the case of *Agent Discovery,* Web automation enabled the services of various photo agencies to be aggregated into a single logical application interface. Figure 17-5

Agent Discovery gives DCI's designers a common user interface for searching for and retrieving images across different photo agencies' Web

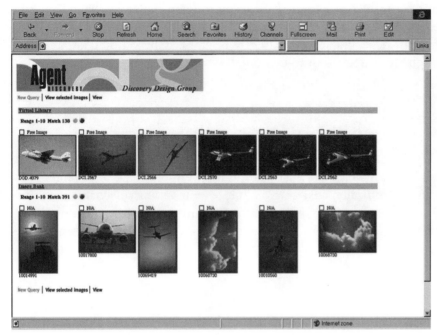

Figure 17-5 *Agent Discovery* enables a "virtual light-box".

sites; it substantially reduces the time an effort required to procure images, and enables more efficient tracking of DCI's digital assets.

17.5 | What about XML?

The introduction of XML promises to accelerate cross-organizational application and data integration, providing a standard for data representation that addresses many of the concerns raised above. However, XML alone is not a total solution.

The *Web Automation Server* was built using an application of XML called the Web Interface Definition Language (WIDL). Together they lower the barriers to cross-organizational integration by removing the requirement that various organizations agree on data formats up front. (See Chapter 38, "WIDL and XML RPC", on page 554 for the details.)

The only requirement is that data be accessible via HTTP, FTP, or HTTPS. The data representation can be either HTML or XML. Most significantly, product is designed to accommodate dynamic change in data representations, so that applications initially deployed with HTML data sources can be migrated transparently to XML. Client side code does not need to be re-generated or re-compiled.

17.6 | Architecture principles

The ability to manage change dynamically is important because target Web sites are periodically changing. While the mapping mechanism within WIDL can "see thorough" a significant amount of change in document representations, it is sometimes necessary to re-map and re-publish a service definition. Figure 17-6

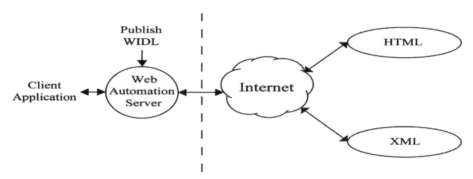

Figure 17-6   WIDL defines a common interface to HTML and XML.

For DCI, the challenge was that each agency presented similar services in different forms. WIDL enabled common interfaces to be defined for different HTML documents. Significantly, WIDL also enables common interfaces to be defined across HTML and XML document structures, and even across different XML DTDs.

Consider the alternative: without the layer of abstraction that WIDL provides, the Agent Discovery application could only have been developed by hard-coding routines to handle each different document structure encountered at the various photo agencies' Web sites. If target document structures changed, application code would have to be modified and recompiled. This is roughly equivalent to the situation experienced by developers of two-tier applications when database changes are made.

17.7 | Conclusion

DCI's Designers wanted a process that was automated and centralized. They wanted one program with one user interface that would search, retrieve, and procure images from multiple sources, thereby reducing the time spent navigating several different Web sites. Agent Discovery delivered on these goals.

The use of Web automation and WIDL logically separated the act of integration from the act of building the client application. This logical separation enabled Agent Discovery to span multiple photo agencies' services, and to be built in record time.

The architecture of the *Agent Discovery* application provides valuable lessons for the development of cross-organizational XML-enabled applications. Waiting for all target systems to support a common format would have significantly slowed the delivery of an application that has had an immediate return on investment.

Just as *Agent Discovery* today must be able to negotiate common interfaces among different HTML document formats, next generation XML-enabled applications may well need to negotiate among different XML DTDs. In addition to removing the barriers to business-to-business application integration, the use of WIDL enforced a three-tier architecture that positions the system for such an eventuality.

Analysis   For all the promise of XML, there is a lurking danger that some developers will fall into the trap of coding applications so that they cannot easily respond to changes in the DTDs. That would effectively be a return to two-tier client/server architecture, where data access methods are embedded in application code.

WIDL or similar interfaces may be a cure for such situations. The best prevention is the employment of late-binding stylesheet-like techniques, such as those successfully employed in publishing by XML and SGML users.

Major Corporation

- Telecommunications equipment industry
- Database publishing
- Migrating from program code to XML
- SQL access from XML documents
- Middle-tier XML application

Chapter 18

Merging data from multiple sources is the essence of middle-tier Web applications, and a key driver in the use of XML. Actually, data capture has been done for years in *print* publications by major corporations, who've developed some useful and broadly-applicable techniques. This chapter is sponsored by ISOGEN International, `http://www.isogen.com`, and was prepared by Carla Corkern, `carla@isogen.com`, and Glenn Deitiker, `deitiker@agave.com`

O ur Major Corporation client[1] transformed its product and price publications from paper to electronic media. In doing so, it radically improved its ability to control document quality and reduce information time-to-market.

Traditionally, the company produced catalogs by manually entering data into large product documents. Data entry errors and constantly shifting page layout created a vicious cycle of self-generated re-work and expanding schedules. Information in the publication was not accurate, timely, or useful.

Now, the catalogs are produced directly from a database using XML with embedded SQL statements. Both the source and the resultant documents are true XML documents and are created without any changes to the legacy database. Replacing the existing database structure was not an option because it would have required re-engineering all of the existing processes that use the database.

Using the Internet, marketing and production engineers, sales support staff, distribution managers, and external distributors and customers can

---

1. "Major Corporation" is a generic identifier, but this case study really happened. SGML was used, but only features that are included in XML, so the text refers to it as "XML".

immediately access accurate product and price information. Users can log in and generate live reports dynamically.

Product adjustments are introduced for approval via this Internet service. Once approved, changes to product and price databases become instantaneously available for use. Although paper publishing is still required, we have already seen substantial savings in time, labor, and cost by using XML in this way.

Let's look at how these results were accomplished.

18.1 | Background

When the migration process started, two publishing specialists were responsible for publication of a single product line twice a year. They worked closely with the organization that was responsible for maintaining pricing information in the product database on a mainframe.

Product descriptions and page layout were maintained by manually editing desktop publishing documents that consisted of multiple files and pages. To publish the catalog, the document was manually updated with price information extracted from the product database (Figure 18-1).

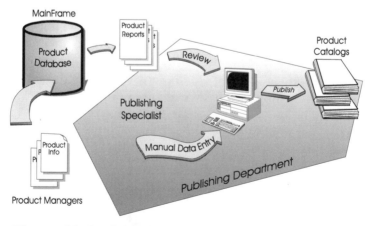

Figure 18-1   Original publishing process.

The process was conducted over a two-week period of excessive overtime, due to the cyclical nature of the work. Since publication was the last step in a long chain of events, it did not begin until information was available from other departments. It was dependent on, among other things, proofing the product database to ensure price accuracy. Once price information was available, the publishing department took over, literally working night and day until the catalog was published.

The migration from a manual to an electronic publication process was executed in the interval between publications by our consulting team. We augmented the client's publishing specialists by providing knowledge of database technology and programming skills. The publishing specialists, in turn, provided corporate business, product knowledge, and publishing skills.

The team initially explored many different ways to publish the price catalog, some of which did not include XML. Ultimately, XML won out as the best method for publishing the catalogs electronically. However, integration with a non-XML data source, specifically the parts and prices database, provided a significant challenge. Solving it required the development of a middle-tier data integration tool named *SQml*.

18.2 | First generation: Client/server

We first conducted several experiments using desktop publishing systems. These led to a working prototype that accessed the database directly, thereby eliminating the need to copy the data manually. Now the workload could be leveled, as proofing of the database could begin immediately after the previous publication was complete.

The first implementation of the database publishing system was built on the concepts proven by the prototype system. A data feed taken from the mainframe product database placed parts price information in a local database on a desktop machine. The mainframe was eventually retired by moving the database structure, intact, onto a UNIX SQL system.

Programs written in C generated documents in a proprietary desktop publishing format. These documents were subsequently imported into a template document. The template contained format definitions, such as font, table, and layout definitions.

These first generation C applications were not elegant. SQL statements that performed data filtering were embedded into the source files along with document structure and format information. As a result, format or content changes to any document required programming skills to edit the C source documents (Figure 18-2).

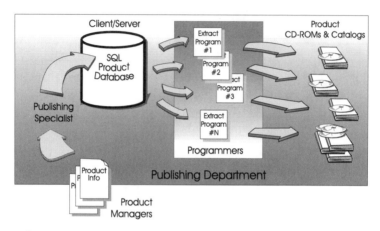

Figure 18-2   First generation database publishing.

In the beginning, there were only four or five documents, each requiring only one simple C program. However, when news spread about the speed and flexibility of the new publication process, an overwhelming demand for new documents resulted.

Suddenly, a multitude of derivative documents were created to satisfy demand. The company began migrating other product lines onto the system. Within a matter of months, approximately 100 different documents were published, each requiring a unique program. Many of the source files differed by only a few characters. The team found itself with a serious configuration management problem on its hands.

Two main issues surfaced that required taking the system back to the drawing board:

- Only programmers could create new documents or modify existing ones. Moreover, many documents were derivatives of a parent document, which meant that changes to a parent might also require changes to its children. Although many of the department's specialists knew SQL (they worked with the SQL database several hours a day), they were not C programmers.

■ It was the nearly impossible to ensure that all documents in a family were kept consistent with changes in the parent. As the requirements for new or one-off documents increased, a document's family tree appeared to grow exponentially, making managing changes more difficult.

On top of all this, the company recognized the cost-saving advantages of CD-ROM over paper publications, and the need to make the product catalog accessible via World Wide Web technology. A new system was needed to solve the problems and satisfy the new requirements.

18.3 | Second generation: Three-tier

For the new system, we recognized the following requirements:

■ There must be a single document representation that is useable for paper, CD-ROM, and the World Wide Web.

■ Publishing specialists must be able to edit and maintain the document source without the help of programmers.

■ Database information must be extractable using SQL queries.

XML, of course, was the basis for our solution, but the extraction of database information using SQL queries posed a challenge because XML did not support it natively. If special programs had to be written, it might jeopardize the ability of publishing specialists to maintain source documents without programmers.

We needed a tool that met three requirements:

It should work within a standard XML editor.

We did not have the time to build an editor. Devising a solution where the source document must be edited in a plain-text editor and validated separately was a step backwards and would be more difficult to use than the non-XML implementation. We wanted a true document mark-up solution and resisted the temptation to fall back on programmer support to maintain documents.

It must work with the existing database.

XML databases are available, but the company had already made a sizable investment in the existing product databases and tools and was not yet ready for a radical departure.

It should not require programming skills outside of some SQL experience.

The use of SQL seemed unavoidable. Even with all of its detractors, it is still a standard and the publishing department was already familiar with it. The team wanted to be sure that the tool did not require additional programming expertise to be operated successfully.

18.3.1 *Data extraction*

Our solution was *SQml*, which Agave Software Design developed for this project and now offers as a commercial tool.

Example 18-1. Embedded SQL in an XML document.

```
<TITLE>Price Book</TITLE>
<SQLCONNECT USER="user" PASSWORD="passwd"/>
<BODY>
   <SQLCURSOR TEXT="select product_line, product_line_desc
      into :prodline, :prodlinedesc
      from product_line"
      <PRODLINE>&prodline;</PRODLINE>
      <PRODLINEDESC>&prodlinedesc;</PRODLINEDESC>
         <SQLCURSOR TEXT="select product_name, product_desc
            into :prodname, :proddesc
            from product
            where product.product_line = :prodline"
            <PRODNAME>&prodname;</PRODNAME>
            <PRODDESC>&proddesc;</PRODDESC>
         </SQLCURSOR>
   </SQLCURSOR>
</BODY>
```

Like other data aggregation notations we have seen in this book, SQml provides some command-like tags that are interspersed in the markup of the source document. These tags don't appear in the generated XML document. Instead, they are interpreted by the SQml middle-tier server, which causes appropriately tagged database data to appear.

In Example 18-1, the SQLCONNECT tag opens a database. Each SQL-CURSOR tag issues an SQL query to that database and iterates on the returned data. The indentions in the example show where the iteration occurs.

The first (outer) SQLCURSOR tag generates one PRODLINE and one PRODLINEDESC element for each product line in the database. For each product line, the second (inner) SQLCURSOR tag generates one PROD-NAME and one PRODDESC element for each product in that product line.

Note that there is no explicit "loop" command, as in scripting languages. The iteration is built into the data source query. And the data sources aren't restricted to SQL: plain-text files, object databases, and XML documents are also supported.

18.3.2 *Database maintenance*

The new system allowed individual product organizations to control their own portions of the product database. Product and price changes could be generated directly by product managers and their staffs, who could immediately generate a copy of the product catalog as it would appear with the changes. As a direct result, the quality of the product catalogs increased because the product information was maintained by those closest to the products themselves (Figure 18-3).

Making product information the responsibility of the product managers helped to eliminate re-authoring of vital information. Now, because all source information necessary to publish the product catalog was resident in the product database, publishing a product catalog was reduced to a three-step process:

1. Create or modify the XML source document, including insertion of *SQml* elements.

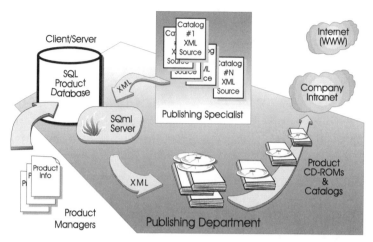

Figure 18-3   Second generation publishing with XML and *SQml.*

2. Generate the XML result document, in which the source document's embedded SQL queries are replaced by the query results.

3. Format and distribute the document through the selected medium: paper, CD-ROM, or the company-wide intranet.

18.4 | Summary

The cooperative effort of our consulting team and the client's publishing specialists has had measurable positive results. The company now has timely access to mission critical product information. Product information systems and catalog publishing processes have undergone substantial changes that have resulted in higher document quality and usability. These improvements also provide benefits in lower maintenance and product costs.

Strategically, the switch to XML was the correct move to make at a critical point in the migration process. XML and SQml provide an environment that bridges the gap between the company's legacy repository of information and the targeted publishing media.

City Of Providence

- Travel industry
- Repurposing content
- Republishing in multiple electronic media
- Linking static and dynamic Web sites

19

This chapter has more information than you ever wanted to know about the nightlife in Providence, Rhode Island. But it has lots that you need to know about publishing that kind of dynamic information in multiple electronic media. The chapter is sponsored by Inso Corporation, http://www.inso.com.

Cities throughout the world have turned the Web into a gigantic rack of travel brochures. But unlike their paper alternatives, Web brochures are expected to be up-to-date, dynamic, and customizable. And cities that want to be competitive have to maintain the Web sites along with the traditional media, which creates new pressures for already overworked staffs and budgets.

19.1 | The *Providence Guide* prototype

City chambers of commerce work to attract local residents, tourists and business travelers to the city to spend their travel and entertainment dollars. Today, they market themselves through multiple media. Paper brochures can be supplemented with Web sites and CD-ROMs mailed to convention planners, travel agents, and others with the potential to bring in hosts of visitors.

Different aspects of a city are of interest to different visitors. Some are interested in historic sites, others in attractions, and the business traveler might only have time to sample a couple of restaurants and night spots during a busy convention. Of particular interest is the question, "what special events are going on during my visit?"

How can a chamber of commerce with a limited marketing budget and staff provide dynamic, up-to-date information for a multitude of visitors with different interests, and on multiple media? Inso Corporation has prototyped a solution for the city of Providence, Rhode Island, where its Electronic Publishing Solutions division is located. This solution **repurposes** the same XML content about Providence that can be **republished** three ways:

- A *Providence Guide* on CD-ROM, viewed with the *DynaText* Browser.
- The same guide served on the Web with *DynaWeb*, which links to...
- A dynamic Web site with current club listings and on-line restaurant reservations, using *DynaBase*.

In addition, XML support in these products enables contextual searching, hypertext navigation aids, and multiple views that allow different readers to **reuse** the publications to meet their own specific needs.

Finally, XML-enabled links between related content in the different publications helps draw the user into a call to action: to visit and spend money at Providence's restaurants, clubs, and other attractions.

To make changes to the *Providence Guide* content in all three forms, the author need only update a single source document with a word processor. These documents are then converted and the content "rescued" (adding XML structure and intelligence) using *DynaTag*.

Extremely volatile data, such as this week's events, are stored and updated in a database and inserted dynamically into the Web pages using DynaBase's built-in scripting language. The city could even allow club promoters to enter their own events directly into the database via a Web-based form, thus reducing work for city employees even further. The club promoters might even be willing to pay an advertising fee for the privilege of listing their events on the city's Web site.

19.2 | Information architecture

The first step in creating the prototype application was to architect the information. Style templates were developed for the word processors with descriptively-named paragraph styles that could easily be converted to XML element-type names.

For example, a club listing consists of three styles: EntertainmentName, EntertainmentLocation, and EntertainmentDescription. These are mapped to similarly named XML element types, inside a containing element type, <ENTERTAINMENT>.

Mapping is not limited to one-to-one mapping of styles to element types. For more information, see Chapter 24, "DynaTag visual conversion environment", on page 326.

19.3 | Conversion to XML

After the *Providence Guide* is written and formatted, it is converted with *DynaTag*.

The initial conversion established the mapping rules for converting word processor styles (and any unstyled formatting) to XML elements. It also generated a DTD for the *Guide*.

This information was saved as a "project", which can be re-used for subsequent conversions as the information in the *Guide* is updated. The same project handles conversion of documents authored in any of the supported word processing formats, as long as they are similar document types.

19.4 | Generating the electronic book

After converting the *Guide* to XML, *DynaText* was used to generate an "electronic book"; that is, a product-specific compiled form of XML with a fulltext index, optimized for online viewing and navigation.

19.4.1 *Using multiple stylesheets*

A stylesheet editor is then used to create stylesheets for viewing the content in various ways. One stylesheet formats the Standard Content view in the *DynaText* Browser, formatting the text for online display (larger fonts, increased line spacing). This stylesheet also provides hypertext cross-reference links and other features unique to online texts, such as icons that pop up graphics and tables in separate windows.

Another stylesheet generates a hypertext table of contents (TOC) for navigating the electronic book. The table of contents is simply a filtered view of the XML content that shows only title elements, and links them to their related chapters and sections.

Figure 19-1 shows the *Providence Guide* as an electronic book, with its TOC and Standard Content views.

A third stylesheet formats the text for on-demand printing, including typical print features such as running headers and footers.

Additional stylesheets were also created for specialized views of the information, such as the "Entertainment only" views for readers who aren't interested in (or don't have time to explore) the city's history or other attractions.

19.4.1.1   Contextual searching and personalization

In addition to providing various views of the content, the *DynaText* Browser also allows the user to search for information, taking full advantage of the XML structure.

Imagine that a visitor to Providence heard that there was a new club opening, but all he knew was that the name was "(something) fish". A simple word search for "fish" would find a slew of seafood restaurants and possibly a listing for the nearby Boston Aquarium.

However, using a *DynaText* search form that restricts the search to club names, the user could quickly find "Blue Fish Red Fish", the new club.

The user can also annotate the site to record his favorite dishes at Al Forno. Or he can create a link between the Trinity Rep theater and L'Elizabeth, his preferred spot for after-theater coffee and dessert.

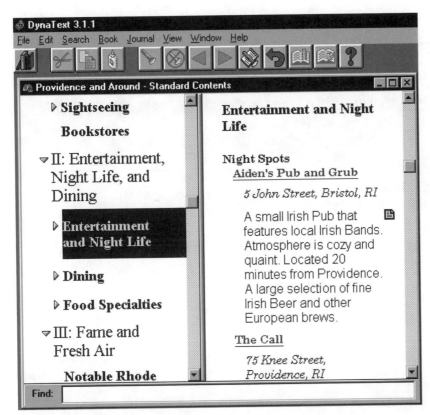

Figure 19-1   The *Providence Guide* electronic book.

19.5 | Web delivery

The same *Providence Guide* is served to Web browsers using *DynaWeb*. For this purpose, a different kind of stylesheet down-translates the XML markup to HTML on the fly. Because this translation is handled in the stylesheet, it is very easy to modify the HTML representation of the data when browsers add support for new tags.

It is not necessary to have a copy of the source tagged as HTML and chunked into small files for serving. The product breaks large documents into chunks based on XML containers such as chapters and sections.

Also provided on the Web is electronic book functionality: fulltext and contextual searching, and an automatically generated table of contents.

Links in the Web version of the *Providence Guide* take the user to related content on the dynamic *This Week in Providence* Web site, described in the following section. Figure 19-2 shows the *Providence Guide* on the Web.

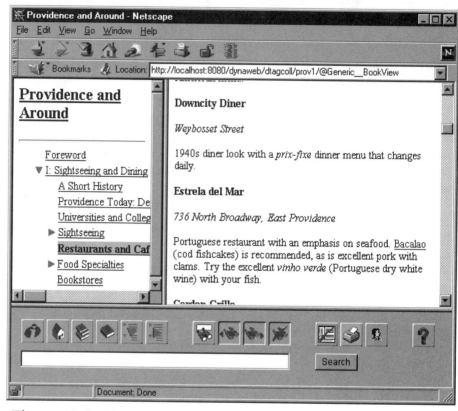

Figure 19-2   The *Providence Guide* on the Web.

19.6 | Dynamic Web delivery

The third deliverable in the three-in-one publishing prototype is the "This Week in Providence" Web site. It contains restaurant listings, online reservations, club listings, and information about this week's performers at each club.

Less volatile information, such as restaurant and club names, locations, and descriptions, are written in word processors and converted to XML as described above. The online restaurant reservations are handled with an HTML form that mails the request to the appropriate restaurant.

The most interesting and unique aspect of the site is the dynamic generation of this week's club listings from the database. The data is integrated with the XML-based club descriptions for presentation. This result is accomplished by a script written in the DynaBase scripting language, which is similar to Visual Basic in its syntax.

Here's how it works. Before serving the XML club listings, a fragment of whose source is shown in Example 19-1, DynaBase processes the file through a script called `buildnite.wbs`. This script looks up each club (tagged as <ENTERTAINMENTNAME>) in the database, and if there are bands scheduled to appear this week, the script puts out the names of the bands and the dates they are scheduled to appear at the bottom of the club listing.

Example 19-1. XML fragment for club listings

```
<?XML VERSION="1.0" ?>
<CHAPTER><CHAPTERTITLE>II: Entertainment, Night Life, and Dining
</CHAPTERTITLE>
...
<ENTERTAINMENT><ENTERTAINMENTNAME>Aiden's Pub and Grub
</ENTERTAINMENTNAME>
<ENTERTAINMENTADDRESS>5 John Street, Bristol, RI
</ENTERTAINMENTADDRESS>
<ENTERTAINMENTDESCRIPTION>
A small Irish Pub that features local Irish Bands.
Atmosphere is cozy and quaint. Located 20 minutes from Providence.
A large selection of fine Irish Beer and other European brews.
</ENTERTAINMENTDESCRIPTION>
</ENTERTAINMENT>
...
</CHAPTER>
```

The script also transforms the relational data and XML document to HTML so that a wide range of Web browsers can display the information. Furthermore, the script inserts HTML "anchor" tags that enable the links from the *Providence Guide* book on *DynaWeb*.

Any time a new band is added to the database, it will appear immediately on the Web page the next time the page is reloaded. Figure 19-3 shows the

Entertainment page from the Web site, with the club listings and this week's scheduled bands.

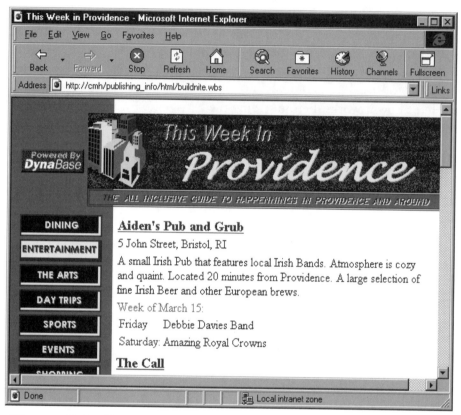

Figure 19-3   The entertainment page is dynamically updated with this week's bands

19.7 | Updating the XML data

The data stored in XML is less volatile than the relational data on this week's bands, but it still needs to be updated whenever a new restaurant or club opens. Let's examine how updates are managed.

The word processing source files for the *Providence Guide* and their XML counterparts (created by *DynaTag*) are stored in the *DynaBase* repository.

When an update is required, an author checks out both files. This checkout process ensures that only one author is updating a file at a time. The interface is shown in Figure 19-4.

The author then opens the word processing file and makes the change. For example, let's say a new club called Blue Fish Red Fish is opening. To ensure consistent use of word processor styles, the author copies an existing club listing and edits the name, location, and description to create a brand new listing.

Next, the author runs the project batch script to convert the updated word processing file to XML. Then, the author checks the XML document and the word processing file back into the repository.

DynaBase updates the revision information for the files and prompts the author for a comment. The author types "added Blue Fish Red Fish" and the checkin process is complete.

The author needs no special training in XML and doesn't need to know all the ways the information will be used. She only needs to know to use the correct word processor styles and to follow the checkin/revise/convert/checkout process.

At this point, the new content may be reviewed by an editor, and additional changes can be made using the same checkout/revise/convert/checkin process. Once all changes are approved, the Web site can be published.

Unlike some file-based Web sites, there aren't separate development and production servers, and no movement of updated files from one server to another. Instead, you simply publish a new "edition" of your Web site, and all the approved content (which may be the latest updates, or previous versions if the latest updates aren't ready for publishing yet) is served as the production site on the Web.

19.8 | Revising the Electronic Book

Now we need to get the latest revisions into the Providence Guide electronic book for Web delivery and publication on CD-ROM. Of course, CD-ROM updates would be published less frequently, but for those without Web access, the CD may be the only way to learn about Providence's attractions.

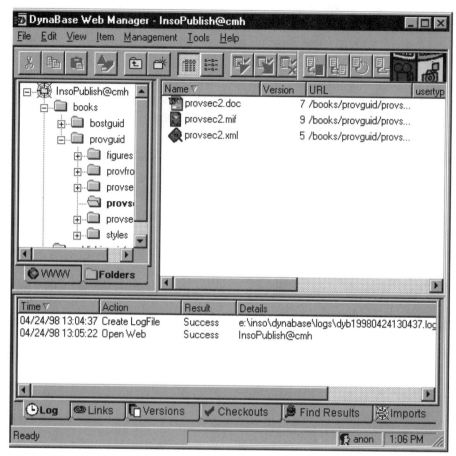

Figure 19-4   The *DynaBase* interface for content management.

Also, the *DynaText* Browser provides features (such as an annotation capability) that are not available in Web browsers. Because the CD and Web versions of the information do not include the dynamically generated club schedules, the information does not become outdated as quickly.

To publish the electronic book, the publisher exports all the XML entities that comprise the book from *DynaBase*. Then, a script is run that builds the electronic book. The various stylesheets for creating different views of the information are also incorporated at this point.

19.9 | Summary

The Providence Guide that we've examined in this chapter illustrates how XML and suitable products (like the Inso Electronic Publishing Solutions suite) can be integrated together to form an XML-based, end-to-end publishing solution that allows for:

- Republishing across media, such as the CD-ROM and Web versions of the *Providence Guide*.
- Repurposing of document components to create multiple publications, such as the club and restaurant descriptions that appear in both the *Providence Guide* and on the "This Week in Providence" Web site.
- Reuse of publications for different user needs, such as the entertainment-only view in the electronic book, and contextual searches that restrict the information to only what is sought.
- Links and navigation aids that lead the reader through your content; for example, the links from club descriptions in the Providence Guide to this week's scheduled bands.

International Organization for Standardization

- Adapting an industry DTD for XML
- *ISO 12083: Electronic Manuscript Preparation and Markup*
- DTD design and modification
- Graphical interface to DTDs

There is a trove of useful industry DTDs out there that can be adapted for use with XML. This chapter, sponsored by Microstar Software Ltd., `http://www.microstar.com`, shows how one organization did it. The chapter was prepared by Dianne Kennedy, the Convenor of the ISO Working Group responsible for the widely-used industry DTD, *ISO 12083*.

Considerable time and resources have been expended in the creation of vertical industry SGML document type definitions, or DTDs. The aerospace, defense, automotive, telecommunications, semiconductor, railroads, health, scholarly journal, and newspaper industries each have their own SGML DTDs.

These DTDs prescribe the rules by which data is represented for interchange within that industry. Now, in order to facilitate direct Web delivery and client-side use of SGML data, there is a need to adapt the standard SGML DTDs so that they are also XML DTDs.

Note the use of the word "adapt" rather than "convert". As XML is a subset of SGML, the modified DTDs will still be SGML DTDs, so they won't have been converted from anything. However, they will now conform to XML as well as to full SGML.

These industry DTDs represent enormous collections of complex data and were often developed only after protracted negotiation among competitive enterprises. It should come as no surprise, then, that the DTDs themselves tend to be quite complex.

As a result, the more automation that can be brought to bear on the adaptation effort, the more likely that these industries will be able to make the transition to Web delivery of XML in the most timely fashion.

One of the oldest and most widely-used industry DTD sets is ISO 12083.

20.1 | ISO 12083; DTDs for publishers

ISO 12083 is also called *Electronic Manuscript Preparation and Markup*. It is meant to provide a framework to be used by authors and publishers.

The DTDs were created by the Association of American Publishers (AAP) in the mid-1980s, around the time that SGML itself was published as an International Standard (ISO 8879). Later these "AAP DTDs" became an American National Standard known as ANSI Z39.59-1988. Finally in the 1990's, the DTDs were re-written and in 1994 were balloted and became an ISO standard.

Currently, a review of ISO 12083 is under way to address the concern that the industry and technology have changed so much that the audience and mission of the standard have changed. Web delivery, not an issue when ISO 12083 was balloted, has become critical to the publishers using the standard. And since XML is the streamlined form of SGML for Web use, it is necessary to modify the ISO 12083 DTDs so that they conform to XML.

20.2 | Adapting ISO 12083 to XML

Microstar's Near & Far Designer 3.0 was used to help automate this activity. It is a new version that incorporates XML into the familiar SGML DTD design tool.

The tool can be used to create a new XML DTD from scratch, using a graphical user interface. But more interesting to those working with ISO 12083, is the ability of the tool to assist with the adaptation of an SGML DTD for use with XML.

XML eliminates a number of options that are possible with full SGML, in order to make the language simpler to understand and easier to parse.

Some of these changes can be handled completely by *Near and Far*, while the product can provide assistance for some others.

20.2.1 *Automated modifications*

These changes are straightforward and are automatically performed when a user selects the "Convert to XML" option in the Tools pull-down menu.

20.2.1.1   XML declaration

Before the DTD begins, an SGML document can declare its concrete syntax and other options with an SGML declaration.

```
<!SGML ... >
```

The syntax of all XML documents is prescribed by the XML specification, and there are no options, so XML documents do not contain an SGML declaration. Instead, it may have the following "XML declaration", which can specify the XML version and character encoding used by the document:

```
<?xml version="1.0" encoding="ISO-8859-1"?>
```

20.2.1.2   Omitted tag minimization rules

An option of full SGML is to allow the omission of selected start- and/or end-tags. As XML does not permit this, the parameter is deleted from the element type declarations.

20.2.1.3   Grouped element type and attribute declarations

In full SGML, a single element type declaration or attribute list declaration can apply to a group of element types. In XML, an element type declaration or attribute list declaration can apply only to a single element type.

20.2.1.4   Comments in other declarations

In full SGML you can add comments inside any of the declarations. In XML DTDs, all comments must stand alone. So full SGML DTDs must be edited to create stand alone comments in place of comments embedded inside other declarations.

20.2.1.5   Quoted default attribute values

In full SGML there is an option for how a default attribute value is specified. In XML, all default attribute values must be surrounded by a pair of quotes.

20.2.1.6   Parameter entity references

In full SGML, the semicolon that closes a parameter entity reference is optional. In XML, the semicolon is required. SGML DTDs must be edited to assure that the semicolon is always used.

20.2.1.7   Example of automated modifications

Example 20-1 illustrates a full-SGML DTD that exhibits all of the above conditions.

Example 20-1. DTD, not compatible with XML.

```
<!DOCTYPE article [
<!ELEMENT bq        - -  %m.pseq                                      >
<!ELEMENT indaddr   - O  %m.name; -- individual address           -->
<!ELEMENT orgaddr   - O  %m.org;  -- organization address         -->
<!ELEMENT artwork   - O  EMPTY                                        >
```

Example 20-2shows the DTD from Example 20-1 after processing by *Near & Far Designer 3.0.* It now conforms to XML as well as to SGML.

Example 20-2. The DTD of Example 20-1, made compatible with XML.

```
<?xml version="1.0" encoding="ISO-8859-1"?>
<!DOCTYPE article [
<!ELEMENT bq  (%m.pseq;) >
<!--individual address-->
<!ELEMENT indaddr  (%m.name;) >
<!--organization address-->
<!ELEMENT orgaddr  (%m.org;) >
<!ELEMENT artwork  EMPTY >
```

20.2.2 *Assisted modifications*

Some adaptations are not automatic, but the product is able to provide some assistance in performing them.

20.2.2.1 Attribute types and defaults

In XML, only CDATA, NMTOKEN, NMTOKENS, ID, IDREF, IDREFS, ENTITY, and ENTITIES are allowed as attribute types. For defaults, only specified values and the keywords #REQUIRED, #FIXED, and #IMPLIED are allowed.

SGML attribute types that are forbidden in XML are:

- NAME and NAMES
- NUMBER and NUMBERS
- NUTOKEN and NUTOKENS

SGML attribute defaults that are not allowed in XML are:

- #CURRENT
- #CONREF

To adapt a DTD to XML, we need to review and change the attribute types and defaults. This is not a completely automatic process, as were the modifications discussed in the previous section. It is rare that the tokenized attribute types won't be replaced by NMTOKEN and NMTOKENS, or that #CURRENT won't become #REQUIRED and #CONREF become #IMPLIED, but it is technically possible. However, the modification can be automated once a mapping has been established.

Near & Far Designer 3.0 enables us to specify standard SGML-to-XML mappings for attribute types and defaults using the "Tools" pull-down menu. Select "Options" and then "XML". At this point you can use check boxes to indicate replacements you wish to make automatically.

For example, you can select "Replace NUTOKENS with NMTOKENS" or you can select "Replace NAMES with NMTOKENS." For the conversion of ISO 12083 to XML, the standard replacements suggested by check boxes in the XML menu were used.

Example 20-3 illustrates two attribute definitions that are not acceptable in XML.

Example 20-3. Before (full SGML).

```
<!ATTLIST chapter   %a.id;
          SDABDY    NAMES      #FIXED          "title h1"
          SDAPART   NAMES      #FIXED          "title h2"
>
```

Example 20-4 shows how they were changed.

Example 20-4. After (XML).

```
<!ATTLIST chapter   %a.id;
          SDABDY    NMTOKENS   #FIXED          "title h1"
          SDAPART   NMTOKENS   #FIXED          "title h2"
>
```

20.2.2.2   Declared content

In XML, declared content of CDATA and RCDATA is not permitted. A completely automatic mapping from SGML to XML does not exist for these, although they are likely to be replaced by (#PCDATA). However, as was the case with attribute types and defaults, this modification can be automated once a mapping has been established.

Near & Far Designer 3.0 enables us to specify standard SGML-to-XML mappings for declared content using the "Tools" pull-down menu. Simply select "Options" and then "XML". At this point you can use check boxes to indicate replacements you wish to make automatically. For ISO 12083, both CDATA and RCDATA were directly replaced with a #PCDATA content model.

20.2.3 *Other modifications*

In addition to the changes that you can automate with *Near & Far Designer 3.0*, there are issues that cannot be resolved either with a one-for-one replacement or with user-defined mappings. In these cases, the product assists you by providing a list of discrepancies (Figure 20-1).

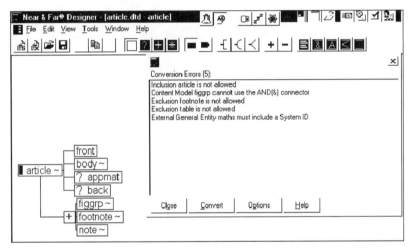

Figure 20-1   Conversion errors report

For ISO 12083, the remaining errors fell into several classes that will be described in the following sections. Types of errors included:

Inclusions not allowed

In XML, inclusions, or elements that can occur anywhere within another element are not allowed. Some other way to model this content must be developed for use with XML.

AND connector not allowed

In XML, the AND connector is not allowed in content models. Some other way to model this content must be developed for use with XML.

Exclusions not allowed

In XML, exclusions, or elements that are banned within certain elements are not allowed. Some other way to model this content must be developed for use with XML.

System identifier required

In XML, a system identifer is required when external entities are declared.

By clicking on an error message in the report in Figure 20-1, you can link to the exact location of the problem in the DTD.

20.2.3.1   Eliminating inclusions

Inclusion exceptions are allowed in SGML DTDs, but not in XML DTDs. Eliminating inclusion exceptions is a relatively easy task if the inclusion falls in the leaf node of the document-type tree (usually the paragraph level). Convert the leaf node content models to mixed content that contains the included element types. Figure 20-2 shows how to accomplish the same result without using paragraph-level inclusions.

Becomes

Figure 20-2   Alternative to paragraph-level inclusions.

Unfortunately, in ISO 12083 inclusions happen at a very high level. In fact, footnotes, notes, and figure groups are inclusions at the article level. This means that these elements can occur within and between any other elements in an article.

While this model quickly solves the end user requirement to have structures such as footnote "anywhere", it is not really what any publisher would do. For example, a figure group would never really fall within a title. Nor would a footnote fall between the front and the body.

So in this case, adapting the DTD to XML by eliminating the inclusions will actually make the article DTD much more precise and usable. For ISO 12083, each content model below article was examined and figure group, footnote, and note were built into the models as appropriate. Figure 20-3 shows the result of eliminating the high-level inclusions.

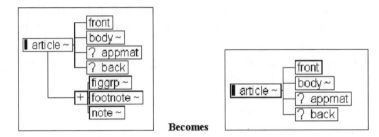

Figure 20-3   Eliminating high-level inclusions.

20.2.3.2   Eliminating AND connectors

In XML, AND connectors are not allowed. AND connectors are used to specify that elements must occur, but in any order.

When AND connectors are used to connect two or three element types, the number of possible combinations is tractable. However, when the AND connector is used with a large group of element types, the possible number of combinations can become staggering. AND was eliminated from XML for this reason. To adapt a DTD for XML, AND connectors must be eliminated.

In ISO 12083, AND connectors are used in the figure group to specify that title or figures can occur in any order. To adapt this model to XML, the AND was replaced by the SEQ connector, requiring the content elements to occur in the specified order. Figure 20-4 shows the result of replacing the AND connectors with SEQ connectors.

Figure 20-4   Replacing the AND connector.

20.2.3.3   Eliminating exclusions

Exclusion exceptions are allowed in full SGML DTDs, but not in XML DTDs. Eliminating exclusions can involve making some hard design decisions.

First let's look at a valid use of an exclusion (the first part of Figure 20-5). In this model a paragraph is either data or footnotes (mixed content). A footnote is defined as being either text or paragraphs. But in this model if we put a paragraph inside a footnote, we also allow a footnote (which can be inside a paragraph) inside a footnote. So to prevent a footnote from falling within a footnote, we use an exclusion to say that a footnote cannot occur within a footnote. Figure 20-5 shows the result of eliminating exclusions.

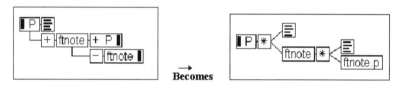

Becomes

Figure 20-5   Eliminating exclusions.

Handling exclusions is usually not straightforward. One solution would be not to rely on XML validation to enforce the exclusion, but to assume that good authoring practice would prevent a footnote from occurring within a footnote.

One form of a more disciplined solution is to name the element type subject to the exclusion differently, perhaps with a "fully qualified" name like "ftnote.para". As a unique element type, "ftnote.para" can have a unique content model that does not permit footnotes.

Unfortunately, this solution modifies the DTD in a way that causes document instances to be incompatible with the original SGML DTD. Documents will need to be transformed for Web delivery in XML.

20.2.3.4   Adding system identifiers

System identifiers are mandatory in XML external entity declarations. The system identifier must be in the form of a URI (Universal Resource Identifier) and is frequently a local file identifier.

```
<!ENTITY x33445 SYSTEM "file://c:/graphics/x3345.tif">
```

To make this task easier, *Near and Far Designer 3.0* notifies us whenever such system identifiers must be added.

20.3 | Conclusion

Industry DTDs, such as those standardized by ISO 12083, represent a valuable resource that should be made available for use in the Web environment with XML. Doing so requires that the DTDs be adapted so that they conform to XML's more stringent requirements. A visual DTD design tool with adaptation aids, such as Near and Far Designer 3.0, has proven to be of help in this process.

Part Four

- Editing and composition
- Content management
- Middle-tier tools

Tools for Working with XML

FrameMaker+ SGML: Editing+ composition

- XML authoring
- Automated WYSIWYG formatting and composition
- Multi-platform publishing
- Free trial version on CD-ROM

21

One approach to XML authoring is modeled on the convenience of word processing. The editing and formatting are integrated, but XML structural facilities are provided. This chapter is sponsored by Adobe Systems Incorporated, `http://www.adobe.com`, and was prepared by Lani Hajagos.

Whether delivering data on the Web or large documents on paper, every corporation today is a publisher. Yet corporations face a daunting publishing challenge: the demand to publish information is quickly surpassing the ability to create, manage, and distribute it.

21.1 | Leveraging information

Delivering content quickly to global markets puts intense pressure on corporate publishing systems. Vast numbers of documents, some thousands of pages long, must be revised, translated, and formatted before business-critical information can reach customers around the globe. Some of these documents must be maintained for many years – far beyond the life-span of any software application or hardware platform.

XML and its parent standard, SGML, have demonstrated the ability to meet this challenge by enabling information reuse. There are many examples of this:

- Multiple outputs can easily be created from a single source. A manufacturer might produce a public parts catalog and a private-label catalog from a common XML source. In addition to the printed versions, electronic versions in HTML and PDF may also be generated, for publishing on CD-ROM and the World Wide Web.

- Information may be shared among numerous documents. A diagnostic and repair procedure for a certain assembly may appear in the trouble-shooting manuals of several devices that incorporate that assembly. The information about the assembly is created and maintained once, and changes are automatically reflected in each manual that references it.

- XML allows users to define markup that identifies components of information within a document. This enables intelligent searching of the information. For example, a user might search for a particular temperature within an "operational tolerances" element. The results from this type of search are far more accurate than simply searching for the string "24°C".

- XML is software and hardware platform-independent, protecting the investment in long-lived information and facilitating the sharing of information in a heterogeneous environment.

When choosing XML tools, you should take into consideration the extent to which the tool can help you obtain those benefits of XML that are important to you. That should be in addition to considerations of how well the tool provides the functionality that you need.

21.2 | XML authoring functions

In this chapter, the discussion of tool capabilities is illustrated by Adobe *FrameMaker+SGML*, an integrated XML authoring and composition product. It is designed to shield the user from the technicalities of XML and to support a workgroup environment. The tool includes a robust composition capability that can handle complex page layouts with a high degree of automation, even such professional graphic arts requirements as spot and process color separations.

21.2.1 *Guided editing*

Guided editing features help authors create documents that conform to the rules for a document type. In Figure 21-1, the element-type catalog shows which element types are valid for the current location in the document. The interactive structure view lets the author manipulate the structure of the document. It graphically advises whether a proposed move will invalidate the structure. These devices make it possible to create and manipulate the structure of the document without ever working directly with, or even looking at, a markup tag.

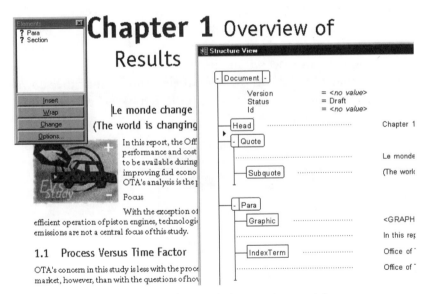

Figure 21-1   Structure view and element-type catalog.

21.2.2 *Authoring flexibility*

When creating type-valid XML documents, an authoring tool might require that the document be valid at all times, even if that means putting in empty elements when information is not yet available. Maintaining validity in this way means that the author has to start at the beginning of the document, and write everything in order, not skipping any required elements.

However, this isn't what happens in the real world. All too often, the information a writer needs simply isn't available. So the writer may skip some parts of the document and write others out of order. As more and more of the information becomes available, the gaps are filled in and eventually the document is complete. This is easy to do in a word processor, but difficult if your authoring tool insists that validity must be maintained.

Some editors address this requirement by allowing information to be entered in any order and allowing required information to be skipped. The document can be saved as a work in progress even if it is not valid. The software keeps track of what is missing and what is in the wrong place, and helps the writer fix things. So the end result is a valid, complete document, without the hassle of having to fight with an inflexible authoring tool.

With *FrameMaker+SGML*, when working in the guided editing mode, the element-type catalog shows only those element types valid at the current location in the document. However, as shown in Figure 21-2, the element-type catalog can also be set to display all element types, or any element type that may be valid within a parent element, even further down in the hierarchy. The valid element types are indicated by a checkmark.

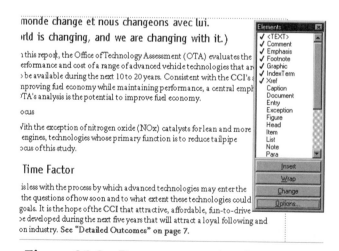

Figure 21-2   Element-type catalog displaying all element types; valid ones are checked.

21.2.3 *Problem correction*

By definition, a product that allows authoring flexibility allows errors, because the user can write a portion of the document out of context when necessary. For example, while working on an introduction, a writer who wants to enter a new term into the glossary can simply insert a glossary element in the middle of the introduction.

As shown in Figure 21-3, from that point the element-type catalog would show the valid element types for a glossary. However, the structure view would indicate, by a dashed vertical line, that the glossary is out of context.

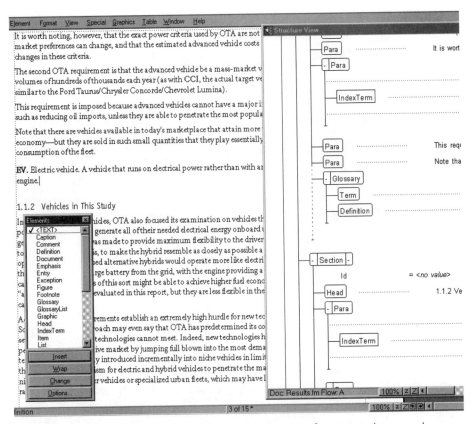

Figure 21-3 Dashed vertical line indicates out-of-context glossary element.

Authoring flexibility also means that a writer can omit required elements. Figure 21-4 indicates that information is missing by an open box in the structure view.

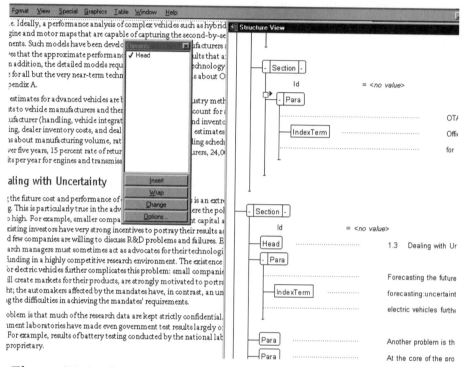

Figure 21-4   Open box indicates missing elements.

A product that allows the writer to bend document rules when creating and manipulating structured information, should also help to fix problems so that the document can become valid with as little effort as possible. In our example, the user should be allowed to move the glossary to its correct location at any time, thereby correcting the structure.

On the other hand, the writer ought not to be obligated to fix problems immediately. It should be possible to save an invalid document and resume work on it later.

As we have seen in Figure 21-3 and Figure 21-4, a product's structure view can indicate problems with visual clues. However, with long documents, it's not very efficient to scroll through the structure view looking for problems.

For this reason, a product might provide a batch validator in addition to interactive validation. A validator scans the document looking for problems, such as elements out of context, missing elements, and illegal or missing attribute values.

In Figure 21-5 we see that when the *FrameMaker+SGML* validator locates a problem, it displays a message and sets the insertion point at the problem area. The element-type catalog displays valid element types for that location, so that the author has help in fixing the problem.

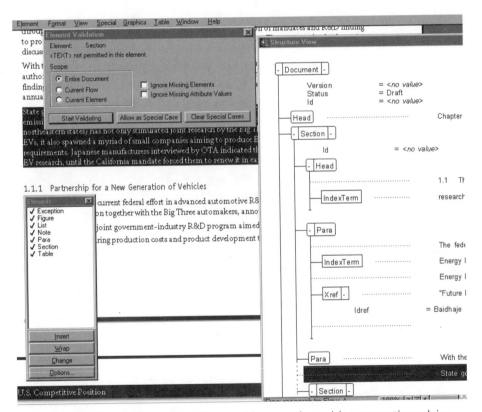

Figure 21-5 Validator identifies problems and provides corrective advice.

21.2.4 *Authoring utilities*

Today's XML authoring tools offer a variety of useful aids for such tasks as spelling checking, indexing, and cross-referencing. A close look at what our illustrative product offers in this area may help you determine your own needs.

For example, *FrameMaker+SGML* users can access an online thesaurus, and also check spelling in 17 languages. The document template can be set to automatically delete redundant spaces, and to turn "straight quotes" into open and close quotes.

21.2.4.1   Cross-references

The cross-reference tool makes it easy to link pieces of information, either within a document or across documents, using standard XML methodology. The user inserts a cross-reference element, and selects a target element type from a list. The tool (Figure 21-6) shows all the instances of that element type in the document.

The user selects the appropriate element and the format of the generated text (e.g., "see table 5 on page 23"), and the generated string is placed in the document. For the XML markup, a unique ID value is automatically generated and placed in the ID attribute of the target element, as well as in the IDREF attribute of the referencing element.

Users can easily modify the generated text, simply by editing the cross-reference format. Table, paragraph, and page numbers are automatically updated as content is inserted into or removed from the document.

21.2.4.2   Indexing

FrameMaker+SGML also provides a powerful index generation utility. This utility can handle complex, multi-level indexes like the following example:

Writers enter index entries at the appropriate locations in the document. These entries are used to compile indexes automatically, either for a single document or a group of documents.

Writers can easily generate trial indexes to check whether use of terms has been consistent. Each item in the generated index is automatically hyper-

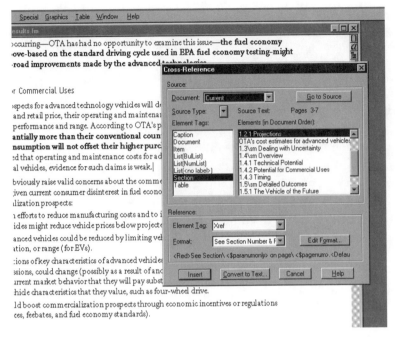

Figure 21-6 Cross-reference interface.

Example 21-1. Multi-level index entry

Continental drift
  Fossil evidence, 57
  Rock structures, 62, 80

linked to its source entry. So, if the writer finds a problem, it is easy to jump directly to the source entry to make modifications.

21.2.4.3 Hypertext

FrameMaker+SGML provides a number of tools for authoring hypertext documents. Many of the links are created automatically. Hyperlinks are automatically created for all cross-references, while generated files such as indexes and tables of contents are also automatically hyperlinked. In addition, users can insert arbitrary hypertext links. A number of link commands are provided to control the behavior of the link, and they can be tested within the product.

21.2.5 *Managing external content*

A good XML authoring tool makes it easy to incorporate external text and graphics into a document. *FrameMaker+SGML* supports a substantial number of text and graphic file formats, allowing input from many different sources. And you can actually see the contents of the external text or graphics in your document, rather than just a reference.

A link is maintained from the reference back to the source document. Any changes made in the source document can automatically be reflected in the referencing document.

To bring in external content, you simply select the appropriate file from a scrolling list. The product automatically creates an entity declaration, if one doesn't already exist, and inserts the entity reference in the XML instance.

21.2.6 *Well-formedness support*

An XML authoring tool normally supports authoring and manipulation of type-valid documents, using structured authoring capabilities such as we've described. You might also need the option of working in a DTD-less mode, creating only well-formed documents.

In FrameMaker+SGML, this is accomplished by using an "unstructured template". Elements of information are identified by applying the product's own style codes in a consistent manner. These codes allow a well-formed XML document to be generated.

21.3 | Automated formatting and composition

The purpose of style is to communicate the content of a document. A rendition must therefore convey the document's structure as well as its words. Because XML documents are well-structured, they allow you to take advantage of rule-based formatting, in which the composition is driven automatically by the document's structure and other attributes. Rule-based formatting not only produces a consistent and communicative result, but it does so with far less effort.

21.3.1 *Rule-based formatting*

Rule-based formatters allow the appearance of the document to be modified easily by importing a new formatting *template*. Writers might initially develop the contents using a simple template with a one-column format. When the contents are complete, they may apply a different template that utilizes more elaborate formatting such as two-column, and then output the document to PostScript for hard copy production.

If additional layouts are desired, other templates can be applied; for instance, one designed specifically for online presentation. The document can then be output to PDF or HTML to create the electronic version.

21.3.2 *Interactive formatting*

On the other hand, interactive formatting allows minute degrees of of adjustment, possibly to communicate in ways too fine-grained to be expressable in rules. More usually, though, interactive styling is used for copyfitting and similar compensations for the medium used, rather than as an expressive device.

An XML formatter should be rule-based. Web browsers are, for example. Interactivity is a plus, but the way in which it relates to the rule-based processing must be considered when evaluating a product.

In *FrameMaker+SGML*, the appearance of the document is fundamentally rule-based. It is controlled through formatting rules stored in the document template. Whenever an element is inserted into the document, the formatting defined for its context is automatically applied. If the element is moved to a new location, its appearance is automatically adjusted to fit its new context.

The product also has an interactive WYSIWYG environment. The user can see what the document will look like and can change the formatting specifications when needed. For example, the user can force a table or graphic to be on the same page with some text by simply selecting several paragraphs and reducing the interline spacing. This can be done without in any way affecting the structure of the document, or by using processing instructions. Therefore, the XML document remains clean.

21.4 | Document fragments

Many enterprises that use XML do so because of a requirement for collaborative authoring and workgroup production. XML's structure provides a disciplined basis for writers to work on various pieces of content and then assemble them into a document. The document type designer specifies which elements in the document can be treated as fragments.

An XML editor can support fragments in many ways, for the benefit of both people and content management systems. FrameMaker+SGML, for example, not only allows elements to be treated as fragments, but also entities, XML's unit of storage. The product maintains a link to the fragment, and if the fragment is modified, the document incorporating that entity is automatically updated. This is demonstrated in Figure 21-7.

FrameMaker+SGML also has a book utility that allows users to divide a long volume into several individual components. The components are arranged in the desired order in a structured book file.

The book generation utility processes all of the components to assign page, section, and figure numbers, and to resolve cross-references among the components. The utility can also compile a table of contents, lists of figures and tables, and indexes for the book. All of the generated lists are automatically hyperlinked to sources in the book, providing an excellent navigation facility for online documents.

21.5 | Publishing the document

As XML documents can be independent of any style or presentation medium, it is easy to publish them in a variety of forms, enabling users to distribute information on many different media using an assortment of tools. Both paper and electronic distribution can be significant considerations when choosing XML products.

Business as Usual

Assuming that gasoline prices rise very gradually in real dollars, to $1.50 a gallon in 2015, OTA believes that new mid-size autos will gradually become more fuel efficient-reaching about 30 mpg by 2005 and 33 mpg in 2015-despite becoming safer, roomier, more powerful, and cleaner in this time period.

Because both the cost effectiveness of fuel economy technologies and customer preference for efficient vehicles will vary with gasoline prices, other gasoline price assumptions will generate different future fleet fuel economies. If gasoline prices were to reach $3 a gallon by 2015, OTA projects that new car fleet fuel economy would increase by 42 percent over 1995, to 39 mpg. In contrast, were gasoline prices to stagnate or decline in real dollars-as they have during the past decade or so-fuel economy improvements would be far less.

Furthermore, fleet fuel economy will depend on a host of additional factors (some of which are influenced by fuel prices) such as government safety and emissions regulations, consumer preferences for high performance, relative sales of autos versus light trucks (when considering the light-duty fleet as a whole), and so forth. OTA's estimate presumes no additional changes in regulations beyond what is already scheduled, gradually weakening demand for higher performance levels, and no major shifts in other factors. Obviously, another set of assumptions would shift the fuel economy estimates.

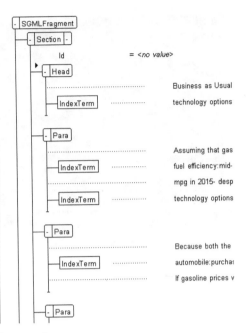

Figure 21-7 Editing a document fragment.

21.5.1 *Paper publishing*

While online distribution is becoming increasingly common, most enterprises still publish a substantial amount of information on paper. An XML product's ability to support paper printing may therefore be important to you.

FrameMaker+SGML, for example, has a composition engine that is quite robust, handling complex formats for both gray-scale and color paper output, as well as simpler online formats. In addition, the product allows you to define colors using Pantone and other standard color libraries. As Figure 21-8 illustrates, spot or process color separations can be created as well, and registration marks can be generated automatically in either Western or Japanese style.

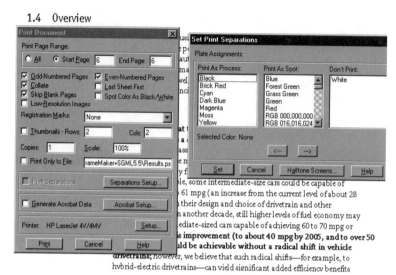

Figure 21-8 The print menu provides numerous options.

21.5.2 *Online publishing*

In addition to XML itself, a composition package should support distribution in other online formats. *FrameMaker+SGML*, for example, supports publishing to CD-ROM or online in *Portable Document Format* (PDF) and HTML.

21.5.2.1 PDF

Hyperlinks and cross-references in the document are automatically converted to PDF links, and hypertext alerts are converted to PDF sticky notes. PDF bookmarks can be generated automatically based on a list of element types. PDF document information, including keywords, can also be generated automatically, resulting in a fully hyperlinked PDF file without post-processing.

21.5.2.2   HTML

FrameMaker+SGML proposes an initial mapping of element types in a document to corresponding HTML elements. The user can review the mapping and make changes as required. In addition, long documents can automatically be divided into smaller files on specified element type boundaries. The files are hyperlinked, and a table of contents is created to aid navigation.

Hyperlinks and cross-references in the document are automatically converted to HREF attributes, and graphics are converted to GIF, JPEG, or PNG. In addition, the product generates a cascading style sheet.

21.6 | Customization and preparation

XML offers much richer possibilities for processing than do unstructured document representations such as word processing files. Couple that fact with the generally rich function set of XML editing and composition products, and you get a sometimes overwhelming set of options as a result. Accordingly, the ability of a product to allow customization and setup can be a major criterion in deciding whether it is right for your environment.

21.6.1   *DTD customization*

Many DTDs are standardized by particular industries for interchange of information among industry members. These DTDs may contain element types that are not used by a particular organization, or within a particular group of documents.

An interchange DTD might also use short, cryptic names, or a terminology that differs from that used at a particular site. (Perhaps because the DTD uses English while the site is in France, or Germany, or Sweden.)

FrameMaker+SGML addresses these situations with a utility that allows the DTD to be customized within the authoring environment without affecting the original. The customizer can create a simple *read/write rule* that will cause specified element types to be dropped as the DTD is brought into the authoring environment. The software also removes references to that element type in all content models.

Similarly, read/write rules can be used to rename element types or attributes. For example, the rule to drop the element type "Foo" is:

```
element "foo" drop;
```

while the rule to rename the element type "Foo" to "Bar" is:

```
element "Foo" is fm element "Bar";
```

All of these changes are made without actually revising the DTD. When the edit is complete, the same read/write rules can be applied in reverse to save the document with its original element type and attribute names.

21.6.2 *Defining formatting rules*

When rule-based formatting is desired, as it almost always is when XML is used, the means by which a product allows formatting rules to be expressed becomes very important. As an example of the techniques employed for this purpose, let's look at those offered by FrameMaker+SGML.

- Page size and layout, column layout, table styles, cross-reference styles, and styles for indexes and tables of contents can be associated with element types and attributes in an *Element Definition Document* (EDD). As the EDD is a structured document, the application developer can take advantage of guided editing to ensure that the format rules are entered properly.

- As an alternative to putting formatting specifications in the EDD, paragraph and character styles can be created in a formatting template (style sheet) and referenced by the format rules of the EDD.

- Attributes can be mapped to object properties. This is especially useful for setting up display of graphics.

- Style association can be context-sensitive. For example, a paragraph element in a table can be associated with different formatting from a paragraph element in a list item.

- Formatting specifications can be inherited. For example, all the items in a list will inherit the formatting specified for the list itself, modified by any specific formatting for the first, last, and/or middle list items.

21.6.3 *Extensibility*

Your applications or business environment may require customization beyond what a product makes available out of the box. XML editing and composition products may offer scripting or programming languages for this purpose. A proprietary language usually offers the advantage of product-specific functions, while a standard language can be utilized more easily by a large body of developers who are already familiar with it.

For example, further customizing or extending the functions of *FrameMaker+SGML* can be accomplished by developing a "plug-in" using a C-based application programming interface (API). The API is accessed through a developers kit that provides an application development environment incorporating a library of function calls and makefiles. The kit supports a machine-independent layer that allows plug-ins to be coded once and then recompiled for multiple platforms.

Analysis   Here's an interesting contradiction. One of the most important aspects of XML is that it can preserve data in the abstract; that is, it won't accidentally intermingle your data with rendition information. On the other hand, the style of a rendition is important, because that is what makes communication of the data effective.

This chapter illustrated an approach to XML editing that seeks to resolve that contradiction. The product is structure-driven, but provides a WYSIWYG rendered view and sophisticated graphic arts functionality. Other XML editors make different trade-offs. Understanding them all will help you determine your own requirements more accurately.

ADEPT·Editor: Edit for content management

- Structured authoring
- Automated document systems
- Batch composition

22

Another approach to XML authoring focuses on structured editing in the context of the total automated document system. This chapter is sponsored by ArborText, Inc., `http://www.arbortext.com`, and was prepared by PG Bartlett.

O rganizations with large amounts of document information typically require an XML authoring and editing tool that easily integrates with content management tools and content delivery tools. That combination yields a complete automated document system.

22.1 | Automated document systems

An automated document system can be the key to an organization gaining significant competitive advantage through improvements in information quality, time to market, and production costs (see Figure 22-1).

The designs of these systems usually emphasize data integrity, data reusability, process automation, and workflow consistency. *Data integrity* is key to the other design factors because without absolutely consistent data, the rest becomes difficult or impossible to achieve.

Two key concepts, *structure* and *content management*, play pivotal roles in the successful deployment and operation of a high-performance automated document publishing system. Let us look at what these terms mean and why they are important.

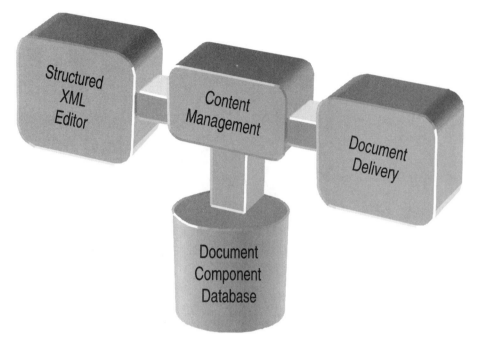

Figure 22-1   Automated document system components.

22.1.1   *Structure*

The contents of documents are often described as *unstructured* information, in contrast to the *structured* information stored in a relational database. But if you look at the right-hand view in Figure 22-2, the rendered document clearly exhibits a structure. It is conveyed to the reader by stylistic conventions, such as type size, numbering, and indentions.

So if the terms "structured" and "unstructured" information aren't really accurate, what then do we mean when we use them?

If you look in the computer file for a word processing document, you will find the style information mixed in with the real information – the *data content* – of the document. In a database, however, there is nothing there but pure abstract data.

So it isn't that documents have no structure, it is that the way most documents are stored obscures the abstract data with information about the way it should look when presented. In a word, while databases contain abstractions, most document files contain *renditions*.

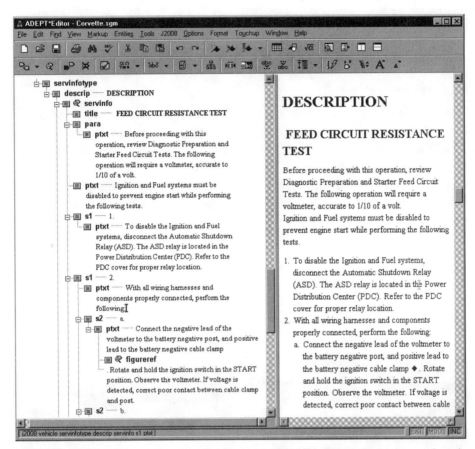

Figure 22-2 Two views of a document: structured and rendered (WYSIWYG).

But what if that could be different? What if you *could* store a document so that its natural structure and data content could always be distinguished from style information? What if you could handle documents as if they were data?

It *can* be different! And XML turns out to be the key, because XML allows you to identify and preserve the structure of any collection of text. With XML, documents and databases are just two different places to keep abstract structured data.

Because XML is a notation that *preserves abstractions*, the data in XML documents can be treated just like other data, which can be automated, processed, reused, protected, classified, and extracted for use in a limitless variety of ways (see Figure 22-3.)

Using XML yields several key benefits:

Multiple outputs

XML document data is often described as "presentation independent" because it is stored in a way that is independent of any particular medium. That allows organizations to deliver their information automatically from a single repository to the Web, CD-ROM, print, and other media. This is a huge contrast to word processing and desktop publishing file formats, which are already rendered with a specific output in mind, usually publishing on paper.

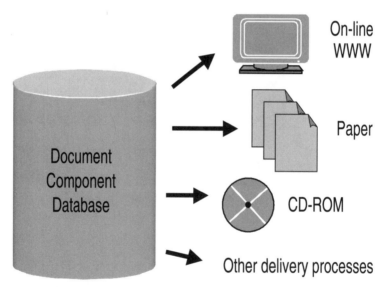

Figure 22-3   Multiple outputs from a single XML source.

Reuse

Many organizations re-create existing information far more often than they reuse existing information. That inefficiency causes inaccuracies, version skew, delivery slips, and inflated costs. One of the primary reasons to build a structured document repository is to eliminate those costs by enabling the maximum possible reuse of existing information. Storing that information in a structured database provides the controls needed to maintain the integrity of the data regardless of when, where, and how often it is used.

Interchange

Organizations can interchange their data freely with suppliers, partners, and customers when the data is based on a standardized document representation like XML.

Automation

Representing your document data in XML and storing it in a repository can yield process improvements through intensive automation that are similar in kind and degree to the benefits of implementing relational databases to replace handwritten ledgers.

22.1.2 Content management

Any organization that manages large amounts of document information should, sooner or later, seek both to structure that information and to store that information in a content management system.

The specific method of content management varies. In some applications, document information is stored directly in a database. In many others, it is stored under the control of a document management system.

Regardless of the specific approach, these systems primarily ensure data integrity through security controls that prevent unauthorized viewing and changing, and revision controls that keep track of changes from one version to the next.

Content management systems for XML documents invariably must keep track of information at a highly granular level (see Figure 22-4). For example, instead of storing complete books in a single chunk, "compound documents" are assembled from small components that are stored separately.

Some components are tiny. For example, individual cells in a table may be stored in various places and appear together only when delivered as a publication.

It can be a challenge to create such documents. Typical document creation tools are designed to create rendered pages, whether they are printed pages or Web pages. But building compound documents out of reusable components requires a structured authoring tool that is designed to handle highly granular unrendered documents. The tool must also integrate tightly

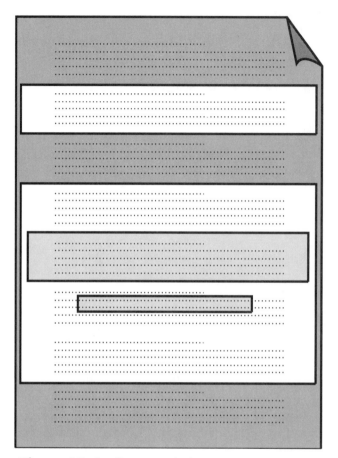

Figure 22-4   Compound documents are composed of a hierarchy of components.

with databases of all kinds, including relational databases, document management systems, and content management systems.

Such systems can display collections of document components *as if they were single documents* while preserving the properties of each individual component. That approach allows an author to view every document component within the context in which it is used, while at the same time ensuring that the author changes only those components for which the author is permitted to make changes, and that are not currently under revision by another author.

22.2 | What information warrants these tools?

Should your organization approach its document applications through the use of structured XML authoring tools integrated with content management systems?

The answer depends on the characteristics of the information you create and the processes you use to create it. There are a number of criteria to consider.

22.2.1 *High volume*

Unless your organization publishes thousands or even millions of pages, current content-management-based products may be too expensive to justify the return. If yours is a manufacturing organization larger than $100 million or a publishing company larger than $25 million, then you are likely to reap sizable rewards from implementing an automated document system.

22.2.2 *Multiple publications*

Most organizations need to publish their information on multiple outputs, the most popular being the Web, CD-ROM, and print. That requirement alone has been sufficient to justify an investment in a new automated document system. But if you are aiming not only to deliver on multiple outputs, but also to leverage the capabilities of electronic media, then it is even more important for you to build a document repository that is media-independent so that you can use each medium to its full advantage.

22.2.3 *High value*

The type of information we are talking about represents a large investment in the "intellectual capital" required to create it, because it is the sort of information that is either vital to a related product or is the product itself. Examples include operating guides, service manuals, parts catalogs, policy and procedure manuals, and reference manuals (e.g., encyclopedias, legal case books, legislation, regulations, and medical drug information).

22.2.4   *Long life*

Closely associated with "high value" is "long life." Most types of information that are worth a significant investment last for years or even decades. In addition to the initial investment, this information often receives additional investment throughout its lifetime in the form of revisions.

22.2.5   *Reusable*

Although there are exceptions, much of the information in a typical publication from a large organization either already existed before within other documents or will be reused in the future.

22.2.6   *Consistent*

Using XML makes the most sense if there are many documents of the same type, or single large documents that have repetitive structures. For example, while it is likely to be worth the investment to create a DTD for service bulletins if you publish 30 every year, it is probably too costly to do the same for a single annual report. On the other hand, single books like dictionaries and catalogs have benefited from the use of XML.

22.2.7   *Created by formal processes*

This is the clearest differentiator of all. Virtually all information that comes out of a process is that is formally defined can benefit from a formal structure. When applied to document information, a "formal" process normally has the following characteristics: defined and repeatable workflow, assigned resources, and mission-critical deliverables.

22.3 | Characteristics to consider

There are a number of important characteristics to look for in a structured XML editor that integrates with content management systems. These characteristics are divided into three main categories:

Authoring issues

These issues affect those who create and revise the information, not only full-time writers but also those who are occasional contributors to the process.

Application development issues

These issues affect those who develop and maintain the products, applications, and infrastructure to support the process.

Business issues

These issues affect those who have to approve the investment in new technologies and who risk the most when an investment goes wrong.

To illustrate these key characteristics, we will use illustrations based on ArborText's ADEPT•Editor, a structured XML authoring tool that has been integrated with several content management systems.

22.3.1 *Authoring issues*

When you look at a structured XML editor, you should look first to see if it provides all the usual editing features such as cut, copy, paste, and drag and drop, and convenience features such as a preferences panel and multi-level undo.

Then you should look for two specific capabilities that are designed specifically for *structured* authoring:

Task-matched authoring tools

Creating highly structured documentation involves more than just typing. An editor with "task-matched" authoring tools provides editing tools that are appropriate for the type of data being entered.

Enforced consistency

To maintain the integrity of your data so that it remains processable and reusable, you should look for a tool that prevents your authors from creating data that is inconsistent or invalid.

Let's take a closer look at these two capabilities.

22.3.1.1   "Task-matched" tools

Writing a user manual involves a lot more than writing paragraphs and heads. Typical technical documentation consists of large amounts of different types of information. A portion of that information, of course, is relatively "free-form" text, such as titles, paragraphs, and lists.

INSTALLATION

For installation, reverse the above procedures. Clean corrosion/dirt from the cable and wire terminals before installing wiring to the solenoid.

STARTER RELAY

The relay is located in the Power Distribution Center (PDC). Refer to the PDC cover for relay location.

OTHER SPECIFICATIONS

Figure 22-5   Rendered view of "free-form" fragment of an XML document.

But even the character data is organized into a structure, and a structured authoring tool should provide a way to navigate and edit the structure itself. This capability should be provided through an alternative "structure view" of the document.

Other information, especially the information in tables, is better suited to a restricted form of data entry such as the various controls you see in the dialog boxes of software programs. These controls include pushbuttons, check boxes, radio buttons, drop-down selection lists, sliders (e.g., volume controls), and other controls. These are shown in Figure 22-7

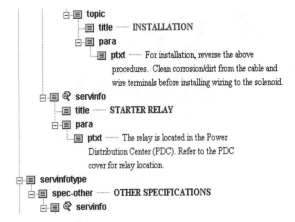

Figure 22-6   Structure view of fragment in Figure 22-5.

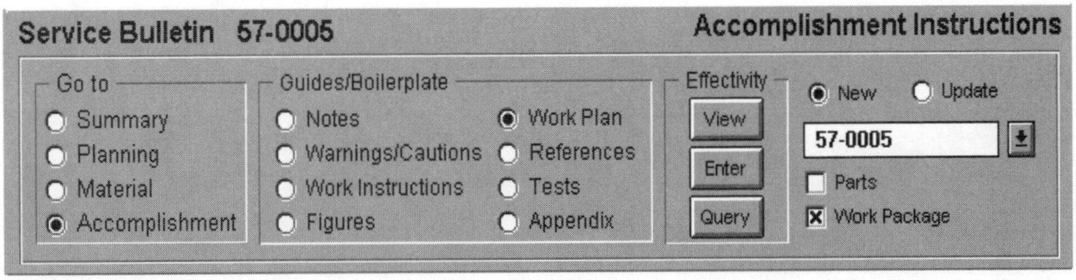

Figure 22-7   Dialog box view for entering specialized data in XML documents.

An authoring tool for structured XML information should allow you to match the type of information to be entered with the best view for the job. In some cases, you will want all three capabilities concurrently for the same document (see Figure 22-8).

22.3.1.2   Structure consistency

Data integrity is the single most important factor in building a highly automated system that is built on top of structured data. The integrity of your data is crucial because automated processes must rely on the validity and consistency of your data in order to perform their functions properly.

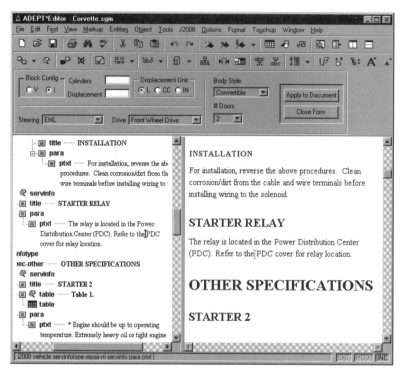

Figure 22-8   *ADEPT•Editor* showing three views concurrently.

One of the most important features of a structured XML editor is its capability to ensure that documents remain consistently structured at all times. This capability is especially important when that structured data is stored in a repository that is accessible to other authors and to automated processing applications.

Data integrity enforcement is illustrated in Figure 22-9, which illustrates that an author is dragging the first step of the "Removal" procedure to the "Starter" title. The cursor "prohibited" symbol shows that the current drop point is invalid and will not be allowed. For valid drop points, the cursor changes to a checkmark or plus sign.

Continuous consistency is also vital to ensure efficient workflow and repeatable processes. Authors who are allowed to create invalid and inconsistent data must either clean up their data later or turn it over to someone else to clean up. Either way, the organization pays the cost of extra work that adds no value but increases costs and time to market.

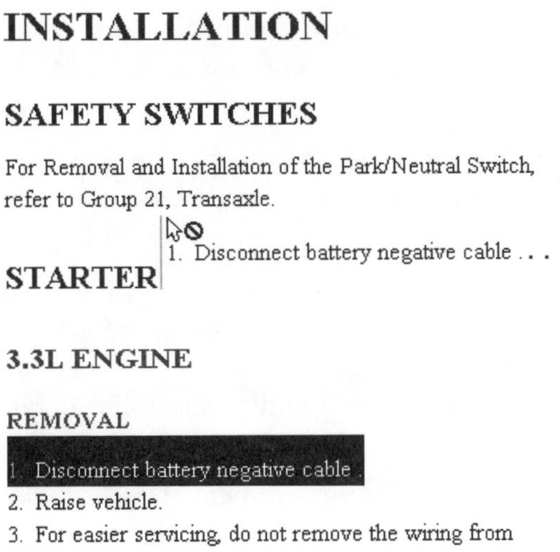

INSTALLATION

SAFETY SWITCHES

For Removal and Installation of the Park/Neutral Switch,
refer to Group 21, Transaxle.

1. Disconnect battery negative cable . . .

STARTER

3.3L ENGINE

REMOVAL

1. Disconnect battery negative cable .
2. Raise vehicle.
3. For easier servicing, do not remove the wiring from

Figure 22-9 *ADEPT•Editor* showing prohibited drop point.

22.3.2 *Development issues*

Developing a powerful system to handle large amounts of structured XML documents is no different from other large automation projects. Building a system to suit your needs will involve a combination of standard products and additional application development work in the form of configuring, programming, and other customizations.

This section describes the key characteristics of a structured XML editor integrated with content management that primarily affect those who have to *develop* systems based on that tool.

22.3.2.1 Content management integration

As Figure 22-1 illustrates, a structured XML authoring tool is just one of several pieces that comprise an enterprise solution for creating, managing, and delivering document information. One of the key additional tools is a content management system.

Organizations can integrate structured XML authoring tools with many different tools for content management. Some start out by building their applications on the file system. Others plunge right into document management or component management. (Some component management systems describe their products as "authoring support" tools because they are specifically designed with information authoring - and not just document management - in mind.)

Whatever system you choose to manage your content, the approach you take to integrating your authoring tools with your content management tool has an enormous impact on performance, scalability, and ease of use.

Ideally, you would choose an authoring tool with an API (Application Program Interface) specifically designed to interface with content management systems. Through that API, the authoring tool can "speak" with the content management system at a component level and not just at a document level.

Let's examine the facilities that this type of connection enables.

Seamless user interface

Instead of switching back and forth between the authoring tool and the user interface of the content management system, it is possible to "build in" to the authoring tool everything the user needs to browse, search, and select documents and document components from the content management system. Figure 22-10 shows an example from *ADEPT•Editor*, which provides an interface that displays the contents of the content management system.

Compound document authoring

There are clear advantages to reusing existing information instead of wasting the time and resources to create it again. To achieve optimum reuse, you should create your information in small, easily reusable components and build "compound documents" that are simply collections of these components.

But when the time comes to edit that information, you should look for a tool that can load compound documents without first combining all the separate components into a single monolithic document. That feature allows the authoring tool to deliver the following benefits:

■ You can open a compound document and check out only those components you want to change, which leaves the remaining components available for other authors to revise.

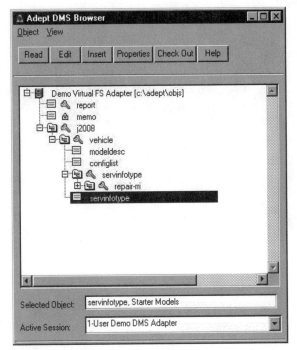

Figure 22-10 Browsing documents and components directly within a structured XML authoring tool.

- You can open enormous documents very quickly because the authoring tool only loads the components necessary to fill the screen.

- You can perform "granular updates", where components that are changed can be reloaded without reloading everything else.

Collaborative authoring

Several users may have the same compound document open for viewing, but by enforcing permissions and checkout at the component level, each user is restricted to editing the components he or she has checked out. This means that in a workgroup authoring environment, all subject matter experts can simultaneously edit their portions of the publication while seeing it in the context of the full publication.

22.3.2.2   Customization

Customizing the document system can provide dramatic improvements in productivity, information quality, and/or performance.

For example, some of the customization that is desirable for an automated document system is to build tools for authors. For example, forms and dialog boxes may provide a faster and easier user interface to certain types of information (see Figure 22-11).

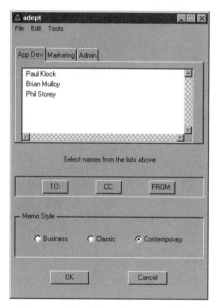

Figure 22-11   Custom dialog box for entering header information.

The key to efficient application development is to choose products that come with appropriate tools for the purpose. For instance, ArborText's ACL Designer product supports customizing the ADEPT•Editor user interface. You can set up forms within the ADEPT window itself (see Figure 22-7) and you can set up dialog boxes that pop up when needed (Figure 22-11).

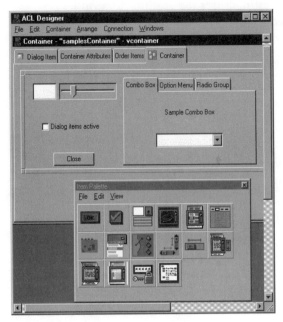

Figure 22-12   ArborText *ACL Designer.*

22.3.3 *Business issues*

Many of the issues surrounding the selection, implementation, and operation of an automated document system represent a significant impact on the business success of the project.

Organizations that have earned outstanding returns from automated document systems built on XML or its parent, SGML, include the following examples:

- Heavy equipment manufacturer improves author productivity by 100%, saving the the hiring of 600 professionals over a five-year period.
- Publisher of daily report reduces 30% of its payroll costs by eliminating regular overtime through streamlining its processes.
- Textbook publisher increases revenues substantially by offering customized versions of its textbooks at prices competitive to standard versions.

■ Electronic equipment manufacturer reduces production lags from three weeks to two days.

Let's consider the characteristics you should look for in an automated document system to help you achieve the sort of business successes described above.

22.3.3.1   Authoring productivity

Have you ever spent ten minutes writing a memo to your boss and another ten minutes formatting it to make it look good? If so, then you know how much time you can waste on tasks that add little value.

With the advent of WYSIWYG word processing and desktop publishing software, authors spend as much as half their time manipulating the appearance of their documents, and only the other half creating content. For many organizations, this is a tremendous unnecessary expense.

In principle, authors are experts in the *subject matter* of the document while graphics designers are experts in the *appearance* of a document. When that principle is violated in practice, the productivity of the subject matter experts - the authors - drops by half or more.

For those organizations that publish only on paper, using authors for document design represents a costly inefficiency. But for many organizations who deliver their information in multiple forms (e.g., in print and on the Web) and who aim to "personalize" documents through automatic assembly of document components to suit individual needs, WYSIWYG no longer makes any sense at all because the information may *never* be delivered in the same form in which it was created.

With some tools, you may find that it is possible to force authors to leave the document design alone but still show them how the printed page will look. The problem with that approach is that the only way an author can affect a page layout is by rewriting to add or remove words. That could lead to an even greater loss of efficiency.

Structured XML authoring tools can separate content from presentation completely by showing a view of the data that uses formatting only to provide cues about meaning, instead of showing the actual rendition. For example, emphasized words are shown in italics and titles are shown in large bold letters, but column breaks and page breaks are *not* displayed (see Figure 22-13).

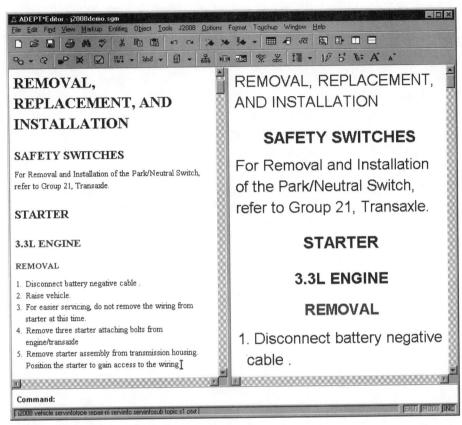

Figure 22-13 Two views of a document, rendered with different stylesheets.

Views designed only for authoring can provide additional assistance by displaying in easy-to-read form information that may be tiny when finally presented. For example, copyright information may be printed in tiny letters but may be displayed in larger letters for authoring without enlarging the entire view.

22.3.3.2   Batch composition

In traditional WYSIWYG environments, authors manually inspect and adjust column breaks and page breaks to keep related elements together and reduce excessive white space. But using a structured XML editor allows you to create a system that automates page layouts and relieves authors from this low-value work. "Batch composition" is the technology that makes this possible.

ADEPT•Publisher from ArborText is one example of a tool that provides batch composition capabilities. By automatically balancing page "fullness" with the need to keep related elements together, the product produces attractive pages with no need for manual intervention or inspection. In addition, it can automatically generate supplemental text, footnotes, endnotes, tables of contents, cross references, indexes, and lists of figures, equations, and tables.

Some organizations must lay out their documents to conform to legal requirements, such as the formatting of safety warnings. For example, it may be a requirement that safety warnings appear in their entirety on the same page as the text to which they are related. *ADEPT•Publisher* can ensure that the document complies with that legal requirement or issue a fatal error if compliance is not possible (for example, if the safety warning exceeds the size of the page). This eliminates manual inspection and eliminates the liability risk from those errors that manual inspection inevitably overlooks.

22.3.3.3   Presentation independence

By its nature, information stored in XML is independent of any particular way of presenting it. That means that through the application of a stylesheet or other transformation method, XML information can be delivered from a single information base to multiple outputs, usually automatically (see Figure 22-3).

The alternative to this approach, which is in common practice today, is to set up a process where authors create the information with the goal of printing it and then hand off the information to another group that handles online delivery. The online group converts the information to the online format and manually adjusts the appearance, sequence, and links to adapt the information for online delivery. In that process, it is common to improve the information itself, but often those improvements are *not* reflected back to the original source.

When the original information is revised, the online group has to make a decision: do they make the same revisions to the online information that were made to the printed information? Or do they convert the printed information to the online format and then make all the manual changes again? No matter which way they go, the result is an expensive and wasteful process.

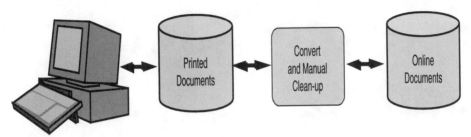

Figure 22-14   Inefficient non-XML alternative to process in Figure 22-3.

22.3.3.4   Standards-based

Structured XML authoring tools are based on open standards that are outside the control of any individual vendor. XML, for example, is an approved recommendation of the World Wide Web Consortium (W3C). With the right choice of technology, you can protect your organization from dependence on any single vendor.

The key to vendor-independence is to build your automated document system based on open standards such as XML and its related specifications, XSL, XLink, the DOM, and other emerging specifications. Many of these are discussed later on in the book and others are in the CD-ROM's XML SPECtacular.

Making the right decision will also ensure high performance and maximum scalability. Choosing overtly standards-based tools, such as those described in this chapter, will ensure that your data remains standards-compliant throughout the entire process of creating, managing, and processing your information.

XMetaL: Friendly XML editing

- Structured authoring
- Familiar interface
- Outside authors

Chapter 23

Another approach to an XML editor is to build on user familiarity with word processors and HTML to provide a friendly environment. The friendly folks at SoftQuad Inc., http://www.sq.com, believe in that approach and have sponsored this chapter.

XML will be a new experience for most of today's Web site developers. If you are in that category, you might welcome a structured editor that is designed to be easy to use and to provide first-time XML editing capabilities right out of the box. Of course, those "friendliness" characteristics will need to be balanced against your functional requirements when choosing a product.

23.1 | Familiar interface

Often, simple differences in the editing interface will cause more problems for users than coping with unfamiliar tags.

One way to increase user comfort with a new technology is to provide the user with a familiar interface. Pull-down menus, the button bar, and short-cut keystrokes should be compatible with the most popular word processing programs. The interface should be designed to provide immediate familiarity and to eliminate the learning curve typically experienced when a user switches to a new editing environment.

Figure 23-1, illustrates the approach taken by SoftQuad's XMetaL to recognize the importance of a comfortable editing environment and make the transition transparent.

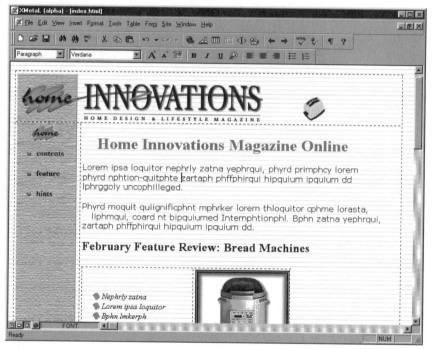

Figure 23-1   XMetaL interface

23.2 | HTML markup transition

Consider how easily an editor can help HTML Web site creators get started with XML. It should be able to import both existing word-processing documents and HTML documents to serve as the basis for new XML documents.

XMetaL, for example, comes with a special XML/HTML rules set to help new users start authoring well-formed XML documents using tags from a familiar HTML baseline element-type set. This HTML foundation can then be extended by adding new element types.

The product supports the development of new element types and attributes by helping users group them into HTML display classes. This immediately provides appropriate screen formatting for ongoing editing sessions.

The user with existing HTML pages has another option as well. The editor has the capability (at least as far as the two languages permit) for automatically making your HTML a well-formed XML document.

23.3 | Structured editing

The XML language was specifically designed to be user-friendly. Yet, because it is expected to carry abstract data between computer programs, it also has to be rigorous.

HTML, on the other hand, was only designed to represent rendered pages for humans to read. We humans are so much smarter than computers that HTML doesn't have to be used quite so rigorously.

For this reason, XML editors need structured editing capabilities, as we have seen. Providing these while maintaining user-friendliness can be a real challenge for a product.

As an example, let's look at how XMetaL steps up to the challenge by examining some of its structured editing features.

23.3.1 *Multiple views*

XMetaL offers views of full document, structured document outline, or XML context. These enable flexible editing, navigating, and manipulating of large portions of your document. The outline view, illustrated in Figure 23-2 will show the new element types that the Web developer has added, and the places where they can be used.

23.3.2 *Tables*

A graphical table editor can be used to produce tables. These can be created in a what-you-see-is-what-you-get mode without intrusive markup requirements.

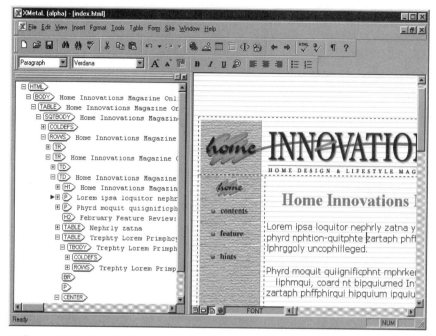

Figure 23-2   Outline view showing element-type hierarchy

23.3.3 *Named bookmarks*

XML pages tend to be larger than typical HTML Web pages. A facility for named bookmarks lets you navigate lengthy XML pages and quickly return to important references.

23.3.4 *Samples and templates*

To help users cope with the Brave New Web of structured information, *XMetaL* provides industry-specific samples and XML DTDs and templates, including one for HTML. Using these resources, Web developers can use or extend the HTML document type, and can employ industry-specific DTDs as well.

23.3.5 *Context-sensitive styles*

You can specify styles for individual elements and for all elements of a given type. You can also associate different styles with an element type, according to the context in which the individual elements of that type occur within your documents. For example, an unordered list item might ordinarily have a round bullet, but if the list occurs nested within another list, a square bullet would be displayed instead.

23.3.6 *Default HTML styles*

For the HTML document type, *XMetaL* provides the default HTML styles out of the box. This eliminates lengthy set up times for those new to XML.

It is also possible for Web developers to use existing HTML styles with newly-developed element types. Doing so can provide familiar user interfaces while preserving data with more descriptive markup. For example, data could be tagged as a "product" element but displayed in the style of an HTML "H3" element.

23.3.7 *Direct DTD processing*

XMetaL can read standard XML document type definitions and immediately configure itself to accept matching XML instance files. There are no lengthy "rules building" setup steps.

23.3.8 *Customization*

With *XMetaL* you can record a common sequence of operations and execute it from a single keystroke combination. You can also customize toolbars and add your own functions through *Visual Basic* and *OLE Automation*.

23.4 | Extend XML capabilities to outside authors

Many organizations that use structured rule-based XML authoring tools within their publication departments are unable to extend the use of these tools to outside authors. Typically, the tools are expensive and complex to learn and use.

As a result, most outside authors rely on using word processors with specialized authoring stylesheets. When an organization brings the work of these outside authors back in-house, conversion into XML is required. This is not only expensive and time consuming, but often problematic because correct stylesheet use is difficult to validate and impossible to enforce.

Overtly "friendly" XML editors that mimic the interface, functionality, and pricing structure of popular word processors may provide a solution to this problem. With such products, it is more likely that outside authors could create XML directly, thereby eliminating the time and expense of conversion.

DynaTag visual conversion environment

■ XML conversion tool

■ Document conversion concepts

24

A lot of the world's documents are in XML, but a lot more aren't and need to be. This chapter is sponsored by Inso Corporation, `http://www.inso.com`, who have a tool for getting them there.

Word processor file formats faithfully record how data should look, but they are useless as reliable sources for processing that data. That's why so many of them need to be converted to XML.

Middle-tier data aggregators need to do it dynamically, and publishers need to do it as part of the authoring process. Both groups can benefit from understanding the concepts involved.

24.1 | Concepts of document conversion

An XML document consists of data intermixed with markup. The purpose of the markup is to describe the data: its meaning, structure, and other attributes.

When data originates in a database, as in middle-tier applications, it is straightforward to incorporate it in an XML document. That is because a database keeps data in an abstract state; it isn't mixed up with reports, entry forms, or other rendition information. Moreover, the database schema knows how to associate meaning with the data – meaning that is easily represented as element types and attributes when creating the XML document.

Creating an XML document is also straightforward with an XML structured editing system. Such systems, like databases, keep the data in an abstract state internally even if they present a rendered WYSIWYG view to the author.

But the real garden variety word processors, beloved of authors and typists the world over, have no concept of data. They exist solely to create renditions and will happily mingle formatting commands with data, given the slightest opportunity.

But despite that fact, many XML-savvy organizations use word processors regularly to create XML documents. They prefer not to invest in the retraining and process changes that switching authoring environments requires.

Which is why XML conversion tools were invented. Many of them are essentially programming languages with varying degrees of XML-awareness. (There are some on the CD-ROM accompanying this book.) They often require a programmer's skills to create rules for parsing word processing formats, and they don't provide visual feedback.

We'll see a different approach later in this chapter, but first we need to look at two key concepts: data rescue and *style serves meaning*.

24.1.1 *Data rescue*

Converting a word processing document to XML typically involves more than just changing from one notation ("file format") to another. Instead of simply translating the document's formatting characteristics and content, it is necessary to isolate the real information content – the abstract data and its structure – from the style information. In other words, the data must be rescued from the rendered form, and stored in a notation – XML – that is capable of preserving structured data as an abstraction.

Data rescue restores rendered content so that it can serve as dynamic information for many uses in a variety of delivery environments. (For an example, see Chapter 19, "City Of Providence", on page 252.)

24.1.2 *Style serves meaning*

The basic principle behind data rescue is that the purpose of the style in word processing documents is to help convey the meaning of the data. In other words, as an example, the reason for using a particular set of formatting instructions (such as bold, centered, 18 point type) is to show that the data in that style is a "title".

By taking advantage of this principle, it is possible to transform word processing styles to XML markup. That task is made easier when the word processing documents use style templates consistently, but even in their absence, combinations of formatting instructions can be used, as we have seen.

24.2 | Converting documents with DynaTag

DynaTag is a graphical environment for converting word processing (WP) documents to XML. (It also contains other components, described later, that prepare the converted documents for electronic publishing on CD-ROM and the Web.) It converts WP documents in Western European languages and Japanese.

The product is designed to simplify the often complex task of mapping word processing style conventions to XML. Once a conversion is defined with *DynaTag*, it can be reused for other documents of the same type.

Figure 24-1 illustrates one view of the product interface. The upper half of the window shows the input word processing file with its original formatting. Names of input formats appear on the left, and output objects (usually element types) appear on the right. The bottom portion of the screen changes depending on the current stage of the process. Here, the input formats tab is displayed.

24.2.1 *Getting started*

In *DynaTag*, the set of rules for transforming a class of WP documents is called a "project". Using the *New Project Wizard* shown in Figure 24-2, the user specifies the project and its initial WP source files. The WP document

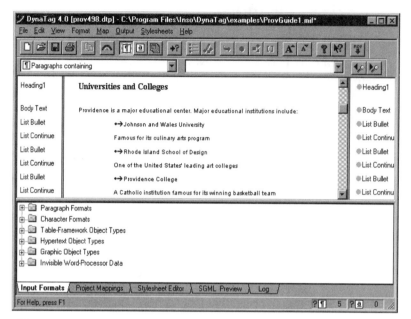

Figure 24-1   *DynaTag* interface to mapping rules

is analyzed and converted into an intermediate tagged form that retains all the content and formatting information. The product then displays a document preview, formatted with the original WP styles. The document is now ready for mapping.

24.2.2 *Mapping*

Document conversion is driven by mapping rules. A *mapping* rule specifies how to convert an input format (a WP style) to the correct output object, which may be an XML element type. Multiple rules may yield the same output object.

Several views are provided for sorting, organizing, and managing these mapping rules. Mapping rules from other projects can be used as a starting point for a new project.

DynaTag's mapping tools provide a number of features for handling different input formats and creating the desired output.

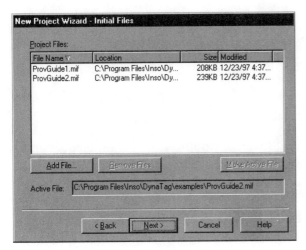

Figure 24-2   New project wizard.

24.2.2.1   Automatic mapping

The product automatically maps WP styles to XML element-types with the same names. This is a fast, easy way to get to well-formed XML when a specific DTD is not a requirement. Those with specific DTD requirements can choose their own element-type names and selectively map each input format to the desired type.

24.2.2.2   Variant detection

DynaTag detects not only WP styles, but also overrides of these styles, or *variants*. Variants can be mapped to unique element types or treated as equivalent to other instances of the WP style.

For example, an author may have used a standard body text style, but applied extra indentation to indicate a block quotation. The product can detect this override and allow the user to map this instance to a <BLOCK-QUOTE> element, while other body text maps to <PARA> elements.

In other instances, the variant formatting may be meaningless. The author may have decreased the space before a paragraph to fit text on the printed page, or inserted a page break to force it to the next page. *DynaTag* can be instructed to ignore such variants.

24.2.2.3   New-mapping helper

A wizard helps users map WP styles to XML element types by guiding the creation of each mapping rule.

24.2.2.4   Conditional mapping

Conditional mappings create different mapping rules for different "conditions" in the text. For example, an initial text pattern, such as the word "Warning" followed by a tab, can be used to map certain instances of the body text style to a <WARNING> element. Context (e.g., the preceding or following element type) and formatting properties can also be used for conditional mappings.

24.2.2.5   List wizard

This wizard, shown in Figure 24-3, helps users map list formatting conventions to element types. It can recognize different kinds of lists (ordered, unordered, term/definition), multiple list levels, and parts of lists (e.g., markers, paragraphs, continuation paragraphs). Different styles and levels of lists in the WP document may be identified and mapped using regular expression matching on the list markers (e.g., different types of bullets, sequence numbers and letters).

24.2.2.6   Tables

Tables are mapped automatically. However, if needed, tables may be divided into classes for special handling. For example, the table's width can be specified with attributes. Later, when the document is rendered in a browser, narrow tables can be formatted to display inline while wide tables are iconized for display in popup windows.

24.2.2.7   Character mapping

Styles that make format changes at the character level (e.g., emphasized text, book titles) can easily be mapped to proper, descriptive XML ele-

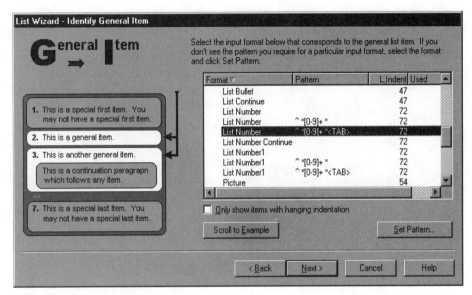

Figure 24-3   List wizard.

ments. In cases where authors simply used formatting overrides to create bold, italic, or underlined text, bulk character mapping can be used to create consistent XML markup for each different format.

For example, in Figure 24-4, bold text is mapped to an output object called EMPH.BOLD, which in turn generates an XML element with the start-tag <EMPH TYPE="BOLD".

24.2.2.8   Cross-references

Each word processor has a recommended way to create automatic cross references, typically printed as a reference to a page or a section title. If authors follow the recommendations of their word processor, *DynaTag* automatically converts the cross-references to hypertext links. In the resulting XML, tags and attributes identify the source and destination of the link.

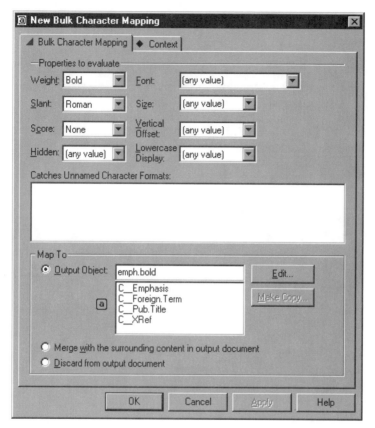

Figure 24-4   Bulk character mapping.

24.2.2.9   Searching

DynaTag provides fulltext searching for finding specific content that needs to be mapped.

24.2.2.10   Comments

All mappings can be annotated with comments for managing mapping tasks and for project documentation.

24.2.2.11   XML markup features

Users can view XML markup inside the user interface. They can also specify attributes, create entities, and use other markup options to enrich the XML output.

24.2.2.12   Capturing structure

XML elements that contain other elements are sometimes called (surprise!) *container elements*. The complete structure of containers and containees can nest to many levels. Computer scientists refer to such a structure as a *hierarchy*, or *tree structure*.

The element structure of an XML document is the basis for much powerful processing. The content of containers can be hidden, or displayed in popup windows in a browser. Containers for chapters and sections are the basis for automatically generating a hypertext table of contents and for selective, on-demand printing.

Most importantly, the concept of containment enables *structured searches*: highly efficient queries that narrow down searching to given elements for maximum precision in finding information.

For example, a boolean search for "chocolate and milk" inside any one <RECIPE> element provides much more precision than searching for the same words across an entire cookbook.

DynaTag's Container Wizard, shown in Figure 24-5, makes makes it easy to assign result element types to their proper level in the document structure. This panel of the Wizard shows that chapter, section, and subsection element types have been created, and illustrates their hierarchical relationship.

24.2.2.13   Reuse

Once a project is finished, its mapping rules can be re-used for similar documents. DynaTag's batch converter processes groups of WP documents that share the same rules. The only human intervention required is starting the batch script and checking the log file upon completion.

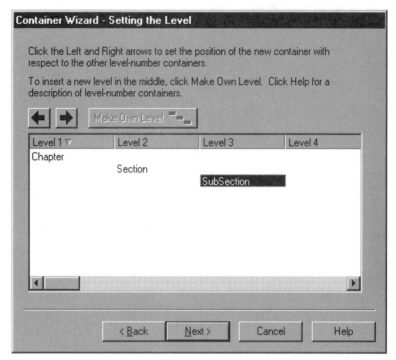

Figure 24-5   Container wizard.

24.3 | Preparing for electronic publishing

DynaTag also includes facilities to prepare a converted document for electronic distribution on CD-ROM and the World Wide Web, using Inso's suite of electronic publishing tools. Those facilities include a stylesheet editor with preview capability, graphics data format conversion to JPEG and TIFF, and a helper for developing contextual search forms. You can see the full suite in action in Chapter 19, "City Of Providence", on page 252.

XML Styler: Graphical XSL stylesheet editor

■ Visual, standards-based design

■ Actions, patterns, and flow objects

■ Free copy on CD-ROM

Chapter 25

Lord Chesterfield said that "style is the dress of thought". With *XML Styler* you can dress up your XML documents in stylesheets without having to weave the cloth yourself. This chapter is sponsored by ArborText, Inc., `http://www.arbortext.com`, and was prepared by Norman Walsh, `http://nwalsh.com/~ndw/`.

he *XML Styler* is a freeware graphical XSL stylesheet editor from ArborText, Inc. The product simplifies the creation and modification of stylesheets for XML documents. It is implemented as a *Java* application that is designed to run on any Java Virtual Machine (JVM). It has been tested on Microsoft's JVM for Windows and Sun's JVM for Solaris.

25.1 | Introduction to XSL

XSL stylesheets separate form from content so that authors can present media-independent XML information. XSL offers powerful features for generating and suppressing content, reordering content, and associating style information with elements in different contexts.

Although *XML Styler* hides most of the complexity of XSL from the stylesheet author, it is useful to have a general understanding of how XSL works. Broadly speaking, an XSL stylesheet consists of a collection of rules. Each rule associates a formatting behavior with an element type.

A rule has two parts: a pattern and an action. The pattern identifies the element types that the rule applies to; for example, all EMPH elements, or all PARA elements occurring within an ABSTRACT. The action defines how the selected elements will be formatted.

25.2 | Creating a stylesheet with *XML Styler*

Before looking at XML Styler and XSL in more detail, let's use XML Styler to create a stylesheet for a simple document type. We'll do this by formatting a particular XML document, `mydoc.xml` in Example 25-1.

Example 25-1. A simple XML document.

```
<?xml version='1.0'?>
<doc><title>A Document</title>
<para>This is a paragraph of text.</para>
<para>Paragraphs can contain <emph>emphasized</emph> text.</para>
</doc>
```

Start *XML Styler* by running `xmlstyler` at the DOS or UNIX shell prompt or by double clicking on the *XML Styler* icon on your desktop. You can get *XML Styler* from the CD that accompanies this book.

XML Styler will start, as shown in Figure 25-1.

Choose "Create a new style sheet" and click "OK". This will start the new-stylesheet wizard.

In order to simplify the creation of a new stylesheet, XML Styler can load the element type names used in your documents from either a plain-text file or an XML document. In this case, we'll get them from `mydoc.xml`, see Figure 25-2.

The next panel in the-new stylesheet wizard lets you set the default font for your documents. Click "Next" to accept the defaults listed.

One of the most useful features in *XML Styler* is the ability to link directly to a test document from within the editor. On the next panel, shown in Figure 25-3, select the preview option and point to the XML document that you would like to preview while editing your stylesheet.

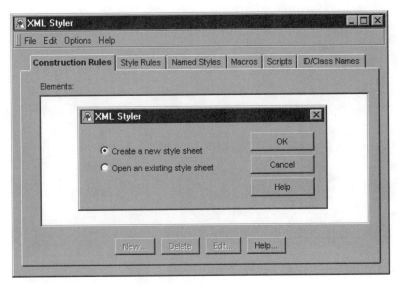

Figure 25-1 Starting *XML Styler.*

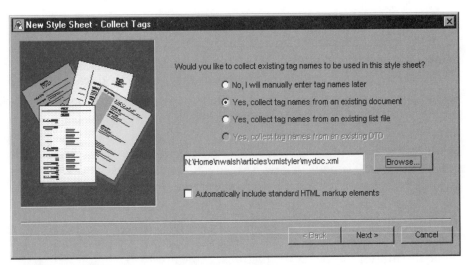

Figure 25-2 Collecting element-type names.

In order to link the stylesheet to the document instance, *XML Styler* has to build a little HTML "glue document". On the next panel of the wizard,

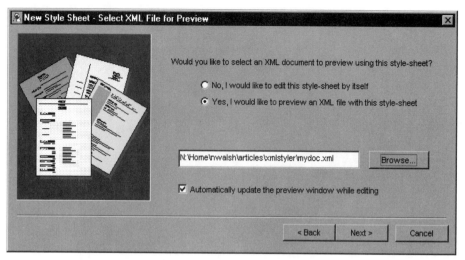

Figure 25-3   Select an XML document for preview.

you can choose the name of the glue document. The default is almost always a good choice.

When the wizard finishes, *XML Styler* will have default rules for all the element types in the document and the browser will display your test document using these default rules. See Figure 25-4.

The default rules are not very useful for presenting this document. Let's add a rule for para. Begin by selecting the para element type in XML Styler and clicking "New...". The dialog box shown in Figure 25-5 will be presented.

Click "Next" to proceed with creating a new rule for the para element type. Each para element in our XML document must be associated with some HTML element type. The obvious choice in this case is P; enter P in the dialog box shown in Figure 25-6 and click "Finish" to proceed.

The resulting document is much improved, see Figure 25-7.

Adding additional rules to associate title elements with H1, and emph elements with EM completes the picture. See Figure 25-8.

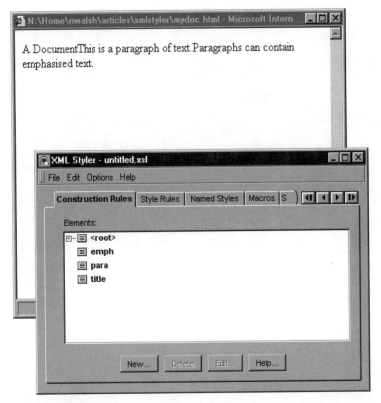

Figure 25-4   Preview using default rules.

25.3 | XSL patterns

In the simple document described above, every element type was used in a unique context. In more complex documents, this is not likely to be the case. Consider the recipe fragment shown in Example 25-2.

Here we see the element type name used in three different contexts, as:

- The recipe name
- The name of a person, and
- The name of a book.

It is likely that each of these will be formatted in a different way.

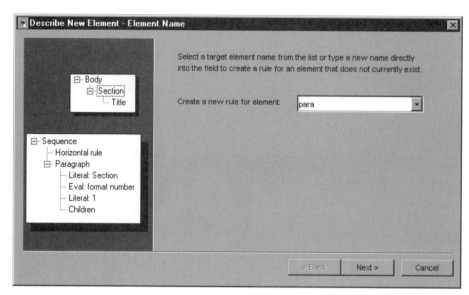

Figure 25-5   Element-type name dialog box.

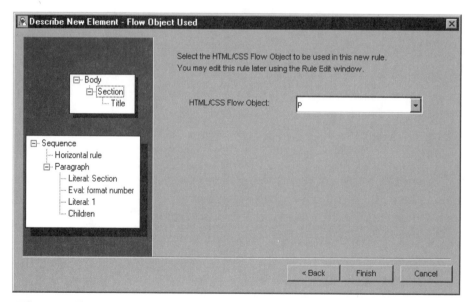

Figure 25-6   Flow object selection dialog box.

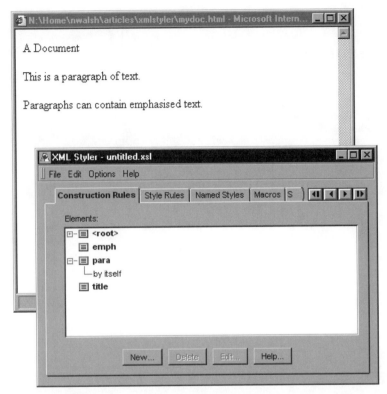

Figure 25-7 Preview using the new rule for para elements.

XSL patterns can identify element types in different contexts in two ways: with attribute tests, and by position.

Figure 25-9 shows the rule that matches only the recipe name.

As you can see, the structure of the pattern on the left-hand side is roughly analogous to the structure of the document. In this case, we see that the rule applies only to name elements within (i.e., that are children of) recipe elements. The dot next to name indicates that it is the element type that is the target of this rule.

A slightly more complex pattern is required to format book names properly. In this case, we want to make the contents of name elements italic if they occur inside of note elements that have a status attribute who's value is "credit". See Figure 25-10.

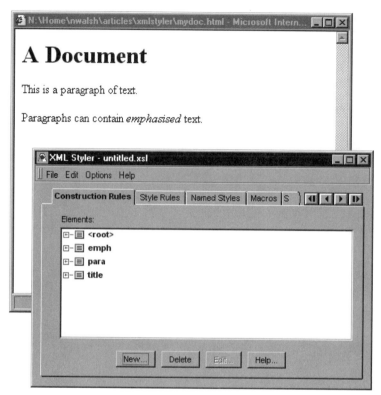

Figure 25-8 Preview using our rules.

Example 25-2. A fragment of a recipe in XML.

```
<recipe>
<name>Corned Beef and Cabbage</name>
<description>A classic New England boiled dinner. This is a
delectable dinner if composed only of beef, onions, and
cabbage. But for authenticity, additional vegetables
are included.</description>
<note>This dish is a Saint Patrick's Day favorite.</note>
<note status="credit">This recipe comes from
<name>The Joy of Cooking</name> by Rombauer and Becker.</note>
<note status="personal"><name>Grandma Luhmen</name> likes it
better without the <ingredient>beets</ingredient>.</note>
<ingredient-list yields="...">
...
</recipe>
```

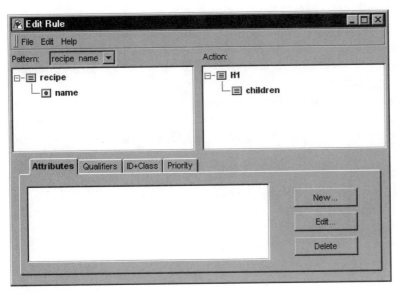

Figure 25-9   The rule for recipe names.

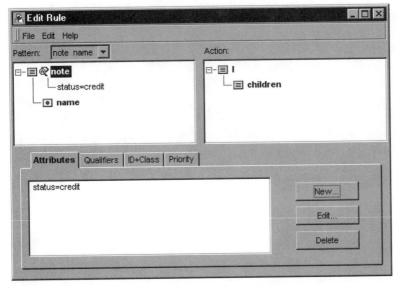

Figure 25-10   The rule for book names.

25.4 | XSL actions

The action part of an XSL rule describes how to format the element type selected by the pattern. XSL describes two sets of formatting objects, "HTML/CSS flow objects" and "DSSSL flow objects".

In addition to the flow objects, there are several "processing elements" that control the behavior of the XSL processor. In these examples, you've already seen the children processing element. This element tells the processor to recursively format the children of the current element (by finding the appropriate rule for each child), and insert the formatted results of that process at the location where *children* occurs.

Other examples of processing elements are *select-elements*, which provides a mechanism for reordering the content, and *eval*, which allows the stylesheet to insert the result of evaluating an expression (calculating the child number of a list item element, for example) into the output.

25.4.1 *HTML/CSS flow objects*

The HTML/CSS flow objects are really nothing more than the HTML element types that you want to use in your output. *Internet Explorer 4.0* and the Microsoft XSL processor both understand the HTML/CSS flow objects.

When you are using XSL to generate HTML from your XML documents, you can use the CSS properties as attributes of the HTML element types. The XSL processor will automatically translate them into the appropriate CSS style attributes. For example, the action shown in Figure 25-11 will format paragraphs in an abstract using the HTML P element type with smaller, italic text.

XML Styler provides simple "tab pages" for easy access the properties of each element type.

25.4.2 *DSSSL flow objects*

The DSSSL flow objects are an abstract representation of formatted output. Each DSSSL flow object has a set of properties that control the details of the formatting for that object. The complete catalog of flow objects and their properties will have well-defined semantics in the final XSL standard.

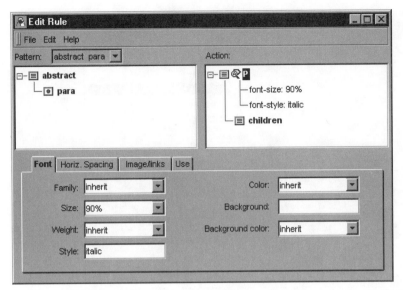

Figure 25-11 The action for paragraphs in abstracts, using HTML.

The XSL processor builds a tree of flow objects and then a rendering engine processes the flow objects and builds the output (on the appropriate media: online, print, aural, etc.). At the time of this writing, Henry Thompson's xslj processor, which works in conjunction with James Clark's Jade engine, offers the only way to process XSL stylesheets that use DSSSL flow objects. Both of these tools are available on the CD-ROM that accompanies this book.

Figure 25-12 shows the same rule for formatting paragraphs within an abstract using DSSSL flow objects.

As in the HTML/CSS case, *XML Styler* has tab pages for each of the DSSSL flow objects.

25.5 | Conclusion

In this chapter, we've seen a brief overview of some of the features of XML Styler and demonstrated how it can be used to quickly and easily create stylesheets without having to learn the syntactic details of XSL. By creating stylesheets for your XML document instances, you can begin to see how

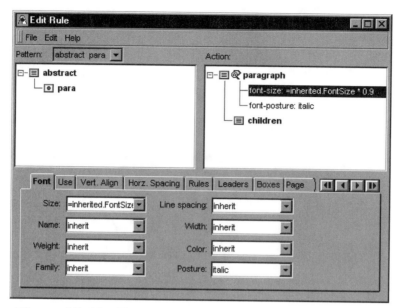

Figure 25-12   The action for paragraphs in abstracts, using DSSSL.

XML plus XSL will allow you to deliver your information the way you want it displayed.

You can find more about XSL in Chapter 35, "Extensible Style Language (XSL)", on page 516.

Astoria: Flexible content management

Document management is about managing documents as a whole, regardless of what is inside them. *Content* management, on the other hand, gets deep down inside and so is far more powerful. This perspective on content management focuses on the business problems it can solve. It is sponsored by Chrystal Software, a Xerox New Enterprise company, `http://www.chrystal.com`, and was prepared by Sean Baird, Robin Gellerman, and Kari Johnson.

Technical publications are critical in today's corporation. Behind these documents are the writers, artists, and editors who develop and maintain the massive amounts of documentation that keep a company running. Now, both publication managers and corporate directors are looking for better ways to leverage this wealth of data for higher returns throughout the enterprise.

Many enterprises have found leverage in managing document content as *components*, rather than as entire publications. This practice is called *content management*, in contrast to *document management*. Middle-tier Web applications, in particular, benefit from the abilty to assemble components with other data for delivery to the client.

26.1 | Components are everywhere

From new cars to software, components are the way we make things today.

In manufacturing industries as much as 80% of products now consist of components drawn from a company's part library or purchased from suppliers. Product designers routinely tap into internal databases and online parts warehouse services in the course of drafting and specifying new models.

In software, most of the new code being written is as objects, self-contained bundles of information and operations with the ability to send and receive messages in standard ways. Programs can be created by assembling a bunch of these object components and making them exchange information and services with each other.

26.1.1 *Components in publishing*

And now components are becoming the trend in publishing as well. Why? Because in publishing, as in other endeavors, components simplify complexity and increase flexibility for adapting to change. Consider these general advantages of components and how they come into play in a content management publishing environment.

26.1.1.1   System simplification

Components make it possible to break down complex systems into pieces that are easier to understand and work with. For publishing groups this means that teams of writers and editors can work on components for the same document simultaneously. Users can more easily locate specific information since components can be explicitly searched for.

26.1.1.2   Easier revision

When something needs to be revised or customized, changes can be made to just the component(s) affected, without having to redesign the whole document. If a single paragraph in a document needs to be revised, the author can check out just that paragraph from the content management system rather than the whole document. Or, if it's important to see the change in context, the author can check out the section the paragraph appears in. After editing, when the section is checked back in, versioning information is applied only to the paragraph that has changed.

26.1.1.3 Efficient authoring

Studies show that at least 30% of the content created by technical publishing groups is reusable – or would be, if people could find the information. Typically, it's buried in documents, scattered here and there in file systems on various desktop systems and servers. Content management eliminates the need to redo work by providing a universal repository for managing published and in-progress documents. The ability to unlock content from structured documents so that individual components of information can be independently accessed, tracked, and versioned enables writers and editors to immediately focus on exactly what they're looking for.

26.1.1.4 Less routine editing

A huge amount of the editing process involves checking documents for consistency and correcting them for corporate style. Content management minimizes editing time and tedium by enabling editors to maintain glossaries as collections of components. This information can be added to or revised rapidly, every day if necessary, with the new material instantly available to all users.

26.1.1.5 Fast, easy customization

Component-level management means that documents can be customized by changing only what is unique about them. This approach makes it possible to rapidly provide markets and customers with tailored information.

26.1.1.6 Universal updates

Each information component exists in the repository as a single object. When authors want to reuse a component, instead of copying it, they simply create a pointer to the object. This approach eliminates the redundant work of having to try to find all places where the information appears and update them independently. Instead authors can revise the component in the repository once, and it will be automatically updated in all documents that contain it.

26.1.1.7   Streamlined translations

Translators typically work with a moving target, a source document that continues to change while translation is going on. Translated versions then have to be returned to translators for a laborious manual process of identifying, changing, and checking new material. Content management can speed this process by providing translators with only those document components that are new, along with information about what has changed and exactly where the revisions should be inserted in the document.

26.1.1.8   Flexible distribution

Content management makes it easy to repurpose content for different media. Users can assign custom attributes to a particular component. For example, an attribute of an element could tell the software whether or not the element should be included when exporting a document for the Web, as opposed to printing it. Users can automate document assembly, including adjustments for target media.

26.1.2   *XML makes components*

XML brings intelligence to data. It breaks up the information into smaller information components. The smaller and more specific the component is, the more addressable and reusable it is.

For example, the document in Figure 26-1 uses descriptive element type names to identify the components and structure of the document. A component is a piece of information that can be used independently, such as a paragraph, chapter, instructional procedure, warning note, part number, order quantity, graphic, side-bar story, video clip, or one of an infinite variety of additional information types.

When managed by a content management system (Figure 26-2), these pieces can be controlled, revised, reused, and assembled into new documents.

Another way XML adds value to information is through attributes, or "metadata" (Figure 26-3). By adding "information about information", users can further describe the information for repurposing. A user assigns attributes to a particular component, for example to specify whether or not

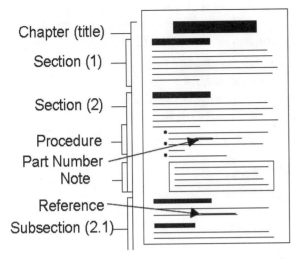

Figure 26-1   Document components described with XML.

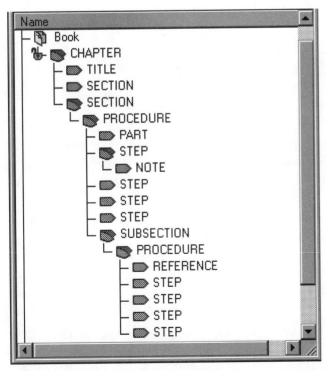

Figure 26-2   Hierarchical structure shown in content management system.

to include it when publishing the document for the Web, as opposed to printing it. When the document is published, the content management system will make the proper adjustments for the target medium.

Metadata can also be used to identify the intended audience for specific components. In this case, a "beginner" requires more information than an "expert". The content management system will assemble a document and publish the information that matches these criteria.

```
<step audience="beginner">Keep the
engine running and park car
on level ground.</step>


<step audience="expert">Keep the
engine running.</step>
```

Figure 26-3   Metadata can identify the intended audience.

26.1.3 *Applications for content reuse*

Reuse, the most compelling feature of content management, allows content within any document to be used elsewhere in the repository. Reuse means writing the information once and linking to it from other documents. This can be very useful when multiple documents contain standard "boilerplate" information. This repurposing of information saves users countless hours of rework and duplication of effort.

Applications for information reuse are everywhere. Reuse can be as simple as finding a description from one document and linking it into a new document. Common content creates an "information pool" of reusable pieces available to individuals or groups inside the company Figure 26-4. Linked reuse, instead of copying, makes updates more efficient and reduces redundant storage.

Organizations that maintain common glossaries of business terms can benefit from reuse. When glossary information stored in a content management system changes, the information is revised only one time. All of the documents containing that information are automatically updated.

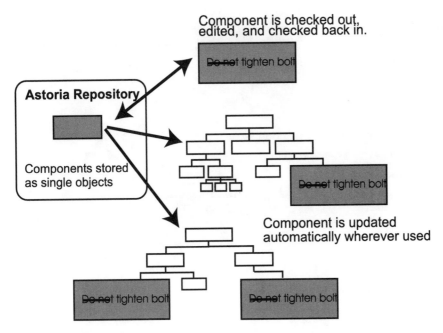

Figure 26-4   Component reuse.

Because warnings and cautions usually require careful wording, organizations strive for uniformity across all documents. Manually locating and changing dozens of these elements in hundreds of contexts can consume countless hours. Content management solves that problem by allowing XML documents to reuse content across documents.

For global business processes, linked reuse helps organizations get to market faster around the world. By identifying the newly revised information in a repair manual, only the new information will be translated into the target languages saving valuable time and money.

26.2 | A content management implementation

To better understand what content management systems provide, it is helpful to look at an actual product in action.

Chrystal Software's Astoria, like other component-based *content* management systems, attempts to provide value beyond that of generalized *document* management systems. It does so by managing the content of the document as a set of components (see Figure 26-5).

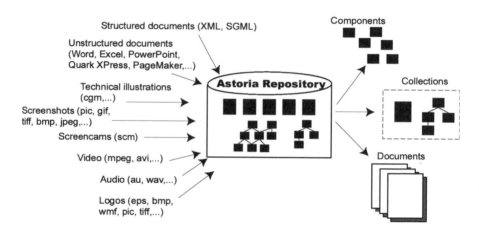

Figure 26-5   The *Astoria* repository.

Some of the product's "off-the-shelf" capabilities are described in the following sections. Customization for specialized requirements is possible through its software development kit, a public C++ application programming Interface.

26.2.1   *Revision tracking*

Astoria automatically collects revision information at each check-in, indicating time, date, author, revision number, and an optional comment. Past versions are available for republishing or to provide an audit trail (see Figure 26-6).

For XML documents, revision history is detected and maintained at the component level, not just at the document level. A sophisticated differencing engine is used to apply revision information to only the content that changes during an editing session.

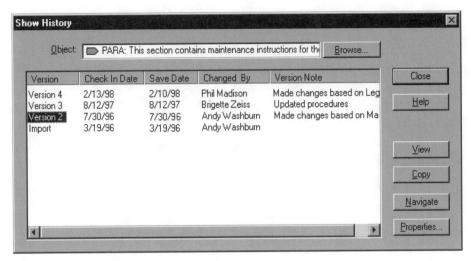

Figure 26-6   Revision history of a paragraph.

At important milestones such as release dates and the beginning of review cycles, users can formalize document versions into "editions". The document state can then be recreated for that point in time by opening the appropriate edition.

26.2.2 *Search*

Astoria's search options let users locate documents created in more than 50 common applications. Advanced indexing enhances search by looking for various forms of the word (e.g., plural, tenses, root). Matching documents can be selected for viewing and editing.

By applying "custom attributes" to documents, users add "information about information." Custom attributes can automatically be created from XML metadata. In addition to custom attributes, document structure, data content, and version information can be used in queries (see Figure 26-7).

Another form of search, "where-used queries", locates content that is reused in multiple XML documents. Users can determine whether changes to that content are appropriate in all contexts before committing to the change.

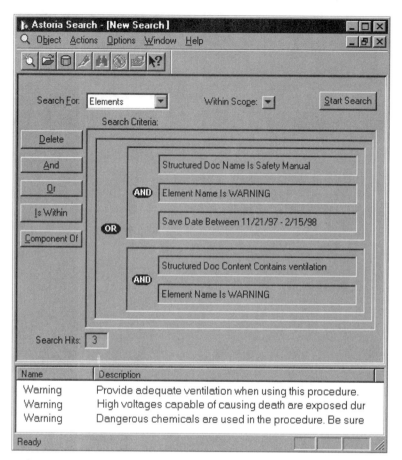

Figure 26-7   Search results refined with XML structure and metadata.

26.2.3 *Dynamic document assembly*

One of the compelling benefits of managing documents at the component level is that users can effectively create an information pool from which to draw. Figure 26-8 shows how users can search for information meeting unique criteria, organize it as they wish, and dynamically create a new deliverable.

For example, a financial portfolio manager could create a series of articles and recommendations which could then be organized dynamically into unique documents based on the profile of each investor.

Analysis   *The management and production of information as components is a powerful idea. Not suitable for a novel, perhaps, but eminently appropriate for the mission-critical data that is part-and-parcel of creating and marketing today's complex products — on the Web and elsewhere.*

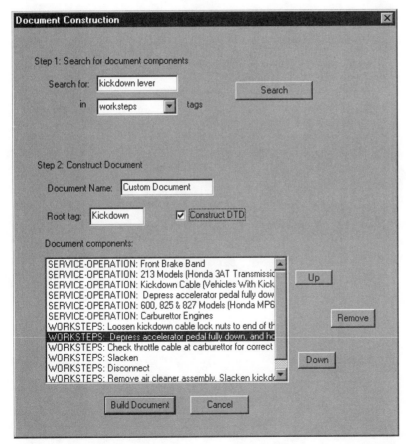

Figure 26-8   Assembling new documents by searching for relevant components.

POET Content Management Suite

■ Information life cycle

■ Object data base

■ Content management system components

Thanks to the Web, the life cycle of information
is shortening even as the volume of information
delivered is growing dramatically. POET Software
Corporation, http://www.poet.com, the sponsors
of this chapter, believe that content management is
the key to meeting this challenge, and that object
database technology is the key to content
management.

Information in general, and written content in particular, has a
life cycle. Managing it has always been a challenge, and the challenge is increasing.

27.1 | Managing the information life cycle

The information content life cycle varies widely, depending on the type of
information being presented. For example, a newspaper might be published
on a daily basis. The information it contains is extremely time sensitive in
the first iteration of its life cycle as breaking news.

The content of a newspaper becomes important again as it is archived for
historical purposes and placed in knowledge bases for research purposes. In
a newspaper's second cycle, the presentation of information moves from
paper-based delivery to electronic delivery. The information may be
indexed and cross-referenced as an aid to research that never existed in its

paper-based form. The actual content of the newspaper is not changed, but the information might be reused in a condensed or edited future reprint.

A medical dictionary has yet another life cycle. Its information needs to be timely, but is not as time-sensitive as a newspaper. Medical terms change, but traditionally this type of publication has a fairly long life cycle. Many terms need to change before a reader feels the need to reinvest in a newer edition of the dictionary. A typical print life cycle for such a dictionary can be as long as four years. It is very expensive to reprint and manage such a large body of information.

27.1.1   *Changes to the information life cycle*

Information life cycles change over time as new media and technologies change the business model of information delivery. The magazine industry is a good example of how technology can affect the delivery and creation of information.

Magazines like *Time* and *Newsweek* were revolutionary in the way they created an entirely new format for disseminating the news. Technology helped make it possible to print magazines on a weekly basis. The proliferation of special interest magazines such as *Men's Health*, and *Outside Magazine* are a direct result of the capabilities of desktop publishing and more efficient national distribution channels.

27.1.2   *The World Wide Web has changed the rules*

Very few changes in the history of information delivery have been as profound as the creation and rise of the World Wide Web. The Web has, in a very short period of time, forced us to radically rethink the information life cycle.

Essentially, there are now two different – yet complementary – life cycles, one for print delivery and one for electronic. The changes that the Web has spawned go beyond just life cycle management. Information is no longer presented in a single format: e.g. newspaper, magazine, manual, dictionary, encyclopedia.

Information needs to be able to change its presentation depending on context. Is the information being presented in an electronic or print medium? Is the information supplemental or being cross-referenced from some other body of information?

For example: In our medical dictionary scenario, medical definitions might be available on-line to insurance claims adjusters who need to look up terms. Or, it might be available in the context of other medical publications like a drug guide.

The print life cycle for a medical dictionary might never be less than 4 years, but the life cycle of the same publication on the World Wide Web or CD-ROM might be far shorter. Web customers would most likely subscribe to this information and would want the most up-to-date information at all times. Most likely the same publication will have more than one distribution medium and a complex life cycle to manage.

Managing today's information requires more flexibility than traditional document management systems can provide. XML provides the appropriate notation for storing and editing information over its entire life cycle. What is needed are new tools and paradigms for managing and enabling XML content.

27.1.3 *Object-oriented components*

The new paradigm for content management with XML is "components". Document components are logical, hierarchical divisions of a document. Through parsing, XML documents are automatically broken down into a component object structure. In a content management system, component objects can be edited, versioned, and shared independently of the document that contains them.

Why are document components more powerful than monolithic documents? By breaking a document down into components, pieces of a single document can be managed as if they were objects. This allows authors to work collaboratively on pieces of a large document while managing the document life cycle through version control.

Document components can be nested inside one another according to the natural structure of the document itself. By reading the document type definition (DTD), a content management system has the necessary information needed to create document components according to user-defined parameters.

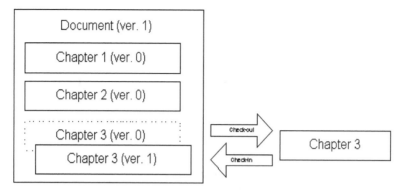

Figure 27-1   Nested document components.

As seen in Figure 27-1, a "document" component can contain "chapter" components. (These components correspond to elements in the XML document.)

A checkout can occur at any level in the hierarchy. Multiple clients can check out different components in the same large document for collaborative authoring.

The component structure of a document looks very much like a table of contents would. Chapters might contains sections and subsections, tables and figures.

Components present the user with a logical view of the document as opposed to a storage-based view of a document. It is not necessary to care how the document is actually stored, whether it be in files or in a database. The most important view of a document is one that reflects the semantic structure of the document itself. Components allow us access to the world of XML structured content in a way never before possible.

27.2 | The *POET Content Management Suite*

One approach to managing document life cycles with content management is the *POET Content Management Suite* (POET CMS).

27.2.1   POET CMS components

The architecture and components of *POET CMS* are shown in Figure 27-2.

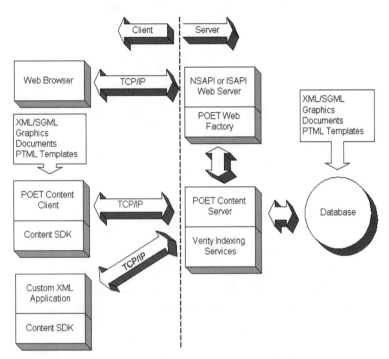

Figure 27-2   *POET Content Management Suite.*

27.2.1.1   POET Content Server

The *POET Content Server* provides the full functionality of the *POET Object Server* database product. However, it is optimized for content access and includes a suite of tools for administering the database.

The product is packaged with a content-enabled version of the *POET Web Factory* server plug-in. It uses server-side templates to dynamically assemble and deliver the latest content to the Web or the corporate intranet. It can deliver HTML, XML, other documents, and graphics, directly from a *POET* database.

27.2.1.2   POET Content Client

The *POET Content Client* provides an immediately deployable solution to managing content in an editorial or delivery environment. The product is a Win95/NT end-user application that provides project management, version control, document component exploration, viewing, querying and component sharing functionality.

27.2.1.3   POET Content SDK

The *POET Content SDK* is a development environment with several application programming interfaces (API).

The *High-level API* provides an interface for performing common tasks such as importing and validating documents, checking components in and out, managing folders and projects, pressing editions and delivering content.

The *Navigation API* provides object-oriented abstractions for traversing, accessing, and querying XML elements, attributes, and components, as well as common graphic and non-XML document files.

The *ActiveX API* provides ready-made tree, list and query controls for embedding in an application, either without programming, by scripting with VBScript and JavaScript, or by interfacing with C++ or Java.

27.2.2   *The POET CMS Architecture*

The *POET Content Management Suite* architecture allows different types of client to access the database at one time. Editors can use the *Content Client* interface while reviewers are viewing the latest draft in Web browsers. Custom applications can run at the same time. A single server can access many different databases at once, and a single client can access many different servers.

27.2.3 *Using POET CMS*

27.2.3.1   Server-side content management

Content management requires control. A database server needs to provide control over concurrent access by multiple clients, management of transactions, user rights, and multi-threaded queries.

Moreover, a content server must be able to address the challenges of structured documents effectively. Fine-grained control of locking and versioning is necessary.

It is tight control of the database that enables flexibility for users.

For example, the *POET Content Server* can operate in editorial and delivery environments concurrently. Users can edit and manage versions on the same system and database that is being used for delivery to the Web or the corporate intranet. Approved editions can be delivered at the same time that new content and versions of the documents are being created.

Moreover, access can be controlled so that different people can access different versions. Web users on the public Internet might only get formally released material, while intranet users might see the most recent version of the information.

27.2.3.2   Client-side editing and viewing

The *POET Content Client* provides a familiar explorer-style interface for managing document components. Documents and components are stored as objects that can be organized into folders, dragged and dropped between projects, checked in and out, viewed, edited, and queried. The product provides the security and power of a traditional version control system with the added power of hierarchical component versioning.

Let's take a closer look at a few of its functions.

Version control

In Figure 27-3 the main window shows the database for a very large document, *Taber's Cyclopedic Medical Dictionary*. In the left-hand window pane is an explorer-style view of the database. Folders and publications can be viewed just as if they were on the file system.

In the case of XML documents, like this one, the document itself is not the smallest unit that can be browsed. Clicking on a document will reveal a new world of document components. This particular document is broken up into the user-defined component levels "MAINENTRY" and "SUBEN-TRY", which are elements of the dictionary.

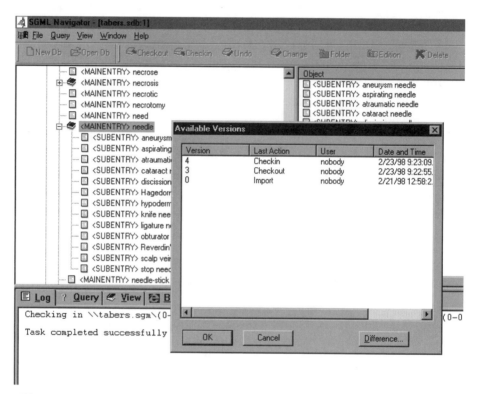

Figure 27-3   Component database with version selection dialog.

Right-clicking on the selected component, in this case the MAINEN-TRY "needle", pops up a menu from which various actions can be taken (Figure 27-4). Clicking on "Change Version" brings up the "Available Versions" dialog that we saw in Figure 27-3, from which a specific version of the component can be selected. Versions are listed along with the last action performed on them and the user who performed the action.

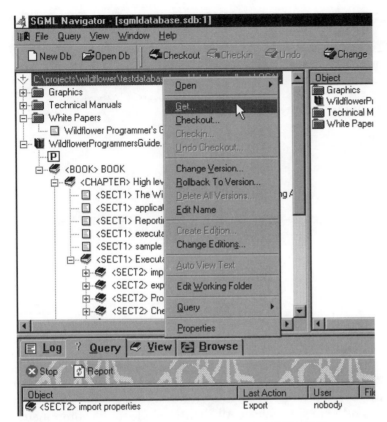

Figure 27-4   Right-click action menu in *POET CMS*.

Checking out a component

The right-click menu offers other actions as well, including the possibility of checking-out the component in order to edit it. In Figure 27-5, the MAINENTRY "neck" in the medical dictionary has been checked out. It and its subcomponents appear in red to indicate that they are checked out and cannot be modified by another user until they are checked back in. check out. All other components are still available for modification by other users.

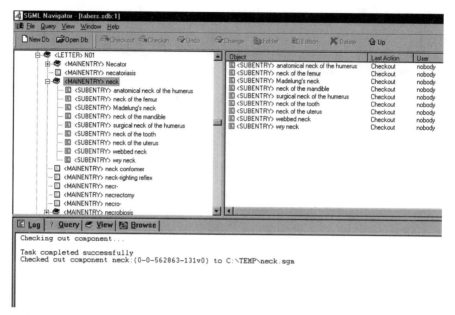

Figure 27-5   Checked-out components.

Sharing a component

A component can be shared by holding down the CTRL-SHIFT keys and dragging it into another project folder. All changes made to the component will be reflected in both projects.

In Figure 27-6 the component "Executable unit properties" is being shared with the "Technical Manuals" folder, as indicated by the curved arrow in the cursor.

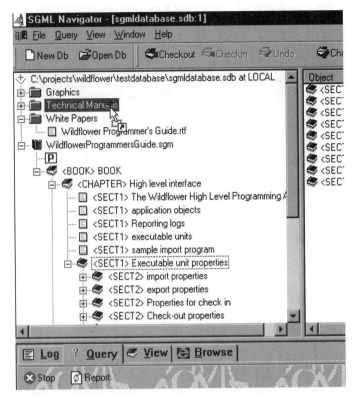

Figure 27-6   Sharing a component.

Viewing a document

An object, such as an XML (or full SGML) component, graphic object, or word processing document, can be viewed by dragging it onto the browser toolbar. Depending on the object type, the browser will either view it directly or launch an external program to view it.

In Figure 27-7 we see the *Softquad Panorama* viewer in the bottom window, viewing the component "microscope".

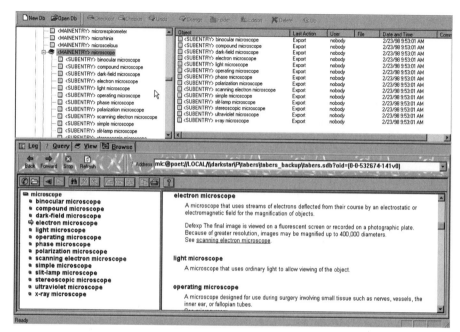

Figure 27-7 Viewing a component.

Full-text search

POET CMS supports several forms of searching. Figure 27-8 illustrates the results of a full text search for the word "migraine". The "Query" tab of the main window lists all of the components that contain the word.

The search was conducted by means of a dialog box, in which the search string was entered. The dialog offers the option of restricting the search to the current version of components that contain the word, or returning all versions that contain it.

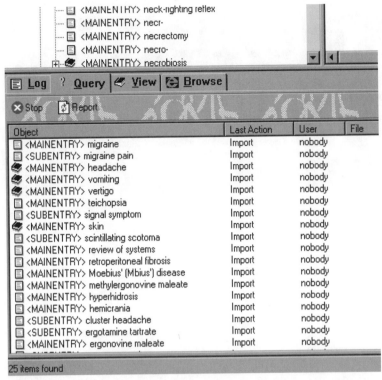

Figure 27-8   Result of querying for components containing "migraine".

The query results can be can be used as a basis for checkout, viewing, and editing by right-clicking on a component as if it were listed in the main pane of the window.

Analysis   *The decreasing life cycles of information brought about by the World Wide Web make a persuasive argument for XML and content management. It is true that content management was originally conceived for large-scale technical publishing. However, it appears likely to play a significant role in middle-tier Web applications as well, particularly as the value of maintaining persistent metadata on the middle tier becomes better appreciated.*

HoTMetaL Application Server

■ Middle-tier server tool

■ Familiar HTML base

■ WYSIWYG development environment

■ Free trial version on CD-ROM

The "leading edge" of the Web today is actually in the middle. That is, on the middle tier, where servers gather data in any format from any source location and serve them up in XML. The friendly folks at SoftQuad Inc., `http://www.sq.com`, believe that this highly technical domain could be a lot friendlier, and have sponsored this chapter to explain how.

T he landscape of the Web is rapidly changing. No longer are static Web pages enough to give an organization the business edge it requires in today's highly competitive world. No matter how well designed and link-intensive your Web page is, it won't make the grade unless it can provide the interactive services that the new generation of "Nintendo" trained, computer-savvy, business-oriented Web users now demand.

Remaining competitive on the Web can be overwhelming for organizations that have struggled just to create today's static Web pages. How can they cope with emerging requirements to provide a "personal experience" on their Web site? This is especially difficult if the organization lacks the technical resources it takes to add interactivity to their site.

28.1 | Dynamic descriptive markup

The solution lies with a new generation of XML-based software for the middle tier that relies on descriptive markup, rather than procedural scripts written in JavaScript, VBscript or C++. Products like SoftQuad's HoT-MetaL Application Server (*HoTMetaL APPS*) seek to introduce new functionality painlessly by leveraging existing user expertise in HTML.

With *HoTMetaL APPS*, for example, Web development is done directly in XML markup, using an extended set of HTML tags. Because the source markup is XML, the product can provide a "what-you-see-is-what-you-get" (WYSIWYG) view of the page as well as the tagged view. (Figure 28-1) Developers new to dynamic Web pages may find it easier to adapt to this familiar paradigm than to deal with scripting code.

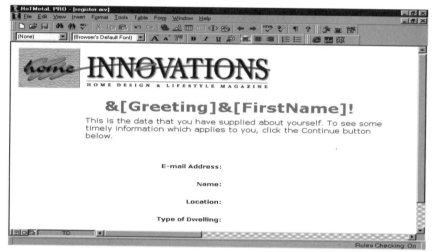

Figure 28-1   WYSIWYG view of a dynamic Web page in *HoTMetaL APPS*.

28.2 | How *HoTMetaL APPS* works

The product has two components. The first is the development interface. The second is the application server itself, which runs on several UNIX platforms as well as IIS, Windows NT, and Apache.

In order to allow the user to work in the familiar HTML Web page development paradigm, the development interface is based on the vendor's HoTMetaL Pro HTML editor, with additional features known as the *Power Pack*. The latter includes support for special "MV" tags (described below), plus documentation and sample applications.

Also included is the *HoTMetaL Personal Server*, which runs under *Windows 95* or *Windows NT. HoTMetaL Personal Server* is a completely self-contained environment that can be used for staging applications before they go to the Web.

A free trial version of *HoTMetaL APPS* can be found on the CD-ROM accompanying this book. It works with existing Web browsers and, for those who have scripting language skills, JavaScript and DHTML can be integrated into its Web pages as well.

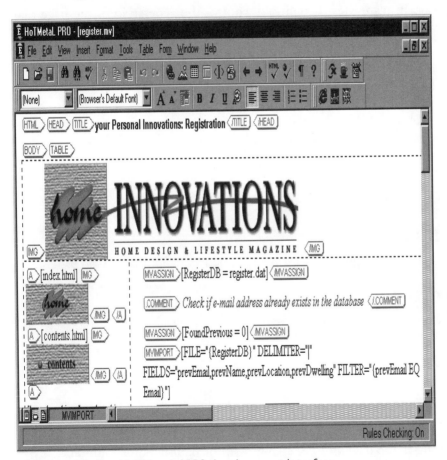

Figure 28-2   *HoTMetaL APPS* development interface.

28.2.1 *Middle-tier server tags*

The major difference between an HTML editor and the *HoTMetaL APPS* development interface (Figure 28-2) is support for a set of special "Middle-tier serVer", or "MV" tags. Normally, XML and HTML tags such as "H1" and "TABLE" identify elements of those types and are rendered by the client browser.

MV tags, however, though resembling normal tags in syntax and method of use, are interpreted by *HoTMetaL APPS* and are never seen by the browser. Instead, they dynamically control the generation of the page that the browser eventually receives.

28.2.1.1   Data access tags

One group of MV tags enables the dynamic inclusion of data from databases and other sources. They include:

MVOPEN

Opens a specified data source.

MVINPUT

Dynamically pulls data from a specified source into the Web page.

MVCLOSE

Closes a specified data source.

28.2.1.2   Conditional logic tags

This set of MV tags enables the Web site developer to perform conditional processing. That is, the generated browser page can depend on conditions occuring in the data or other changing information. Some examples are:

MVIF

Causes following text to be processed if a specified statement is true.

MVELSE

Causes alternative text to be processed when the MVIF statement is false.

Note that the text that is processed because of the above tags can include both MV tags to be processed on the server and ordinary text to be included in the generated page.

28.2.2 *Guided construction of dynamic pages*

When creating dynamic Web pages with a procedural scripting language, the developer must know the language commands and parameters and where they can be used. In contrast, markup-based development is governed by an XML document type definition that allows entry of tags only where appropriate.

In *HoTMetaL APPS*, for example, MV tags are entered in the Web page via the "add markup" pull-down menu in the same manner as normal tags can be entered. The available tag selection dynamically changes based on document context, so adding tags in the right spot is automatic.

Moreover, since the programming parameters for MV tags are specified as attributes, the *HoTMetaL APPS Attribute Inspector* can guide the developer in their correct use. For example, in Figure 28-3, the *Attribute Inspector* indicates required parameters in boldface.

Figure 28-3   The *Attribute Inspector*

28.3 | Functionality can be friendly

The business requirement to engage the customer in the Web site experience is growing each day. No longer is it enough simply to present informa-

Figure 28-4   Dynamic XML-based Web Pages

tion to those who visit your site. You must include them in the business process (Figure 28-4).

XML is the enabling technology that will make such interaction pervasive. And there is no need for it to be limited to those with large budgets or huge technical staffs. Products like HoTMetaL Application Server offer the non-programmer the potential to build highly interactive Web sites in a tag-based environment, where today's Webmasters are already comfortable and proficient.

Junglee Virtual DBMS

- Middle-tier server tool
- Virtual database technology
- Wrappers and extractors

29

One view of the middle tier is that it should appear to be a single relational database, one whose data can be delivered by packaging it as XML documents. This chapter is sponsored by Junglee Corporation, `http://www.junglee.com`, and was prepared by Anand Rajaraman, STS Prasad, and Debra Knodel.

With the explosive growth of the Internet, corporate intranets, and the World Wide Web, a vast resource of data is now available. This data is scattered across Web sites, file systems, database systems and legacy applications. Writing applications to query and combine data from this wide variety of sources is a complex and difficult process.

29.1 | Why virtual database technology?

All of the middle-tier approaches described in this book can integrate data from multiple sources and deliver it to the client in the form of XML documents. Some users, however, may find a compelling logic in going even further, as Junglee Corporation has.

Their *Virtual Database Management System* (VDBMS) is designed to make the World Wide Web and other external data sources behave as a single relational database – as part of your enterprise or Web application infrastructure. The relational database view makes it possible to execute powerful queries using the industry-standard *Structured Query Language* (SQL), and results can be presented as relational tables or XML documents, as required by the application.

The VDBMS leverages the power of XML to deliver results in a form that can be manipulated by the browser without round trips to the Web server. For example, XML allows browser-side sorting and filtering of data, and presentation of the data to suit specific user preferences based on style sheets. Figure 29-1 illustrates the core functionality of the VDBMS.

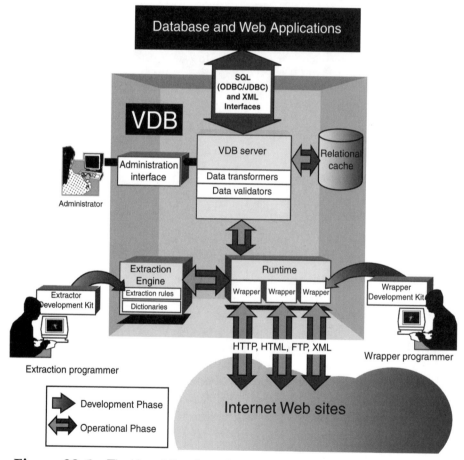

Figure 29-1   The *Virtual Database Management System* (VDBMS).

29.2 | How the VDBMS works

The *Virtual Database Management System* is an integrated Java-based system that enables you to develop and operate a "virtual database", a relational view over large collections of Web sites and other data sources. Database and Internet applications can access a virtual database using SQL, through ODBC and JDBC interfaces.

The VDBMS provides a comprehensive set of tools for transforming the Internet into a database:

- Wrapper Development Kit (WDK)
- Extractor Development Kit (EDK)
- VDB Server and Data Quality Kit
- Administration Interface

29.2.1 *Wrapper Development Kit (WDK)*

Wrappers are Java programs designed to extract data from data sources (such as Web sites) on demand, and present the data in a tabular format. Figure 29-2 shows the wrapper development process.

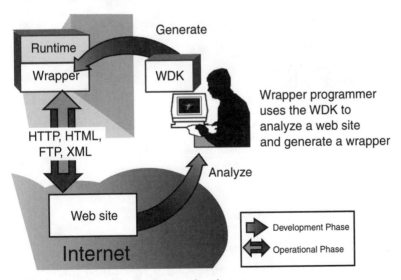

Figure 29-2   The wrapper development process.

The *Wrapper Development Kit* provides *wrapper frameworks*, which are collections of Java classes. Using these frameworks, the wrapper programmer can easily customize data retrieval. The WDK provides a high-level abstraction for network access, HTML parsing, pattern-matching and relational data output, allowing the programmer to focus on the core issues of data manipulation.

29.2.2 *The Extractor Development Kit (EDK)*

Data integration often involves extracting structured data from "unstructured" text; that is, text whose computer representation intermixes style information with the abstract data. To do this, a wrapper uses a program called an extraction rule, a set of rules and dictionaries created by the programmer using the *Extractor Development Kit* (EDK). Figure 29-3 illustrates the extractor development process.

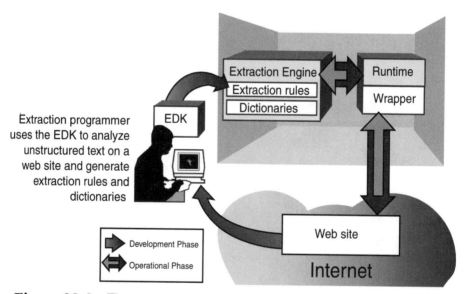

Figure 29-3   The extractor development process

Extraction rules are expressed in a high level language called the Junglee Extraction Language (JEL). JEL allows programmers to specify complex textual patterns and linguistic structures to identify the context in which specific terms are used. Individual terms are listed in the dictionaries, and can be tagged with flags and values using the EDK compilers. Extraction rules and dictionaries are interpreted by the EDK Extraction Engine.

29.2.3 *VDB Server and Data Quality Kit*

The *VDB Server* combines a collection of wrappers – and the necessary extractors – and presents them as a coherent relational database that can be queried using SQL through JDBC or ODBC. The VDB server can present results as tables or XML documents, as required by the application.

The VDB Server can be configured with a relational cache (see Figure 29-4), to improve query performance over Web data sources. The cache can be preloaded and refreshed depending on the application requirements.

Virtual databases often deal with highly irregular data from sources that are outside the control of the VDB administrator, and are subject to large-scale changes without notice. For this reason data transformation and data validation are key issues.

The *Data Quality Kit* provides the capability to set up data transformers that map attribute values from different sources to a common representation and vocabulary. In addition, data validators can be set up to monitor conditions or enforce constraints at various levels – row, column, or table.

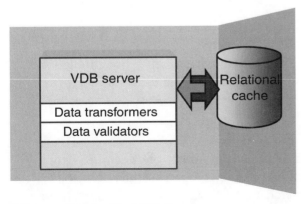

Figure 29-4   The VDB Server

Stability tests are unique to data from wrappers. Since wrappers often export data from Web sites that are subject to change, these tests are a vital first line of defense against corrupt data. These tests compare statistics of the data in a table against historical statistics for that table and report large deviations from historical trends.

29.2.4 *Administration interface*

The administration utility is used in conjunction with the VDB server to register or unregister each data source and the associated wrapper used to access it. Registration enables the data source to become visible as a set of one or more tables in the virtual database.

The registration command permits the system administrator to set up authentication mappings between a VDB server user and the corresponding name to be used when accessing the data source. Registration also allows the system administrator to distribute the work load on the system over a number of workstations on the LAN.

29.3 | Applications of VDB technology

The increasing use of the Internet to deliver information and provide sources leads to innovative applications of VDB technology, based on its capability to normalize disparate Web sites. Two such applications are described in this book.

online recruitment

Job seekers can utilize a powerful search capability through a virtual database of jobs aggregated from hundreds of corporate Web sites. See Chapter 15, "The Washington Post", on page 202.

Web commerce

Online shoppers can find products in dozens of categories – from hundreds of online merchants – and compare features, availability and pricing among merchants. See Chapter 9, "Comparison shopping service Web site", on page 132.

But many more come to mind, including:

corporate procurement
> Enable employees to find and compare products and services from approved suppliers.

engineering design databases
> Provide engineers with integrated catalogs of design components from manufacturers, searchable by specific attributes.

information management
> Integrate content from Web sites, news feeds, digital libraries and document databases to deliver value to the knowledge worker.

Free XML
software

- ■ Editors
- ■ Browsers
- ■ Parsers
- ■ ... and More!

The best things in life are free ... and 55 of them are on our CD-ROM!

Although XML is a new specification, it has a long history of free software for the SGML family of standards (including HyTime and DSSSL) to draw on. As a result, we could be selective about what we included.

The CD-ROM has over 55 free software titles, collected for The XML Handbook by Lars Marius Garshol. There is other useful software as well, as we'll see.

30.1 | What do we mean by "free"?

To meet our requirements for genuinely free software, a product must:

- Allow the user to do useful processing of the user's own documents.
- Have no time limit on its use.

These requirements are easily met by software that is written only for free distribution. In the case of shareware and "lite" versions of commercial software, though, the free version might have less function than the full-fledged offering, or it may have a restriction that it is only for personal use, or some similar legal constraint to prevent commercial abuse. It can be shareware that gently nags, as long as it doesn't expire.

Many of the programs are available under the GNU General Public License. That license meets all of our criteria and is available on the CD.

We have included executable files for both Win32 and Macintosh when available. In the Unix world, we only provide binaries for Linux, not every variant under the Sun.

Anything else doesn't meet our definition of free, but free isn't everything.

Demos, time-limited "trialware", and software that won't save the output or is otherwise unsuitable for production work, can still be useful. It can save you hours of product research and phone calls, and provide definitive answers about whether a product meets your requirements.

Our sponsors have provided lots of software in the CD-ROM Sponsor Showcase. Some of their goodies will surprise and delight you, so be sure to take a look.

And remember that the product descriptions only apply to the release being discussed. If you've tried out the software on the CD-ROM and you like it, be sure to visit the author's web site for the latest version.

30.2 | The best XML free software

30.2.1 *Parsers and engines*

30.2.1.1   Xlink engines

xmllink, 17.Mar.98 release

Bert Bos

Information on web:
http://www.w3.org/XML/notes.html
Software on web:
http://www.w3.org/XML/xmllink.zip

Software included on CD-ROM (Java):
./freesw/others/xmllib.tar.gz

This is a Java XML parser which also implements Xlink and an experimental proposal for SQL-like typing. There are command-line utilities for showing how links are interpreted and ESIS-like output.

30.2.1.2   XSL engines

Sparse, 28.Feb.98 release

Jeremie Miller

Information on web:
http://www.jeremie.com/Dev/XSL/index.phtml
Software on web:
http://www.jeremie.com/Dev/XSL/sparse.js
Software included on CD-ROM (JavaScript):
./freesw/others/sparse.zip

This is an XSL processor written in JavaScript. According to the author, it "is still of alpha quality and missing most of the features of the XSL Proposal".

The Microsoft XSL Processor, 7.Jan.98 release

Microsoft

Information on web:
http://www.microsoft.com/xml/xsl/msxsl.htm
Software on web:
http://www.microsoft.com/xml/xsl/downloads/msxsl.zip

The Microsoft XSL processor is a command-line utility that can process XSL style sheets and deliver HTML output. This processor can also be used as an ActiveX control from MSIE 4.0. It requires MSIE 4.0.

docproc, 07.Feb.98 release

Sean Russell

Information on web:
http://javalab.uoregon.edu/ser/software/docproc/index.xml
Software on web:
http://javalab.uoregon.edu/ser/software/distributions/docproc_full.jar
Software included on CD-ROM (Java):
./freesw/others/docproc.zip

docproc is a Java servlet that can be used to automatically convert XML documents to HTML and serve them on the web. docproc also comes as an application that can be run separately from any web server. docproc uses XSL, with Pnuts for scripting (Pnuts is similar to ECMAScript). The parser used by docproc is Lark.

xslj, 0.4

Henry Thompson

Information on web:
http://www.ltg.ed.ac.uk/~ht/xslj.html
Software on web:
ftp://ftp.cogsci.ed.ac.uk/pub/XSLJ/
Software included on CD-ROM (Source):
./freesw/xslj/xslj-0.4.tar.gz
Software included on CD-ROM (Win 32):
./freesw/xslj/xslj-0.4-bin-win32.tar.gz

xslj is an XSL processor with support for nearly all of the XSL proposal. It converts the XSL stylesheets to DSSSL stylesheets for further processing with Jade, and so requires Jade to be installed.

30.2.1.3   DSSSL engines

Jade, 1.1 (General SGML/XML tool)

James Clark

Information on web:
http://www.jclark.com/jade/
Software on web:
ftp://ftp.jclark.com/pub/jade/
Software included on CD-ROM (Source):
./freesw/jade/jade1_1.zip
Software included on CD-ROM (Win32):
./freesw/jade/jadew1_1.zip

Jade is James Clark's excellent DSSSL engine, which is really a general SGML tool for conversion from SGML to other SGML DTDs or to output formats like RTF and TeX. Jade can process XML documents and can also output XML.

DAE SDK

Copernican Solutions

Information on web:
http://www.copsol.com/products/dae/
Software on web:
http://www.copsol.com/products/dae/downloadreq.html
Software included on CD-ROM (Java):
./freesw/others/dae_install.class

This is a collection of Java tools from Copernican Solutions, which includes a DSSSL engine, a grove API, a Scheme interpreter (Kawa) and an XML parser.

DAE Server SDK

Copernican Solutions

Information on web:
http://www.copsol.com/products/daeserver/
Software on web:
http://www.copsol.com/products/daeserver/downloadreq.html
Software included on CD-ROM (Java):

./freesw/others/daeserver_install.class

This is an extended version of the DAE SDK that has been integrated with the Jigsaw web server from the W3C.

30.2.1.4   SGML/XML parsers

SGMLSpm, 1.03ii (General SGML/XML tool)

David Megginson

Information on web:
http://home.sprynet.com/sprynet/dmeggins/software.html
Software on web:
http://home.sprynet.com/sprynet/dmeggins/SGMLSpm-1.03ii.tar.gz
Software included on CD-ROM (Perl):
./freesw/others/sgmlspm-1.03ii.tar.gz

SGMLSpm reads ESIS output (from parsers like SP) and offers an event-based interface to the parser. As long as the parser can parse XML this also works for XML.

SP, 1.3 (General SGML/XML tool)

James Clark

Information on web:
http://www.jclark.com/sp/
Software on web:
http://www.jclark.com/sp/howtoget.htm
Software included on CD-ROM (Win32):
./freesw/sp/sp1_3.zip
Software included on CD-ROM (Source):
./freesw/sp/sp-1.3.tar.gz

SP is an SGML/XML parser, and is fast, complete, highly conformant and very stable. SP has been the parser of choice for most of the SGML community for many years and has been embedded in many other applications.

The SP package includes the SX program, which can adapt arbitrary SGML documents to XML automatically.

30.2.1.5   XML parsers

Windows Foundation Classes, Release 34
Sam Blackburn

Information on web:
http://ourworld.compuserve.com/homepages/sam_blackburn/wfc.htm
Software on web:
http://ourworld.compuserve.com/homepages/sam_blackburn/wfc.zip
Software included on CD-ROM (Win32):
./freesw/others/wfc.zip

WFC is a collection of C++ classes for Windows programming. Included are classes to parse and create XML documents.

RXP, beta6
Richard Tobin

Software on web:
ftp://ftp.cogsci.ed.ac.uk/pub/richard/rxp.tar.gz
Software included on CD-ROM (Source):
./freesw/others/rxp.tar.gz

RXP is a non-validating parser written in C. It is distributed as C source and must be compiled before use. It supports Unicode and comes with a command-line application that prints out the parsed document.

Dan Connolly's XML parser, 1.8
Dan Connolly

Information on web:
http://www.w3.org/XML/9705/hacking
Software on web:

http://www.w3.org/XML/9705/xml.py
Software included on CD-ROM (Python):
./freesw/others/dc_parser.zip

This is a simple well-formedness (not complete) parser written in Python that handles both XML and HTML and can output lout.

XML-Toolkit, 0.7
David Schere

Information on web:
http://csmctmto.interpoint.net/didx/xml.html
Software on web:
http://csmctmto.interpoint.net/didx/archive/xmltoolkit.tar.gz
Software included on CD-ROM (Python):
./freesw/others/xmltoolkit.tar.gz

The XML-Toolkit provides a non-validating XML parser, a WIDL implementation and the parser can also be used in a client/server model.

LTXML, 0.9.5
Edinburgh Language Technology Group

Information on web:
http://www.ltg.ed.ac.uk/software/xml/
Software on web:
http://www.ltg.hcrc.ed.ac.uk/software/research_xml.html
Software included on CD-ROM (Source):
./freesw/ltxml/ltxml-0.9.5.tar.gz
Software included on CD-ROM (Linux):
./freesw/ltxml/ltxml-0.9.5-bin-linux.tar.gz
Software included on CD-ROM (Mac):
./freesw/ltxml/ltxml-0.9.5-bin-mac.sea.hqx
Software included on CD-ROM (Win32):
./freesw/ltxml/ltxml-0.9.5-bin-win32.zip

LTXML is a set of tools (including a parser) written in portable C. Included are: a program to strip out all XML markup, an XML normalizer (mainly useful for well-formedness checking), an ESIS outputter, an element occurrence counter, a tokenizer, a down-translation tool, a grep tool, a sorting tool, some linking tools as well as some other minor utilities. The executables are mainly intended to be pipelined to produce various kinds of output, but provide a C API that can be used to extend them for other purposes.

expat, 19980405

James Clark

Information on web:
http://www.jclark.com/xml/expat.html
Software on web:
ftp://ftp.jclark.com/pub/xml/expat.zip
Software included on CD-ROM (C source):
./freesw/others/expat.zip

expat is written in C, and is the parser previously known as XMLTok. It is used in Mozilla 5.0 and in a Perl parser module written by Larry Wall. expat does no validation, but aims to be a fully conforming well-formedness parser. This is a beta release.

Tcl Support for XML, 1.0a1

Steve Ball

Information on web:
http://tcltk.anu.edu.au/XML/
Software on web:
http://tcltk.anu.edu.au/XML/XML-1.0a1.tcl.gz
Software included on CD-ROM (tcl):
./freesw/others/tclxml.zip

TCLXML is a validating XML parser written entirely in tcl, but is an alpha release that has not been tested much. The parser offers several ways to access the in-memory document structure after parsing, but only one is documented.

Xparse, 0.91

Jeremie Miller

Information on web:
http://www.jeremie.com/Dev/XML/index.phtml
Software on web:
http://www.jeremie.com/Dev/XML/xparse.js
Software included on CD-ROM (JavaScript):
./freesw/others/xparse.zip

Xparse is a very simple XML parser for use in web pages. It reads an XML document and produces a document tree consisting of elements, PIs, comments and character data.

XP, 0.2

James Clark

Information on web:
http://www.jclark.com/xml/xp/
Software on web:
ftp://ftp.jclark.com/pub/xml/xp.zip
Software included on CD-ROM (Java 1.1):
./freesw/others/xp.zip

XP is written to be fully-conforming and as fast as possible. The emphasis is on server-side production use. There is no validation, only well-formedness checking. Even though 0.2 is an alpha release it is very stable and extremely fast.

DataChannel XML Parser (DXP), 1.0 beta1a

DataChannel

Information on web:
http://www.datachannel.com/products/xml/DXP/
Software on web:
http://www.datachannel.com/products/xml/reg1.htm
Software included on CD-ROM (Java):

./freesw/others/DXP.zip

DXP is based on NXP, which was one of the first XML parsers, written by Norbert Mikula. It is validating and written for server-side use. There are both ESIS and SAX interfaces and support for SGML Open entity catalogs.

A full DOM interface and sophisticated error checking may appear in the full 1.0 version, so you may want to check the web site.

XML::Parse, 25.Mar.98 release

Larry Wall

Information on web:
ftp://www.wall.org/pub/larry/
Software on web:
ftp://www.wall.org/pub/larry/xmlparser-0.0.tar.gz
Software included on CD-ROM (Perl):
./freesw/others/xmlparser-0.0.tar.gz

This is a Perl wrapper around James Clark's XMLTok C parser (now known as expat). It is intended to be compiled into the Perl interpreter. It is undocumented and is not a final, official release.

PyXMLTok, 13.Mar.98 release

Jack Jansen

Information on web:
http://www.python.org/pipermail/1998q1.doc-sig/03eba1bbb5c3.html
Software on web:
ftp://ftp.cwi.nl/pub/jack/pyxmltok.tar.gz
Software included on CD-ROM (Python):
./freesw/others/pyxmltok.tar.gz

This is James Clark's XMLTok C parser module (now called expat) wrapped up as a Python module. This means that by compiling this into the Python interpreter (which is much easier than it sounds) one can have a fast C parser available from within Python. The interface is non-standard (i.e. not SAX).

Lark, 1.0 final beta
Tim Bray

Information on web:
http://www.textuality.com/Lark/
Software on web:
http://www.textuality.com/Lark/lark.tar.gz
Software included on CD-ROM (Java):
./freesw/others/lark.tar.gz

Lark was one of the two first XML parsers to appear, written by XML spec co-editor Tim Bray, but was non-validating for a long time. Tim Bray has now added Larval, a validating parser, to the package.

Lark is fast, small and thread-safe. Larval is in version 0.8 and not yet finished. The interface is non-standard, but there is a SAX driver in the SAX package.

Microsoft XML Parser in Java, 1.8
Microsoft

Information on web:
http://www.microsoft.com/workshop/author/xml/parser/
Software on web:
http://www.microsoft.com/xml/parser/msxml.tar.gz

This parser is validating, and has a non-standard interface, although a SAX driver is available in the SAX driver package. The parser implements the complete November 17, 1997, XML Working Draft, but has not been updated since the final recommendation. Lots of examples and documentation are bundled with the parser.

XML for Java, 9.Feb.98 release
IBM alphaWorks

Information on web:
http://www.alphaworks.ibm.com/formula/xml
Software on web:
http://www.sil.org/sgml/xml4j-19980206.zip

Software included on CD-ROM:
./freesw/others/xml4j-19980206.zip

This parser was written by Kento Tamura and Hiroshi Maruyama of the Tokyo Research Laboratory, IBM Japan. It is a validating parser that conforms to the 08.Dec.97 XML Working Draft and has not been updated since the release of the XML Recommendation.

The parser builds a tree structure object from an XML document, and can generate an XML document from a tree structure. There is also a SAX interface.

Use of this product is subject to the IBM alphaWorks license distributed with the software. However, the 90-day time limit is waived for purchasers of this book.

Ælfred, 1.1

Microstar

Information on web:
http://www.microstar.com/XML/index.htm
Software on web:
http://www.microstar.com/XML/aelfred-1.1.zip
Software included on CD-ROM (Java):
./freesw/others/aelfred-1.1.zip

Ælfred is designed to be small and fast, and is especially intended for use in Java applets (uses only two .class files). It has a non-standard interface, but comes with a SAX driver. Ælfred also handles a large number of different Unicode encodings.

Ælfred reads the DTD, but does not validate the document.

xmlproc, 0.30

Lars Marius Garshol

Information on web:
http://www.stud.ifi.uio.no/~larsga/download/python/xml/xmlproc.html
Software on web:
http://www.stud.ifi.uio.no/~larsga/download/python/xml/xmlproc.zip
Software included on CD-ROM (Python):

./freesw/others/xmlproc.zip

xmlproc is a validating parser written in Python. It implements most of the XML Recommendation, but not all. Some validation checks are not performed, illegal characters are accepted in some places, and some input transforms are not performed.

xmlproc has a non-standard interface, but comes with a SAX driver.

xmllib, 0.1

Sjoerd Mullender

Information on web:
http://www.python.org/doc/lib/
node162.html#SECTION001210000000000000000000
Software on web:
http://www.cwi.nl/ftp/sjoerd/xmllib.tar.gz
Software included on CD-ROM (Python):
./freesw/others/xmllib.tar.gz

The xmllib parser is part of the Python 1.5 distribution. The version included here is a newer version than the one in the standard distribution. xmllib is non-validating, but a fairly complete well-formedness parser with a simple and intuitive interface. A SAX driver is available in saxlib.

30.2.1.6   XML middleware

XPublish, 1.0

Media Design in*Progress

Information on web:
http://interaction.in-progress.com/xpublish/index
Software included on CD-ROM (Mac):
./freesw/others/xpublish10.sit

XPublish is a web content management system based on XML. XPublish lets you write your documents in XML (and hybrids of HTML and XML) and publish them on the web as HTML. The XPublish editor is an Emacs clone, with Lisp as an extension language. XPublish also helps you create a DTD and simplifies XML to HTML conversion.

Frontier, 5.0.1

Userland Software

Information on web:
http://www.scripting.com/frontier5/
Software on web:
http://www.scripting.com/frontier5/downloads/default.html
Software included on CD-ROM (Mac):
./freesw/frontier/frontier5.0.1.sit.hqx
Software included on CD-ROM (Win32):
./freesw/frontier/frontier501.zip

Frontier is a scripting environment for web content management. It works with a lot of different data sources, including XML. Frontier is rather unique and difficult to describe, so be sure to check the information at the Frontier web site. An XML package called blox is also included.

blox, 1.0b7

Technology Solutions

Information on web:
http://www.techsoln.com/frontier/blox/
Software on web:
http://www.techsoln.com/frontier/blox/download/
Software included on CD-ROM (Mac):
./freesw/frontier/blox.sit
Software included on CD-ROM (Win32):
./freesw/frontier/blox.zip

blox is an XML tool suite for Frontier that includes a parser and tools for manipulating XML documents.

PyDOM, 0.1
Stephane Fermigier

Information on web:
http://www.math.jussieu.fr/~fermigie/python/PyDOM/
Software on web:
http://www.math.jussieu.fr/~fermigie/python/PyDOM/dom-0.1.zip
Software included on CD-ROM (Python):
./freesw/others/dom-0.1.zip

PyDOM can build the DOM tree from a supplied XML parser (Dan Connolly's), an ESIS outputter, any SAX-compliant parser, the Python HTML parser (htmllib) or the Python SGML parser (sgmllib).

This online version of this list was produced by a Python script that used PyDOM for navigation through the parsed document. PyDOM is preliminary software and may have some bugs.

XML::Grove, 0.03
Ken MacLeod

Information on web:
http://bitsko.slc.ut.us/~ken/perl-xml/
Software on web:
http://bitsko.slc.ut.us/~ken/perl-xml/XML-Grove-0.03.tar.gz
Software included on CD-ROM (Perl):
./freesw/others/xml-grove-0.03.tar.gz

XML::Grove uses XML::Parse to build a tree structure from the parsed document that programs can access and change. Similar to DOM, that is, but based on ISO standards.

saxlib, 0.92
Lars Marius Garshol

Information on web:
http://www.stud.ifi.uio.no/~larsga/download/python/xml/
Software on web:
http://www.stud.ifi.uio.no/~larsga/download/python/xml/saxlib.zip

Software included on CD-ROM (Python):
./freesw/others/saxlib.zip

saxlib is a Python translation of the SAX parser interface. It has drivers for the xmllib parser and for the XML-Toolkit parser. There are also two demo applications: saxdemo.py, which produces canonical XML output and saxtimer.py, which measures the time used to parse a document with an empty document handler.

SAX, 27.Jan.98 release

David Megginson

Information on web:
http://www.microstar.com/XML/SAX/java-implementation.html
Software on web:
http://www.microstar.com/XML/SAX/sax-java-19980127.zip
Software included on CD-ROM (Java):
./freesw/others/sax-java-19980127.zip

SAX is a simple event-based API for XML parsers. It is not an official standard, since it was developed by the participants of the xml-dev mailing list instead of a standards body. However, SAX is very much a de facto standard, since it is supported by at least 9 parsers.

This library contains the Java implementation of SAX, but no drivers.

SAX drivers for Lark and MSXML, 13.Mar.98 release

David Megginson

Information on web:
http://www.microstar.com/XML/SAX/drivers.html
Software on web:
http://www.microstar.com/XML/SAX/sax-java-drivers-19980313.zip
Software included on CD-ROM (Java):
./freesw/others/sax-java-drivers-19980313.zip

This is a package consisting of two SAX drivers for Java parsers that do not support SAX natively, namely Lark and the Microsoft parser.

SAXDOM, 6.Apr.98 release

Don Park

Information on web:
http://www.docuverse.com/personal/saxdom.html
Software on web:
http://www.docuverse.com/personal/saxdom040698.zip
Software included on CD-ROM (Java):
./freesw/others/saxdom040698.zip

SAXDOM is a Java implementation of the Document Object Model that uses any SAX client (just use the SAX package and any parser you like) to build the DOM document tree. SAXDOM will continue to change as SAX and the DOM evolve. You may want to check the website to see if there is a new version.

30.2.2 *Editing and composition*

30.2.2.1   XML editors

PSGML, 1.0.1 with XML patch (General SGML/XML tool)

Lenart Staflin
   David Megginson

Information on web:
http://www.lysator.liu.se/projects/about_psgml.html
Software on web:
ftp://ftp.lysator.liu.se/pub/sgml/
Software included on CD-ROM:
./freesw/others/psgml-xml.zip (Elisp source)

Emacs is easily one of the most powerful (if not the most powerful) text editors in the world. It has an internal Lisp programming language, which means that new modes are easy to write, and as a consequence Emacs has usage modes for most programming languages, as well as a web browser with CSS (and budding DSSSL) support and a world-class news reader.

The user interface is quite unlike most modern editors, but Emacs comes with internal documentation that can help you out.

PSGML is a full SGML mode that has been patched to support XML. It reads the DTD, can use an external parser to validate documents, does syntax coloring, and a lot of other things.

Visual XML, beta 1

Pierre Morel

Information on web:
http://www.pierlou.com/visxml/
Software on web:
http://www.pierlou.com/visxml/download.htm
Software included on CD-ROM (Java):
./freesw/others/visual-xml-b1.zip

Visual XML is an XML editor written in Java with JFC (Swing). It lets you edit a tree view of the XML document. This is a test version and may have bugs.

XED, 19.Mar.98 release

Henry Thompson

Information on web:
http://www.ltg.ed.ac.uk/~ht/xed.html
Software on web:
ftp://ftp.cogsci.ed.ac.uk/pub/ht/
Software included on CD-ROM (Win32):
./freesw/xed/xed.zip
Software included on CD-ROM (Solaris 2.5):
./freesw/xed/xed-solaris2.5.tar.gz

XED is a simple XML editor written in C, Python and Tk. It tries to ensure that the author cannot write a document that is not well-formed and reads the DTD in order to be able to suggest valid elements to be inserted at any point in the document.

The document is shown as text, not as a tree view.

XML < PRO >, 1.0b

Vervet Logic

Information on web:
http://www.vervet.com/
Software on web:
http://www.vervet.com/beta.html

XML < PRO > is a tree-based XML editor, with validation.

Amaya, 1.2a

World Wide Web Consortium

Information on web:
http://www.w3.org/Amaya/
Software on web:
http://www.w3.org/Amaya/User/BinDist.html
Software included on CD-ROM (Win32):
./freesw/amaya/amaya-1.2a.exe
Software included on CD-ROM (Java (Linux)):
./freesw/amaya/amaya-java-LINUX-1.1c.tar.gz
Software included on CD-ROM (Linux):
./freesw/amaya/amaya-LINUX-ELF-1.2a.tar.gz

Amaya is the W3C testbed browser, and is an HTML browser (and editing tool) with CSS support. It also supports the MathML XML DTD and can edit and display presentational MathML graphically.

30.2.3 *Control information development*

30.2.3.1   XSL editors

ArborText XML Styler, 2.0

ArborText

Information on web:

http://www.arbortext.com/xmlstyler/
Software on web:
http://www.arbortext.com/xmlstyler/registration.html
Software included on CD-ROM (Win32):
./freesw/xmlstyler/xmlstyler2c.exe
Software included on CD-ROM (Java):
./freesw/xmlstyler/xmlstyler2c.zip

XML Styler lets you create XSL style sheets for your XML documents using a visual editor. The Windows version allows previewing with the XSL ActiveX control in MSIE 4.0.

30.2.3.2 DTD editors

tdtd, revision 0.4

Tony Graham

Information on web:
ftp://ftp.mulberrytech.com/pub/mulberrytech/tdtd/
Software on web:
ftp://ftp.mulberrytech.com/pub/mulberrytech/tdtd/tdtd.zip
Software included on CD-ROM:
./freesw/others/tdtd.zip (Elisp files)

This is an Emacs major mode for editing DTDs. It does syntax coloring and has some convenience macros for inserting commonly-typed constructs.

30.2.3.3 DTD documenters

perlSGML, 18.Sep.97 (General SGML/XML tool)

Earl Hood

Information on web:
http://www.oac.uci.edu/indiv/ehood/perlSGML.html
Software on web:

http://www.oac.uci.edu/indiv/ehood/tar/perlSGML.1997Sep18.tar.gz
Software included on CD-ROM (Perl):
./freesw/others/perlSGML.1997Sep18.tar.gz

perlSGML is a collection of Perl tools for working with full SGML, but they also work with XML. Included are DTD documentation tools, a DTD diff tool and several useful related libraries.

30.2.4 *Conversion*

30.2.4.1 General S-converters

OmniMark LE, 4.0e2 (General SGML/XML tool)
OmniMark Technologies

Information on web:
http://www.omnimark.com/develop/omle40/
Software on web:
http://www.omnimark.com/develop/omle40/download/omle40e2.exe

OmniMark is a well-known tool in the SGML industry, where it is much used for SGML conversions and also non-SGML conversions due to its superb regular expression and SGML support. This prerelease version of OmniMark LE (a free, but limited version of the program) is the first version of OmniMark to support XML.

30.2.4.2 Specific N-converters

RDF for XML, 9.Apr.98 release
IBM alphaWorks

Information on web:
http://www.alphaWorks.ibm.com/formula/rdfxml
Software included on CD-ROM (Java):

./freesw/others/rdf.zip

RDF for XML is an RDF implementation for building, querying and manipulating RDF structures as well as reading them from and writing them to the XML representation. This implementation follows the 16.Feb.98 RDF working draft.

RDF for XML requires the XML for Java XML parser.

Use of this product is subject to the IBM alphaWorks license distributed with the software. However, the 90-day time limit is waived for purchasers of this book.

30.2.4.3   General N-converters

DataChannel XML Generator, 0.1 beta1
DataChannel

Information on web:
http://www.datachannel.com/press_room/xml_gen/
Software on web:
http://www.datachannel.com/products/xml/dxp/xmlgenerator.zip
Software included on CD-ROM (Java):
./freesw/others/xmlgenerator.zip

The DataChannel XML Generator takes a character-delimited file (such as an exported spreadsheet or database) and an XML template as input and produces XML output based on the template and input.

30.2.5   *Electronic delivery*

30.2.5.1   XML browsers

Mozilla, 8.Apr.98 release
The Mozilla team

Information on web:

http://www.mozilla.org/
Software on web:
http://www.uwasa.fi/~e75644/mozilla/MozFAQ.html
Software included on CD-ROM (Win32 sources):
./freesw/mozilla/win_19980408.zip
Software included on CD-ROM (Mac sources):
./freesw/mozilla/mac_19980408.sit.bin
Software included on CD-ROM (Unix sources):
./freesw/mozilla/unix_19980408.tar.gz

This is version 5 of Netscape Navigator, which can display XML documents with CSS stylesheets. Please note that this is a very preliminary test version and is known to have bugs.

Jumbo, 9801a1

Peter Murray-Rust

Information on web:
http://ala.vsms.nottingham.ac.uk/vsms/java/jumbo/
Software on web:
http://ala.vsms.nottingham.ac.uk/vsms/java/jumbo/jan9801/jumbo9801a/
Software included on CD-ROM (Java):
./freesw/others/jumbo9801a1.zip

Jumbo was the first XML browser to appear, but does not support stylesheets, so documents are currently shown in a tree view. (There is built-in support for some DTDs, notably CML.) Jumbo is not delivered with a parser, but installing a parser with a SAX driver in your class path will automatically enable Jumbo to parse XML documents.

DataChannel XML Viewer, 28.Jul.97 release

DataChannel

Information on web:
http://xml.datachannel.com/XMLTreeViewer/demo.html
Software on web:
http://www.datachannel.com/products/xml/xmlviewerappletkit.zip
Software included on CD-ROM (Java):

./freesw/others/xmlviewerappletkit.zip

This is an applet (and an application) that shows a tree-based view of XML documents.

Prototype, I

Pierre Morel

Information on web:
http://www.pierlou.com/prototype/
Software on web:
http://www.pierlou.com/prototype/download.htm
Software included on CD-ROM (Java):
./freesw/others/proto-full.zip

Prototype is a program that reads a structured description of an application, in the form of an XML document corresponding to a particular DTD. It produces the look and feel of the application.

30.2.6 *Resources*

30.2.6.1   Useful programs

This is a collection of software that is needed to run some of the packages included, but which does not have XML capabilities natively. We've linked to them here to help you find these packages if you don't have them already.

Emacs

- *Web page*:
  http://www.geek-girl.com/emacs/emacs.html
- *Win32 version*:
  http://www.cs.washington.edu/homes/voelker/ntemacs.html
- *Software on CD-ROM (Win32)*:
  ./freesw/utils/emacs-19.34.zip

- *Software on CD-ROM (Linux)*:
  ./freesw/utils/emacs-MBSK-X11-20.2-4.i386.rpm
- *Software on CD-ROM (Source)*:
  ./freesw/utils/emacs-20.2.tar.gz
- Sadly, Emacs has not been available for the Mac since version 18.59.

Python

- *Web page*:
  http://www.python.org/
- *Software on CD-ROM (Win32)*:
  ./freesw/utils/pyth151.exe
- *Software on CD-ROM (Mac)*:
  ./freesw/utils/macpython15b3.bin
- *Software on CD-ROM (Linux)*:
  ./freesw/utils/python-1.5.1-1.i386.rpm
- *Software on CD-ROM (Source)*:
  ./freesw/utils/pyth151.tgz

Perl

- Web page: http://www.perl.com/.
- *Software on CD-ROM (Win32)*:
  ./freesw/utils/Pw32i316.exe
- *Software on CD-ROM (Mac)*:
  ./freesw/utils/Mac_Perl_519r4_appl.bin
- *Software on CD-ROM (Linux)*:
  ./freesw/utils/perl-5.004_03-1.i386.rpm
- *Software on CD-ROM (Source)*:
  ./freesw/utils/perl5.004_04.tar.gz

Other tools

- Java Development Kit: http://java.sun.com/products/jdk/1.1/
- The Tcl interpreter: http://sunscript.sun.com/TclTkCore/

30.2.6.2   Archiving software

Most of the software is distributed as a collection of files combined (or "archived") into a single file for easier network delivery. The utilities used to create these archives often originated on the UNIX operating system as standard UNIX tools, or as free software from the Free Software Foundation's GNU collection, but all are available in Windows and DOS versions as well:

- Win95/NT gunzip, unzip, tar: ftp://ftp.cs.washington.edu/pub/ntemacs/latest/i386/utilities/i386/
- DOS unzip and gzip (gzip also unzips *.gz files): ftp://ftp.uu.net/pub/archiving/zip/MSDOS/
- DOS untar: ftp://wuarchive.wustl.edu/systems/ibmpc/garbo.uwasa.fi/unix/
- NT/Win 95 unzip and gzip: ftp://ftp.uu.net/pub/archiving/zip/WIN32/
- NT/Win 95 tar (tar program also untars): ftp://sunsite.doc.ic.ac.uk/pub/packages/simtel/win95/archiver/

Part Five

- XML markup
- Document type definitions
- Linking and addressing
- Style sheets
- XML-Data
- Web Interface Definition Language (WIDL)

The Technology of XML

XML basics

- Syntactic details
- The prolog and the document instance
- XML declaration
- Elements and attributes

31

XML's central concepts are quite simple, and this chapter outlines the most important of them. Essentially, it gives you what you need to know to actually create XML documents. In subequent chapters you will learn how to combine them, share text between them, format them, and validate their structure.

Before looking at actual XML markup (don't worry, we'll get there soon!) we should consider some syntactic constructs that will recur throughout our discussion of XML documents. By *syntax* we mean the combination of characters that make up an XML document. This is analogous to the distinction between sounds of words and the things that they mean. Essentially, we are talking about where you can put angle brackets, quote marks, ampersands, and other characters and where you cannot! Later we will talk about what they mean when you put them together.

After that, we will discusses the components that make up an XML document instance[1]. We will look at the distinction between the prolog (information XML processors need to know about your document) and the instance (the representation of the real document itself).

---

1. Roughly, what the XML spec calls the "root element".

31.1 | Syntactic details

XML documents are composed of characters from the *Unicode* character set. Any such sequence of characters is called a *string*. The characters in this book can be thought of as one long (but interesting) string of text. Each chapter is also a string. So is each word. XML documents are similarly made up of strings within strings.

Natural languages such as English have a particular syntax. The syntax allows you to combine words into grammatical sentences. XML also has syntax. It describes how you combine strings into well-formed XML documents. We will describe the basics of XML's syntax in this section.

31.1.1 *Case-sensitivity*

XML is *case-sensitive*. That means that if the XML specification says to insert the word "ELEMENT", it means that you should insert "ELEMENT" and not "element" or "Element" or "ElEmEnT".

For many people, particularly English speaking people, case-insensitive matching is easier than remembering the case of particular constructs. For instance, if a document type has an element type named img English speakers will often forget and insert IMG. They confuse the two because they are not accustomed to considering case to be significant. This is also why some people new to the Internet tend to TYPE IN ALL UPPER CASE. Most applications of SGML, including HTML, are designed to be case-insensitive. They argue that this eliminates case as a source of errors.

Others argue that the whole concept of case-insensitivity is a throwback to keypunches and other early text-entry devices. They also point out that case-sensitivity is a very complicated concept in an international character set like Unicode for a variety of reasons.

For instance, the rules for case conversion of certain accented characters are different in Quebec from what they are in France. There are also some languages for which the concept of upper-case and lower-case does not exist at all. There is no simple, universal rule for case-insensitive matching. In the end, internationalization won out in XML's design.

So mind your "p's" and "q's" and "P's" and "Q's". Our authoritative laboratory testing by people in white coats indicates that exactly 74.5% of all XML errors are related to case-sensitivity mistakes. Of course XML is also spelling-sensitive and typo-sensitive, so watch out for these and other byproducts of human fallibility.

Note that although XML is case-sensitive it is not case-prejudiced. Anywhere that you have the freedom to create your own names or text, you can choose to use upper- or lower-case text, as you prefer. So although you must type XML's keywords exactly as they are described, your own strings can mix and match upper- and lower-case characters however you like.

For instance, when you create your own document types you will be able to choose element type names. A particular name could be all upper-case (SECTION), all lower-case (section) or mixed-case (SeCtION). But because XML is case-sensitive, all references to a particular element type would have to use the same case. It is good practice to create a simple convention such as all lower-case or all upper-case so that you do not have to depend on your memory.

31.1.2 *Markup and data*

The constructs such as tags, entity references, and declarations are called *markup*. These are the parts of your document that are supposed to be understood by the XML processor. The parts that are between the markup are typically supposed to be understood only by other human beings. That is the *character data*. Here is what the XML specification says on this issue:

Spec. Reference 31-1. Markup

Markup takes the form of start-tags, end-tags, empty-element tags, entity references, character references, comments, CDATA section delimiters, document type declarations, and processing instructions.

We haven't explained what all of those things are yet, but they are easy to recognize. All of them start with less-than ("<") or ampersand ("&") characters. Everything else is character data.

31.1.3 *White space*

There is a set of characters called *white space* characters that XML processors treat differently in XML markup. They are the "invisible" characters: space (Unicode/ASCII 32), tab (Unicode/ASCII 9), carriage return (Unicode/ASCII 13) and line feed (Unicode/ASCII 10). These correspond roughly to the spacebar, tab, and Enter keys on your keyboard.

When the XML specification says that white space is allowed at a particular point, you may put as many of these characters as you want in any combination. Just as you might put two lines between paragraphs in a word processor to make a printed document readable, you may put two carriage returns in certain places in an XML document to make your source file more readable and maintainable. When the document is processed, those characters will be ignored.

In other places, white space will be significant. For instance you would not want the processor to strip out the spaces between the words in your document! Thatwouldmakeithardtoread. So white space outside of markup is always preserved in XML and white space within markup may be preserved, ignored, and sometimes combined in weird, and wonderful ways. We will describe the combination rules as we go along.

31.1.4 *Names and name tokens*

When you use XML you will often have to give things names. You will name logical structures with element type names, reusable data with entity names, particular elements with IDs, and so forth. XML names have certain common features. They are not nearly as flexible as character data:

Spec. Reference 31-2. Names

A Name [begins] with a letter or one of a few punctuation characters, and [continues] with letters, digits, hyphens, underscores, colons, or full stops, together known as name characters. Names beginning with the string "xml", [matched case-insensitively] are reserved for standardization in this or future versions of this specification.

In other words, you cannot make names that begin with the string "xml" or somecase-insensitive variant like "XML" or "XmL". Letters or underscores can be used anywhere in a name. You may include digits, hyphens and full-stop (".") characters in a name, but you may not start the name with one of them. Other characters, like various symbols and white space, cannot be part of a name.

There is another related syntactic construct called a *name token*. Name tokens are just like names except that they *may* start with digits, hyphens, full-stop characters, and the string XML.

Spec. Reference 31-3. Name tokens

An Nmtoken (name token) is any mixture of name characters.

In other words every valid name is also a valid name token, but here are some name tokens that are not valid names:

Example 31-1. Name tokens

```
.1.a.name.token.but.not.a.name
2-a-name-token.but-not.a-name
XML-valid-name-token
```

Like almost everything else in XML, names, and name tokens are matched case-sensitively. Names and name tokens do not allow white space, most punctuation or other "funny" characters. The remaining "ordinary" characters are called *name characters*.

31.1.5 *Literal strings*

The data (text other than markup) can contain almost any characters. Obviously, in the main text of your document you need to be able to use punctuation and white space characters! But sometimes you also need these characters *within* markup. For instance an element might represent a hyperlink and need to contain a URL. The URL would have to go in markup, where characters other than the name characters are not usually allowed.

Literal strings allow users to use funny (non-name) characters within markup, but only in contexts in which it makes sense to specify values that might require those characters. For instance, to specify the URL in the hyperlink, we would need the slash character. Here is an example of such an element:

```
<REFERENCE URL="http://www.documents.com/document.xml">
```

The string that defines the URL is the literal string. This one starts and ends with double quote characters. Literal strings are always surrounded by either single or double quotes. The quotes are not part of the string. Here is what the XML spec says:

Spec. Reference 31-4. Literal data

Literal data is any quoted string not containing the quotation mark used as a delimiter for that string. Literals are used for specifying the content of internal entities, the values of attributes, and external identifiers.

You may use either single ("'") or double (""") quotes to mark (*delimit*) the beginning and end of these strings in your XML document. Whichever type of quote the string starts with, it must end with. The other type may be used within the literal and has no special meaning there. Typically you will use double quotes when you want to put an actual single-quote character in the literal and single quotes when you want to embed an actual double quote. When you do not need to embed either, you can take your pick. Here are some examples:

```
"This is a double quoted literal."
'This is a single quoted literal.'
"'tis another double quoted literal."
'"And this is single quoted" said the self-referential example.'
```

The ability to have quotes within quotes is quite useful when dealing with human speech or programming language text:

```
"To be or not to be"
'"To be or not to be", quoth Hamlet.'
"'BE!', said Jean-Louis Gassee."
'B = "TRUE";'
```

Note that there *are* ways of including a double quote character inside of a double-quoted literal. This is important because a single literal might (rarely) need both types of quotes.

31.1.6 *Grammars*

Natural language syntax is described with a grammar. XML's syntax is also. Some readers will want to dig in and learn the complete, intricate details of XML's syntax. We will provide grammar rules for them as we go along. These come right out of the XML specification. If you want to learn how to read them, you should skip ahead to Chapter 37, "Reading the XML specification", on page 546. After you have read it, you can come back and understand the rules as we present them. Another strategy is to read the chapters without worrying about the grammar rules, and then only use them when you need to answer a particular question about XML syntax.

You can recognize grammar rules taken from the specification by their form. They will look like this:

Spec. Reference 31-5. An example of a grammar rule

```
xhb ::= 'a' 'good' 'read'
```

We will not specifically introduce these rules, because we do not want to interrupt the flow of the text. They will just pop up in the appropriate place to describe the syntax of something.

31.2 | Prolog vs. instance

Most document representations start with a header that contains information about the real document and how to interpret its representation. This is followed by the representation of the real document.

For instance, HTML has a HEAD element that can contain the TITLE and META elements. After the HEAD element comes the BODY. This is where the representation of the real document resides. Similarly, email messages have "header lines" that describe who the message came from, to whom it is addressed, how it is encoded, and other things.

An XML document is similarly broken up into two main parts: a *prolog* and a *document instance*. The prolog provides information about the interpretation of the document instance, such as the version of XML and the document type to which it conforms. The document instance follows the prolog. It contains the actual document data organized as a hierarchy of elements.

Spec. Reference 31-6. Document production

```
document ::=  prolog element Misc*
```

31.3 | The logical structure

The actual content of an XML document goes in the document instance. It is called this because if it has a DTD, it is an instance of a class of documents defined by the DTD. Just as a particular person is an instance of the class of "people", a particular memo is an instance of the class of "memo documents". The formal definition of "memo document" is in the memo DTD.

Here is an example of a small XML document.

Example 31-2. Small XML Document

```
<?xml version="1.0"?>
<!DOCTYPE MEMO SYSTEM "memo.dtd">
<memo>
<from>
   <name>Paul Prescod</name>
   <email>papresco@prescod.com</email>
</from>
<to>
   <name>Charles Goldfarb</name>
   <email>charles@sgmlsource.com</email>
</to>
<subject>Another Memo Example</subject>
<body>
<paragraph> Charles, I wanted to suggest that we
<emphasis>not</emphasis> use the  typical memo example in
our book. Memos tend to be used anywhere a small, simple
document type is needed, but they are just
<emphasis>so</emphasis> boring!
</paragraph>
</body>
</memo>
```

Because a computer cannot understand the data of the document, it looks primarily at the *tags*, the markup between the less-than and greater-than symbols. The tags delimit the beginning and end of various elements. The computer thinks of the elements as a sort of tree.

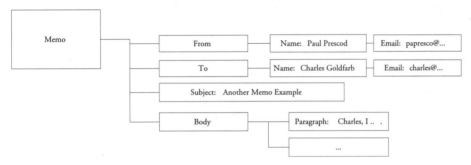

Figure 31-1   The memo XML document viewed as a tree.

Figure 31-1 shows a graphical view of the logical structure of the document. The MEMO element is called either the *document element* or the *root element*.

The document element (memo) represents the document as a whole. Every other element represents a component of the document. The from and to elements are meant to indicate the source and target of the memo. The name elements represent people's names. Continuing in this way, the logical structure of the document is apparent from the element-type names.

Experts refer to an element's real-world meaning as its semantics. In a particular DTD, the semantics of a P element might be "paragraph" and in another it might mean pence. If you find yourself reading or writing markup and asking: "But what does that *mean?*" or "What does that look like?" then you are asking about semantics.

Computers do not know anything about semantics. They do not know an HTTP protocol from a supermodel. Document type designers must describe semantics to authors some other way. For instance they could send email, write a book or make a major motion picture (well, maybe some day). What the computer does care about is how an element is supposed to look when it is formatted, or how it is to behave if it is interactive, or what to do with the data once it is extracted. These are specified in *stylesheets* and computer programs.

31.4 | Elements

XML elements break down into two categories. Most have content, which is to say they contain characters, elements or both, and some do not. Those that do not are called *empty elements*.

Here is an example of an element with content:

Example 31-3. Simple element

```
<title>This is the title</title>
```

Most elements have content. Elements with content begin with a start-tag and finish with an end-tag. The "stuff" between the two is the element's content. In Example 31-3, "This is the title" is the content.

Spec. Reference 31-7. Element with content

```
[39] element ::=   start-tag content End-tag
```

XML start-tags consist of the less-than (<) symbol ("left angle bracket"), the name of the element's type, termed a generic identifier (gi), and a greater-than (>) symbol ("right angle bracket"). Start-tags can also include attributes. We will look at those later in the chapter. The start-tag in Example 31-3 is <TITLE> and its generic identifier is "TITLE".

Spec. Reference 31-8. Start-tag

```
[40] STag ::=   '<' Name (S Attribute)* S? '>'
```

XML end-tags consist of the string "</", the same generic identifier (or *GI*) as in the start-tag, and a greater-than (>) symbol. The end-tag in Example 31-3 is </TITLE>.

You must always repeat the GI in the end-tag. This helps you to keep track of which end-tags line up with which start-tags. If you ever forget one or the other, the processor will know immediately, and will alert you that the document is not well-formed. The downside of this redundancy is that it requires more typing. Some people like belts and some prefer suspenders. The XML Working Group likes belts *and* suspenders.

Spec. Reference 31-9. End-tag

```
[42] ETag ::=  '</' Name S? '>'
```

Note that less-than symbols in content are always interpreted as beginning a tag. If the characters following them would not constitute a valid tag, then the document is not well-formed.

> **Caution**   Use the word "tag" precisely
> Many people use the word "tag" imprecisely. Sometimes they mean "generic identifier", sometimes "element-type name", sometimes "element type" and sometimes they actually mean "tag". This leads to confusion. In XML, tags always start with less-than symbols and end with greater-than symbols. Nothing else is a tag. Tags are not defined in DTDs; element types are defined in DTDs.

It is possible for an element to have no content at all. Such an element is called an *empty element*. One way to denote an empty element is to merely leave out the content. But as a shortcut, empty elements may also have a different syntax. Because there is no content to delimit, they may consist of a single empty-element tag. That looks like this: `<EmptyTag/>`.

The slash at the end indicates that this is an empty-element tag, so there is no content or end-tag coming up. The slash is meant to be reminiscent of the slash in the end-tag of an element with both tags.

Spec. Reference 31-10. Empty-element tag

```
[44]  EmptyElemTag ::=  '<' Name (S Attribute)* S? '/>'
```

Usually empty elements have *attributes*. Occasionally an empty element without attributes will be used to flag a particular location in a document. Here is an example of an empty element with an attribute:

```
<EMPTY-ELEMENT ATTR="ATTVAL"/>
```

In summary, elements are either empty or have content. Elements with content are represented by a start-tag, the content, and an end-tag. Empty elements can either have a start-tag and end-tag with nothing in between, or a single empty-element tag. An element's type is always identified by the generic identifiers in its tags.

The reason we distinguish element types from generic identifiers is because the term "generic identifier" refers to the syntax of the XML document – the characters that represent the real document. The term "element type" refers to a property of a component of the real document.

31.5 | Attributes

In addition to content, elements may have *attributes*. Attributes are a way of attaching characteristics or properties to elements of a document. Attributes have *names*, just as real-world properties do. They also have values. For instance, two possible attributes of people are their "shoe size" and "IQ" (the attributes' names), and two possible values are "12" and "12" (respectively).

In a DTD, each attribute is defined for a specific element type and is allowed to exhibit a certain type of value. Multiple element types could provide attributes with the same name and it is sometimes convenient to think of them as the "same attribute" even though they technically are not.

Attributes have semantics also. They always *mean* something. For example, an attribute named `height` might be provided for `person` elements (allowed occurrence), exhibit values that are numbers (allowed values), and represent the person's height in centimeters (semantics).

Here is how attributes of `person` elements might look.

Example 31-4. Elements with attributes

```
<person height="165cm">Dale Wick</person>
<person height="165cm" weight="165lb">Bill Bunn</person>
```

As you can see, the attribute name does not go in quotes, but the attribute value does.

Spec. Reference 31-11. Attributes

```
[41]  Attribute ::=  Name Eq AttValue
[25]  Eq ::=  S? '=' S?
```

Like other literals (see page 429), attributes can be surrounded by either single (') or double (") quotes. When you use one type of quote, the other can be used within that attribute value. As we discussed earlier, this makes it convenient to create attribute values that have the quote characters within them:

Example 31-5. Attribute values can have quotes in them

```
<PERSON HEIGHT='80"'>
<PERSON QUOTE="'To be or not to be'">
```

There are other ways of getting special characters into attribute values and we will discuss them in 36.2, "Character references", on page 535.

A DTD constrains an attribute's allowed occurrence and values. One possibility is to require an attribute to be specified for all elements. For example, a military document might require section elements to have a security attribute with the value unclassified, classified, or secret.

```
<!ATTLIST SECTION
          SECURITY (unclassified | classified | secret) #REQUIRED >
```

The attribute would need to be specified for each section element:

```
<SECTION SECURITY="unclassified">...</SECTION>
```

It would be a validity error to create a section element without a security attribute.

Usually empty elements have attributes. Sometimes an element with sub-elements can be modeled just as well with an empty element and attributes. Here are two ways of modeling a person element in an email message:

Example 31-6. Alternative person element

```
<FROM><NAME>Paul Prescod</NAME>
      <EMAIL>"papresco@prescod.com"</EMAIL>
</FROM>
vs.
<FROM NAME="Paul Prescod" EMAIL="papresco@prescod.com"/>
```

Yet another way to do it would be to let the person's name be data content:

As you can see, there can be many different ways to represent the same construct. There is no one right way to do so. In the case of person, the last

Example 31-7. Another alternative person **element**

```
<FROM><PERSON EMAIL="papresco@prescod.com">Paul Prescod
      </PERSON>
</FROM>
```

version shown is the most typical because the character data of a document generally represents what you would expect to see in a "print-out".

But that is not a hard and fast rule (after all, renditions vary widely). Because there are so many ways to represent the same thing, it is advisable to use a DTD. The constraints in a DTD can maintain consistency across a range of documents, or even within a single large document. There may be many ways to represent a particular concept, but once you choose one, let the DTD help you stick to it.

31.6 | The prolog

XML documents should start with a prolog that describes the XML version ("1.0", for now), document type, and other characteristics of the document.

The prolog is made up of an *XML declaration* and a *document type declaration*, both optional. Though an author may include either, neither, or both, it is best to try to maximize the amount of prolog information provided. This will make later processing more reliable.

The XML declaration must precede the document type declaration if both are provided. Also, comments, processing instructions, and white space can be mixed in among the two declarations. The prolog ends when the first start-tag begins.

Here is a sample prolog as a warm-up:

Example 31-8. A simple prolog

```
<?xml version="1.0"?>
<!DOCTYPE DOCBOOK SYSTEM "http://www.davenport.org/docbook">
```

This DTD says that the document conforms to XML version 1.0 and declares adherence to a particular document type, DOCBOOK.

Here are the grammar rules for the prolog:

Spec. Reference 31-12. **Prolog**

```
[22]   prolog ::=  XMLDecl? Misc* (doctypedecl Misc*)?
[27]   Misc ::=  Comment | PI |  S
```

31.6.1 *XML declaration*

The XML declaration is fairly simple. It has several parts and they fit together one after another.

Spec. Reference 31-13. **XML declaration**

```
[23]   XMLDecl ::=   '<?xml' VersionInfo EncodingDecl? SDDecl? S? '?>'
```

A minimal XML declaration looks like this:

Example 31-9. **Minimal XML declaration**

```
<?xml version="1.0"?>
```

Here is a more expansive one, using all of its parts:

Example 31-10. **More expansive XML declaration**

```
<?xml version="1.0" encoding="UTF-8" standalone="yes"?>
```

There is one important thing to note in the last example. It looks like a start-tag with attributes, but it is *not*. The different parts of the XML declaration just happen to look like attributes. Well, not quite "just happen": it could have had a completely different syntax, but that would have been harder to memorize. So the parts were chosen to look like attributes to reduce the complexity of the language. One important difference between XML declaration parts and attributes is that the parts are strictly ordered whereas attributes can be specified in any order.

31.6.1.1   Version info

The *version info* part of the XML declaration declares the version of XML that is in use. It is required in all XML declarations. At the time of writing, the only valid version string is "1.0". But if you always use the version string, you can be confident that future XML processors will not think that your document was meant to conform to XML version 2.0 or 3.0 when and if those languages become available. Since they do not exist yet, you cannot know if your documents will be compatible with them.

In fact, the only reason that the XML declaration is optional is so that some HTML and SGML documents can be used as XML documents without confusing the software that they usually work with. You can imagine that an older browser would not react nicely to an HTML document with an XML declaration. But this "backwards compatibility" consideration is only temporary. Future versions of XML may require the XML declaration.

The XML version information is part of a general trend towards information representations that are *self-identifying*. This means that you can look at an XML document and (if it has the declaration) know immediately both that it is XML and what version of XML it uses. As more and more document representations become self-identifying, we will be able to stop relying on error-prone identification schemes like file extensions.

31.6.1.2   Encoding declaration

An XML declaration may also include an *encoding declaration*. It describes what character encoding is used. This is another aspect of being self-identifying. If your documents are encoded in the traditional 7-bit-ASCII used on most operating systems and with most text editors, then you do not need to worry about the encoding-declaration. 7-bit-ASCII is a subset of a Unicode encoding called *UTF-8* which XML processors can automatically detect and use. If you use 7-bit ASCII and need to encode a character outside of 7-bit-ASCII, such as the trademark sign or a non-English character, you can do so most easily by using a numeric character reference, as described in 36.2, "Character references", on page 535.

Spec. Reference 31-14. **Encoding declaration**

```
[80]EncodingDecl::= S 'encoding'
                    Eq ('"' EncName '"' | "'" EncName "'" )
[81]EncName::= [A-Za-z] ([A-Za-z0-9._] |'-')*
```

31.6.1.3   Standalone document declaration

An XML declaration can include a *standalone document declaration*. It declares what components of the document type definition are necessary for complete processing of the document. This declaration is described in 36.4, "Standalone document declaration", on page 541.

31.6.2 *Document type declaration*

Somewhere after the XML declaration (if present) and before the first element, the *document type declaration* declares the document type that is in use in the document. A "book" document type, for example, might be made up of chapters, while a letter document type could be made up of element types such as ADDRESS, SALUTATION, SIGNATURE, and so forth.

The document type declaration is at the heart of the concept of *structural validity*, which makes applications based on XML robust and reliable. It includes the markup declarations that express the *document type definition (DTD)*.

The DTD is a formalization of the intuitive idea of a document type. The DTD lists the element types available and can put constraints on the occurrence and content of elements and other details of the document structure. This makes an information system more robust by forcing the documents that are part of it to be consistent.

31.7 | Markup miscellany

This section contains information on some more useful markup constructs. They are not as important or as widely used as elements, attributes and the XML declaration, but they are still vital parts of a markup expert's toolbox.

31.7.1 *Predefined entities*

Sometimes when you are creating an XML document, you want to protect certain characters from markup interpretation. Imagine, for example, that you are writing a user's guide to HTML. You would need a way to include an example of markup. Your first attempt might be to create an example element and do something like this:

Example 31-11. An invalid approach to HTML examples in XML

```
<p>HTML documents must start with a DOCTYPE, etc. etc. This
is an example of a small HTML document:
<example>

  <!DOCTYPE HTML PUBLIC "-//W3C//DTD HTML 3.2 Final//EN">
  <HTML>
  A document's title
  <H1>A document's title</H1>
  </HTML>

</example>
```

This will not work, however, because the angle brackets that are supposed to represent HTML markup will be interpreted as if they belonged to the XML document you are creating, not the mythical HTML document in the example. Your XML processor will complain that it is not appropriate to have an HTML DOCTYPE declaration in the middle of an XML document! There are two solutions to this problem: predefined entities and CDATA sections.

Predefined entities are XML markup that authors use to represent characters that would otherwise be interpreted as having a special meaning, such as a start-tag or an entity reference. There are five *predefined* ("built-in") entities in XML. These were included precisely to deal with this problem. They are listed in Table 31-1.

Table 31-1   Predefined entities

Entity reference	Character
&amp;	&
&lt;	<
&gt;	>
&apos;	'
&quot;	"

Why these specific five characters?

Spec. Reference 31-15. **Predefined entities**

The ampersand character (&) and the left angle bracket (<) may appear in their literal form only when used as markup delimiters, or within a comment, a processing instruction, or a CDATA section. [...] If they are needed elsewhere, they must be escaped using either numeric character references or the strings "&" and "<" respectively.

Spec. Reference 31-16. **Attribute values**

To allow attribute values to contain both single and double quotes, the apostrophe or single-quote character (') may be represented as "'", and the double-quote character (") as """.

An entity for the right angle bracket is also provided because it is sometimes useful to avoid putting a special string called *CDEnd* (discussed later) into your document. But you do not have to use this entity in most cases.

We can use references to the predefined entities to insert these characters, instead of typing them directly. Then they will not be interpreted as markup:

When your XML processor parses the document, it will replace the entity references with actual characters. It will not interpret the characters it inserts as markup, but as "plain 'ol data characters" (character data).

Example 31-12. Writing about HTML in XML

```
<p>HTML documents must start with a DOCTYPE, etc. etc. This
is an example of a small HTML document:
<EXAMPLE>
   &lt;!DOCTYPE HTML PUBLIC "-//W3C//DTD HTML 3.2 Final//EN">
   &lt;HTML>
   &lt;HEAD>
   &lt;TITLE>A document's title
   &lt;/TITLE>
   &lt;/HEAD>
   &lt;/HTML>
</EXAMPLE>
```

31.7.2 *CDATA sections*

While predefined entities are convenient, human beings are not as good at decoding them as computers are. Your readers will get the translated version, so they will be fine. But as the author, you will spend hours staring at character entity references while you are editing your XML document. You may also spend hours replacing special characters with character entity references. This can get annoying.[1]

Another construct, called a CDATA section, allows you to ask the processor not to interpret a chunk of text as containing markup: "Hands off! This isn't meant to be interpreted." CDATA stands for "character data". You can mark a section as being character data using this special syntax:

Example 31-13. CDATA section

```
'<![CDATA[' content ']]>'
```

Here are some examples:

As you can see, it does not usually matter what you put in CDATA sections because their content is not scanned for markup. There is one obvious exception (and one not-so-obvious corollary). The string that ends the CDATA section, "]]>" (known as *CDEnd*) cannot be used inside the section:

```
<![CDATA[
 JavaScript code: if( a[c[5]]> 7 ) then...
]]>
```

---

1. This is especially nasty when you are writing an XML book, where examples tend to contain may angle brackets.

Example 31-14. Writing about HTML in a CDATA section

```
<![CDATA[
<HTML>
This is an example from HTML for Dumbbells!
<p>It may be a pain to write a book about HTML in HTML,
but it is easy in XML!
</HTML>
]]>
```

Example 31-15. Java code in a CDATA section

```
<![CDATA[
if( foo.getContentLength() < 0  && input = foo.getInputStream() )
    open = true;
]]>
```

The first occurrence of CDEnd in the middle of the JavaScript expression will terminate the section. You simply cannot use a CDATA section for content that includes CDEnd. You must end the section and insert the character:

```
<![CDATA[
 JavaScript code: if( a[c[5]]]]>><![CDATA[ 7 ) then...
]]>
```

This is quite painful and can cause a problem for embedding programming languages. But even in those languages, CDEnd is probably a fairly rare character string, so you should just keep an eye out for it.

The non-obvious corollary is:

Caution   *CDEnd ("]]>") should only be used to close CDATA sections. It must not occur anywhere else in an XML document.*

This is an absolute requirement, not just a recommendation. Because of it you can easily check that you have closed CDATA sections correctly by comparing the number of CDEnd strings to the number of sections. If you do not close a CDATA section correctly, some of your document's markup may be interpreted as character data. Since ("]]>") is not something that typical documents contain, this restriction is rarely a problem.

With all of these warnings, CDATA sections may sound tricky to use, but they really aren't. This book, for example, has several hundred. Mistakes involving CDATA sections are usually quite blatant, because either markup will show up in your rendered document, or data characters will be interpreted as markup and probably trigger an error message.

Predefined entities and CDATA sections only relate to the interpretation of the markup, not to the properties of the real document that the markup represents.

31.7.3 *Comments*

Sometimes it is useful to embed information about a document or its markup in a manner that will be ignored by computer processes and renditions of the document. For example, you might insert a note to yourself to clean up the wording of a section, a note to a co-author explaining the reason for a particular section of the document, or a note in a DTD describing the semantics of a particular element. This information can be hidden from the application in a *comment*. Comments should never be displayed in a browser, indexed in a search engine, or otherwise processed as part of the data of the real document. They may, however, be treated as metadata.

Example 31-16. A comment

```
<!-- This section is really good! Let's not change it. -->
```

Comments consist of the characters "<!--" followed by almost anything and ended by "-->". The "almost anything" in the middle cannot contain the characters "--". This is a little bit inconvenient, because people often use those two characters as a sort of dash, to separate thoughts. This is another point to be careful of, lest you get bitten.

Spec. Reference 31-17. Comment

```
[15]  Comment ::= '<!--'((Char - '-')|('-'(Char - '-')))*'-->'
```

Comments can go just about anywhere in the instance or the prolog. However, they cannot go within declarations, tags, or other comments. Here is a document using some comments in several correct places:

Example 31-17. Comments all over the place

```
<?xml version="1.0"?>
<!-- There is no other version yet! -->
<!-- Now on to the doctype ->
<!DOCTYPE EXAMPLE [
  <!-- This is a comment in the
  doctype declaration internal subset! -->
  <!ELEMENT EXAMPLE (#PCDATA)>
  <!-- This is a very simple DTD. -->
]> <!-- Here comes the "root" or "document" element. -->
<EXAMPLE>This is some character data.
<!-- That was some character data. -->
</EXAMPLE>
<!-- That's all folks -->
```

Markup is not recognized in comments. You can put less-than and ampersand symbols in them, but they will not be recognized as the start of elements or entity references.

Comments are a good place to describe the semantics of element types and attributes. So you might use a comment to tell other DTD maintainers and authors that an element type with a cryptic name like p is actually intended to model paragraphs and not (for example) British currency. Comments are not just about being helpful to other people. After all, even expert document type designers have a limited and imperfect memory. Some day even you will wonder exactly what it was you meant by a particular element-type name. The DTD comments will help. The job that you are saving might be your own!

31.8 | Summary

An XML document is composed of a prolog and a document instance. The prolog is optional, and provides information about how the document is structured both physically (where its parts are) and logically (how its elements fit together). Elements and attributes describe the logical structure. Entities describe the physical structure. To use a rough analogy, the entities are like a robot's body parts, the elements are his thoughts, and stylesheets and software provide his behavior.

Creating a document type definition

- Document type declaration
- Element type declarations
- Attribute list declarations

32

reating your own document type definition is like creating your own markup language. If you have ever chafed at the limitations of a language with a fixed set of element types, such as HTML, TEI or LaTeX, then you will embrace the opportunity to create your own language.[1]

We should note again that it is possible to keep a document type definition completely in your head rather than writing the declarations for a DTD. Sometimes DTD designers do that while they are testing out ideas. Usually, though, you actually commit your ideas to declarations so that a validating processor can help you to keep your documents consistent.

Note also that, for the present, we are maintaining the distinction, discussed in 4.4.3, "Document type, DTD, and markup declarations", on page 61, between a document type, the XML markup rules for it (DTD), and the markup declarations that declare the DTD. Those *DTD declarations* are connected to the big kahuna of markup declarations – the *document type declaration*.

---

1. With its own set of limitations!

32.1 | Document type declaration

A document type declaration for a particular document might say "This document is a concert poster." The document type definition for the document would say "A concert poster must have the following features." As an analogy: in the world of art, you can *declare* yourself a practitioner of a particular movement, or you can *define* the movement by writing its manifesto.

The XML spec uses the abbreviation DTD to refer to document type definitions because we speak of them much more often than document type declarations. The DTD defines the allowed element types, attributes and entities and can express some constraints on their combination.

A document that conforms to its DTD is said to be *valid*. Just as an English sentence can be ungrammatical, a document can fail to conform to its DTD and thus be *invalid*. That does not necessarily mean, however, that it ceases to be an XML document. The word valid does not have its usual meaning here. An artist can fail to uphold the principles of an artistic movement without ceasing to be an artist, and an XML document can violate its DTD and yet remain a well-formed XML document.

As the document type declaration is optional, a well-formed XML document can choose not to declare conformance to any DTD at all. It cannot then be a valid document, because it cannot be checked for conformance to a DTD. It is not invalid, because it does not violate the constraints of a DTD.

XML has no good word for these merely well-formed documents. Some people call them "well-formed", but that is insufficiently precise. If the document were not well-formed, it would not be XML (by definition). Saying that a document is well-formed does not tell us anything about its conformance to a DTD at all.

For this reason, we prefer the terms used by the ISO for full-SGML: *type-valid*, meaning "valid with respect to a document type", and *non-type-valid*, the converse.

Example 32-1 is an XML document containing a document type declaration and document type definition for mailing labels, followed by an instance of the document type: a single label.

The document type declaration starts on the first line and ends with "]>". The DTD declarations are the lines starting with "<!ELEMENT". Those are *element type declarations*. You can also declare attributes, entities and notations for a DTD.

Example 32-1. XML document with document type declaration

```
<!DOCTYPE label[
    <!ELEMENT label (name, street, city, state, country, code)>
    <!ELEMENT name (#PCDATA)>
    <!ELEMENT street (#PCDATA)>
    <!ELEMENT city (#PCDATA)>
    <!ELEMENT state (#PCDATA)>
    <!ELEMENT country (#PCDATA)>
    <!ELEMENT code (#PCDATA)>
]><label>
<name>Rock N. Robyn</name>
<street>Jay Bird Street</street>
<city>Baltimore</city>
<state>MD</state>
<country>USA</country>
<code>43214</code>
</label>
```

Recall from 3.4, "Entities: The physical structure", on page 38 that an XML document can be broken up into separate objects for storage, called "entities".[1] The document type declaration occurs in the first (or only) entity to be parsed, called the "document entity".

In Example 32-1, all of the DTD declarations that define the label DTD reside within the document entity. However, the DTD could have been partially or completely defined somewhere else. In that case, the document type declaration would contain a reference to another entity containing those declarations.

A document type declaration with only external DTD declarations looks like Example 32-2.

Example 32-2. Document type declaration with external DTD declarations

```
<?xml version="1.0"?>
<!DOCTYPE LABEL SYSTEM "http://www.sgmlsource.com/dtds/label.dtd">
<LABEL>
...
</LABEL>
```

They keyword SYSTEM is described more completely in 33.9.1, "System identifiers", on page 495. For now, we will just say that it tells the processor

---

1. Loosely, an entity is like a file.

to fetch some resource containing the external information. In this case, the external information is made up of the declarations that define the label DTD. They should be exactly the ones we had in the original label document. The big difference is that now they can be reused in hundreds, thousands, or even millions of label documents. Our simple DTD could be the basis for the largest junk mailing in history!

All document type declarations start with the string "<!DOCTYPE". Next they have the name of an element type that is defined in the DTD. The root element in the instance (described in 31.4, "Elements", on page 434) must be of the type declared in the document type declaration. If any of the DTD declarations are stored externally, the third part of the document type declaration must be either "SYSTEM" or "PUBLIC". We will cover "PUBLIC" later. If it is "SYSTEM", the final part must be a *URI* pointing to the external declarations. A URI is, for all practical purposes, a URL. URIs are discussed in 34.4, "Uniform Resource Identifier (URI)", on page 512.

Spec. Reference 32-1. DOCTYPE declaration

```
[28] doctypedecl ::= '<!DOCTYPE' S Name (S ExternalID)? S? ('['
                     (markupdecl | PEReference | S)* ']' S?)? '>'
[75] ExternalID ::=  'SYSTEM' S SystemLiteral
                     | 'PUBLIC' S PubidLiteral S SystemLiteral

[29] markupdecl ::= elementdecl | AttlistDecl | EntityDecl
                    | NotationDecl | PI | Comment
```

32.2 | Internal and external subset

In Example 32-1, the DTD declarations were completely *internal*. They were inside of the document type declaration. In Example 32-2, they were completely external. In many cases, there will be a mix of the two. This section will review these options and show how most XML document type declarations combine an internal part, called the *internal subset* and an external part, called the *external subset*.

From now on, as we'll almost always be writing about DTD declarations, we'll refer to them as "the DTD". We'll resort to the finer distinctions only when necessary for clarity.

We will start with another example of a DTD:

Example 32-3. Garage sale announcement DTD.

```
<!ELEMENT GARAGESALE (DATE, TIME, PLACE, NOTES)>
<!ELEMENT DATE (#PCDATA)>
<!ELEMENT TIME (#PCDATA)>
<!ELEMENT PLACE (#PCDATA)>
<!ELEMENT NOTES (#PCDATA)>
```

These markup declarations would make up an ultra-simple DTD for garage sale announcements.[1] As you may have deduced, it declares five element types. We will get to the syntax of the declarations soon. First we will look at how they would be used. These could reside in a separate file called garage.dtd (for instance) and then every document that wanted to conform to them would declare its conformance using a document type declaration. This is shown in Example 32-4.

Example 32-4. Conforming garage sale document.

```
<!DOCTYPE GARAGESALE SYSTEM "garage.dtd">
<GARAGESALE>
<DATE>February 29, 1998</DATE>
<TIME>7:30 AM</TIME>
<PLACE>249 Cedarbrae</PLACE>
<NOTES>Lots of high-quality junk for sale!</NOTES>
</GARAGESALE>
```

Instead of a complete URL, we have just referred to the DTD's file name. Actually, this is still a URL. It is a relative URL. That means that in a standard Web server setup, the XML document entity and its DTD entity reside in the same directory. You could also refer to a full URL as we did in Example 32-2.

Example 32-5. Specifying a full URL

```
<!DOCTYPE GARAGESALE SYSTEM
          "http://www.tradestuff.com/stuff.dtd">
<GARAGESALE>
...
</GARAGESALE>
```

1. A garage sale is where North Americans spend their hard-earned money on other people's junk, which they will eventually sell at their own garage sales.

The relative URL is more convenient while you are testing because you do not need to have a full server installed. You can just put the two entities in the same directory on your hard drive. But your DTD and your instance can get even more cozy than sharing a directory. You can hoist your DTD into the same entity as the instance:

Example 32-6. Bringing a DTD into the instance

```
<!DOCTYPE GARAGESALE
[
<!ELEMENT GARAGESALE (DATE, PLACE, NOTES)>
<!ELEMENT DATE (#PCDATA)>
<!ELEMENT TIME (#PCDATA)>
<!ELEMENT PLACE (#PCDATA)>
<!ELEMENT NOTES (#PCDATA)>
]>
<GARAGESALE>
...
</GARAGESALE>
```

The section between the square brackets is called the *internal subset* of the document type declaration. For testing, this is very convenient! You can edit the instance and the DTD without moving between entities. Since entities usually correspond to files, this means that instead of moving between two files, you need only edit one.

Although this is convenient, it is not great for reuse. The DTD is not available anywhere but in this file. Other documents cannot conform to this DTD without copying the declarations into their internal subset.

Often you will combine both approaches. Some of the DTD declarations can go in an external entity where it can be reused, and some of it can go in the same entity as the instance. Often graphic entities (see 33.6, "Unparsed entities", on page 486) would be declared in the internal subset because they are specific to a document. On the other hand, element type declarations would usually be in the *external subset*, the external part of the document type declaration:

Example 32-7. Reference to an external subset

```
<!DOCTYPE GARAGESALE SYSTEM "garage.dtd">
<!ENTITY LOGO SYSTEM "logo.gif">
]><GARAGESALE> ... </GARAGESALE>
```

The declarations in the internal subset are processed before those in the external subset. This gives document authors the opportunity to override[1] some kinds of declarations in the shared portion of the DTD.

Note that the content of both the internal subset and the external subset makes up the DTD. `garage.dtd` may have a `.dtd` extension but that is just a convention we chose to emphasize that the file contains DTD declarations. It is *not* necessarily the full set of them. The full set of DTD declarations is the combination of the declarations in the internal and external subsets.

Caution   *Many people believe that the file containing the external subset is "the DTD". Until it is referenced from a document type declaration and combined with an internal subset (even an empty one) it is just a file that happens to have markup declarations in it. It is good practice, however, when an external subset is used, to restrict the internal subset to declarations that apply only to the individual document, such as entity declarations for graphics.*

It is often very convenient to point to a particular file and refer to it as "the DTD" for a given document type. As long as the concepts are straight in your mind, it does seem a trifle simpler than saying "the file that contains the markup declarations that I intend to reference as the external subset of the document type declaration for all documents of this type".

32.3 | Element type declarations

Elements are the foundation of XML markup. Every element in a valid XML document must conform to an element type declared in the DTD. Documents with elements that do not conform could be well-formed, but not valid. Here is an example of an element type declaration:

Element type declarations must start with the string "<!ELEMENT", followed by the name (or *generic identifier* of the element type being

---

1. Actually, preempt.

Example 32-8. Element type declaration.

```
<!ELEMENT memo (to, from, body )>
```

declared. Finally they must have a *content specification*. The content specification above states that elements of this type must contain a to element followed by a from element followed in turn by a body element. Here is the rule from the XML grammar:

Spec. Reference 32-2. Element type declaration

```
<!ELEMENT' S Name S contentspec S? '>'
```

Element type names are XML *names*. That means there are certain restrictions on the characters allowed in them. These are described in 31.1.4, "Names and name tokens", on page 428. Each element type declaration must use a different name because a particular element type cannot be declared more than once.

Caution   Unique element type declaration
Unlike attribute and entities, element types can be declared only once.

32.4 | Element type content specification

Every element type has certain allowed content. For instance a document type definition might allow a chapter to have a title in its content, but would probably not allow a footnote to have a chapter in its content (though XML itself would not prohibit that!).

There are four kinds of content specification. These are described in Table 32-1.

Table 32-1 *Content specification types*

Content specification type	Allowed content
EMPTY content	May not have content. They are typically used for their attributes.
ANY content	May have any content at all.
Mixed content	May have character data or a mix of character data and sub-elements specified in mixed content specification.
Element content	May have only sub-elements specified in element content specification

---

32.4.1 *Empty content*

Sometimes we want an element type that can never have any content. We would give it a content specification of EMPTY. For instance an image element type like HTML's img would include a graphic from somewhere else. It would do this through an attribute and would not need any sub-elements or character data content. A cross-reference element type might not need content because the text for the reference might be generated from the target. A reference to an element type with the title "More about XML" might become "See *More about XML* on page 14".

You can declare an element type to have empty content by using the EMPTY keyword as the content specification:

Example 32-9. Empty element type

```
<!ELEMENT MY-EMPTY-ELEMENT EMPTY>
```

32.4.2 *ANY content*

Occasionally, you want an element type to be able to hold any element or character data. You can do this if you give it a content spec of ANY:

This is rarely done. Typically we introduce element type declarations to express the structure of our document types. An element type that has an

Example 32-10. Element type with ANY content.

```
<!ELEMENT LOOSEY-GOOSEY ANY>
```

ANY content specification is completely unstructured. It can contain any combination of character data and sub-elements. Still, ANY content element types are occasionally useful, especially while a DTD is being developed. If you are developing a DTD for existing documents, then you could declare each element type to have ANY content to get the document to validate. Then you could try to figure out more precise content specifications for each element type, one at a time.

32.4.3 *Mixed content*

Element types with *mixed content* are allowed to hold either character data alone or character data with child elements interspersed. A paragraph is a good example of a typical mixed content element. It might have character data with some mixed in emphasis and quotation sub-elements. The simplest mixed content specifications allow data only and start with a left parenthesis character ("("), followed by the string #PCDATA and a final close parenthesis (")"):

Example 32-11. Data-only mixed content.

```
<!ELEMENT emph (#PCDATA)>
<!ELEMENT foreign-language ( #PCDATA ) >
```

You may put white space between the parenthesis and the string #PCDATA if you like. The declarations above create element types that cannot contain sub-elements. Sub-elements that are detected will be reported as validity errors.

In other words, these elements do not really have "mixed" content in the usual sense. Like the word "valid", XML has a particular meaning for the word that is not very intuitive. Any content specification that contains #PCDATA is called mixed, whether sub-elements are allowed or not.

We can easily extend the DTD to allow a mix of elements and character data:

Example 32-12. Allow a mix of character data and elements

```
<!ELEMENT paragraph (#PCDATA|emph)*>
<!ELEMENT abstract (#PCDATA|emph|quot)*>
<!ELEMENT title ( #PCDATA | foreign-language | emph )* >
```

Note the trailing asterisks. They are required in content specifications that allow a mix of character data and elements. The reason that they are there will be clear when we study content models. Note also that we can put white space before and after the vertical bar ("|") characters.

These declarations create element types that allow a mix of character data and sub-elements. The element types listed after the vertical bars ("|"), are the allowed sub-elements. The following would be a valid `title` if we combine the declarations in Example 32-12 with those in Example 32-11

```
<title>this is a <foreign-language>tres gros</foreign-language>
       title for an <emph>XML</emph> book</title>
```

The `title` has character data ("This is a"), a `foreign-language` sub-element, some more character data ("title for an"), an `emph` sub-element and some final character data "book". We could have reordered the `emph` and `foreign-language` elements and the character data however we wanted. We could also have introduced as many (or as few) `emph` and `foreign-language` elements as we needed.

32.5 | Content models

The final kind of content specification is a "children" specification. This type of specification says that elements of the type can contain only child elements in its content. You declare an element type as having *element content* by specifying a *content model* instead of a mixed content specification or one of the keywords described above.

A content model is a pattern that you set up to declare what sub-element types are allowed and in what order they are allowed. A simple model for a `memo` might say that it must contain a `from` followed by a `to` followed by a `subject` followed by a `paragraph`. A more complex model for a `question-and-answer` might require `question` and `answer` elements to alternate.

A model for a `chapter` might require a single `title` element, one or two `author` elements and one or more `paragraphs`. When a document is validated, the processor would check that the element's content matches the model.

A simple content model could have a single sub-element type:

```
<!ELEMENT WARNING (PARAGRAPH)>
```

This says that a WARNING must have a single PARAGRAPH within it. As with mixed content specifications, you may place white space before or after the parentheses. We could also say that a WARNING must have a TITLE and then a PARAGRAPH within it:

```
<!ELEMENT WARNING (TITLE, PARAGRAPH)>
```

The comma (",") between the "TITLE" and "PARAGRAPH" GIs indicates that the "TITLE" must precede the "PARAGRAPH" in the "WARNING" element. This is called a *sequence*. Sequences can be as long as you like:

```
<!ELEMENT MEMO (FROM, TO, SUBJECT, BODY)>
```

You may put white space before or after the comma (",") between two parts of the sequence.

Sometimes you want to have a *choice* rather than a sequence. For instance a document type might be designed such that a FIGURE could contain either a GRAPHIC element (inserting an external graphic) or a CODE element (inserting some computer code).

```
<!ELEMENT FIGURE (GRAPHIC|CODE)>
```

The vertical bar character ("|") indicates that the author can choose between the elements. You can put white space before or after the vertical bar. You may have as many choices as you want:

```
<!ELEMENT FIGURE (CODE|TABLE | FLOW-CHART| SCREEN-SHOT)>
```

You may also combine choices and sequences using parenthesis. When you wrap parenthesis around a choice or sequence, it becomes a *content particle*. Individual GIs are also content particles. You can use any content particle where ever you would use a GI in a content model:

```
<!ELEMENT FIGURE (CAPTION, (CODE|TABLE|FLOW-CHART|SCREEN-SHOT) )>
<!ELEMENT CREATED ((AUTHOR | CO-AUTHORS), DATE )>
```

The content model for FIGURE is thus made up of a sequence of two content particles. The first content particle is a single element type name. The second is a choice of several element type names. You can break down the content model for CREATED in the same way.

You can make some fairly complex models this way. But when you write a DTD for a book, you do not know in advance how many chapters the book will have, nor how many paragraphs each chapter will contain. You need a way of saying that the part of the content specification that allows captions is *repeatable* – that you can match it many times.

Sometimes you will also want to make an element optional. For instance, some figures may not have captions. You may want to say that part of the specification for figures is optional.

XML allows you to specify that a content particle is optional or repeatable using an *occurrence indicator*. There are three occurrence indicators:

Table 32-2   *Occurrence Indicators*

Indicator	Content particle is...
?	Optional (0 or 1 time).
*	Optional and repeatable (0 or more times)
+	Required and repeatable (1 or more times)

Occurrence indicators directly follow a GI, sequence or choice. The occurrence indicator cannot be preceded by white space.

For instance we can make captions optional on figures:

```
<!ELEMENT FIGURE (CAPTION?, (CODE|TABLE|FLOW-CHART|SCREEN-SHOT))>
```

We can allow footnotes to have multiple paragraphs:

```
<!ELEMENT FOOTNOTE (P+)>
```

Because we used the "+" indicator, footnotes must have at least one paragraph. We could also have expressed this in another way:

```
<!ELEMENT FOOTNOTE (P, P*)>
```

This would require a leading paragraph and then 0 or more paragraphs following. That would achieve the same effect as requiring 1 or more paragraphs. The "+" operator is just a little more convenient than repeating the preceding content particle.

We can combine occurrence indicators with sequences or choices:

```
<!ELEMENT QUESTION-AND-ANSWER (INTRODUCTION,
                              (QUESTION, ANSWER)+,
                              COPYRIGHT?)>
```

It is also possible to make all of the element types in a content model optional:

```
<!ELEMENT IMAGE (CAPTION?)>
```

This allows the IMAGE element to be empty sometimes and not other times. The question mark indicates that CAPTION is optional. Most likely these IMAGE elements would link to an external graphic through an attribute. The author would only provide content if he wanted to provide a caption.

In the document instance, empty IMAGE elements look identical to how they would look if IMAGE had been declared to be always empty. There is no way to tell from the document instance whether they were declared as empty or are merely empty in a particular case.

32.6 | Attributes

Attributes allow an author to attach extra information to the elements in a document. For instance a code element for computer code might have a lang attribute declaring the language that the code is in. On the other hand, you could also use a lang sub-element for the same purpose. It is the DTD designer's responsibility to choose a way and embody that in the DTD. Attributes have strengths and weaknesses that differentiate them from sub-elements so you can usually make the decision without too much difficulty.

The largest difference between elements and attributes is that attributes cannot contain elements and there is no such thing as a "sub-attribute". Attributes are always either text strings with no explicit structure (at least as far as XML is concerned) or simple lists of strings. That means that a chapter should not be an attribute of a book element, because there would be no place to put the titles and paragraphs of the chapter. You will typically use attributes for small, simple, unstructured "extra" information.

Another important difference between elements and attributes is that each of an element's attributes may be specified only once, and they may be specified in any order. This is often convenient because memorizing the order of things can be difficult. Elements, on the other hand, must occur in the order specified and may occur as many times as the DTD allows. Thus you must use elements for things that must be repeated, or must follow a certain pattern or order that you want the XML parser to enforce.

These technical concerns are often enough to make the decision for you. But if everything else is equal, there are some usability considerations that can help. One rule of thumb that some people use (with neither perfect success nor constant abject failure) is that elements usually represent data that is the natural content that should appear in every print-out or other rendition, Most formatting systems print out elements by default and do not print out attributes unless you specifically ask for them. Attributes represent data that is of secondary importance and is often information about the information (*"metainformation"*).

Also, attribute names usually represent properties of objects, but element-type names usually represent parts of objects. So given a `person` element, sub-elements might represent parts of the body and attributes might represent properties like weight, height, and accumulated karma points.

We would advise you not to spend too much of your life trying to figure out exactly what qualifies as a part and what qualifies as a property. Experience shows that the question "what is a property?" ranks with "what is the good life?" and "what is art?". The technical concerns are usually a good indicator of the philosophical category in any event.

32.6.1 *Attribute-list declarations*

Attributes are declared for specific element types. You declare attributes for a particular element type using an *attribute-list declaration*. You will often see an attribute-list declaration right beside an element type declaration:

```
<!ELEMENT PERSON (#PCDATA)>
<!ATTLIST PERSON EMAIL CDATA #REQUIRED>
```

Attribute declarations start with the string "<!ATTLIST". Immediately after the white space comes an element type's generic identifier. After that comes the attribute's name, its *type* and its *default*. In the example above, the attribute is named EMAIL and is valid on PERSON elements. Its value must be *character data* and it is required – there is no default and the author must supply a value for the attribute on every PERSON element.

Spec. Reference 32-3. Attribute-list declarations

```
[52]  AttlistDecl ::=  '<!ATTLIST' S Name AttDef* S? '>'
[53]  AttDef ::=  S Name S AttType S DefaultDecl
```

You can declare many attributes in a single attribute-list declaration.[1]

You can also have multiple attribute-list declarations for a single element type:

---

1. That's why it is called a list!

Example 32-13. Declaring multiple attributes

```
<!ATTLIST PERSON EMAIL CDATA #REQUIRED
                 PHONE CDATA #REQUIRED
                 FAX CDATA #REQUIRED>
```

Example 32-14. Multiple declarations for one element type

```
<!ATTLIST PERSON HONORIFIC CDATA #REQUIRED>
<!ATTLIST PERSON POSITION CDATA #REQUIRED
                 ORGANIZATION CDATA #REQUIRED>
```

This is equivalent to putting the declarations altogether into a single attribute-list declaration.

It is even possible to have multiple declarations for the same attribute of the same element type. When this occurs, the first declaration of the attribute is binding and the rest are ignored. This is analogous to the situation with entity declarations.

Note that two different element types can have attributes with the same name without there being a conflict. Despite the fact that these attributes have the same name, they are in fact different attributes. For instance a SHIRT element could have an attribute SIZE that exhibits values SMALL, MEDIUM and LARGE and a PANTS element in the same DTD could have an attribute also named SIZE that is a measurement in inches:

```
        <!-- These are -->
<!ATTLIST SHIRT SIZE (SMALL|MEDIUM|LARGE) #REQUIRED>

        <!-- two different attributes -->
<!ATTLIST PANTS SIZE NUMBER #REQUIRED>
```

It is not good practice to allow attributes with the same name to have different semantics or allowed values in the same document. That can be quite confusing for authors.

32.6.2 *Attribute defaults*

Attributes can have *default values*. If the author does not specify an attribute value then the processor supplies the default value if it exists. A DTD designer can also choose not to supply a default.

Specifying a default is simple. You merely include the default after the type or list of allowed values in the attribute list declaration:

```
<!ATTLIST SHIRT SIZE (SMALL|MEDIUM|LARGE) MEDIUM>
<!ATTLIST SHOES SIZE NUMBER "13">
```

Any value that meets the constraints of the attribute list declaration is legal as a default value. You could not, however, use "abc" as a default value for an attribute with declared type `number` any more than you could do so in a start-tag in the document instance.

Sometimes you want to allow the user to omit a value for a particular attribute without forcing a particular default. For instance you could have an element SHIRT which has a SIZE attribute with a declared type of NUMBER. But some shirts are "one size fits all". They do not have a size. You want the author to be able to leave this value out and you want the processing system to *imply* that the shirt is "one size fits all". You can do this with an *impliable* attribute:

```
<!ATTLIST SHIRT SIZE NUMBER #IMPLIED>
```

The string "#IMPLIED" gives any processing program the right to insert whatever value it feels is appropriate. This may seem like a lot of freedom to give a programmer, but typically implied attributes are simply ignored. In the case of our SHIRT, there is no need to worry about "one size fits all" shirts because anybody can wear them. Authors should only depend upon the implied value when they do not care or where there is a well-defined convention of what the lack of a value "really" means. This is again a case of semantics and would be communicated to the author through some other document, DTD comment or other communication mechanism.

It is easy for an author to not specify a value for an attribute that is not required: just do not mention the attribute. Note that specifying an attribute value that is an empty string is *not* the same as not specifying an attribute value:

```
<SHIRT>          <!-- This conforms to the declaration above. -->
<SHIRT SIZE=""> <!-- This does *not* conform to the declaration. -->
```

The opposite situation to providing a default is where a document type designer wants to force the author to choose a value. If a value for an attribute is important and cannot reliably be defaulted, the designer can require authors to specify it with a *required* attribute default:

```
<!ATTLIST IMAGE URL CDATA #REQUIRED>
```

In this case, the DTD designer has made the URL attribute required on all IMAGE elements. This makes sense because without a URL to locate the image file, the `image` element is useless.

It may be surprising, but there are even times when it is useful to supply an attribute value that cannot be overriden at all. This is rare, but worth knowing about. Imagine, for instance, that an Internet directory maintainer like *Yahoo*™ decides to write a robot [1] that will automatically extract the first section title of every document indexed by the directory. The difficulty is that different DTDs will have different element-type names for titles. HTML-like DTDs use H1 etc. DocBook-like DTDs use title. TEI-like DTDs use head. Even if the robot knows about these DTDs, what about all of the others? There are potentially as many DTDs in existence as there are XML documents! It is not feasible to write a robot that can understand every document type.

The vendor needs to achieve some form of standardization. But it cannot force everyone to conform to the same DTD: that is exactly what XML is supposed to avoid! Instead, they can ask all document creators to label the elements that perform the *role of* section titles. They could do this with an attribute, such as title-element. The robot can then use the content of those elements to generate its index.

Each DTD designer thinks through the list of element types to add the attribute to. They specify what their element types mean in terms of the indexing system understood by the robot. They may not want authors changing the value on an element by element basis. They can prevent this with *fixed* attributes:

```
<!ATTLIST H1 TITLE-ELEMENT CDATA #FIXED "TITLE-ELEMENT">
<!ATTLIST HEAD TITLE-ELEMENT CDATA #FIXED "TITLE-ELEMENT">
<!ATTLIST TITLE TITLE-ELEMENT CDATA #FIXED "TITLE-ELEMENT">
```

Now all of the appropriate elements are marked with the attribute. No matter what else is in the DTD, the robot can find what it is looking for.

32.6.3 *Attribute types*

An important feature of attributes is that attributes have *types* that can enforce certain *lexical* and *semantic* constraints. *Lexical* constraints are constraints like "this attribute must contain only numerals". Semantic constraints are along the lines of "this attribute must contain the name of a declared entity". These constraints tend to be very useful in making robust DTDs and document processing systems.

However, it is vital to remember that **the value of an attribute is not necessarily the exact character string that you enter between the quotation marks**. That string first goes through a process called *attribute-*

---

1. A *robot* is an automatic Web information gatherer.

value normalization on its way to becoming the attribute value. Since attribute types apply to the *normalized value*, we had better digress for a moment to master normalization.

32.6.3.1   Attribute value normalization

XML processors normalize attribute values to make author's lives simpler. If it were not for normalization, you would have to be very careful where you put white space in an attribute value. For instance if you broke an attribute value across a line:

```
<GRAPHIC ALTERNATE-TEXT="This is a picture of a penguin
    doing the ritual mating dance">
```

You might do this merely becuse the text is too long for a single line in a text editor.

This sort of thing is normalized by the XML processor. The rules for this are a little intricate, but most times they will just do what you want them to. Let's look at them.

All XML attribute values are entered as quoted strings. They start and end with either single-quotes ("'") or double-quotes ('""'). If you want to embed a single-quote character into an attribute value delimited by single quotes or a double-quote character into an attribute value delimited by double quotes, then you must use an entity reference as described in 31.7.1, "Predefined entities", on page 442.

The first thing the XML parser does to prepare for normalization is to strip off the surrounding quotes.

Then, character references are replaced by the characters that they reference. As we discussed earlier, character references allow you to easily insert "funny" characters.

Next, general entity references are replaced. This is important to note. While it is true that entity references are not allowed in markup, unnormalized attribute values are *text* – a mixture of markup and data. After normalization, only the data remains.[1]

If the expansion for an entity reference has another entity reference within it, that is expanded also, and so on and so forth. This would be rare in an entity used in an attribute value. After all, attribute values are usually

---

1. Philosophically, attribute values are metadata, but it is an article of faith in the XML world that metadata is data.

very short and simple. An entity reference in an attribute value cannot be to an external entity.

Newline characters in attribute values are replaced by spaces. *If* the attribute is known to be one of the tokenized types[1] (see below), then the parser must further remove leading and trailing spaces. So " token " becomes "token". It also collapses multiple spaces between tokens into a single space, so that "space   between" would become "space between". The distinction between *unnormalized attribute value text* and *normalized attribute value data* trips up even the experts. Remember, when reading about attribute types, that they apply to the normalized data, not the unnormalized text.

32.6.3.2   CDATA and name token attributes

The simplest type of attribute is a *CDATA* attribute. The CDATA stands for "character data". The declaration for such an attribute looks like this:

Example 32-15. CDATA Attributes

```
<!DOCTYPE ARTICLE[
<!ELEMENT ARTICLE>
<!ATTLIST ARTICLE DATE CDATA #REQUIRED>
...
]>
<ARTICLE DATE="January 15, 1999">
...
</ARTICLE>
```

Character data attribute values can be any string of characters. Basically anything else is legal in this type of attribute value.

Name token (NMTOKEN) attributes are somewhat like CDATA attributes. The biggest difference is that they are restricted in the characters that name tokens allow. Name tokens were described in 31.1.4, "Names and name tokens", on page 428. To refresh your memory, they are strings made up of

---

1. If, in other words, attribute-list declarations were provided and the processor is either a validating processor or a non-validating processor that decides to read them.

letters, numbers and a select group of special characters: period ("."), dash
("-"), underscore ("_") and colon (":").

Example 32-16. Name token attribute type

```
<!DOCTYPE PARTS-LIST[
...
<!ATTLIST PART DATE NMTOKEN #REQUIRED>
...
]>
<PARTS-LIST>
...
<PART DATE="1998-05-04">...</PART>

</PARTS-LIST>
]>
```

An empty string is not a valid name token, whereas it would be a valid
CDATA attribute value.

Name tokens can be used to allow an attribute to contain numbers that
need special characters. They allow the dash, which can be used as a minus
sign, the period, which can be a decimal point, and numbers. These are useful for fractional and negative numbers. You can also use alphabetic characters to specify units.

Name tokens can also be used for naming things. This is similar to how
you might use variable names in a programming language. For instance, if
you used XML to describe the structure of a database, you might use name
tokens to name and refer to fields and tables. The restrictions on the name
token attribute type would prevent most of the characters that would be
illegal in field and table names (spaces, most forms of puncutation, etc.). If
there is a reason that all fields or record names must be unique, then you
would instead use the *ID* attribute type discussed in 32.6.3.4, "ID and
IDREF attributes", on page 470.

If it is appropriate to have more than one name token, then you can use
the NMTOKENS attribute type which stands for "name tokens". For instance
in describing a database:

One other difference between CDATA attributes and NMTOKEN attributes is
in their *normalization*. This was discussed in 32.6.3.1, "Attribute value normalization", on page 467.

Example 32-17. Name tokens attribute type

```
<!DOCTYPE DATABASE [
...
<!ELEMENT TABLE EMPTY>
<!ATTLIST TABLE NAME NMTOKEN #REQUIRED
                FIELDS NMTOKENS #REQUIRED>
...
]>
<DATABASE>
...
<TABLE NAME="SECURITY" FIELDS="USERID PASSWORD DEPARTMENT">
...
</DATABASE>
```

32.6.3.3   Enumerated and notation attributes

Sometimes as a DTD designer you want to create an attribute that can only exhibit one of a short list of values: "small/medium/large", "fast/slow"; "north/south/east/west". *Enumerated attribute types* allow this. In a sense, they provide a choice or menu of options.

The syntax is reminiscent of choice lists in element type declarations:

```
<!ATTLIST CHOICE (OPTION1|OPTION2|OPTION3) #REQUIRED>
```

You may provide as many choices as you like. Each choice is an XML *name token* and must meet the syntactic requirements of name tokens described in 31.1.4, "Names and name tokens", on page 428.

There is another related attribute type called a notation attribute. This attribute allows the author to declare that the element's content conforms to a declared notation. Here is an example involving several ways of representing dates:

```
<!ATTLIST DATE NOTATION (EUROPEAN-DATE|US-DATE|ISO-DATE) #REQUIRED>
```

In a valid document, each notation allowed must also be declared with a notation declaration.

32.6.3.4   ID and IDREF attributes

Sometimes it is important to be able to give a name to a particular occurrence of an element type. For instance, to make a simple hypertext link or cross-reference from one element to another, you can name a particular section or figure. Later, you can refer to it by its name. The target element is labeled with an *ID* attribute. The other element refers to it with an *IDREF* attribute. This is shown in Example 32-18

Example 32-18. ID and IDREF used for cross-referencing

```
<!DOCTYPE BOOK [
...
<!ELEMENT SECTION (TITLE, P*)>
<!ATTLIST SECTION MY-ID ID #IMPLIED>
<!ELEMENT CROSS-REFERENCE EMPTY>
<!ATTLIST CROSS-REFERENCE TARGET IDREF #REQUIRED>
...
]>
<BOOK>
...
<SECTION MY-ID="Why.XML.Rocks"><TITLE>Features of XML</TITLE>
...
</SECTION>


...
If you want to recall why XML is so great, please see
the section titled <CROSS-REFERENCE TARGET="Why.XML.Rocks"/>.
...
</BOOK>
```

The style sheet would instruct browsers and formatters to replace the cross-reference element with the name of the section. This would probably be italicized and hyperlinked or labeled with a page number if appropriate.

Note that we made the section's MY-ID optional. Some sections will not need to be the target of a cross-reference, hypertext link or other reference and will not need to be uniquely identified. The TARGET attribute on CROSS-REFERENCE is required. It does not make sense to have a cross-reference that does not actually refer to another element.

IDs are XML names, with all of the constraints described in 31.1.4, "Names and name tokens", on page 428. Every element can have at most one ID, and thus only one attribute per element type be an ID attribute. All IDs specified in an XML document must be unique. A document with two ID attributes whose values are the same is invalid. Thus "chapter" would not be a good name for an ID, because it would make sense to use it in many places. "introduction.chapter" would be a logical ID because it would uniquely identify a particular chapter.

IDREF attributes must refer to an element in the document. You may have as many IDREFs referring to a single element as you need. It is also possible to declare an attribute that can potentially exhibit more than one IDREF by declaring it to be of type IDREFS:

```
<!ATTLIST RELATED-CHAPTERS TARGETS IDREFS #REQUIRED>
```

Now the TARGETS attribute may have one or more IDREFs as its value. There is no way to use XML to require that an attribute take two or more, or three or more, (etc.) IDREFs. You will recall that we could do that sort of thing using content models in element type declarations. There is no such thing as a content model for attributes. You could model this same situation by declaring RELATED-CHAPTERS to have content of one or more or two or more (etc.) CHAPTER-REF elements that each have a single IDREF attribute (named TARGET in this example):

Example 32-19. IDREF attributes

```
<!DOCTYPE BOOK[
...
<!ELEMENT RELATED-CHAPTERS (CHAPTER-REF+)>
<!ELEMENT CHAPTER-REF EMPTY>
<!ATTLIST CHAPTER-REF TARGET IDREF #REQUIRED>
...
]>
<BOOK>
...
<RELATED-CHAPTERS>
<CHAPTER-REF TARGET="introduction.to.xml">
<CHAPTER-REF TARGET="xml.rocks">
</RELATED-CHAPTERS>
...
</BOOK>
```

As you can see, element type declarations have the benefit of having content models, which can define complex structures, and attributes have the benefit of attribute types, which can enforce lexical and semantic constraints. You can combine these strengths to make intricate structures when this is appropriate.

32.6.3.5   ENTITY attributes

External unparsed entities are XML's way of referring to objects (files, CGI script output, etc.) on the Web that should not be parsed according to XML's rules. Anything from HTML documents to pictures to word processor files fall into this category. It is possible to refer to unparsed entities using an attribute with declared type ENTITY. This is typically done either to hyperlink to, reference or include an external object:

Example 32-20. Entity attribute type

```
<!DOCTYPE ARTICLE[
<!ATTLIST BOOK-REF TARGET ENTITY #REQUIRED>
...
<!ENTITY another-book SYSTEM
          "http://www.buyOurBooks.com/TheOtherBook.html">
...
]><BOOK>
...
<BOOK-REF target="another-book">
...
</BOOK>
```

You can also declare an attribute to be of type *ENTITIES*, in which case its value may be the name of more than one entity. It is up to the application or stylesheet to determine whether a reference to the entity should be treated as a hot link, embed link or some other kind of link. The processor merely informs the application of the existence and notation of the entity. You can find information on unparsed entities and notations in Chapter 33, "Entities: Breaking up is easy to do", on page 476 and 32.7, "Notation Declarations", on page 474.

32.6.3.6   Summary of attribute types

There are two *enumerated* attribute types: *enumeration* attributes and NOTATION attributes.

Seven attribute types are known as *tokenized* types because each value represents either a single token (ID, IDREF, ENTITY, NMTOKEN) or a list of tokens (IDREFS, ENTITIES, and NMTOKENS).

The final type is the CDATA string type which is the least constrained and can hold any combination of XML characters as long as "special characters" (the quote characters and ampersand) are properly entered.

Table 32-3   Summary of attribute types

Type	Lexical constraint	Semantic constraint
CDATA	None	None
Enumeration	Nmtoken	Must be in the declared list.
NOTATION	Name	Must be in the declared list and a declared notation name.
ID	Name	Must be unique in document.
IDREF	Name	Must be some element's ID.
IDREFS	Names	Must each be some element's ID.
ENTITY	Name	Must be a declared entity name.
ENTITIES	Names	Must each be a declared entity name.
NMTOKEN	Name Token	None
NMTOKENs	Name Tokens	None

32.7 | Notation Declarations

Notations are referred to in various parts of an XML document, for describing the data content notation of different things. A data content notation is the definition of how the bits and bytes of class of object should be interpreted. According to this definition, XML is a data content notation, because it defines how the bits and bytes of XML documents should be interpreted. Your favorite word processor also has a data content notation. The notation declaration gives an internal name to an existing notation so that it can be referred to in attribute list declarations, unparsed entity declarations, and processing instructions.

The most obvious place that an XML document would want to describe the notation of a data object is in a reference to some other resource on the web. It could be an embedded graphic, an MPEG movie that is the target of a hyperlink, or anything else. The XML facility for linking to these data resources is the entity declaration, and as we discussed earlier, they are referred to as *unparsed entities*. Part of the declaration of an unparsed entity is the name of a declared notation that provides some form of pointer to the external definition of the notation. The external definition could be a public or system identifier for documentation on the notation, some formal specification or a helper application that can handle objects represented in the notation.

Example 32-21. Notations for unparsed entities

```
<!NOTATION HTML SYSTEM "http://www.w3.org/Markup">
<!NOTATION GIF SYSTEM "gifmagic.exe">
```

Another place that notations arise are in the notation attribute type. You use this attribute type when you want to express the notation for the data content of an XML element. For instance, if you had a date element that used ISO or EU date formats, you could declare notations for each format:

Example 32-22. Notations for unparsed entities

```
<!NOTATION ISODATE PUBLIC +//APPROPRIATE-IDENTIFIER-HERE//>
<!NOTATION EUDATE PUBLIC +//APPROPRIATE-IDENTIFIER-HERE//>
<!ELEMENT TODAY (#PCDATA)>
<!ATTLIST TODAY DATE-FORMAT NOTATION (ISODATE|EUDATE) #REQUIRED>
```

Now the DATE-FORMAT attribute would be restricted to those two values, and would thus signal to the application that the content of the TODAY element conforms to one or the other.

Finally, notations can be used to give XML names to the targets for processing instructions. This is not strictly required by XML, but it is a good practice because it provides a sort of documentation for the PI and could even be used by an application to invoke the target.

This seems like a good way to close this chapter. DTDs are about improving the permanence, longevity, and wide reuse of your data, and the predictability and reliability of its processing. If you use them wisely, they will save you time and money.

Tip   *Learning the syntax of markup declarations so that you can write DTDs is important, but learning how to choose the right element types and attributes for a job is a subtle process that requires a book of its own. We suggest David Megginson's* Structuring XML Documents, *also in this series (ISBN 0-13-642299-3).*

Entities: Breaking up is easy to do

- Parameter and general
- Internal and external
- Parsed and unparsed

33

XML allows flexible organization of document text. The XML constructs that provide this flexibility are called *entities*. They allow a document to be broken up into multiple storage objects and are important tools for reusing and maintaining text.

33.1 | Overview

In simple cases, an entity is like an abbreviation in that it is used as a short form for some text. We call the "abbreviation" the *entity name* and the long form the *entity content*. That content could be as short as a character or as long as a chapter. For instance, in an XML document, the entity dtd could have the phrase "document type definition" as its content. Using a reference to that entity is like using the word DTD as an abbreviation for that phrase – the parser replaces the reference with the content.

You create the entity with an *entity declaration*. Here is an entity declaration for an abbreviation:

Entities can be much more than just abbreviations. There are several different kinds of entities with different uses. We will first introduce the differ-

Example 33-1. Entity used as an abbreviation

```
<!ENTITY dtd "document type definition">
```

ent variants in this overview and then come back and describe them more precisely in the rest of the chapter. We approach the topic in this way because we cannot discuss the various types of entity entirely linearly. Our first pass will acquaint you with the major types and the second one will tie them together and provide the information you need to actually use them.

Another way to think of an entity is as a box with a label. The label is the entity's name. The content of the box is some sort of text or data. The entity declaration creates the box and sticks on a label with the name. Sometimes the box holds XML text that is going to be parsed (interpreted according to the rules of the XML notation), and sometimes it holds data, which should not be.

If the content of an entity is XML text that the processor should parse, the XML spec calls it a *parsed entity*. The name is badly chosen because it is, in fact, unparsed; it will be parsed only if and when it is actually used.

If the content of an entity is data that is not to be parsed, the XML spec calls it an unparsed entity. This name isn't so great either because, as we just pointed out, an XML text entity is also unparsed.

We'll try to minimize the confusion and to avoid saying things like "a parsed entity will be parsed by the XML parser". But we sure wish they had named them "text entity" and "data entity".

The abbreviation in Example 33-1 is a parsed entity. Parsed entities, being XML text, can also contain markup. Here is a declaration for a parsed entity with some markup in it:

Example 33-2. Parsed entity with markup

```
<!ENTITY dtd "<term>document type definition</term>">
```

The processor can also fetch content from somewhere on the Web and put that into the box. This is an *external* entity. For instance, it could fetch a chapter of a book and put it into an entity. This would allow you to reuse the chapter between books. Another benefit is that you could edit the chapter separately with a sufficiently intelligent editor. This would be very useful if you were working on a team project and wanted different people to work on different parts of a document at once.

Example 33-3. External entity declaration

```
<!ENTITY intro-chapter SYSTEM "http://www.megacorp.com/intro.xml">
```

Entities also allow you to edit very large documents without running out of memory. Depending on your software and needs, either each volume or even each article in an encyclopedia could be an entity.

An author or DTD designer refers to an entity through an *entity reference*. The XML processor replaces the reference by the content, as if it were an abbreviation and the content was the expanded phrase. This process is called *inclusion*. After the operation we say either that the entity reference has been *replaced* by the entity content or that the entity content has been *included*. Which you would use depends on whether you are talking from the point of view of the entity reference or the entity content. The content of parsed entities is called their *replacement text*.

Here is an example of a parsed entity declaration and its associated reference:

Example 33-4. Entity Declaration

```
<!DOCTYPE MAGAZINE[
...
<!ENTITY title "Hacker Life">
...
]>
<MAGAZINE>
<TITLE>&title;</TITLE>
...
<P>Welcome to the introductory issue of &title;. &title; is
geared to today's modern hacker.
...
</MAGAZINE>
```

Anywhere in the document instance that the entity reference "&title;" appears, it is *replaced* by the text "Hacker Life". It is just as valid to say that "Hacker Life" is *included* at each point where the reference occurs. The ampersand character starts all general entity references and the semicolon ends them. The text between is an entity name.

Spec. Reference 33-1. General entity reference

```
[68]   EntityRef ::=   '&' Name ';'
```

We have looked at entities that can be used in the creation of XML documents. Others can only be used to create XML DTDs. The ones we have been using all along are called *general* entities. They are called general entities because they can generally be used anywhere in a document. The ones that we use to create DTDs are called *parameter* entities.

We would use parameter entities for most of the same reasons that we use general entities. We want document type definitions to share declarations for element types, attributes and notations, just as we want documents to share chapters and abbreviations. For instance many DTDs in an organization might share the same definition for a paragraph element type named *para*. The declaration for that element type could be bundled up with other common DTD components and used in document type definitions for memos, letters and reports. Each DTD would include the element type declaration by means of a parameter entity reference.

Unparsed entities are for holding data such as images or molecular models in some data object notation. The application does not expect the processor to parse that information because it is not XML text.

Although it is an oversimplification, it may be helpful in your mind to remember that unparsed entities are often used for pictures and parsed entities are usually used for character text. You would include a picture through an unparsed entity, since picture representations do not (usually!) conform to the XML specification. Of course there are many kinds of non-XML data other than graphics, but if you can at least remember that unparsed entities are used for graphics then you will remember the rest also.

Example 33-5. Unparsed entity declaration

```
<!ENTITY picture SYSTEM "http://www.home.org/mycat.gif" NDATA GIF>
```

We use unparsed entities through an entity attribute. A processor does not expand an entity attribute, but it tells the application that the use occurred. The application can then do something with it. For instance, if the application is a Web browser, and the entity contains a graphic, it could display the graphic. Entity attributes are covered in 32.6.3.5, "ENTITY attributes", on page 472.

33.2 | Entity details

Caution   *Like other names in XML, entity names are case-sensitive: &charles; refers to a different entity from &Charles;.*

It is good that XML entity names are case-sensitive because they are often used to name letters. Case is a convenient way of distinguishing the upper-case version of a letter from the lower-case one. "Sigma" would represent the upper-case version of the Greek letter, and "sigma" would be the lower-case version of it. It would be possible to use some other convention to differentiate the upper- and lower-case versions, such as prefixes. That would give us "uc-Sigma" and "lc-Sigma".

Entities may be declared more than once, but only the first declaration is *binding*. All subsequent ones are ignored as if they did not exist.

```
<!ENTITY abc "abcdefghijklmnopqrst"> <!-- This is binding. -->
<!ENTITY abc "ABCDEFGHIJKLMNOPQRST"> <!-- This is ignored. -->
<!ENTITY abc "AbCdEfGhIjKlMnOpQrSt"> <!-- So is this.       -->
```

Declarations in the internal DTD subset are processed before those in the external subset, as described in Chapter 32, "Creating a document type definition ", on page 448. In practice, document authors can override parameter entities in the external subset of the DTD by declaring entities of the same name in the internal subset.

Entities are not difficult to use, but there are several variations and details that you should be aware of. We have already covered the major varieties, but only informally.

There is one special entity, called the *document entity* which is not declared, does not have a name and cannot be referenced. The document entity is the entity in which the processor started the current parse. Imagine you download a Web document called `catalog.xml`. Before a browser can display it, it must start to parse it, which makes it the document entity. It may include other entities, but because parsing started with `catalog.xml`, those others are not the document entity. They are just ordinary external entities.

If you click on a link and go to another XML Web page, then the processor must parse that page before it can display it. That page is the document entity for the new parse. In other words, even the simplest XML document has at least one entity: the document entity. The processor starts parsing the document in the document entity and it also must finish there.[1]

The document entity is also the entity in which the XML declaration and document type declaration can occur.

You may think it is strange for us to call this an entity when it is not declared as such, but if we were talking about files, it would probably not surprise you. It is common in many computer languages to have files that include other files. Even word processors allow this. We will often use the word entity to refer to a concept analogous to what you would think of as a file, although entities are more flexible. Entities are just "bundles of information". They could reside in databases, zip files, or be created on the fly by a computer program.

33.3 | Classifications of entities

There are many interesting things that you can do with entities. Here are some examples:

- You could store every chapter of a book in a separate file and link them together as entities.
- You could "factor out" often-reused text, such as a product name, into an entity so that it is consistently spelled and displayed throughout the document.
- You could update the product name entity to reflect a new version. The change would be instantly visible anywhere the entity was used.
- You could create an entity that would represent "legal boilerplate" text (such as a software license) and reuse that entity in many different documents.
- You could integrate pictures and multimedia objects into your document.
- You could develop "document type definition components" that could be used in many document type definitions. These would allow you to reuse the declarations for common

---

1. To put it mystically: it is the alpha and the omega of entities.

element types (such as paragraph and emphasis) across several document types.

Because XML entities can do so many things, there are several different varieties of them. But XML entities do not break down into six or eight different types with simple names. Rather, you could think of each entity as having three properties that define its type. This is analogous to the way that a person could be tall or short and at the same time male or female and blonde or brunette.

Similarly, entities can be *internal* or *external*, *parsed* or *unparsed* and *general* or *parameter*. There is no single word for a short, male, brunette, and there is similarly no single word for an internal, parsed, parameter entity.

Caution   *Some combinations of entity types are impossible. Obviously an entity cannot be both internal and external, just as a person could not be both blonde and brunette. It turns out that due to restrictions on unparsed entities, there are five combinations that are valid and three that are not.*

Most of the rest of this chapter will describe the five types of entities in greater depth. We will use one convention that might be confusing without this note. In a section on, for instance, internal parsed general entities, we may describe a constraint or feature of all general entities. When we do so, we will use the word "general entity" instead of "internal general entity". This convention will allow us to avoid repeating text that is common among entity types. We will refer back to that text from other sections when it becomes relevant.

33.4 | Internal general entities

Internal parsed general entities are the simplest type of entity. They are essentially abbreviations defined completely in the document type declaration section of the XML document.

All internal general entities are parsed entities. This means that the XML processor parses them like any other XML text. Hence we will leave out the redundant word "parsed" and refer to them simply as internal general entities.

The content for an internal general entity is specified by a string literal after the entity's name. The string literal may contain any markup, including references to other entities. An example is in Example 33-6.

Example 33-6. Internal general entity

```
<?xml version="1.0"?>
<!DOCTYPE EXAMPLE SYSTEM "example.dtd"[
    <!ENTITY xml "Extensible Markup Language">
]>
<EXAMPLE>
    &xml;
</EXAMPLE>
```

Internal general entities can be referenced anywhere in a document instance. They can also be referenced in the content of another general entity. Because they are general entities, they cannot be used to hold markup declarations for expansion in the DTD. They can only hold document content. Because of this, Example 33-7 is not well-formed.

Example 33-7. Illegal: General entities cannot be reference in the DTD

```
<?xml version="1.0"?>
<!DOCTYPE EXAMPLE[
    <!ENTITY xml "Extensible Markup Language">
    &xml;
]>
```

The grammar rules for internal general entities are described in Specification reference 33-2.

Spec. Reference 33-2. Internal general entities

```
[70]   EntityDecl ::=   GEDecl | PEDecl
[71]   GEDecl ::=   '<!ENTITY' S Name S EntityDef S? '>'
[73]   EntityDef ::=   EntityValue | (ExternalID NDataDecl?)
[9]    EntityValue ::=   '"' ([^%&"] | PEReference | Reference)* '"'
                    |   "'" ([^%&'] | PEReference | Reference)* "'"
```

33.5 | External parsed general entities

Every XML entity is either internal or external. The content of internal entities occurs right in the entity declarations. External entities get their content from somewhere else in the system. It might be another file on the hard disk, a Web page or an object in a database. Wherever it is, it is located through an *external identifier*. Usually this is just the word SYSTEM followed by a URI (see 34.4, "Uniform Resource Identifier (URI)", on page 512).

In this section, we are interested specifically in external parsed general entities. Here is an example of such an entity:

```
<!ENTITY ent SYSTEM "http://www.house.gov/Constitution.xml">
```

It is the keyword SYSTEM that tells the processor that the next thing in the declaration is a URI. The processor gets the entity's content from that URI. The combination of SYSTEM and the URI is called an external identifier because it identifies an external resource to the processor. There is another kind of external identifier called a PUBLIC identifier. It is denoted by the keyword PUBLIC. External identifiers are described in 33.9, "External identifiers", on page 494

External parsed general entities can be referenced in the same places that internal general entities can be – the document instance and the replacement text of other general entities – except not in the value of an attribute.

33.5.1 *External parsed entity support is optional*

XML processors are allowed, but not required, to validate an XML document when they parse it. The XML specification allows a processor that is not validating a document to completely ignore declarations of external parsed entities (both parameter and general). There is no way to control this behavior with the standalone document declaration or any other XML markup.

The reason for this is improved Web surfing performance. The XML working group thought that it was important for processors to be able to download the minimum amount of data required to do their job and no more. For instance, a browser could display unresolved external parsed entities as hypertext links that the user could click on to receive. Because the entity would only be downloaded on demand, the original page might display faster.

Unfortunately this is very inconvenient for authors, because it means that external parsed entities are essentially unreliable in systems that you do not completely control (e.g. the Internet vs. an intranet).

Caution   *External parsed entity processing is optional XML processors can ignore external parsed entities. If you use them to store parts of your documents, those parts will only show up at the browser vendor's option.*

In practice this probably means that you should not put documents that use external entities on the Web until a pattern for browser behavior emerges. In the meantime, tools like James Clark's sgmlnorm (part of SP) (see 400) can read an XML document that uses external entities and expand all of the entities for you. Hopefully future versions of the XML specification will make external entity inclusion mandatory.

33.6 | Unparsed entities

Every XML entity is either an *unparsed<>* entity or a *parsed<>* entity. Unparsed entities external entities that the XML processor does not have to parse. For example a graphic, sound, movie or other multimedia object would be included through an unparsed entity. You can imagine the number of error messages you would get if an XML processor tried to interpret a graphic as if it were made up of XML text!

It is occasionally useful to refer to an XML document through an unparsed entity, as if it were in some unparsable representation. You might embed a complete letter document in a magazine document in this way. Rather than extending the magazine DTD to include letter elements, you would refer to it as an unparsed entity. Conceptually, it would be handled in the same way a picture of the letter would be handled. If you refer to it as an unparsed entity, the processor that handles the magazine does not care that the letter is actually XML.

All unparsed entities are external entities because there is no way to express non-XML information in XML entities. They are also all general entities because it is forbiddent (and senseless) to embed data in XML DTDs. Hence, the term "unparsed entity" implies the terms "general" and "external".

Syntactically, declarations of unparsed entities are differentiated from those of other external entities by the keyword NDATA followed by a *notation* name.

Spec. Reference 33-3. Non-XML data declaration

```
NDataDecl ::=   S 'NDATA' S Name
```

The name at the end is the name of a declared notation. Notation declarations are described in 32.7, "Notation Declarations", on page 474. The processor passes this to the application as a hint about how the application should approach the entity.

If the application knows how to deal with that sort of entity (for instance if it is a common graphics notation) then it could do so directly. A browser might embed a rendition of the entity. It might also make a hyperlink to the entity. If it needs to download or install some other handler such as a Java program or Active-X control, then it could do so. If it needs to ask the user what to do it could do that also. The XML specification does not say what it must do. XML only expects processors to tell applications what the declared notation is and the applications must figure out the rest.

In the rare case that the entity is an XML document, the application might decide to process it, create a rendition of it, and then embed it. Alternatively, it might decide to make a hyperlink to it.

33.7 | Internal and external parameter entities

XML entities are classified according to whether they can be used in the DTD or in the document instance. Entities that can only be used in the DTD are called *parameter* entities. For instance, you might want to wrap up a few declarations for mathematical formuale element types and reuse the declarations from DTD to DTD.

The other entities can be used more generally (throughout the entire document instance), and are called *general* entities. Authors can use general entities as abbreviations, for sharing data among documents, including pictures, and many similar tasks.

There is an important reason why the two types are differentiated. When authors create documents, they want to be able to choose entity names without worrying about accidently choosing a name that was already used by the DTD designer. If there were no distinction between entities specific to the DTD and general to the document instance, according to XML's rules, the first declaration would win. That means that either the author would accidently take the place of ("clobber") a declaration that was meant to be used in the DTD, and thus trigger a cryptic error message, or the DTD designer's entity would clobber the entity that was meant to go in the document instance, and a seemingly random string of DTD-text would appear in the middle of the document! XML prevents this by having two different types of entities with distinct syntaxes for declaration and use.

Parameter entities are distinguished from general entity declarations by a single percent symbol in their declaration, and by a different syntax in their use. Here is an example of a parameter entity declaration and use

Example 33-8. Parameter entity

```
<!DOCTYPE EXAMPLE[
    <!-- parameter entity declaration -->
<!ENTITY % example-entity "<!ELEMENT EXAMPLE (#PCDATA)>">
    <!-- parameter entity use -->
%example-entity;
]>
<EXAMPLE>
</EXAMPLE>
```

The entity in Example 33-8 is declared with a syntax similar to that of general entities, but it has a percent sign between the string `<!ENTITY` and the entity's name. This is what differentiates parameter entity declarations from general entity declarations. If you want a general entity you just leave the percent character out.

The entity contains a complete element type declaration. It is referenced on the line after it is declared. Parameter entity references start with the percent-sign and end with the semicolon. The parser replaces the entity reference with the entity's content. In Example 33-8, the processor replaces the reference with the element type declaration "<!ELEMENT EXAMPLE (#PCDATA)>". It then parses and interprets the element type declaration as if it had occurred there originally. The element type is declared and so the example is valid.

Spec. Reference 33-4. Parameter Entity Declaration

```
[72]   PEDecl ::=   '<!ENTITY' S '%' S Name S PEDef S? '>'
[74]   PEDef ::=   EntityValue | ExternalID
[75]   ExternalID ::=   'SYSTEM' S SystemLiteral
              | 'PUBLIC' S PubidLiteral S SystemLiteral
[69]   PEReference ::=   '%' Name ';'
```

Parameter entities can be external, just as general entities can be. But they can never be unparsed. Parameter entities exist to provide building blocks for reusing markup declarations and making DTDs more flexible. It would not make sense to tell the XML processor not to process one! An example of an external parameter entity is in Example 33-9.

Example 33-9. External parameter entity

```
<!DOCTYPE EXAMPLE[
    <!-- parameter entity declaration -->
<!ENTITY % example-entity SYSTEM "pictures.ent">
    <!-- parameter entity use -->
%example-entity;
]>
<EXAMPLE>
</EXAMPLE>
```

Parameter entities cannot be referenced in the document instance. In fact, the percent character is not special in the document instance, so if you try to reference a parameter entity in the instance, you will just get the entity reference text in your data, like "%this;".

Parameter entities can only be referenced after they have been declared. General entities, in contrast, may be referenced before they are declared:

This works because the entity replacement for &usee; does not take place until the point where the user entity is *referenced*. Remember that general entities can only be expanded in the document instance. So the fact

Example 33-10. General entity usage

```
<!ENTITY user "This entity uses &usee;.">
<!ENTITY usee "<em>another entity</em>">
```

that user refers to *usee* is recorded, but the replacement is not immediately done. Later, in the document instance, the author will refer to the user entity using the general entity reference, &user;. At that point, the inclusion of its replacement text will trigger the expansion of the &usee; entity reference and the inclusion of its replacement text.

As you know, all entity declarations are in the DTD. The document instance comes after the DTD. The general entity expansions do not take place until they are referenced in the document instance, so general entity reference expansions will always take place after all of the declarations have been processed, no matter what the order of the general entity declarations in the DTD. Hence, the content of general entities can contain references to other general entities that are declared after them, but the content of parameter entities cannot.

33.8 | Markup may not span entity boundaries

Parsed entities may contain markup as well as character data, but elements and other markup must not span entity boundaries. This means that a particular element may not start in one entity and end in another. If you think of entities as boxes, then an element cannot be half in one box and half in another. This is an example of illegal entity use:

Example 33-11. Elements spanning entity boundaries.

```
<!DOCTYPE EXAMPLE[
    <!ENTITY start "<title>This is a">
    <!ENTITY finish "title</title>">
]>

&start;&finish;
```

This document is not well-formed. When the entity references are replaced with their text, they create a title element. This element spans the entities.

Other markup cannot span entities either. Declarations, comments, processing instructions and entity references must all finish in the entity in which they started. This applies to the document entity as much as any other. Markup strings and elements may not start in the document entity and finish in an included entity. This is a subtle but important rule. Documents which fail to conform are not well-formed.

In Example 33-12, entities are used in ways that are illegal. They are all illegal because they start markup without finishing it or finish it without starting it.

Example 33-12. Illegal entities

```
<!DOCTYPE TEST[
    <!ENTITY illegal1 "This will soon be <em>illegal">
    <!ENTITY illegal2 "This will too <em>">
    <!ENTITY illegal3 "This will also </em>">
    <!ENTITY illegal4 "And so will <!-- this">
    <!ENTITY illegal5 "And this &too">
    <!-- note that none of these are illegal yet. -->
...
]><TEST>
<!-- These references are all illegal -->
&illegal1; <!-- Start-tag in entity with no end-tag there. -->
&illegal2; <!-- Start of tag in entity -->
&illegal3; <!-- End-tag in entity with no start-tag there. -->
&illegal4; <!-- Comment start but no end in entity. -->
&illegal5; <!-- Entity reference starts in entity. -->
</TEST>
```

The entities in Example 33-13 can be used legally or illegally. They do not necessarily represent the start or end of elements or markup, because they do not contain the strings that are used to start a tag ("<"), comment ("<!--"), general entity reference ("&") or other markup. Entity content is interpreted as markup if the replacement text would be interpreted as markup in the same context. In other words, the processor expands the entity and then looks for markup. If the markup it finds spans entity boundaries, then it is illegal.

In this case, it is not the declared entities themselves that are causing the problem, but the fact that elements, entities and markup started in the doc-

Example 33-13. Sometimes legal entities

```
<?xml version="1.0"?>
<!DOCTYPE TEST[
<!ELEMENT TEST (#PCDATA)>
<!ENTITY maybelegal1 "em>"> <!-- May not be part of tag -->
<!ENTITY maybelegal2 "-->"> <!-- May not be part of comment -->
<!ENTITY maybelegal3 "ph>"> <!-- May not be part of tag -->
]>
<TEST>
&maybelegal1; <!-- Legal: Interpreted as character data -->
&maybelegal2; <!-- Legal: Interpreted as character data -->
&maybelegal3; <!-- Legal: Interpreted as character data -->

<&maybelegal1; <!-- Illegal: Markup (tag) spans entities -->
<!-- &maybelegal2; <!-- Ignored: entity ref ignored in comment -->
<em&maybelegal3;   <!-- Illegal: Markup (tag) spans entities -->
</TEST>
```

ument entity must end there, just as in any other entity. The context of an entity reference is very important. That is what decides whether it is legal or illegal.

This is true even of entities that hold *complete* tags, elements, comments, processing instructions, character references, or entity references. References to those entities are legal anywhere their replacement text would be legal. The same applies to *validity* (conformance to a document type definition). Example 33-14 is well-formed, but not valid, because the fully expanded document would not be valid. Validity is covered in Chapter 32, "Creating a document type definition ", on page 448.

Example 33-14. Well-formed but not valid

```
<?xml version="1.0"?>
<!DOCTYPE TEST[
  <!ELEMENT EVENT (TIME, DESCRIPTION)>
  <!ELEMENT TIME (#PCDATA)>
  <!ELEMENT DESCRIPTION (#PCDATA)>
  <!ENTITY accident "<ERROR>Error</ERROR>">
]>
<EVENT>&accident;</EVENT>
```

The document in the example is well-formed. Both the EVENT and ERROR elements start and end in the same entity. It meets all of the other rules required for it to be well-formed. But it is not valid, because accident's replacement text consists of an ERROR element which is not valid where the entity is referenced. (in the EVENT element).

Conceptually, validation occurs after all entities have been parsed.

Spec. Reference 33-5. General entity definition

```
[70]   EntityDecl ::=  GEDecl | PEDecl
[71]   GEDecl ::=  '<!ENTITY' S Name S EntityDef S? '>'
[73]   EntityDef ::=  EntityValue | (ExternalID NDataDecl?)
[72]   PEDecl ::=  '<!ENTITY' S '%' S Name S PEDef S? '>'
[74]   PEDef ::=  EntityValue | ExternalID
```

33.8.1 *Legal parameter entity reference*

Neither general entities nor parameter entities may span markup boundaries, but parameter entities have other restrictions on them. There are precise places that parameter entity references are allowed. Within the internal subset, the rules are simple: parameter entities can only be expanded in places where full markup declarations are allowed. For them to be legal in these contexts they must always contain one or more markup declarations.

Example 33-15. Multiple markup declarations in one parameter entity

```
<!ENTITY % several-declarations
              "<!ELEMENT FOO (#PCDATA)>
              <!ELEMENT BAR (#PCDATA)>
              <!ELEMENT BAZ (#PCDATA)>"
%several-declarations;
```

Because of the way XML handles white space, this entity declaration's replacement text is parsed as it would if the entity declaration had occurred on a single line. In this case we have defined the literal entity value over several lines to make the DTD more readable. When we refer to the parameter entity "several-declarations", the three element types are declared.

The rules for parameter entities in the external subset are much more complex. This is because parameter entities in the external subset are not restricted to complete markup declarations. They can also be parts of a markup declaration. XML restricts parameter entities in the internal subset to full declarations because the internal subset is supposed to be very easy to process quickly by browsers and other processors. The external subset allows more complex, powerful parameter entity references. For instance, in the external subset, this would be a legal series of declarations:

Example 33-16. Entities in the external subset

```
<!ENTITY ent-name "the-entity">
<!ENTITY ent-value "This is the entity">
<!ENTITY %ent-name; %ent-value;>
```

Both the name and the replacement text of the final entity declaration are specified through parameter entity references. Their replacement texts become the entity's name and replacement text.

The tricky part is that there are only particular places that you can use parameter entity references in markup declarations. You might wonder, for instance, if you could replace the string "<!ENTITY" with a parameter entity reference. You might guess that this is impossible because XML does not allow a markup declaration to start in one entity and end in another. You would guess correctly. It would be harder to guess whether you could use an entity reference to fill in the string "ENTITY" which follows the "<!" It turns out that this is illegal as well.

To be safe, we would advise you to stick to using parameter entities only to hold full markup declarations until you are familiar with the text of the XML specification itself. The specification uses a special convention in the grammar to describe the places that parameter entity replacement is allowed in the external subset. There are just too many places for us to list them here.

33.9 | External identifiers

External identifiers refer to information outside the entity in which they occur. There are two types. System identifiers use URIs to refer to an object based on its location. Public identifiers use a publicly declared name to refer to information.

Spec. Reference 33-6. External identifier

```
[75]   ExternalID ::=   'SYSTEM' S SystemLiteral
                      | 'PUBLIC' S PubidLiteral S SystemLiteral
```

33.9.1 *System identifiers*

The *SystemLiteral* that follows the keyword SYSTEM is just a URI. Here is another example of that:

```
<!ENTITY ent SYSTEM "http://www.entities.com/ent.xml">
```

You can also use relative URIs to refer to entities on the same machine as the referring entity. A relative URI is one that does not contain a complete machine name and path. The machine name and part of the path are implied from the context.

Example 33-17. Local external general entity

```
<!ENTITY local SYSTEM "local.xml">
```

If this were declared in a document at the URI http://www.baz.org/, then the processor would fetch the replacement text from http://www.baz.org/local.xml.

These URIs are relative to the location of the referring entity (such as an external parameter entity or the external subset of the DTD) and not necessarily to the document entity. If your document entity is on one machine, and it includes some markup declarations from another machine, relative URIs in the included declarations are interpreted as being on the second machine.

For example, your document might be at http://www.myhome.com. It might include a DTD component with a set of pictures of playing cards from http://www.poker.com/cards.dtd. If that DTD component had a URI, 4Heartss.gif, it would be interpreted relative to the poker site, not yours.

33.9.2 *Public identifiers*

It is also possible to refer to a DTD component or any entity by a name, in addition to a URI. This name is called a "public identifier". If a few entities become widely used in XML circles then it would be inefficient for everyone to fetch the entities from the same servers. Instead, their software should come with those entities already installed (or else it should know the most efficient site from which to download them, perhaps from a corporate intranet). To enable these smarter lookup mechanisms, you would refer to those DTDs by public identifiers, like this:

Example 33-18. Referencing a DTD by public identifier

```
<!DOCTYPE MEMO PUBLIC "-//SGMLSOURCE//DTD MEMO//EN"
                "http://www.sgmlsource.com/dtds/memo.dtd">
<MEMO> </MEMO>
```

The public identifier is a unique name for the entity. It should be unique world-wide. Usually they contain corporate or personal names to make them more likely to be unique. If the software knows how to translate the public identifier into a URI, it will do so. If not, it will use the system identifier.

Right now, the translation from public identifier to URI is typically either hard-wired into a processor or controlled through files called "entity catalogs". Entity catalogs list public identifiers and describe their URIs, in the same way that phone books allow you to look up a name and find a number. Documentation for XML software should mention the format of the catalogs it supports, if any.

In the future there may be intranet- and Internet-wide systems that will look up a public identifier and download the DTD from the site that is closest to you. The Web's designers have been promising this feature for years and XML is ready when they deliver. In the meantime, the system identifier following the public identifier will be used.

33.10 | Conclusion

As you can see, XML separates issues of logical structure from those of the physical storage of the document. This means that document type designers do not have to forsee every possible reasonable way of breaking up a document when they design the document type. This is good, because that sort of decision is best made by those who know their system resource limits, bandwidth limits, editor preferences, and so forth. The document type designer, in contrast, takes responsibility for deciding on a good structure for the document.

XML Linking Language(XLink

- Linking and addressing
- Simple links
- Extended links

34

Hypertext links are the backbone of the World Wide Web. Documents were shuffled around the Internet long before today's Web existed, but it was the ease of moving from page to page with hypertext links that made the Web into the mass market phenomenon it is today.

However, despite their centrality, Web links have many weaknesses. The linking system that we use today is essentially unchanged from the earliest version of the Web. Unfortunately, market inertia has prevented anything more powerful from coming along ... until now.

The second specification in the XML family is XLink. It allows links that go far beyond those provided by HTML. XLinks can have multiple end points, be traversed in multiple directions, and be stored in databases and groups independently of the documents they refer to.

XLink is exciting, but we cannot take full advantage of it yet. It is still being refined by the World Wide Web consortium.

 **Note**   The current version of XLink, and its companion specification, XPointer, are working drafts and will change before they are completed. The basic concepts are well understood and will not change, but the specifics may change between now and then. We will cover only the parts we consider most stable.

34.1 | Basic concepts

The most important (and sometimes subtle) distinction in any discussion of hyperlinking is that of *linking* versus *addressing*. Linking is simply declaring a relationship between two things. If we say "George Washington and Booker T. Washington share a last name" then we have linked those two people in some way.

Addressing, on the other hand, is about describing how to find the two things being linked. There are many kinds of addresses, such as mail addresses, email addresses and URLs. When you create a link in XML, you declare a relationship between two objects referred to by their addresses (URIs). We refer to these objects as *resources*. We will discuss the addresses (URIs) more in 34.3, "Addressing", on page 511.

If you have created Web pages before, you are probably familiar with HTML's simple A element. Whether or not you are familiar with HTML, that link is a good starting point for understanding hyperlinking in general.

The A stands for anchor. Anchor is essentially the HTML term for resource. An HTML link has two ends, termed the *source* and *destination*. When you click on the source end, (designated with an A element and HREF attribute), the Web browser transports you to the other end. Example 34-1 shows how this works.

Example 34-1. An HTML (not XML) link

```
<A HREF="http://www.mysite.com">Go to my site!</A>
```

In this case, the A element itself describes a link, and its HREF attribute points to one of the resources (the destination). As we know, links connect resources, so there must be at least one more resource involved. The other resource, the source, is actually the text that forms the content of the A element. As we will see, XML *simple* links also use the content of the link as one of the resources.

The destination of the link in Example 34-1 does not necessarily know that it is a destination. If you want to link to the Disney home page, you do not need to inform Disney. If a particular document has fifty A elements with HREF attributes, then you know that it has fifty links out. But the Web provides no way to know how many links into it there are.

In the more general *extended* link case, we will link two things such that *neither* end will "know" that it is being linked. The link exists in some third location (or fourth, or fifth, for multi-ended links). This is intuitive if you go back to the definition of linking as defining a relationship. In a real-world sense, I can "link" Jenny Jones and Oprah Winfrey just by speaking of them in the same sentence. Unless they are interested in careers as web-masters, they will probably never know. XLink provides a standardized way to express this in markup.

We might even want to link something that is not explicitly labeled. For instance, we might want to link the third paragraph of the fourth sub-point of the second section of a legal document to the transcript of a relevant court case.

This is analogous to the real world situation where you can either send something to a labeled location ("Please take this to the White House.") or you can give directions to the destination. In hyperlinking terms, we would consider either one of these to be an "address." Obviously there must be some way of locating a resource from a link, but it could be either an address, a label or a combination of the two: "The building is 5 blocks down the street from the White House."

34.1.1 *Simple links*

Although XLink allows more flexible links than does HTML, it also offers simple links that are not much more complicated than HTML's links are. This sort of link is referred to as a simple link. A simple link has two ends, a source and a destination, just like an HTML link. One end has content that represents a resource (usually the source) and it refers to the other end through a URI.

Example 34-2. XML Simple Link

```
. . . for more information, consult
<citation xml:link="simple" href="http://www.uw.ca/paper.xml">
    Biemans(1997)
</mylink>
```

The biggest difference between this link and the HTML link is that this element is not designated a link by its element type name. It is not called A or any special element type name specified in the XML specification. You can call your linking elements whatever you want to. This is an important feature, because it allows you to have many different types of linking elements in a document, perhaps with different declarations, attributes and behaviors. Just as XML allows you to use any element-type name for paragraphs or figures, it allows you flexibility in your linking element-type names.

The link is actually designated an XML link by its `xml:link` attribute. The `xml:` prefix indicates that this attribute's allowed values and semantics are specified by the World Wide Web consortium. This attribute describes what kind of link it is. In this case, it is a simple link.

34.1.2 *Link roles*

In HTML, link resources are either sources or destinations. The element that describes the link is always the source. The resource referred to is always the destination. In XML, this rigid distinction is not hard-wired. An application can make either or both links into sources or destinations. Consider, for instance, if a Web browser made it possible to create notes about someone else's Web site and "stick" them on to it like Post-It notes. These annotations might be represented as XLink *extended* links.

In this case, we actually want the application to make some form of clickable "hotspot" at the other end, on the newspaper's Web page. Of course we don't want them to have control of the actual linking element, or else they might just choose not to show our link. So we want the link to exist in one

Example 34-3. XLink annotations.

```
<annotation xml:link="extended"
        href="http://www.mynewspaper.com">
As usual, your editorial is filled with the kind of claptrap and
willywag that gives me the heebie-jeebies!
</annotation>
```

spot and create a "hotspot" at another. This is the opposite of traditional HTML links.

In order to reverse linking roles, we must somehow tell the application that we want it to do so. One way would be to use an element-type name that the application is hard-coded to understand as having that semantic. For instance an "annotation server" might only deal with annotation elements, or perhaps a few different variants, and would thus know exactly how to handle it.

Another way would be to use some form of stylesheet. But you would still need to have something special in the document that would differentiate annotations from other links (perhaps the annotation element-type name). The stylesheet would provide an extra level of translation to allow your private element-type names to be interpreted as annotations by software.

Yet another way to solve this problem would be to provide an attribute that describes the role of the link in the document and hypertext system. Any of these are valid implementation approaches, and the XLink specification provides a special role attribute to handle the last case. Example 34-4 is an example of that attribute in action.

Example 34-4. Role attribute

```
<hlink role="annotation"
        xml:link="extended"
href="http://www.mynewspaper.com">
As usual, your editorial is filled with the kind of claptrap and
willywag that gives me the heebie-jeebies!
</hlink>
```

In this case, the role designation has moved from the element-type name (now hlink instead of annotation) to the role attribute. Which is more appropriate will depend on your DTD, your software and your taste. XLink could perhaps dictate one style or the other, but real world usage is not that simple. For instance you might need to use an industry standard DTD and thus have no control over element-type names. In another application, you might need to constrain the occurrence of certain kinds of linking elements, and thus need to use element-type names and content models.

34.1.3 *Is this for real?*

You might well ask whether all of this annotation stuff is likely to happen. After all, there are all sorts of social, technical and financial difficulties related to being able to annotate someone else's Web page. Imagine annotation spam: "Tired of reading this boring technical Web page? Click here for HOT PICS!!!" It turns out that early versions of the pre-Netscape Mosaic browser allowed remote annotations (using a proprietary linking scheme), and you could share your annotations with friends or co-workers, but not with everybody on the Web. There are various other experimental services and products that provide the same ability for the modern-day Web. However, each uses a distinct link description notation so that they cannot share.

We may or may not get to the point where everybody can publish annotations to the whole world, but we already have the technology to create annotations that can be shared by other people we know. Unfortunately, this technology has never been widely deployed. Perhaps XLink will solve the link incompatibility problem and allow Web pages to become readable, writeable, and even more linkable.

So what can you do without a world-wide link database? Well let's say that your organization was considering buying a very expensive software product. You and your co-workers might agree to submit your opinions of the product specifications published on the vendor's Website. You could make a bunch of external links from the vendor's text to your comments on it and submit that to your organizational link database. When your co-workers go to see the page, their browsers can fetch your links and actually display them as if they were part of the original document. When your co-workers click on them, the browser will take them to your annotations.

In fact, with a reasonably big link database, you could annotate any Web page you came upon in this manner. When others from your organization came upon the page, they would see your annotations. In one sense, you are editing the entire Web! Of course, the bigger your organization is, the more points of view you can see on each page. On the other hand, sometimes you might not want to share all of your comments with the entire company, so you might have a smaller departmental database which is separate, and only shared by your direct co-workers. And of course at the opposite end of the spectrum, there might be a database for everyone on the Web (if we can make link database software that scales appropriately and find someone to run it).

External links can be useful even without a link database. Without such a database, there is no easy way to distribute your links to other people, so you must communicate the links' existence in some other way. For instance, you could include a critique of a Web page as an attachment to an email. You could also build a document full of links that annotated one of your own Web pages with links to glossary and bibliographic information. We might term each collection a link sheet. Depending on which link sheet the reader used, he would get either the glossary links or the bibliographic links or both sets of links overlapping.

If it makes sense to "project" a link from your home computer onto an existing Website, then surely it makes just as much sense to link two existing Websites. For instance, we could make a link that is targeted towards members of the SGML newsgroup that links the World Wide Web consortium's XML Web page to a related page we know about on the Web. This link would still have two ends, but both could be sources and destinations at the same time. If so, we would term that link bidirectional, because you could *traverse* it from either end. Because the link would exist on your Web site, but link two other pages, we would call it *out-of-line*. And if it makes sense to link two pages, then why not three, or four, or five? Extended links allow this.

34.1.4 *Link behaviors*

XML authors usually go out of their way to avoid putting information about formatting and other types of document behavior into XML documents. We've already been through all of the benefits of keeping your information "pure". As we have said, if you just mark up your documents according to their abstractions, you can apply formatting and other behavior through stylesheets.

On the other hand, there are a few link behaviors that are so common – almost universal – that the XML working group decided that it would be easier to provide some attributes to specify them directly. This takes a layer of abstraction out and thus makes hyperlinking a little bit easier. The concepts of hyperlinking are already abstract, so anything that makes life a little bit easier will help XLink to become popular.

The most interesting type of link behavior is *traversal*. When you click on a hyperlink, you are *traversing* it. If a link is intended to embed information from one resource in another, then the process of actually accomplishing the embedding is a traversal.

The behavioral descriptions are still "abstract enough" to allow a variety of specific behaviors, depending on the situation. The XLink spec says:

Spec. Reference 34-1. Behavior

The mechanism that XLink provides allows link authors to signal certain intentions as to the timing and effects of traversal. Such intentions can be expressed along two axes, labeled *show* and *actuate*. These are used to express policies rather than mechanisms; any link-processing application software is free to devise its own mechanisms, best suited to the user environment and processing mode, to implement the requested policies.

What this means is that different types of software applications are allowed to interpret these suggestions differently. For instance, you might not think of a printer as a machine that would care about hyperlinks, but it might be useful to have a printer that could directly print Web pages and their annotations, or that could resolve graphics embedded through XLink.

34.1.4.1   Show

As the name implies, the show attribute describes how the results of a link traversal should be shown. When you click on a Web link, that is a link traversal — one initiated by your click. On the other hand, if you have ever been to a site where a Web page comes up and says: "You will be forwarded to another page in just a few seconds", then that is a link traversal that is automatic. Typically on the Web, when a link is traversed (manually or automatically) it replaces the previous document in the Web browser window. XLink allows an author to request this behavior with the replace value of the show attribute:

For example:

Occasionally you will also come across a link that actually opens a new window, so that after traversal there is a window for the new page in front

Spec. Reference 34-2. Replace

"replace" indicates that upon traversal of the link, the designated resource should, for the purposes of display or processing, replace the resource where the traversal started.

Example 34-5. A replace link

```
<A xml:link="simple" show="replace" href="http://www.gop.org/">
Click here to visit the GOP</A>
```

of the window for the old page. XLink allows this through the new value of the show attribute.

Spec. Reference 34-3. New

"new" indicates that upon traversal of the link, the designated resource should be displayed or processed in a new context, not affecting that of the resource where the traversal started.

Example 34-6. A new link

```
<A xml:link="simple" show="new" href="http://www.democrats.org/">
Click here to launch a new window and visit the the Dems.</A>
```

As we discussed before, a link can in fact represent *any* relationship. Consider the relationship between a document and an embedded graphic or even text fragment. This can be represented as a link also! Of course there are ways to embed graphics and text using only XML entities, but XLink provides another way of doing the same thing, which can be used in situations where the entity mechanism is not expressive enough by itself.

In this case, you can use the embed value:

Spec. Reference 34-4. Embed

"embed" indicates that upon traversal of the link, the designated resource should be embedded, for the purposes of display or processing, in the body of the resource and at the location where the traversal started.

Example 34-7. An embed link

```
<A xml:link="simple" show="embed"
    href="http://www.democrats.org/logo.gif">
```

34.1.5 *Actuate*

The `actuate` attribute allows the author to describe when the link traversal should occur. For instance it could be user-triggered, such as by a mouse click or a voice command. Or else it could be automatic, such as the automatic embedding of a graphic, or an automatic forward to another Web page (e.g. "This page has moved. You will be directed to the new page momentarily.")

The `user` value indicates that the traversal should be user-triggered. When it is combined with a a `show` attribute of `replace`, it is a typical, click-here-to-go-there link, at least in a graphical browser. On a text-based browser, it might be a type-this-number-to-go-there link. On a spoken-word browser it might be a say-this-number-to-go-there link.

When it is combined with a value of `new` it opens a new "context" (usually a browser window) at user command and leaves the old one open. When it is combined with a value of `embed`, it would make a link that expands into the embedded object. For instance a footnote or graphic might expand in-place when you click on them.

The `auto` value of the `actuate` attribute is used to specify that traversal should be automatic. For instance, most `show="embed"` links would specify automatic traversal. If you combine `show="new"` with `actuate="auto"`, then you can create a Web page that immediately opens another Web page. Perhaps with a stylesheet or other attribute, you could make them be side by side. The final combination is `show="replace"` with `actuate="auto"`. You would use this to set up a "forwarding" link, such as the one we have described, and thus forward users from one page to another.

34.1.6 *Behavior*

XLink also provides a `behavior` attribute for specifying more precise behaviors than the policies described above. You could fill this attribute with commands provided by a browser vendor, or with "hooks" to invoke rules in your stylesheet.

You should be careful with an attribute that is as vaguely defined as this one. Wait until some conventions for its use arise before you fill your documents with markup that could be misinterpreted by confused software.

Spec. Reference 34-5. Behavior attribute

A link author can also optionally use an attribute called behavior to communicate detailed instructions for traversal behavior. The contents, format, and meaning of this attribute are unconstrained.

34.2 | Extended links

In this section, we will discuss more features of the *extended links*. One that we have already discussed is the ability to specify them out-of-line. Extended links also allow for more link ends, more advanced link roles, and other good stuff. We will also be able to re-describe the simple links that we have already seen in the terminology of the more general extended link system.

34.2.1 *Locator elements*

The first extension we will undertake is links with more than two link ends. Consider, for example, that you are redirecting users to several different interpretations of a text. For instance if there were two competitive schools of thought on a topic, each hotspot in the document might allow traversal to a different interpretation of the topic. Now you have three link ends, one for the source and one for each of the interpretations of it. Just as in real life, XLink allows you to make logical links among two or more concepts.

The first big difference between simple links and extended links is that we need to figure out how to specify the address of more than one destination link. We do this by putting *locator* sub-elements into the extended link element. Here is an example:

Example 34-8. Multi-ended link

```
<commentary xml:link="extended">
    <locator href="roberts.xml" role="Roberts"/>
    <locator href="beam.xml" role="Beam"/>
    <locator href="goodwin.xml" role="Goodwin"/>
<P>My fellow Americans, this speech will go down in history...
</commentary>
```

In this case, the three locators each address a resource. A sufficiently sophisiticated browser displaying this document might represent each with an icon or supply a popup menu that allows access to each of the resources. It could even open a small window for each interpretation when the hotspot is selected. This could be controlled by a stylesheet or a behavior attribute. As you can see, each locator can have a different role, but they could also share roles. The role just specifies a semantic for processing the resource when processing the link, not some sort of unique identifier.

Locators can also have some other associated attributes. They can have titles, specified through a `title` attribute. These provide information for human consumption. The browser does not act on them. It merely passes them on to the human in some way, such as a popup menu, or text on the status bar. Locators can also have `show`, `actuate` and `behavor` attributes with the same semantics as for a simple link. Locators seem very similar to simple links because a simple link is a combination of a link and a locator. In fact, this is how they are defined in the XML spec:

Spec. Reference 34-6. Simple links

Simple links can be used for purposes that approximate the functionality of a basic HTML A link, but they can also support a limited amount of additional functionality. Simple links have only one locator and thus, for convenience, combine the functions of a linking element and a locator into a single element. As a result of this combination, the simple linking element offers both a locator attribute and all the link and resource semantic attributes.

It is both useful and convenient that simple links combine these two things, but it means that we must be careful to keep the ideas separate in our heads. The link describes a relationship. The locators say what resources are being related. A simple link uses its content as one resource and the target of its `href` as the other.

34.2.2 *Link groups*

It is often useful to be able to process a group of hyperlinked documents all together. For instance, if one document contains some text and another contains a rebuttal of the text, the browser might want to show them "side by side". It could also allow link traversals in one window to trigger the correct portion of the rebuttal in the other.

Such processing can only work if the browser knows about both documents at the same time. Extended link groups allow you to tell the browser about all of the nodes that should be processed together.

An *extended link group* element is a special kind of extended link. It describes a list of other documents that should be seen to be in this *link group*. Here is an example of such a link:

Example 34-9. Extended link group

```
<related-documents xml:link="group">
<doc xml:link="document" href="annotation.html">
<doc xml:link="document" href="rebuttal.html">
<doc xml:link="document" href="support.html">
</related-documents>
```

In one sense, a link group is a small database of hyperlinks. A browser, editor or other application could look in the link group to see which elements are hyperlink resources and what their behaviors and roles are.

34.3 | Addressing

Now that you know how to make all kinds of neat-o links, you might wonder if XML also features neat-o addressing. Good guess! Of course, XML allows the usual kinds of URLs that you use to navigate the Web. But now that those have found their way onto everything from milk cartons to television advertisments, it is time for something new: *XPointers*. XPointers allow sophisticated addressing into the contents of XML documents. That means that you can make a link to an element, or even a span of elements, based on things like position, element type and ID.

Like XLink and XSL, XPointers are still under development. But the concepts are not likely to change much. They are well established in existing projects like the *Text Encoding Initiative* and the *HyTime* International Standard.

34.4 | Uniform Resource Identifier (URI)

The basic form of address for XLink is a *URI*, which stands for Uniform Resource Identifier. Today's most important form of URI is an extended form of the URL or *Uniform Resource Locator*.[1]

URLs are uniform, in that they have the same basic syntax no matter what specific type of resource (e.g. Web page, newsgroup) is being addressed or what mechanism is described to fetch it. They describe the locations of Web resources much as a physical address describes a person's location. URLs are hierarchical, just as most physical addresses are. A land mail address is resolved by sending a letter to a particular country, and from there to a local processing station, and from there to an individual. URLs are similar.

The first part of a URL is the *protocol*. It describes the mechanism that the Web browser or other client should use to get the resource. Think of it as the difference between Federal Express, UPS, and the other courier services. The most common such protocol is http which is essentially the "official" protocol of the World Wide Web. The ftp file transfer protocol is also widely used, chiefly for large downloads such as new browser versions.

After the protocol, there is a *hostname* and then a *datapath*. The datapath is broken into chunks separated by slash ("/") characters, as you have no doubt seen in hundreds of URLs. Technically, a URL ends at that point.

In a URI, the URL can be followed by an optional *query* and then an optional *fragment identifier*. For instance you may have seen links into HTML documents that look like this:

http://www.megabank.com/banking#about

"#about" is a fragment identifier. It refers to a particular HTML element. XPointers are a similar concept for XML documents, but they are much more flexible. Essentially, XPointers are an extension to URLs to allow you to point not just *to* a document, but into the content of one.

For instance, on today's Web, if you wanted to quote a particular paragraph out of another document, you would go to that document and cut and paste the text into yours. If, in the future, the text on the Web changes,

---

1. When URIs are finalized by the *Internet Engineering Task Force* (IETF RFC 1738 and IETF RFC 1808), they will also allow *Universal Resource Names*, which aren't location-dependent and perhaps will reduce the number of broken links.

yours does not. If that is what you want, that is fine. But XPointers allow you to construct a "living document" that quotes and refers to the very latest version of the paragraph. You can understand how important this ability is for the types of annotations we have discussed. Without it, you could only annotate complete documents.

34.5 | Referring to IDs

The simplest form of XPointer allows you to refer to a particular element named with an ID. This is also the most robust form of XPointer, because it does not at all depend on the location of the referenced text within its document. Consider this XML document:

```
<?xml version="1.0"?>
<!DOCTYPE HEATWAVE SYSTEM "heatwave.dtd">
<HEATWAVE>
<WAVE ID="summer.92">
    <DURATION>July 22 to August 2</DURATION>
    <TEMPERATURE>101 Degrees</TEMPERATURE>
</WAVE>
<WAVE ID="summer.96">
    <DURATION>June 15 to July 18</DURATION>
    <TEMPERATURE>103 Degrees</TEMPERATURE>
</WAVE>
</HEATWAVE>
```

If this document resides at `http://www.hotdays.com/heatwave.xml`, then we could refer to the second HEATWAVE with this URI:

`http://www.hotdays.com/heatwave.xml#id(summer.92)`

The XPointer is the last little bit of the URI, after the pound-sign ("#"). An important thing to note is that this XPointer does not *do* anything. It refers to something. Whether the object is included, hyperlinked, or downloaded is competely a function of the context of reference.

For instance, you could use the XPointer in an XLink to create a hyperlink to something, or in a browser to download a particular object. It is also up to the software to decide whether the referred to element is returned alone, or in the context of its document. For instance, if you use an XPointer in a browser window, it would probably present the whole document and highlight the referenced element. But if you use it in an XLink to include a paragraph, it would probably take that paragraph out of its context and present it alone in the new context.

34.6 | Location terms

In the URI:

`http://www.hotdays.com/heatwave.xml#id(summer.92)`

The string id(summer.92) is called a *location term*. Another simple XPointer location term is the *root* location term. You use this to refer to the root element of a referenced document. For example:

`http://www.hotdays.com/heatwave.xml#root()`

That might seem strange, because you can implicitly refer to the root of a document just by leaving off the XPointer. But with more advanced location terms, we will actually be able to use the root (or an ID) as the starting point for a location ladder. That means that we could, for example, ask for the URI's second sub-element, that element's third sub-element of type p and so forth. These types of XPointers are more fragile because document reorganizations can break them. On the other hand, they allow you to refer to things that have not been identified with an ID. This is important if you are referring to text you cannot change, such as a document elsewhere on the Web, or on a read-only medium.

For example, to refer to the root element's third sub-element of type WAVE, you would do this:

`http://.../heatwave.xml#root().child(3, WAVE)`

Elements of other types would be ignored.

The child location term is called a *relative* location term because it depends upon a starting location identified by root() or id() which are *absolute* location terms. The child location term is the most common type of relative location term, but there are others. When you string them together, they allow you to "navigate" around a document from absolute or relative points. Here is the complete list:

The word "node", used in the spec, is more general than "element", because it includes constructs like comments, processing instructions and character strings.

So for instance, to refer to the element of type H1 that follows the parent of the node with the ID graceland, you would create the following location ladder:

`http://.../something.xml#id(graceland).parent().following(1, H1)`

You can read the ladder like this: "Go to the element named graceland. Go to its parent. Find the H1 following it." Each statement represents a step down the metaphoric ladder. By combining them, you can address any element in an XML document.

Spec. Reference 34-7. Relative location terms

child

> Identifies direct child nodes of the location source.

descendant

> Identifies nodes appearing anywhere within the content of the location source.

ancestor

> Identifies element nodes containing the location source.

preceding

> Identifies nodes that appear before (preceding) the location source.

following

> Identifies nodes that appear after (following) the location source.

psibling

> Identifies sibling nodes (sharing their parent with the location source) that appear before (preceding) the location source.

fsibling

> Identifies sibling nodes (sharing their parent with the location source) that appear after (following) the location source.

XPointers have more advanced and esoteric features, but they are still under development and may change in the future.

34.7 | Conclusion

XLink and XPointer have the power to change the Web, and our lives, in unforseeable ways. For more of the vision, see Chapter 13, "Extended linking", on page 176. For the current version of the specs, see the *XML SPECtacular* on the CD-ROM.

Extensible Style Language (XSL)

- Stylesheets for XML
- Style rules
- Actions
- Flow objects

he *Extensible Style Language* (*XSL*) is a specification being developed within the World Wide Web consortium for applying formatting to XML documents in a standard way. Under the covers, XSL is based on *DSSSL*, a more powerful International Standard from the ISO. However, XSL stylesheets do not look much like DSSSL stylesheets at all. The basic concepts of XSL are similar to DSSSL's, but they have been simplified and "prettified" for Web use. Here are some of the design principles that are being used to create XSL:

- XSL should be straightforwardly useable over the Internet.
- XSL stylesheets should be human-legible and reasonably clear.
- XSL stylesheets shall be easy to create.

As you can see, usability is an important concern in its design!

As our verb tense implies, XSL is still under development. It is likely to change quite a bit. The latest set of design goals includes features for animation, interactivity and other very advanced features. XSL will be the topic of many books all by itself!

The important thing is that the central concepts will be the same as those of DSSSL and the current XSL proposal. These concepts are the focus of this chapter.

Note   *XSL is changing quickly. This chapter outlines the important ideas that are not likely to change.*

The most important thing to get out of this chapter is a feeling for how XML documents are actually processed. We have worked with them purely as abstractions, but now we are going to put them to work. XSL's mechanism for doing this is very similar to that of most XML processing tools.

35.1 | XSL overview

As we discussed earlier, XSL is used to apply style to XML documents. These will usually be marked up entirely according to their abstract structure without (in theory) markup specifically tailored for style application or any other particular kind of processing. Thus XSL is the "missing link" between the data that has been encoded for computer processing and the formatted rendition required for comfortable reading. If you are trying to build a Web page, style languages are very important. Even if you are not, they provide a good example of how processing of XML documents proceeds.

35.1.1 *XSL stylesheets*

Most XSL code looks more or less like "ordinary" XML. Simple XSL stylesheets are merely a specialized form of XML markup designed for formatting other XML documents. XSL is not defined in terms of a formal DTD, but you can still think of it as a document type. The XSL language defines element types and attributes, constrains them to occurring in particular places, and gives them semantics.

Let's start simply and consider a stylesheet that would say that "Paragraphs should use a 12pt font" and "Titles should be 20 point and bolded."

These types of simple declarations are sufficient for many easy tasks. We say that XSL is a "declarative" language because declarations are so important. Declarative languages are easier to learn and use than are programming languages. They do not require complicated logical operations for simple tasks. Here is an XSL stylesheet to accomplish these tasks:

Example 35-1. XSL Example

```
<xsl>
  <rule>
    <target-element type="p"/>
    <paragraph font-size="12pt">
      <children/>
    </paragraph>
  </rule>

  <rule>
    <target-element type="title"/>
    <sequence font-size="20pt" font-weight="bold">
      <children/>
    </sequence>
  </rule>
</xsl>
```

Each `rule` element contains a `target-element` and an action. They say that whenever the XSL processor encounters a `p` element in an XML document, it should create a paragraph in the browser or word processor and give it a font-size of 12 points. Similarly, it should look for `title` elements and make them bold and 20pt. These are simple declarative rules. You do not have to think about the order in which things will be processed, where they are stored or other housekeeping tasks that programming languages usually require you to look after.

35.2 | Referencing XSL stylesheets

There is currently a proposal to allow XML documents to refer to their stylesheets. It has no official standing but it is short, simple and does the job it claims to, so it will probably become a defacto standard. Here is the relevant text of that proposal:

Spec. Reference 35-1. `xml:stylesheet` **processing instruction**

The xml:stylesheet processing instruction is allowed anywhere in the prolog of an XML document. The processing instruction can have pseudo-attributes href (required), type (required), title (optional), media (optional), charset (optional).

These are called "pseudo-attributes" instead of attributes because, although they use attribute syntax, they do not describe properties of an element. The only real syntactic difference between pseudo-attributes and attributes is that you must use pseudo-attributes in the order they are described. You can use attributes in any order.

The most important pseudo-attributes are `href`, which supplies a URI for the stylesheet, and `type`, which says that the stylesheet is in XSL and not DSSSL, CSS, or some other stylesheet language. You can also supply a `title` that the browser might use when offering a list of stylesheet choices. The `media` option allows you to specify what medium the stylesheet is for. You could, for example, have different stylesheets for print (with footnotes and page breaks), online (with clickable links), television (large text and easy scroll controls) and telephone (read aloud with inflection representing emphasis). XSL is not powerful enough yet to handle all of these media equally well, but it will be one day.

Here is an example stylesheet processing instruction (PI):

Example 35-2. Stylesheet PI

```
<?xml:stylesheet href="http://www.sgmlsource.com/memo.xsl"
                 type="text/xsl"?>
```

You can also provide multiple PIs to allow for choice by media, title or stylesheet language:

35.3 | Rules, patterns and actions

Every style sheet language consists of a series of statements that convert structural elements (from the source document) into formatting objects. Even the "Style" menu in Word for Windows consists of such a mapping. It

Example 35-3. Alternative stylesheets

```
<?xml:stylesheet rel=alternate
                 href="mystyle1.xsl"
                 title="Fancy"
                 type="text/xsl"?>
<?xml:stylesheet
                 rel=alternate
                 href="mystyle2.css"
                 title="Simple"
                 type="text/css"?>
<?xml:stylesheet
                 rel=alternate
                 href="mystyle2.aur"
                 title="Aural"
                 type="text/aural"?>
```

takes "paragraph" elements and "maps" them to fonts, colors and other typographic effects. LaTeX users and professional publishers are probably quite comfortable with this idea of a stylesheet.

In XSL, this construct is called a *rule*. Rules have *actions* associated with them. The actions translate elements into formatting constructs called *flow objects*. Each element in a document matches a single rule. The entire point of an XSL stylesheet is to look at each element in the document and apply the correct rule.

Example 35-4. A simple rule

```
<rule>
  <!-- pattern -->
  <target-element type="emph"/>

  <!-- action -->
  <font font-weight="bold">
    <children/>
  </sequence>
</rule>
```

This rule describes a pattern that matches emph elements and makes them bold.

35.4 | Flow Objects

Of course we are going to need commands that actually describe the layout of the finished product. XML provides a set of *flow objects* that represent the components of the rendered document.

Imagine a typist taking an XML "manuscript" and typing it into a word processor. He would have to use the constructs provided by the word processor, such as paragraphs, bulleted lists, hypertext links and so on. In XSL terms, those constructs are "flow objects". They are so-called because text flows from one to another, and they are each individual objects representing things like characters, paragraphs, clickable links and pages.

Simple XSL stylesheets will typically contain paragraph flow objects, external graphic flow objects, rule flow objects (for horizontal rules), table flow objects and so forth. A table flow object might in turn contain paragraphs. The paragraphs would contain character flow objects, and also "sequence" flow objects that would apply formatting like italics and bold to sequences of characters.

Conceptually, these objects form a tree. The page (or Web page) is the root. Paragraphs, tables, sequences and other "container" objects are the branches, and characters, graphics and other "atomic" objects are the leaves. The leaf objects are called "atomic" because they are not made up of any other objects, just as atoms are not made up of other atoms. The tree of flow objects is called the "flow object tree."

There is usually a relationship between your document's parse tree and the output flow object tree, but they are not identical. You could suppress elements so that they do not appear in the flow object tree. You could add text, such as boilerplate copyright text. You could combine or re-order elements and so forth. For instance, you would re-order and suppress elements to generate an index. XSL code for creating an index would surpress all elements other than those bound for the index, and reorder them alphabetically.

Every flow object has characteristics. The exact set of characteristics that a flow object exhibits depends on its *class*. For example, Web pages have scroll bars, clickable links have destinations, fonts have font sizes, and pictures have heights and widths.

The current version of XSL also has special flow objects that take advantage of many Web designers' knowledge of HTML. These are called the "HTML flow objects" and they correspond to the element types in the HTML DTD. If you format a document using them, it will look as if it had been created in HTML directly. You can think of this process as a conversion from XML markup to HTML markup.

The goal is usually not to create an actual HTML file, but rather to describe the formatting of the document in terms that authors are already familiar with. In theory, the HTML document exists only conceptually. In practice, browsers do not support XSL yet, so XSL processors really do output HTML documents that you can use on the Web as if you had created them by hand.

Caution   *At the time of writing, the future of the HTML flow objects is unclear. Many people are confused by them. Some think that XSL is related to HTML, depends on HTML, or is some kind of XML to HTML conversion language. This confusion may be enough to encourage the working group to provide DSSSL-inspired flow objects exclusively.*

Right now, however, the HTML flow objects are much more widely supported than the DSSSL ones. This is because there is so much software around that already knows how to handle HTML. We will use these flow objects for that reason. We will restrict our usage to only two of them. We will use the HTML P flow object to create new paragraphs and the FONT flow object to apply a typographic style to a series of characters.

35.5 | Using XSL

The easiest way to get started with XSL is to use the simple XSL implementation called *Sparse* that is on the CD-ROM and is also available on the Web. The Web version is very easy to use and more up-to-date than the CD-ROM version. Sparse is nice because it is interactive, fast and user friendly.

Sparse has two windows, one for XML text, and one for XSL text. You type an XML document into one window, and an XSL stylesheet into the other. To get started, you can type the following document and stylesheet into the correct windows:

XML	XSL
``` <?XML version="1.0"?> <para>This is a paragraph.</ para> <para>This is too, but it has <emph>emphasis</emph>.</para> ```	``` <rule> <!-- look for paragraphs --> <target-element type="para"/> <!-- turn them into paragraph flow objects --> <P color="blue"> <children/> </P> </rule> <rule> <!-- look for emphasis --> <target-element type="emph"/> <FONT color="red"><children/ ></FONT> </rule> ```

This formats `para` elements as blue paragraphs, and makes `emph` elements red.

35.6 | Patterns

Patterns allow the XSL processor to choose which elements to apply which style rules to. Every pattern has a `target-element` that specifies the elements to be matched in the document. You can supply a `type` attribute to force the `target-element` to only match elements of a certain element type. So this rule bolds only `emph` elements:

```
<rule>
  <target-element type="emph"/>

  <FONT font-weight="bold">
    <children/>
  </FONT>
</rule>
```

On the other hand, the following rule bolds elements of *any* type:

```
<rule>
  <target-element/>

  <FONT font-weight="bold">
    <children/>
  </FONT>
</rule>
```

If a rule matches elements of any type, we call it the *default rule,* because it is the rule that gets called when no other rule matches. You should almost always have a default rule. If you do not have a default rule, and you forget to supply a rule for a particular case, then elements of that type are cycled-through but do not appear in the output.

We can also choose to match only elements with certain attributes:

```
<rule>
  <target-element>
    <attribute name=security value="top-secret"/>
  </target-element>

  <sequence color="red">
    <children/>
  </sequence>
</rule>
```

An `attribute` element has attributes `name`, `value` and `has-value`. You must always specify the name, but you can either require the attribute to conform to a particular value (`top-secret` in our example), or you can merely ask whether it conforms or not.

It is possible to match based on an element's context. For instance if we wanted to change the color of all elements inside of a `warning` element, we could do so with the following rule:

```
<rule>
  <warning>
    <target-element type="p"/>
   </warning>

  <sequence color="red">
</rule>
```

Essentially, the elements that surround the `target-element` define a pattern that is matched against elements in the document. We can do the same with the target element's sub-elements.

```
<rule>
  <warning>
    <target-element type="p"/>
      <footnote>
    </target-element>
  </warning>

  <sequence color="red">
</rule>
```

This rule would only match elements of type p that contain at least one footnote and are inside a warning.

XSL's patterns are very powerful and convenient. But it is when you pair them with actions that you can actually make something exciting.

35.7 | Actions

After the XSL processor chooses a rule based on a pattern match, it looks at the action part of the rule. The action says what objects to create in the output tree. The actions can directly create flow objects, add literal text (such as boilerplate text), and tell the XSL processor to process the source element's content to get access to its flow objects. We can start with the simplest case first. Let's assume that the input document had an hr element that was to be turned into a horizontal-rule flow object. You can do that this way:

```
<rule>
    <target-element type="hr"/>

    <horizontal-rule/>
</rule>
```

That is simple because we can assume that hr is an empty element and has no content. But most elements do have content. The content is made up of character data and sub-elements. We call each such character string or sub-element a *child*. We can process children by using the children element. For instance if we want to put a horizontal rule before and after sections, and then process the children of the section, we would do this:

```
<rule>
    <target-element type="section"/>

    <horizontal-rule/>
    <children>
    <horizontal-rule/>
</rule>
```

We can also mix in literal text:

```
<rule>
    <target-element type="warning"/>

    <horizontal-rule/>
    <sequence font-size="20" font-weight="bold">
        WARNING:
    <sequence>
    <children>
    <horizontal-rule/>
</rule>
```

We've almost covered enough to do interesting things now. The last step is actually the easiest. You just have to learn which flow objects and characteristics are available for use in your XSL stylesheets.

35.8 | Flow objects and characteristics

As we described earlier, there are two major sets of flow objects. There are those based upon HTML and those based upon DSSSL. They are not meant to be used together. The HTML ones are easy to use if you already know HTML, because they look and behave exactly as HTML elements do on the Web. Here is the list of HTML element types that are available:

These element types can be created with the attributes that they would usually have according to the HTML spec. You can also provide them with attributes that represent style properties from the *Cascading Style Sheet Language*. You can get that full list from the *XML SPECtacular* on the CD-ROM.

The DSSSL flow objects provided are:

Information about these flow objects is available through a link on the CD-ROM. Each of them is described in a chapter of the DSSSL specification.

35.9 | XSL and JavaScript

Sometimes formatting tasks can be quite tricky. They can be so tricky that you need the full power of a programming language to solve them. For instance, as a visual aid you might want every second row in a table to be blue, or every title with a numeric attribute in a particular range to be in a

Spec. Reference 35-2. HTML flow objects in XSL

```
SCRIPT
    PRE
    HTML
            TITLE
            META
            BASE
        BODY
        DIV
        BR
        SPAN
        TABLE
            CAPTION
            COL
            COLGROUP
            THEAD
            TBODY
            TFOOT
            TR
            TD
        A
        FORM
            INPUT
            SELECT
            TEXTAREA
        HR
        IMG
            MAP
            AREA
        OBJECT
            PARAM
            FRAMESET
```

particular font, and other titles to be in a different font. These more complicated tasks must be solved with the help of a full programming language. Declarations alone are not enough.

XSL embeds such a language in the form of ECMAScript, a standardized version of JavaScript. Although XSL technically uses the standardized form, which is slightly different from JavaScript, we will refer to it as JavaScript for familiarity. The differences are minor. The JavaScript variant in XSL is essentially the same language used to make many Web pages interactive, but with new features designed for applying style to documents. JavaScript itself is beyond the scope of this book, and there are many good books that already cover it. We will just demonstrate how XSL and JavaScript fit together.

Spec. Reference 35-3. DSSSL flow objects in XSL

```
scroll--used for online display
paragraph, paragraph-break--used for paragraphs
character--used for text
line-field--used for lists
external-graphic--used for including graphic images
horizontal-rule, vertical-rule--used for rules
score--used for underlining and scoring
embedded-text--used for bi-directional text
box--used for borders
flow objects for tables
    table
    table-part
    table-column
    table-row
    table-cell
    table-border
sequence--used for specifying inherited characteristics
display-group--used for positioning flow objects
simple-page-sequence--used for simple page layout
link--used for hypertext links
```

Just as you can use JavaScript on a Web page when HTML "runs out of steam", you can use it in your stylesheets to solve the harder problems that simple declarations cannot handle.

When JavaScript is used in XSL documents, it has access to many advanced features of the underlying XML system, and this makes style application easier. For instance, there is a query language for selecting and returning document components. This is analogous to the way that database query languages such as SQL select and return particular rows from a database.

For instance, you might want to generate text at the source of a cross-reference based on data at the target. A typical cross reference would say something like: "See Chapter 1.1 'Intro to Foobar'". Of course the chapter number and title must be fetched from that other part of the document. XSL's query features give you this access to information anywhere in the document.

Here is an example of an XSL stylesheet with JavaScript code in it:

Now you can understand the reason for two other XSL design principles:

- XSL should provide a declarative language to do all common formatting tasks.

Example 35-5. JavaScript stylesheet

```
<xsl>
  <define-script>
    var defaultFontSize = "12pt";

    function hierarchicalIndent(elementType, element){
    return length(hierarchicalNumberRecursive(
               elementType, element)) * 12pt;
    }

  </define-script>
  <rule>
   <element type="list">
    <target-element type="item">
    </element>
    <DIV font-size="=defaultFontSize"
     margin-left='=1in+hierarchicalIndent(element, "item")'>
     <children/>
    </DIV>
   </rule>
</xsl>
```

■ XSL should provide an "escape" into a scripting language to
accommodate more sophisticated formatting tasks and to
allow for extensibility and completeness.

Tip   *You may find the XML Styler helpful when create XSL
stylesheets. The software is free and is described in detail in
Chapter 25, "XML Styler: Graphical XSL stylesheet editor", on
page 338.*

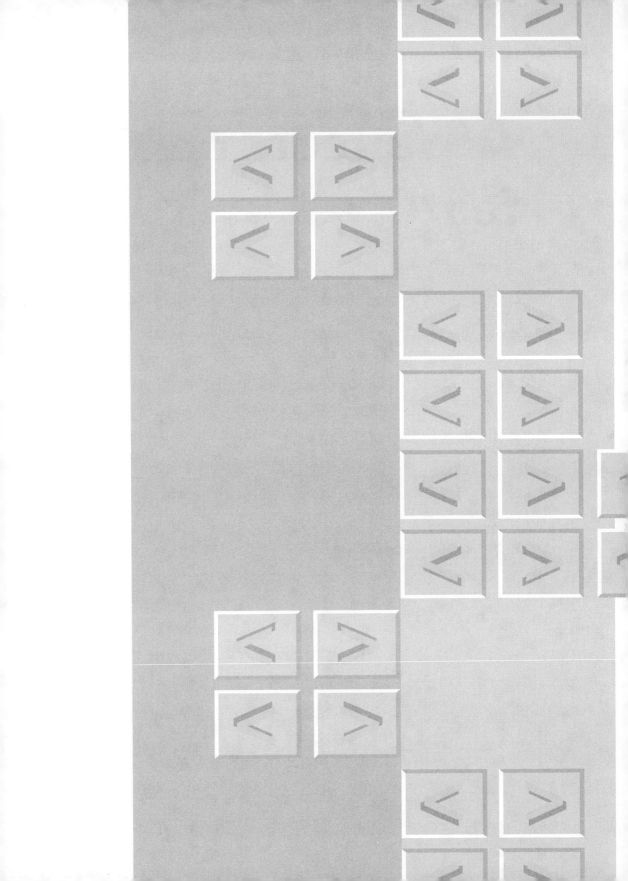

Advanced features

- Conditional sections
- Character references
- Processing instructions
- Standalone declaration

36

The features in this chapter are advanced in the sense that only advanced users will get around to reading them. They do not require advanced degrees in computer science or rocket science to understand. They are just a little esoteric. Most XML users will get by without ever needing to use them.

36.1 | Conditional sections

Conditional sections can only occur in the external subset of the document type declaration, and in external entities referenced from the internal subset. The internal subset proper is supposed to be quick and easy to process. In contrast, the external subset is supposed to retain some of the full-SGML mechanisms that make complicated DTDs easier to maintain. One of these mechanisms is the conditional section, which allows you to turn on and off a series of markup declarations.

Like the internal and external subsets, conditional sections may contain one or more complete declarations, comments, processing instructions, or nested conditional sections, with optional white space between them.

A conditional section is turned on and off with a keyword. If the keyword is INCLUDE, then the section is processed just as if the conditional section markers did not exist. If the keyword is IGNORE, then the contents are ignored by the processor as if the declarations themselves did not exist.

Example 36-1. Conditional sections

```
<![INCLUDE[
  <!ELEMENT magazine (title, article+, comments* )>
]]>
<![IGNORE[
  <!ELEMENT magazine (title, body)>
]]>
```

This is a useful way of turning on and off parts of a DTD during development.

The real power in the feature derives from parameter entity references. These are described in 33.7, "Internal and external parameter entities", on page 487.

If the keyword of the conditional section is a parameter entity reference, the processor replaces the parameter entity by its content before the processor decides whether to include or ignore the conditional section. That means that by changing the parameter entity in the internal subset, you can turn on and off a conditional marked section. In that way, two different documents could reference the same set of external markup declarations, but get slightly (or largely) different DTDs. For instance, we can modify the example above:

Example 36-2. Conditional sections and parameter entities

```
<![%editor[
  <!ELEMENT magazine (title, article+, comments* )>
]]>
<![%author[
  <!ELEMENT magazine (title, body)>
]]>
```

Now editors will have a slightly different DTD from authors. When the parameter entities are set one way, the declaration without comments is chosen:

Example 36-3.

```
<!DOCTYPE MAGAZINE SYSTEM "magazine.dtd"[
   <!ENTITY % editor "IGNORE">
   <!ENTITY % author "INCLUDE">
]>
```

Authors do not have to worry about comments elements that they are not supposed to use anyway. When the document moves from the author to the editor, the parameter entity values can be swapped, and the expanded version of the DTD becomes available. Parameter entities can also be used to manage DTDs that go through versions chronologically, as an organiztion's needs change.

Conditional sections are also sometimes used to make "strict" and "loose" versions of DTDs. The loose DTD can be used for compatibility with old documents, or documents that are somehow out of your control, and the strict DTD can be used to try to encourage a more precise structure for future documents.

36.2 | Character references

It is not usually convenient to type in characters that are not available on the keyboard. With many text editors, it is not even possible to do so. XML allows you to insert such a character with a *character reference*. If, for instance, you wanted to insert a character from the "International Phonetic Alphabet", you could spend a long time looking for a combination of keyboard, operating system and text editor that would make that straightforward. Rather than buying special hardware or software, XML allows you to refer to the character by its Unicode number.

Here is an example:

Example 36-4. Unicode character

```
<P>Here is a special character from Unicode: &#161;.
```

That includes the character numbered 161 in Unicode, which happens to be the inverted exclamation mark. If you happen to know it, you could also use that character's hex value, by using a slightly different form of reference:

Example 36-5. Unicode character

```
<P>Here is a special character from Unicode: &#xA1; .
```

Hex is a numbering system often used by computer programmers that translates naturally into the binary codes that computers use. The *Unicode Standard book* uses hex, so those that have that book will probably prefer this type of character reference over the other (whether they are programmers or not).

Here are the specifics on character references from the XML spec:

Spec. Reference 36-1. Character reference

```
CharRef ::=  '&#' [0-9]+ ';'
    |  '&#x' [0-9a-fA-F]+ ';'
```

Spec. Reference 36-2. Interpreting character references

If the character reference begins with "&#x", the digits and letters up to the terminating ; provide a hexadecimal representation of the character's code point in ISO/IEC 10646. If it begins just with "&#", the digits up to the terminating ; provide a decimal representation of the character's code point.

For our purposes, ISO/IEC 10646 is essentially Unicode. Think of Unicode as industry market-speak for the ISO version of the standard.

Note that character references are not entity references, though they look similar to them. Entities have names and values, but character references only have numbers. In a well-formed document, all entities except the predefined ones must be declared and in a valid document even the predefined ones must be declared. But numeric references are never declared.

Because Unicode numbers are hard to remember, it is often useful to declare entities that stand in for them:

```
<!ENTITY inverted-exclamation "&#161;">
```

Most likely this is how most XML users will refer to obscure characters. There will probably be popular character entity sets that can be included in a DTD through a parameter entity. This will free them from learning obscure character numbers and probably even from learning how to use character references.

36.3 | Processing instructions

XML comments are for those occasions where you need to say something to another human being without reference to the DTD, and without changing the way the document looks to readers or applications. Processing instructions are for those occasions where you need to say something to *a computer program* without reference to the DTD and without changing the way that the document is processed by other computer programs. This is only supposed to happen rarely.

Many people argued that the occasions would be so rare that XML should not have processing instructions at all. But as one of us (Charles) said in *The SGML Handbook*: "In a perfect world, they would not be needed, but, as you may have noticed, the world is not perfect." It turns out that processing instruction use has changed over the years and is not as frowned upon as it was in the early days of SGML.

Processing instructions are intended to reintroduce software-specific markup. You might wonder why you would want to do that. Imagine that you are creating a complex document, and, like a good user of a generalized markup language, you are concentrating on the structure rather than the formatting. Close to the deadline you print the document using the proprietary formatting system that has been foisted on you by your boss. There are many of these systems, some of which are of fantastic quality and others which are not.

Your document looks reasonable, but you need a way to make the first letter of each paragraph large. However, reading the software's manual, you realize that the formatter does not have a feature that allows you to modify the style for the first letter of a word. The XML Purist in you might want to go out and buy a complete formatting system but the Pragmatist in you knows that that is impossible.

Thinking back to the bad-old days of "What You See is All You Get" word processors, you recall that all you really needed to do is to insert a code in the beginning of each paragraph to change the font for the first let-ter. This is not good "XML Style" because XML Purists do not insert for-matting codes and they especially do not insert codes specific to a particular piece of software – that is not in the "spirit" of generalized markup. Still, in this case, with a deadline looming and stubborn software balking, a process-ing instruction may be your best bet. If the formatter has a "change font" command it may be accessible through a processing instruction:

Example 36-6. Processing instruction

```
<CHAPTER>The Bald and the Dutiful
<P><?DUMB-FORMATTER.FONT="16PT"?>N<?DUMB-FORMATTER.ENDFONT?>ick
took Judy in his arms</P>
```

If you find yourself using many processing instructions to specify format-ting you should try to figure out what is wrong with your system. Is your document's markup not rich enough? Is your formatting language not pow-erful enough? Are you not taking advantage of the tools and markup you have available to you? The danger in using processing instructions is that you can come to rely on them instead of more reusable structural markup. Then when you want to reuse your information in another context, the markup will not be robust enough to allow it.

Processing instructions start with a fixed string "<?". That is followed by a name and, after that, any characters except for the string that ends the PI, "?>".

Here are the relevant rules from the XML specification:

Spec. Reference 36-3. Processing Instruction

```
[16]   PI ::=  '<?' PITarget (S (Char* - (Char* '?>' Char*)))? '?>'
[17]   PITarget ::=  Name - (('X' | 'x') ('M' | 'm') ('L' | 'l'))
```

This name at the beginning of the PI is called the *PI target*. This name should be standardized in the documentation for the tool or specification. After the PI target comes white space and then some totally proprietary command. This command is not processed in the traditional sense at all. Characters that would usually indicate markup are totally ignored. The command is passed directly to the application and it does what it wants to with it. The command ends when the processor hits the string "?>". There is absolutely no standard for the "stuff" in the middle. Markup is not recognized there. PIs could use attribute syntax for convenience, but they could also choose not to.

It is possible that more than one application could understand the same instructions. They might come from the same vendor or one vendor might agree to accept another vendor's commands. For instance in the early days of the Web, the popular NCSA (National Center for Supercomputing Activities) Web Server introduced special commands into HTML documents in the form of special HTML comments. Because the NCSA server was dominant in those days, many servers now support those commands.

Under XML we would most likely use processing instructions for the same task. The virtue of XML processing instructions in this case is that they are explicitly instructions to a computer program. In our opinion, one of the central tenets of generalized markup is that it is important to be *explicit* about what is going on in a document. Reusing markup constructs for something other than what they were intended for is not explicit.

For instance, since comments are meant to be instructions to users, an ambitious Web Server administrator might decide to write a small script that would strip them out to save download time and protect internal comments from being read by others. But if instructions to software (like the NCSA server commands) were hidden in comments, they would be stripped out as well. It would be better to use the supplied processing instruction facility, which was designed for the purpose.

Better still (from a purist's point of view) would be a robust XML-smart mechanism for accomplishing the task. For instance, one thing that the NCSA servers do is include the text of one HTML file into another. XML's entity mechanism (see Chapter 33, "Entities: Breaking up is easy to do", on page 476) can handle this, so you do not need processing instructions in that case.

If you want to insert the date into a document, then you could connect the external entity to a CGI[1] that returns the date. If you want to insert information from a database then you could have software that generates XML entities with the requested information.

Sometimes, though, the processing instruction solution may be the most expedient. This is especially the case if your application vendor has set it up

---

1. CGI is the "Common Gateway Interface", a specification for making Web pages that are generated by the server when the user requests them, rather than in advance.

that way. If your document is heavily dependent on a database or other program, then it is not very "application independent" in any case. If a document is inherently dependent on an application then you may decide that strictly adhering to generalized markup philosophy is just too much work. In the end you must choose between expediency and purity. Most people mix both.

Processing instructions are appropriate when you are specifying information about a document that is unrelated to the actual structure of the document. Consider, for instance, the problem of specifying which stylesheets go with which XML documents on a web site. Given enough money and time you could erect a database that kept track of them. If you already had your XML documents in a text database then this would probably be the most efficient mechanism. If you did not have a text database set up, then you could merely keep the information in a flat text file. But you would have to keep that external information up-to-date and write a program to retrieve it in order to do formatting. It would probably be easier to simply stick the information somewhere in the file where it is easy to find (such as at the beginning).

You could add a STYLESHEET element or attribute to each document, but that could cause three problems. First, it would violate the XML Purist principle that elements should represent document components and not formatting or other processing information. Second, if you are using DTDs with your documents then you must add the element or attribute to each DTD that you will be using. This would be a hassle.

The third reason to use processing instructions instead of elements is the most concrete: you may not be able to change those DTDs. After all, DTDs are often industry (or international!) standards. You cannot just go monkeying around with them even if you want to. Instead, you could put a processing instruction at the start of each document. Processing instructions are not associated with particular DTDs and they do not have to be declared. You just use them.

As we described in an earlier chapter (page 519), XML provides a processing instruction for including stylesheets:

Example 36-7. Stylesheet PI

```
<?xml:stylesheet
         href="http://www.sgmlsource.com/memo.xsl"
         type="text/xsl"?>
```

Note that the stylesheet processing instruction does not really add anything to the content or structure of the document. It says something about how to *process* the document. It says: "This document has an associated stylesheet and it is available at such and such a location." It is not always obvious what is structural information and what is merely processing information. If your instruction must be embedded in documents of many types, or with DTDs that you cannot change, then processing instructions are typically your best bet.

The XML encodingPI is an example of another processing instruction. It says what character encoding the file uses. Again this information could be stored externally, such as in a database, a text file or somewhere else, but XML's designers decided (after weeks of heated discussion) that it would be most convenient to place it in the XML document itself rather than require it to be stored (and transmitted across the Internet) externally.

If you go back to 31.6.1, "XML declaration", on page 439 you will also notice that the XML declaration has the same prefix ("<?") and suffix ("?>") as processing instructions do. Formally speaking, the XML declaration is a special form of processing instruction. From an SGML processor's point of view, it is a processing instruction that controls the behavior of a particular class of software: XML processing software. Software that treats XML as just another kind of SGML will ignore it, as they do other types of processing instructions.

To summarize: PIs (processing instructions) were invented primarily for formatting hacks but based on our experience with SGML we know that they are more widely useful. There are already predefined processing instructions in the XML specification for some kinds of processing. Processing instructions will probably be used for other things in the future. Everything that can be accomplished with PIs would be accomplished by other means in a perfect world of pure generalized markup, but in the real world they are often convenient.

36.4 | Standalone document declaration

We should start by saying that the standalone document declaration is only designed for a small class of problems, and these are not problems that most XML users will run into. We do not advise its use. Nevertheless, it is part of

XML and we feel that you should understand it so that you can understand why it is seldom useful.

A DTD is typically broken into two parts, an external part that contains declarations that are typically shared among many documents, and an internal part that occurs within the document and contains declarations that only that document uses (see Chapter 32, "Creating a document type definition ", on page 448). The external part includes all external parameter entities, including both the external subset of the document type declaration and any external entities referenced from the internal subset.

The DTD describes the structure of the document, but it can also control the interpretation of some of the markup and declare the existence of some other entities (such as graphics or other XML documents) that are required for proper processing. For instance, a graphic might only be used in a particular document, so the declaration that includes it (an *entity declaration*) would usually go in the internal subset rather than the external one.

Processors that validate a document need the entire DTD to do so. A document is not valid unless it conforms to both the internal and external parts of its DTD. But sometimes a system passes a document from program to program and it does not need to be validated at each stage. For instance, two participants in an electronic data interchange system might agree that the sender will validate the document once, instead of having both participants validate it.

Even though the receiving processor may not be interested in full validation, it may need to know if it understands the document in exactly the same way that the sender did. Some features of the DTD may influence this slightly. Documents with defaulted attributes would be interpreted differently if the attribute declarations are read rather than ignored. Entity declarations would allow the expansion of entity references. Attribute values can only be normalized according to their type when the attribute declarations are read. Some white space in content would also be removed if the DTD would not allow it to be interpreted as text.

If a process can reliably skip a part of the DTD dedicated exclusively to validation, then it would have less data to download and process and could let the application do its work (browsing, searching, etc.) more quickly. But it would be important for some "mission critical" applications to know if they are getting a slightly different understanding of the document than they would if they processed the entire DTD.

The *standalone document declaration* allows you to specify whether a processor needs to fetch the external part of the DTD in order to process the document "exactly right." The Standalone document declaration may take the values (case sensitive) of yes and no.

A value of yes says that the document is *standalone* and thus does not depend on the external part of the DTD for correct interpretation. A value of *no* means that it either depends on the external DTD part or it might, so the application should not trust that it can get the correct information without it. You could always use no as the value for this attribute, but in some cases applications will then download more data than they need to do their jobs. This translates into slower processing, more network usage and so forth.

Example 36-8. A standalone document declaration that forces processing of the internal subset.

```
<?xml version="1.0" standalone="no"?>
<!DOCTYPE MEMO SYSTEM "http://www.sgmlsource.com/memo.dtd" [
<!ENTITY % pics SYSTEM "http://www.sgmlsource.com/pics.ent">
 %pics;
]>
<MEMO></MEMO>
```

Example 36.4, "Standalone document declaration", on page 541 will tell the application that unless the processor fetched the pictures, the application might get a slightly different understanding of the document than it would if it processed the whole document. For instance, the MEMO element might have defaulted attributes.

But if the value is *yes*, the receiving application may choose not to get the external part of the DTD. This implies that it will never know what was in it. Still, it needs to be able to trust the accuracy of the declaration. What if the security level for a document is set in an attribute and the default level is top-secret? It would be very bad if a careless author could obscure that with a misleading standalone document declaration. In the scenario we outlined, the sender has already validated the document. So the sender has enough information to check that the information is correct. The XML specification requires a validating processor to do this (see Specification reference 36-4).

The last one is very likely to happen. Often people use white space between tags to make the source XML document readable, but that can slightly change the interpretation of the document. Validating processors will tell applications that there are some contexts where character data is not

Spec. Reference 36-4. Standalone document declaration

The standalone document declaration must have the value "no" if any external markup declarations contain declarations of:

- attributes with default values, if elements to which these attributes apply appear in the document without specifications of values for these attributes, or
- entities (other than amp, lt, gt, apos, quot), if references to those entities appear in the document, or
- attributes with values subject to normalization, where the attribute appears in the document with a value which will change as a result of normalization, or
- element types with element content, if white space occurs directly within any instance of those types.

legal, so the white space occuring in those places must be merely formatting white space (see 32.5, "Content models", on page 459). If an application that does not want to validate a document is to get exactly the same information out of the document, it must know whether there are any elements where white space should be interpreted just as source formatting. We say that this sort of white space is *insignificant*.

The standalone document declaration warns the application that this is the case so that mission critical applications may download the DTD just to get the right information out of the document, even when they are not interested in validating it.

The standalone document declaration is fairly obscure and it is doubtful if it will get much use outside of a few mission critical applications. Even there, however, it is safest to just get the external data and do a complete validation before trusting a document. You might find that it had been corrupted in transit.

36.5 | Is that all there is?

We've pretty much covered all the details of XML, certainly all that are likely to see extensive use. There are some things we didn't touch on, such as restrictions that must be observed if you are using older SGML tools to process XML. As the generalized markup industry is retooling rapidly for XML, such restrictions will be short-lived and, we felt, did not warrant complicating our XML tutorial.

In any case, you are now well-prepared – or will be after reading Chapter 37, "Reading the XML specification", on page 546 – to tackle the XML spec yourself. You'll find it in the XML SPECtacular section of the CD-ROM that accompanies this book.

Reading the
XML
specification

- Grammars
- Rules
- Symbols

37

The XML specification is a little tricky to read, but with some work you can get through it by reading and understanding the glossary and applying the concepts described so far in this book. One thing you'll need to know is how to interpret the production rules that make up XML's grammar. This chapter teaches how to read those rules.

When discussing a particular string, like a tag or declaration, we often want to discuss the parts of that string individually. We call each part of the string a *token*. Tokens can always be separated by white space as described above. Sometimes the white space between the tokens is required. For instance we can represent the months of the year as tokens:

Example 37-1. Tokens

```
JANUARY FEBRUARY   MARCH      APRIL       MAY          JUNE
```

White space between tokens is *normalized* (combined) so that no matter how much white space you type, the processor treats it as if the tokens were separated by a single space. Thus the example above is equivalent to the following:

Example 37-2. Tokens after normalization

```
JANUARY FEBRUARY MARCH APRIL MAY JUNE
```

Whenever we discuss strings made up of tokens, you will know that you can use as much white space between tokens as you need and the XML processor will normalize it for you.

37.1 | A look at XML's grammar

There are two basic techniques that we could use to discuss XML's syntax precisely. The first is to describe syntactic constructs in long paragraphs of excruciatingly dull prose. The better approach is to develop a simple system for describing syntax. In computer language circles, such systems are called grammars. Grammars are more precise and compact. Although they are no less boring (as you may recall from primary school), you can skip them easily until you need to know some specific detail of XML's syntax.

As a bonus, once you know how to read a grammar, you can read the one in the XML specification and thus work your way up to the status of "language lawyer".[1] As XML advances, an ability to read the specification will help you to keep on top of its progress.

The danger in this approach is that you might confuse the grammar with XML markup itself. The grammar is just a definitional tool. It is not used in XML applications. You don't type it in when you create an XML document. You use it to figure out what you can type in. Before "the new curriculum", students were taught grammar in primary school. They would be taught parts of speech and how they could combine them. XML's grammar is the same. It will tell you what the parts of an XML document are, and how you can combine them.

Grammars are made up of production *rules* and *symbols*. Rules are simple: they say what is allowed in a particular place in an XML document.

---

1. You too can nitpick about tiny language details and thus prove your superiority over those who merely use XML rather than obsess over it.

Rules have a symbol on the left side, the string "::=" in the middle and a list of symbols on the right side:

```
people ::= 'Melissa, ' 'Tiffany, ' 'Joshua,' 'Johan'
```

If this rule were part of the grammar for XML (which it is not!) it would say that in a particular place in an XML document you could type the names listed.

The symbols on the right (the names, in the last example) define the set of allowed values for the construct described by the rule ("people"). An allowed value is said to *match*. Rules are like definitions in a dictionary. The left side says what is being defined and the right side says what its definition is. Just as words in a dictionary, are defined in terms of other words, symbols are defined in terms of other symbols. Rules in the XML grammar are preceded by a number. You can look the rule up by number. If an XML document does not follow all of the XML production rules, it is not *well-formed*.

37.2 | Constant strings

The most basic type of symbol we will deal with is a *constant string*. These are denoted by a series of characters in between single quote characters. Constant strings are matched case-sensitively (as we discussed earlier). Here are some examples:

```
AlphabetStart ::= 'ABC'
Example1 ::= '<!DOCTYPE'
```

This would match (respectively) the strings

```
ABC
<!DOCTYPE
```

When we are discussing a constant string that is an English word or abbreviation, we will refer to it as a keyword. In computer languages, a keyword is a word that is interpreted specially by the computer. So your mother's maiden name is not (likely) a keyword, but a word like #REQUIRED is.

Symbols in XML's grammar are separated by spaces, which means that you must match the first, and then the second, and so on in order.

```
AlphabetStartAndEnd ::= 'ABC' 'XYZ'
NumbersAndLetters ::= '123' 'QPZ'
```

These would match:

```
ABCXYZ
123QPZ
```

Note that a space character in the grammar does not equate to white space in the XML document. Wherever white space can occur we will use the symbol "S". That means that wherever the grammar specifies "S", you may put in as much white space as you need to make your XML source file maintainable.

```
SpacedOutAlphabet ::= 'ABC' S 'XYZ'
```

matches:

```
ABC XYZ
ABC       XYZ
ABC                 XYZ
```

This is the first example we have used where a single rule matches multiple strings. This is usually the case. Just as in English grammar there are many possible verbs and nouns, there are many possible strings that match the rule SpacedOutAlphabet, depending on how much white space you choose to make your XML source file maintainable.

Obviously XML would not be very useful if you could only insert predefined text and white space. After all, XML users usually like to choose the topic and content of their documents! So they need to have the option of inserting their own content: a *user defined string*. The simplest type of user defined string is character data. This is simply the text that isn't markup. You can put almost any character in character data. The exceptions are characters that would be confused with markup, such as less-than and ampersand symbols.

37.3 | Names

The XML specification uses the symbol "Name" to represent names. For example:

```
PersonNamedSmith :: = Name S 'Smith'
```

When we combine the name, the white space and the constant string, the rule matches strings like these:

```
Christina Smith
Allan       Smith
Michael       Smith
Black          Smith
Bla_ck           Smith
_Black           Smith
```

37.4 | Occurrence indicators

Sometimes a string is *optional*. We will indicate this by putting a question mark after the symbol that represents it in a rule:

```
Description ::= 'Tall' S? 'dark'? S? 'handsome'? S? 'person'
Tall person
Tallperson
Tall handsomeperson
Tall dark person
Talldarkhandsomeperson
```

Notice that optionality does not affect the order of the tokens. For example, dark can never go before tall. We can also allow a part of a rule to be matched multiple times. If we want to allow a part to be matched one or more times, we can use the plus symbol and make it *repeatable*.

```
VeryTall ::= 'A' S ('very' S)+ 'tall' S 'person.'
A very tall person.
A very very tall person.
A very very very tall person.
```

An asterisk is similar, but it allows a string to be matched zero or more times. In other words it is both repeatable and optional.

```
VerySmall ::= 'A' S ('very' S)* 'small' S 'person.'
A small person.
A very small person.
A very very small person.
A very very very small person.
```

Symbols can be grouped with parentheses so that you could, for instance, make a whole series of symbols optional at once. This is different from making them each optional separately because you must either supply strings for all of them or none:

```
Description2 ::= 'A' S ('tall' S 'dark' S 'handsome' S)? 'man.'
```

This rule matches these two strings (and no others):

```
A tall dark handsome man.
A man.
```

We will sometimes have a choice of symbols to use. This is indicated by separating the alternatives by a vertical bar:

```
Description3 ::= 'A' S ('short'|'tall') S
                 ('fair'|'tan'|'dark') S ('man'|'woman') '.'
A tall dark man.
A short fair woman.
A short tan man.
A tall dark woman.
```

Note that we broke a single long rule over two lines rather than having it run off of the end of the page. This does not in any way affect the meaning of the rule. Line breaks are just treated like space characters between the symbols.

We can combine all of these types of symbols. This allows us to make more complex rules.

```
Book ::= (('Fascinating'|'Intriguing') S ('XML'|'SGML') S 'Book')
                   | ('Yet another HTML' S 'Book')
Fascinating XML Book
Yet another HTML Book
Intriguing SGML Book
```

So in this case, you should treat the first large parenthesized expression (saying good things about SGML and XML books) as one option, and the second (saying not as good things about HTML books) as another. Inside the first set, you can choose different adjectives and book types, but the ordering is fixed and there must be white space between each part.

37.5 | Combining rules

Finally, rules can refer to other rules. Where one rule refers to another, you just make a valid value for each part and then put the parts together like building blocks.

```
FunnyDate ::= Month S Day ',' Year
Month ::= 'Jan'|'Feb'|'Mar'|'Apr'|'May'|'Jun'
                |'Jul'|'Aug'|'Sep'|'Oct'|'Nov'|'Dec'
Day ::= ('1'|'2'|'3')?
                ('1'|'2'|'3'|'4'|'5'|'6'|'7'|'8'|'9'|'0')
Year ::= '1998'|'1999'|'2000'|'2001'|'2002'
```

This would match strings such as:

```
Jan 21,1998
May 35,2000
Sep 2,2002
```

As you can see, this is not quite a strict specification for dates, but it gets the overall form or *syntax* of them right.

37.6 | Conclusion

We've explained the bulk of what is needed to understand XML's production rules. There are a few more details that you can find in section 6 of the XML spec itself. It is included in the XML SPECtacular on the CD-ROM.

WIDL and XML RPC

- Application interoperability

- Web Interface Definition Language (WIDL)

- XML Remote Procedure Call (RPC)

- WIDL specification on CD-ROM

38

XML goes a long way toward allowing applications to interoperate, but some think it needs to go a WIDL further. Among them are webMethods, Inc., `http://www.webmethods.com`, who sponsor this chapter, and Joe Lapp, who prepared it.

Engineers *numbered 12-345-68 through 23-457-89 at Oops E-Commerce Corporation say "XML is the solution to interoperability." These engineers gang up on the managers until the corporate gears succumb and reverse direction. Soon the sales reps are saying the words "universal data format" more often than the words "object-oriented." Oops XML-enables its popular Loops product, renames the product to Xoops, and then ships Xoops out the door.*

Over the following weeks we eavesdrop on the support engineers: "Well, if you have Company Q's product you can use our XML feature with it... Well, to get it to talk to your purchasing system, you'll have to XML-enable the purchasing system... Well, their program uses a different DTD from ours, so Xoops won't interoperate with it."

Woops, Oops goofed with Xoops: XML alone is not quite enough.

38.1 | XML alone is not quite enough

A client that hands a server data must tell the server what to do with the data. The client does this by naming a service. A client must also understand the data that the service returns. Two applications may communicate only if they agree on the names of the services and on the types of the input and the output data.

Furthermore, applications must agree on how to represent this data in the messages that transfer between them. XML provides a way to represent the data, but it does not associate input data and output data with service names, and it does not provide a way to map between message types. Something is missing.

38.1.1 *The missing piece*

The obvious solution to the problem is to associate input DTDs with output DTDs and to give these associations service names. This does provide enough information for two applications to communicate, but it requires both applications to be XML-enabled and it requires the applications to conform to the same DTDs. While there may not be many XML-enabled applications right now, eventually there will be, but it is unlikely that all will agree on the same DTDs.

A better solution to the interoperability problem is to define application interfaces in an abstract way. CORBA, DCOM, and DCE have all taken this approach, and in these systems the abstractions are known as interface specifications.

Interface specifications allow developers to create different but compatible implementations of interfaces. In CORBA, DCOM, and DCE interface specifications allow applications written in different programming languages to communicate. We need to take this a step further. We must also bridge between applications whose XML messages conform to different DTDs.

The missing piece is an IDL - an *Interface Definition Language*. An IDL is a language in which interface specifications are written.

webMethods, Inc. has specified an IDL for this purpose, an IDL called WIDL. WIDL interface specifications enable middleware to map transparently between application interfaces and XML message DTDs. By delegating XML intelligence and accessibility issues to IDL-aware middleware, we also simplify the application. An IDL such as WIDL allows us to maximize an application's accessibility.

38.1.2 *The role of WIDL*

WIDL is an acronym for *Web Interface Definition Language*. It is an IDL that is expressed in XML. OMG IDL and Microsoft IDL are other examples of IDLs, but there are important differences between WIDL and conventional IDLs.

WIDL differs from other IDLs primarily because it satisfies the 80/20 rule. It provides 80% of the capability of a conventional IDL with only 20% of the complexity. WIDL is consequently easy to learn, easy to read, and relatively easy to implement.

This fact provides WIDL with a potentially large user base, but still leaves room for more sophisticated IDLs, including new ones based on XML. WIDL also goes a step further than conventional IDLs by requiring all data items to have names, which simplifies the process of translating documents into interfaces.

webMethods originally developed WIDL to wrap Web sites within APIs, thereby giving applications programmatic access to the Web. Consequently, the WIDL 1.x and 2.x specifications defined a single language that both specified interfaces and defined how interface specifications map onto a Web site.

WIDL 3.0 places the interface specification and the document-mapping implementation in separate XML documents. WIDL 3.0 therefore defines two components: an IDL component and a document-mapping component. Together these components allow applications to communicate over a network regardless of the programming languages in which the applications are written, regardless of whether the applications speak XML, and regardless of the DTDs to which XML-speaking applications conform.

38.2 | WIDL the IDL

Let's take a look at the IDL component of WIDL 3.0. Example 38-1 shows a short but complete example of a WIDL 3.0 interface specification.

Example 38-1. A WIDL 3.0 interface specification.

```
<WIDL NAME="com.Fortunes-R-Us.Purchasing" VERSION="3.0">
  <RECORD NAME="FortuneOrder">
    <VALUE NAME="accountID" TYPE="i4"/>
    <VALUE NAME="zodiacSign"/>
  </RECORD>
  <RECORD NAME="FortuneReceipt">
    <VALUE NAME="orderNumber" TYPE="i4"/>
    <VALUE NAME="fortune"/>
    <VALUE NAME="accountBalance" TYPE="r4"/>
  </RECORD>
  <METHOD NAME="orderFortune" INPUT="FortuneOrder"
      OUTPUT="FortuneReceipt" RETURN="orderNumber"/>
</WIDL>
```

A WIDL document specifies a single interface. Example 38-2 is a DTD that defines WIDL documents sufficiently for our purposes.

Interfaces should have names that are unique within their scope of use. Naming an interface relative to the reverse order of a domain name provides one way to accomplish this. A client may then identify interfaces by name.

A WIDL element contains one or more RECORD or METHOD elements.

38.2.1 *Methods*

The METHOD element identifies a service that the client may invoke.

Method names must be unique within the document. Methods may optionally have input and output parameters, as indicated by the optional INPUT and OUTPUT attributes.

The INPUT attribute provides a link to a RECORD element that enumerates the method's input parameters. The OUTPUT attribute provides a link to a RECORD element that enumerates the method's output parameters. The tag may optionally indicate that one of the output parameters is the return value of the method when the interface is implemented in a programming language. Methods may also identify the exceptions that they raise in order to report method invocation failures.

Example 38-2. WIDL interface DTD.

```
<!ELEMENT WIDL      (RECORD | METHOD)+ >
<!ATTLIST WIDL
         NAME       CDATA #REQUIRED
         VERSION    CDATA #FIXED "3.0"
>
<!ELEMENT METHOD    EMPTY>
<!ATTLIST METHOD
         NAME       CDATA #REQUIRED
         INPUT      CDATA #IMPLIED
         OUTPUT     CDATA #IMPLIED
         RETURN     CDATA #IMPLIED
>
<!ELEMENT RECORD    (VALUE | LIST | RECORDREF)* >
<!ATTLIST RECORD
         NAME       CDATA #REQUIRED
         BASE       CDATA #IMPLIED
>
     <!-- Parameters -->
<!ELEMENT VALUE     EMPTY >
<!ATTLIST VALUE
         NAME       CDATA #REQUIRED
         TYPE       CDATA "string"
         DIM        NMTOKEN 0
>
<!ELEMENT LIST      EMPTY >
<!ATTLIST LIST
         NAME       CDATA #REQUIRED
         DIM        NMTOKEN 0
>
<!ELEMENT RECORDREF EMPTY >
<!ATTLIST RECORDREF
         NAME       CDATA #REQUIRED
         RECORD     CDATA #IMPLIED
         DIM        NMTOKEN 0
>
```

38.2.2 *Records*

A RECORD element represents a record and conforms to the DTD shown in Example 38-2. Record names must be unique within a document. A record consists of a collection of zero or more parameter elements, each of which must have a unique name within the scope of the record. If the record provides a BASE attribute, the record inherits all of the named parameter elements found within the RECORD element to which the attribute points.

The parameter element types are VALUE, LIST, and RECORDREF.

VALUE

An element that represents lexical data and has an optional TYPE attribute that identifies the datatype. Datatypes include strings ("string"), integers ("i4"), and floats ("r4").

LIST

A LIST element represents a vector of arbitrary size consisting of an arbitrary set of types.

RECORDREF

The RECORDREF element identifies a RECORD element that nests within the RECORDREF's parent record.

Parameters have an optional DIM attribute. When DIM has a value of "1" or "2" the parameter represents a single- or two-dimensional array. When the attribute is absent, the value defaults to "0" to indicate that the parameter is a single data item and not an array.

WIDL provides only a small number of simple data types. These data types are sufficient to represent most of the types available to programming languages. WIDL is compatible with other data definition languages such as XML-Data and Resource Description Framework (RDF), so WIDL may accommodate the sophisticated schema languages that are emerging. This allows WIDL to support complex data types without itself becoming complex.

38.3 | Remote procedure calls

WIDL provides the information that applications need to communicate, but it does not perform the actual communication. An application that requests a service of another application must issue a Remote Procedure Call, or RPC, to the other application. An application issues an RPC by packaging a message, sending the message to the other application, and then waiting for the reply message.

The RPC mechanism requires the applications to agree on the form of the messages and on the transfer protocol by which the messages travel. HTTP provides a POST method that allows a client to submit a document to a server and to receive a document in response, so HTTP is a candidate protocol. Since HTTP is nearly ubiquitous and since it tunnels through firewalls, it's obvious that we should use HTTP. The question is, should XML be the message form?

IIOP and DCE are both industry standards for RPC messages. Either of these would work, as it is possible to send them over HTTP. We might notice that these message representations are inflexible: senders and receivers must agree on how a message decomposes data into arguments, including the positions of the individual arguments and the structures of these arguments.

Yet if the message representation were XML, the applications would still have to agree on the DTDs to which the messages conformed. Just as applications that use different IIOP or DCE message types cannot communicate, applications that use different DTDs cannot communicate. Without looking more closely, we might be inclined to conclude that XML is all hype after all.

However, we *are* going to look more closely. These problems do afflict XML, IIOP, and DCE alike. No reneging here. When we take that closer look we find that, unlike IIOP and DCE, XML provides a way to solve the problem.

That is, XML provides a way to ensure that so long as two applications agree to conform to the same abstract interface specification, then those two applications may communicate – even if the applications are hard-coded to use different DTDs.

38.3.1 *Representing RPC messages in XML*

XML is an ideal notation for RPC messages because it allows us to label the individual data constituents of a message semantically. These labels are XML's tags.

The only semantic labels available in IIOP and DCE are the numeric positions of the constituents. IIOP and DCE do not allow data to move to new positions and they do not allow data to grow or shrink in unforeseen ways. They also do not allow applications to discover the absence of data from a message or to introduce new data items into a message independently.

But the greatest benefit that XML brings to RPC is that XML moves a significant amount of information about a message into the message itself. It is a benefit because it moves an equal amount of information out of the programs that process the messages. This simplifies the programs that integrate applications.

In all probability, industries will never completely agree on standard interfaces or standard DTDs, so it will always be necessary to translate between interfaces. XML provides interoperability by enabling a new class of middleware to serve as generic application integrators.

38.3.2 *Generic and custom message DTDs*

There are two ways to represent RPC messages in XML. A generic document type is capable of representing any message. The interface specification determines the form that a message takes in a generic document type.

More specifically, the definition of a method uniquely determines the DTDs of the request and reply messages that correspond to the method.

On the other hand, a custom document type is designed only to contain the inputs or the outputs of a particular kind of service. There are many possible custom document type definitions for a given interface method.

Let's look at a few examples that are based on the Fortunes-R-Us purchasing interface shown in Example 38-1. Example 38-3 contains three RPC messages.

The first portrays what an instance of a generic document type might look like for a message that invokes the "orderFortune" method. The same document type scheme might be used for the reply message, which is the second message of Example 38-3. The third message shown is an instance of a custom-DTD reply.

There are many possible generic XML document types, and we can expect to see industries creating them and using them. There are also many possible custom document types for any given method. We can also expect to see applications using custom document types to message other applications.

The trick is to ensure that we can integrate applications that use different document types to represent the same information. Without this we do not have interoperability. XML makes it feasible to provide large-scale interop-

Example 38-3. Generic- and custom-DTD RPC messages.

```
<RPC TYPE="REQUEST">
  <VALUE NAME="accountID" TYPE="i4">2001</NUMBER>
  <VALUE NAME="zodiacSign">Aquarius</VALUE>
</RPC>

<RPC TYPE="REPLY">
  <VALUE NAME="orderNumber" TYPE="i4">438553</NUMBER>
  <VALUE NAME="fortune">You will use XML for RPC</VALUE>
  <VALUE NAME="accountBalance" TYPE="r4">65.00</NUMBER>
</RPC>

<FORTUNE-RECEIPT>
  <orderNumber>438553</orderNumber>
  <fortune>You will use XML for RPC</fortune>
  <accountBalance>65.00</accountBalance>
</FORTUNE-RECEIPT>
```

erability, but only if we design our messages so that integration middleware may robustly identify data constituents by label.

38.4 | Integrating applications

WIDL and XML RPC together enable middleware to integrate applications. We'll use the term integration server to refer to middleware that assumes this kind of responsibility.

A WIDL interface specification supplies an integration server with the information the server needs to map between XML RPC messages and native application interfaces. Interface specifications do not themselves define the mappings, but they provide a common language in which to express them.

Figure 38-1 shows how integration servers connect applications.

Integration servers need to integrate a wide variety of application interfaces. One application may implement an interface as a set of Java or C++ methods. Another may implement an interface as a set of functions in C.

Another application may input and output XML documents conforming to custom DTDs. Still another may input and output XML documents in the form of generic RPC messages. Integrating applications requires bridging between programming languages and document representations.

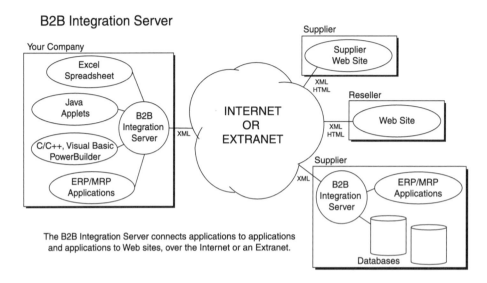

Figure 38-1   Connecting applications with XML RPC and integration servers.

38.4.1 *Stubs*

Conventional RPC bridges programming languages through code snippets known as *stubs*. A stub translates between the details of an interface and a common data representation. One side of a stub speaks the language that is native to an application and the other side speaks a common data representation.

By connecting the data representation ends of two stubs, one may bridge between any two programming languages. In a client stub, the language-specific side consists of a set of APIs (functions) that the client may call. In a server stub, the language-specific side calls APIs that the server itself exposes.

Figure 38-2 illustrates this property of stubs by portraying four stub pairings. Here, XML is the common data representation, but in the usual case intervening middleware will hide knowledge of XML from the stubs.

In diagram (a) an application written in Java is communicating with another application written in Java. Diagrams (b) and (c) show that the same application may also communicate with applications written in C++ or C. Diagram (d) depicts the Java application communicating with an application that speaks XML. In this last scenario the XML-speaking application has no stub, since the XML messages pass directly to the application.

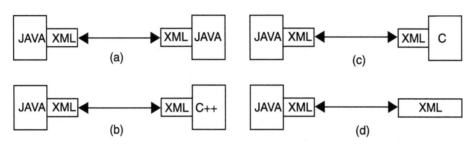

Figure 38-2   Using stubs to make applications interoperable.

Figure 38-3 portrays how a developer uses stubs to integrate applications. A developer generates an interface specification in WIDL and then runs the specification through a WIDL compiler.

The WIDL compiler generates two source files in a programming language of the developer's choice. Both files are stubs, but one file is a client stub and the other is a server stub. The developer then links the appropriate stub into the client or server application. The stubs free the application from knowledge of XML and allow middleware to map transparently between interfaces and different XML document types.

38.4.2 *Document mapping*

The document-mapping component of WIDL defines mappings between interfaces and XML or HTML documents. This is the portion that provides the bridge between XML RPC messages and application APIs; that is, the portion that makes the different XML document types indistinguishable to the application. webMethods originally developed this facility to encapsulate HTML-based Web sites within APIs, but because XML does a better job of labeling data than HTML does, the technology reaps more benefits from XML.

WIDL document-mapping does its job through *bindings*. A binding specifies how to map raw data into an RPC message or vice versa, where "raw data" means "data represented in a way that is natural to a program-

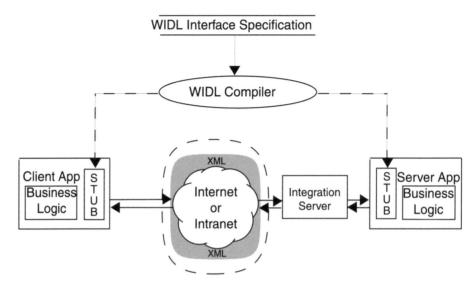

Figure 38-3   Using WIDL for RPC over the Web.

ming language". The best way to make sense of this is to look at an example, so consider Example 38-4.

Example 38-4. A WIDL binding.

```
<OUTPUT-BINDING NAME="OrderReplyBinding">
  <VALUE NAME="orderNumber" TYPE="i4">
         doc.orderNumber[0].text</VALUE>
  <VALUE NAME="fortune">doc.fortune[0].text</VALUE>
</OUTPUT-BINDING>
```

This binding applies to the custom-DTD reply message of Example 38-3. Each VALUE element corresponds to a data item that the binding extracts from the message. In this case the binding extracts two strings, but bindings may extract other data types, including records and even XML documents.

Upon receiving the reply message, middleware applies this binding and passes the two strings to the application. Since the application ordered the fortune by issuing a function call on a client stub, the stub returns the strings to the application as output parameters of the function. Middleware completely shields the application from knowledge of XML and from dependence on a specific XML document type.

In this example, the binding only retrieves the order number and the fortune from the reply message, indicating that the application cannot utilize the account balance. The content of each VALUE element is a query, expressed in a document query language, that specifies where to find these items within the message. In this particular case, the query uses the web-Methods Object Model, but WIDL is compatible with other query languages as well.

A binding may also define how to translate data into an RPC message. WIDL supports several forms of messages. For request messages, the binding may have the data submitted via the HTTP GET or POST methods, thus providing the data as CGI query parameters. The binding may also have the data submitted as an XML or an HTML message, constructing the message from a particular template. Templates are a straightforward way to generate XML.

Bindings provide a simple way to make applications compatible with a variety of XML message DTDs. Bindings are most useful with custom document types, since it is possible to hard-code document-mapping for generic document types. Generic document types do not require the flexibility that bindings provide, and by hard-coding them middleware can provide more efficient document-mapping.

An integration server puts bindings to work by using them to mask differences in XML document types. By connecting the variable names of bindings to parameter names in interface specifications, an integration server may map any XML document type into any programming language.

To get a feel for the benefits of this capability, take a look at Figure 38-4. Here industries and businesses have defined a variety of DTDs to which different RPC document types conform. The interface defined with WIDL captures a superset of the services and data available through the DTDs. Although different client applications use different XML document types, the integration server is able to bridge these differences to make the application universally accessible.

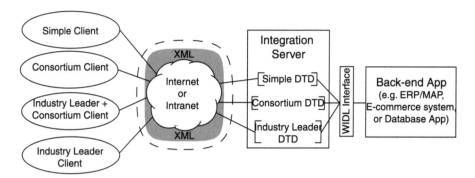

Figure 38-4   Using WIDL to make different XML messages interoperable.

38.5 | Interoperability attained

WIDL, XML RPC, and integration servers are the pieces that provide application interoperability. With them one can make any application accessible over a network via XML and HTTP.

One can also make a single application available to client applications that use different XML message formats. Or one can upgrade an application, or substitute one application for another, and still allow all previous clients to communicate with the new application.

These capabilities should give us second thoughts about hard-coding servers to use specific XML document types. Servers should leave document type decisions to middleware, empowering middleware to make the server widely accessible.

XML-Data

- DTD schemas
- Aliases
- Combining multiple schemas
- Datatypes

XML-Data is the name of a proposal for a DTD schema language, a new way to create and augment document type definitions. This chapter is sponsored by Microsoft Corporation, `http://www.microsoft.com`.

The Internet holds within it the potential for integrating all information into a global network (with many private but integrated domains), promising access to information any time and anywhere. However, this potential has yet to be realized. At present, the Internet is merely an access medium.

To realize the Internet's potential, we need to add intelligent search, data exchange, adaptive presentation, and personalization. The Internet must go beyond setting an information access standard and must set an information *understanding* standard, which means a standard way of representing data so that software can better search, move, display, and otherwise manipulate information currently hidden in contextual obscurity.

XML is an important step in this direction. XML is a standardized notation for representing structured information. It is well-founded theoretically and is based on extensive industry experience. Although XML documents are simple, readily-transmitted character strings, the notation easily depicts a tree structure. A tree is a natural structure that is richer than a simple flat list, yet also respectful of cognitive and data processing requirements for economy and simplicity.

Valid XML documents belong to classes – document types – that determine the tree structure and other properties of their member documents. The properties of the classes themselves comprise their document type definitions, or DTDs, which serve the same role for documents that schemas do for databases.

And that is where the potential for enhancing the Web lies.

Today, the only standardized method of creating document type definitions is through the use of markup declarations, a specialized syntax used only for this purpose. What is needed is a method of augmenting the existing set of DTD properties with additional properties that will enable the goal of true information understanding.

Fortunately, there are ways to accomplish this goal by using XML itself. The W3C XML Working Group has agreed to work on a *DTD schema language* for XML. The DTD schema language will provide a means of using XML instances to define augmented DTDs.

As a contribution to this effort, ArborText, DataChannel, Inso, and Microsoft have co-authored the *XML-Data* submission to the W3C.

XML-Data is a notation, in the form of an XML document, that is both an alternative to markup declarations for writing DTDs and a means of augmenting DTDs with additional capabilities. For example:

- *XML-Data* supports rich data types, allowing for tighter validation of data and reduced application effort. Developers can use a list of standard data types, such as numbers or ISO 8601 dates, or define their own.
- Through the namespaces facility, *XML-Data* improves expressiveness, ensuring the existence of uniquely qualified names.
- *XML-Data* provides for greater and more efficient semantic facilities by incorporating the concept of inheritance, enabling one schema to be based on another. For instance, a bookstore purchase order schema could be based on a general purpose electronic-commerce purchase order schema.

Since *XML-Data* uses XML instance syntax, there are a number of other benefits:

- The same tools that are used to parse XML can be used to parse the *XML-Data* notation.

- As the syntax is very similar to HTML, it should be easy for HTML authors to learn and read.

- It is easily extensible.

The text of the *XML-Data* proposal follows, as contained in *W3C Note 05 Jan 1998*. A browseable version, can be found on the CD-ROM and at `http://www.w3.org/TR/1998/NOTE-XML-data`. That version identifies the individual authors and others whose help and contributions to the proposal the authors acknowledged.

39.1 | Introduction

Schemas define the characteristics of classes of objects. This paper describes an XML vocabulary for schemas, that is, for defining and documenting object classes. It can be used for classes which as strictly syntactic (for example, XML) or those which indicate concepts and relations among concepts (as used in relational databases, KR graphs and RDF). The former are called "syntactic schemas;" the latter "conceptual schemas."

For example, an XML document might contain a "book" element which lexically contains an "author" element and a "title" element. An XML-Data schema can describe such syntax. However, in another context, we may simply want to represent more abstractly that books have titles and authors, irrespective of any syntax. XML-Data schemas can describe such conceptual relationships. Further, the information about books, titles and authors might be stored in a relational database, in which XML-Data schemas describe row types and key relationships.

One immediate implication of the ideas in this paper is that XML document types can now be described using XML itself, rather than DTD syntax. Another is that XML-Data schemas provide a common vocabulary for ideas which overlap between syntactic, database and conceptual schemas. All features can be used together as appropriate.

Schemas are composed principally of declarations for:

Concepts

Classes of objects

- Class hierarchies
- Properties

Relationships

- Indicated by primary key to foreign key matching
- Indicated by URI

XML DTD Grammars and Compatibility

- grammatical rules governing the valid nesting of the elements and attributes
- attributes of elements
- internal and external entities, represented by intEntityDecl and extEntityDecl
- notations, represented by notationDcl

Datatypes giving parsing rules and implementation formats.

Mapping rules allowing abbreviated grammars to map to a conceptual data model.

39.2 | The Schema Element Type

All schema declarations are contained within a schema element, like this:

```
<?XML version='1.0' ?>
<?xml:namespace
    name="urn:uuid:BDC6E3F0-6DA3-11d1-A2A3-00AA00C14882/"
    as="s"/?>
<s:schema id='ExampleSchema'>
  <!-- schema goes here. -->
</s:schema>
```

The namespace of the vocabulary described in this document is named "urn:uuid:BDC6E3F0-6DA3-11d1-A2A3-00AA00C14882/".

39.3 | The *ElementType* Declaration

The heart of an XML-Data schema is the *elementType* declaration, which defines a class of objects (or "type of element" in XML terminology). The *id* attribute serves a dual role of identifying the definition, and also naming the specific class.

```
<elementType id="author"/>
```

Within an elementType, the *description* subelement may be used to provide a human-readable description of the elements purpose.

```
<elementType id="author">
  <description>The person, natural or otherwise, who wrote
               the book.</description>
</elementType >
```

39.4 | Properties and Content Models

Subelements within *elementType* define characteristics of the classs members. An XML "content model" is a description of the contents that may validly appear within a particular element type in a document instance.

```
<elementType id="author">
    <string/>
</elementType>

<elementType id="Book">
    <element type="#author" occurs="ONEORMORE"/>
</elementType>
```

The example above defines two elements, author and book, and says that a book has one or more authors. The author element may contain a string of character data (but no other elements). For example, the following is valid:

```
<Book>
    <author>Henry Ford</author>
    <author>Samuel Crowther</author>
</Book>
```

Within an elementType, various specialized subelements (element, group, any, empty, string etc.) indicate which subelements (properties) are allowed/required. Ordinarily, these imply not only the cardinality of the subelements but also their sequence. (We discuss a means to relax sequence later.)

39.4.1 *Element*

Element indicates the containment of a single element type (property). Each *element* contains an *href* attribute referencing another *elementType*, thereby including it in the content model syntacticly, or declaring it to be a property of the object class conceptually. The element may be required or optional, and may occur multiple times, as indicated by its *occurs* attribute having one of the four values "REQUIRED", "OPTIONAL", "ZEROOR-MORE" or "ONEORMORE". It has a default of "REQUIRED".

```
<elementType id="Book">
    <element type="#title" occurs="OPTIONAL"/>
    <element type="#author" occurs="ONEORMORE"/>
</elementType>
```

The example above describes a book element type. Here, each instance of a book *may* contain a title, and *must* contain one or more authors.

```
<Book>
    <author>Henry Ford</author>
    <author>Samuel Crowther</author>
    <title>My Life and Work</title>
</Book>
```

When we discuss type hierarchies, later, we will see that an element type may have subtypes. If so, inclusion of an element type in a content model permits elements of that type directly and all its subtypes.

39.4.2 *Empty, Any, String, and Mixed Content*

Empty and *any* content are expressed using predefined elements *empty* and *any*. (*Empty* may be omitted.) *String* means any character string not containing elements, known as "PCDATA" in XML. *Any* signals that any mixture of subelements is legal, but no free characters. *Mixed* content (a mixture of parsed character data and one or more elements) is identified by a *mixed* element, whose content identifies the element types allowed in addition to parsed character data. When the content model is mixed, any number of the listed elements are allowed, in any order.

```
<?XML version='1.0' ?>
<?xml:namespace
        name="urn:uuid:BDC6E3F0-6DA3-11d1-A2A3-00AA00C14882/"
        as="s"/?>
<s:schema>

    <elementType id="name">
        <string/>
    </elementType>

    <elementType id="Person">
        <any/>
    </elementType>

    <elementType id="author">
        <string/>
    </elementType>

    <elementType id="titlePart">
        <string/>
    </elementType>

    <elementType id="title">
        <mixed><element type="#titlePart"/></mixed>
    </elementType>

    <elementType id="Book">
        <element type="#title" occurs="OPTIONAL"/>
        <element type="#author" occurs="ONEORMORE"/>
    </elementType>

</s:schema>

...

<Book>
    <author>Henry Ford</author>
    <author>Samuel Crowther</author>
    <title>My Life and<titlePart>Work</titlePart></title>
</Book>
```

Here, *book* is defined to have an optional *title* and one or more *authors*. The *name* element has content model of *any*, meaning that free text is not allowed, but any arrangement of subelements is valid. The *content model* of *title* is *mixed*, allowing a free intermixture of characters and any number of *titleParts*. The author, *name* and *titleParts* elements have a *content model* of *string*.

39.4.3 *Group*

Group indicates a set or sequence of elements, allowing alternatives or ordering among the elements by use of the groupOrder attribute. The group as a whole is treated similarly to an element.

```
<elementType id="Book">
    <element type="#title"/>
    <element type="#author" occurs="ONEORMORE"/>
    <group occurs="OPTIONAL">
        <element type="#preface"/>
        <element type="#introduction"/>
    </group>
</elementType>
```

In the above example, if a preface or introduction appears, both must, with the preface preceding the introduction. Each of the following is valid:

```
<Book>
    <author>Henry Ford</author>
</Book>


<Book>
    <author>Henry Ford</author>
    <preface>Prefatory text</preface>
    <introduction>This is a swell book.</introduction>
</Book>
```

Sometimes a schema designer wants to relax the ordering restrictions among elements, allowing them to appear in any order. This is indicated by setting the groupOrder attribute to "AND":

```
<elementType id="Book">
    <element type="#title"/>
    <element type="#author" occurs="ONEORMORE"/>
    <group groupOrder="AND" occurs="OPTIONAL">
        <element type="#preface"/>
        <element type="#introduction"/>
    </group>
</elementType>
```

Now the following is also valid:

```
<Book>
    <author>Henry Ford</author>
    <introduction>This is a swell book.</introduction>
    <preface>Prefatory text</preface>
</Book>
```

Finally, a schema can indicate that any one of a list of elements (or groups) is needed. For example, either a preface *or* an introduction. The groupOrder attribute value "OR" signals this.

```
<elementType id="Book">
    <element type="#title"/>
    <element type="#author" occurs="ONEORMORE"/>
    <group groupOrder="OR">
        <element type="#preface"/>
        <element type="#introduction"/>
    </group>
</elementType>
```

Now each of the following is valid:

```
<Book>
    <author>Henry Ford</author>
    <preface>Prefatory text</preface>
</Book>

<Book>
    <author>Henry Ford</author>
    <introduction>This is a swell book.</introduction>
</Book>
```

39.4.4 *Open and Closed Content Models*

XML typically does not allow an element to contain content unless that content was listed in the model. This is useful in some cases, but overly in others in which we would like the listed content model to govern the cardinality and other aspects of whichever subelements are explicitly named, while allowing that other subelements can appear in instances as well.

The distinction is effected by the *content* attribute taking the values "OPEN" and "CLOSED." The default is "OPEN" meaning that all element types not explicitly listed are valid, without order restrictions. (This idea has a close relation to the Java concept of a final class.)

For example, the following instance data for a book, including the unmentioned element *copyrightDate* would be valid given the content models declared so far, because they have all been *open*.

```
<Book>
    <author>Henry Ford</author>
    <author>Samuel Crowther</author>
    <title>My Life and Work</title>
    <copyrightDate>1922</copyrightDate>
</Book>
```

However, had the content model been declared closed, as follows, the *copyrightDate* element would be invalid.

```
<elementType id="Book" content="CLOSED">
    <element type="#title"/>
    <element type="#author" occurs="ONEORMORE"/>
    <group groupOrder="SEQ" occurs="OPTIONAL">
        <element type="#preface"/>
        <element type="#introduction" occurs="REQUIRED"/>
    </group>
</elementType>
```

A closed content model does not allow instances to contain any elements or attributes beyond those explicitly listed in the elementType declaration.

39.5 | Default Values

An element with occurs of REQUIRED or OPTIONAL (but not ONE-ORMORE or ZEROORMORE) can have a default value specified.

```
<elementType id="Book">
    <element type="#title"/>
    <element type="#author" occurs="ONEORMORE"/>
    <element type="#ageGrp" occurs="OPTIONAL">
        <default>adult</default>
    </element>
</elementType>
```

The default value is implied for all element *instances* in which it is syntactically omitted.

To indicate that the default value is the only allowed value, the *presence* attribute is set to "FIXED".

```
<elementType id="Book">
    <element type="#title"/>
    <element type="#author" occurs="ONEORMORE"/>
    <element type="#ageGrp" occurs="OPTIONAL" presence="FIXED">
        <default>ADULT</default>
    </element>
</elementType>
```

Presence has values of "IMPLIED," "SPECIFIED," "REQUIRED," and "FIXED" with the same meanings as defined in XML DTD.

39.6 | Aliases and Correlatives

ElementTypes can be know be different names in different languages or domains. The equivalence of several names is effected by the sameAs attribute, as in

```
<elementTypeEquivalent id="livre" type="#Book"/>
<elementTypeEquivalent id="auteur" type="#author"/>
```

Elements are used to represent both primary object types (nouns) and also properties, relations and so forth. Relations are often known by two names, each reflecting one direction of the relationship. For example, husband and wife, above and below, earlier and later, etc. The *correlative* element identifies such a pairing.

```
<elementType id= "author">
    <string/>
</elementType>

<elementType id= "wrote">
    <correlative type="#author" />
    <string/>
</elementType>
```

This indicates that "wrote" is another name for the "author" relation, but from the perspective of the person, not the book. That is, the two fragments below express the same fact:

```
<Person>
    <name>Henry Ford</name>
</Person>

<Book>
    <title>My Life and Work</title>
    <author>Henry Ford</author>
</Book>

...

<Person>
    <name>Henry Ford</name>
    <wrote>My Life and Work</wrote>
</Person>

<Book>
    <title>My Life and Work</title>
</Book>
```

A correlative may be defined simply to document the alternative name for the relation. However, it may also be used within a content model where it permits instances to use the alternative name. Further it may to establish constraints on the relation, indicate key relationships, etc.

39.7 | Class Hierarchies

ElementTypes can be organized into categories using the *superType* attribute, as in

```
<elementType id="price">
    <string/>
</elementType>

<elementType id="ThingsIveBoughtRecently">
    <element type="#price"/>
</elementType>

<elementType id="PencilsIveBoughtRecently">
    <superType type="#ThingsIveBoughtRecently"/>
    <element type="#price"/>
</elementType>

<elementType id="BooksIveBoughtRecently">
    <superType type="#ThingsIveBoughtRecently"/>
    <element type="#price"/>
</elementType>
```

This simply indicates that, in some fashion, *PencilsIveBoughtRecently* and *BooksIveBoughtRecently*are subsets of *ThingsIveBoughtRecently.* It implies that every valid instance of the subset is a valid instance of the superset. The superset type must have an *open* content model.

There are restrictions that should be followed, based on the principle that all instances of the species (subtype) must be instances of the genus (supertype):

- The genus type must have content="OPEN".
- It must have either no groups or only groups with groupOrder="AND" (that is, no order constraints).
- You can add new elements and attributes.
- Occurs cardinality can be decreased but not increased.
- Ranges and other constraints are cummulative, that is, all apply (though the exact effect of this depends on the semantics of the constraint type).
- Default values can be made FIXED defaults.

To indicate that the content model of the subset should inherit the content model of a superset, we use a particular kind of superType called "genus" of which only one is allowed per ElementType. This copies the content model of the referenced element type and permits addition of new elements to it. Further, sub-elements occurring in the superset type, if declared again, are replaced by the newer declarations.

```
<elementType id="Book">
    <element type="#title"/>
    <element type="#author" occurs="ONEORMORE"/>
</elementType>

<elementType id="BooksIveBoughtRecently">
    <genus type="#Book"/>
    <superType type="#ThingsIveBoughtRecently"/>
    <element type="#price"/>
</elementType>
```

The above has the same effect as

```
<elementType id="Book">
    <element type="#title"/>
    <element type="#author" occurs="ONEORMORE"/>
</elementType>

<elementType id="BooksIveBoughtRecently">
    <superType type="#Book"/>
    <superType type="#ThingsIveBoughtRecently"/>
    <element type="#title"/>
    <element type="#author" occurs="ONEORMORE"/>
    <element type="#price"/>
</elementType>
```

39.8 | Elements which are References

ElementTypes and the content model elements defined so far are sufficient to declare a tree structure of elements. However, some elements such as "author" are *not only* usable on their own, they also act as references to other elements. For example, "Henry Ford" is the value of the *author* subelement of a *book* element. "Henry Ford" is also the value of the *name* element in a *person* element, and it can be used to connect these two.

```
<Book>
    <author>Henry Ford</author>
    <author>Samuel Crowther</author>
    <title>My Life and Work</title>
</Book>

<Person><name>Henry Ford</name></Person>

<Person><name>Samuel Crowther</name></Person>
```

In this capacity, such subelement are often referred to as *relations* when using "knowledge representation" terminology or "keys" when using database terms. (The meaning of "relation" and "key" are slightly different, but the fact which the terms recognize is the same.)

To make such references explicit in the schema, we add declarations for *keys* and *foreign keys*.

```
<elementType id="name">
    <string/>
</elementType>

<elementType id="Person">
    <element id="p1" type="#name"/>
    <key id="k1"><keyPart href="#p1"/></key>
</elementType>

<elementType id="author">
    <string/>
    <foreignKey range="#Person" key="#k1"/>
</elementType>

<elementType id="title">
    <string/>
</elementType>

<elementType id="Book">
    <element type="#title"/>
    <element type="#author" occurs="ONEORMORE"/>
</elementType>
```

The *key* element within *person* tells us that a person can be uniquely identified by his *name*. The *foreignKey* element within the *author* element definition says that the contents of an author element are a foreign key indentifying a person by *name*.

An uninformed user agent can still display the string "Henry Ford" even if it cannot determine that is supposed to be a person. A savvy agent that reads the schema can do more. It can locate the actual person.

This is the information needed for a *join* in database terminology.

This mechanism not only handles the typical way in which properties are expressed in databases, it also handles all cases in which the contents of an element are to be interpreted as strings from a restricted vocabulary, such as enumerations, XML nmtokens, etc.

```
<Book>
    <author>Henry Ford</author>
    <author>Samuel Crowther</author>
    <title>My Life and Work</title>
    <lccn>HD9710.U54 F58 1973</lccn>
    <dewey>629.2/092/4 B</dewey >
    <isbn>0405050887</isbn>
    <series>Business<series>
</Book>
```

Although not shown here, presumably *lccn*, *dewey* and *isbn* are declared in the schema to be foreign keys to corrresponding fields of catalog records. *Series* is a foreign key to a categorization of books, of which "Business" is one category.

Keys can contain URIs, as in

```
<Book>
    <author>http://SSA.gov/blab/people/Henry+Ford</author>
    <author>http://SSA.gov/blab/people/Samuel+Crowther</author>
    <title>My Life and Work</title>
</Book>
```

This is indicated in the schema by a datatype of "URI".

```
<elementType id="author">
    <string/>
    <datatype dt="uri"/>
</elementType>
```

39.8.1 *One-to-Many Relations*

Element relations are binary. That is, we never express an n-to-1 relationship directly. We do not, for example, list within *books* a single relation that somehow resolves to all the *authors*. Instead, we always write the relationship on the 1-to-n side, but allow multiple occurrences of the *subelement*, for example, allowing *books* to have multiple occurrences of *author*.

```
<Person><name>Henry Ford</name></Person>

<Person><name>Samuel Crowther</name></Person>

<Person><name>Harvey S. Firestone</name></Person>

<Book>
    <author>Henry Ford</author>
    <author>Samuel Crowther</author>
    <title>My Life and Work</title>
</Book>

<Book>
    <author>Harvey S. Firestone</author>
    <author>Samuel Crowther</author>
    <title>Men and Rubber</title>
</Book>
```

This example shows a book with several persons as author, and also a person who is author of several books. We discussed such many-to-many relations more under the topic of *correlations*.

39.8.2 *Multipart Keys*

When the foreignKey element does not have foreignKeyPart sub-elements (as it does not above) then the entirety of the elements contents (e.g. "Henry Ford") should be used as the key value. However, for multipart foreign keys, or cases where the element has several sub-elements, foreignKey-Part is used, as shown below.

```
<elementType id="firstName">
    <string/>
</elementType>

<elementType id="lastName">
    <string/>
</elementType>

<elementType id="Person">
    <element id="pp1" type="#firstName"/>
    <element id="pp2" type="#lastName"/>
    <key id="k1">
        <keyPart href="#pp1"/>
        <keyPart href="#pp2"/>
    </key>
</elementType>

<elementType id="author">
```

```
    <element id="ap1" type="#firstName"/>
    <element id="ap2" type="#lastName"/>
    <domain type="#Book"/>
    <range type="#Person"/>
    <foreignKey range="#Person" key="#k1">
        <foreignKeyPart href="#ap1"/>
        <foreignKeyPart href="#ap2"/>
    </foreignKey>
</elementType>

...

<Book>
    <title>My Life and Work</title>
    <author>
        <firstName>Henry</firstName>
        <lastName>Ford</lastName>
    </author>
</Book>
```

39.9 | Attributes as References

An alternative way to express a reference is with an attribute.

```
<person id="person1"><name>Henry Ford</name></Person>

<person id="person2"><name>Samuel Crowther</name></Person>

<Book>
    <author name="Henry Ford"/>
    <author name="Samuel Crowther"/>
    <title>My Life and Work</title>
</Book>
```

This allows us to link a book to a person, through the author relation, using an attribute of the relation. This exactly parallels the construction we saw above under "multipart keys," where a *subelement* of author contained the authors name. Here, an *attribute* of author contains the name. We can express this in our schema as

```
<elementType id="author">
    <attribute name="name" id="authorname"/>
    <foreignKey range="#Person" key="#k1">
        <foreignKeyPart href="#authorname"/>
    </foreignKey>
</elementType>
```

A widely-used variant of this is to use a URI as a foreign key:

```
<Book>
    <author href="http://SSA.gov/blab/people/Henry+Ford"/>
    <author href="http://SSA.gov/blab/people/Samuel+Crowther"/>
    <title>My Life and Work</title>
</Book>
```

In this case, we are using the *href* attribute to contain a URI. This is a particular kind of foreign key, where the *range* is any possible resource, and where that resource is not identified by some combination of its properties but instead by a name-resolution service. We indicate this by using an attribute element, with dt= "URI".

```
<elementType id="author">
    <attribute name="href" id="authorhref" dt="uri"/>
</elementType>
```

39.10 | Constraints & Additional Properties

39.10.1 *Min and Max Constraints*

Elements can be limited to restricted ranges of values. The *min* and *max* elements define the lower and upper bounds.

```
<elementType id="age">
    <string/>
</elementType>
```

```
<elementType id="Person">
    <element hef="#age"><min>0</min><max>131</max></element>
</elementType>
```

Such intervals are *half-open* (that is, the *min* value is in the interval, and the *max* value is the smallest value not in the interval).

This rule leads to the simplest calculation in most cases, and is unambiguous with respect to precision. In the above example, it is clear by these rules the 130.9999 is in the interval and 131 is not. However, had we said "all numbers from 0 to 130.99," in practice we would have some ambiguity regarding the status of 130.9999. Or interpretation would depend on the precision that we inferred for the original statement. The issue is particularly ambiguous for dates. (What exactly does "From December 5 to December 8" mean? The use of half-open intervals for representation does not, however, put any requirements on how processors must display intervals. For example, dates in some contexts display differently than their storage. That is, the interval `<min>1997-12-05</min><max>1997-12-09</max>` might be displayed as "December 5 through December 8".

In certain cases this rule for a half-open interval is impractical (for example, what letter follows "z" in the latin alphabet?) If so, use *maxInclusive*:

```
<elementType id="student">
    <element type="#grade">
        <min>A</min><maxInclusive>Z</maxInclusive>
    </element>
</elementType>
```

39.10.1.1   Domain and Range Constraints

We can use the *domain* and *range* elements to add constraints to an elements use or value. The *domain* element, if present, indicates that the element may only be used as a property of certain other elements. That is, syntactically it may appear only in the content model of those other element types. It constrains the sorts of schemas that can be written with the element.

```
<elementType id="author">
    <string/>
    <domain type="#Book"/>
    <attribute name="href" dt="uri"/>
</elementType>
```

The *domain* property above permits *author* elements to be used only within elements which are either *books* or subsets of *books*. Use of domain is optional. If omitted, there is simply no restriction.

The *range* element is used with elements which are references and declares a restriction on the types of elements to which the relation may refer. Graphically, it describes the target end of a directed edge. Each *range* element references one elementType, any of which are valid. In this case, below, we have said that an *author* element must have an *href* attribute which is a URI reference to a *Person* or to an element type which is *Person* or a subset of *Person*.

```
<elementType id="author">
    <string/>
    <domain type="#Book"/>
    <attribute name="href" dt="uri" range="#Person" />
</elementType>
```

39.10.2 *Other useful properties*

Element and attribute types can have an unlimited amount of further information added to them in the schema due to the open nature of XML with namespaces.

39.11 | Using Elements from Other Schemas

A schema may use elements and attributes from other schemas in content models. For example, a subelement named "http://books.org/date" could be used within a *book* element as follows:

```
<?XML version='1.0' ?>
<?xml:namespace
      name="urn:uuid:BDC6E3F0-6DA3-11d1-A2A3-00AA00C14882/"
      as="s"/?>
<s:schema>
    <elementType id="author">
        <string/>
    </elementType>

    <elementType id="title">
        <string/>
    </elementType>

    <elementType id="Book">
        <element type="#title" occurs="OPTIONAL"/>
        <element type="#author" occurs="ONEORMORE"/>
        <element href="http://books.org/date" />
    </elementType>
</s:schema>
```

This can be abbreviated by adopting the rule that namespace-qualified names may be used within the *href attribute* value of an *element* or *attribute* element.

```
<?XML version='1.0' ?>
<?xml:namespace
        name="urn:uuid:BDC6E3F0-6DA3-11d1-A2A3-00AA00C14882/"
        as="s"/?>
<?xml:namespace name=" http://books.org/" as="bk"/?>
<s:schema>
    <elementType id="author">
        <string/>
    </elementType>

    <elementType id="title">
        <string/>
    </elementType>

    <elementType id="Book">
        <element type="#title" occurs="OPTIONAL"/>
        <element type="#author" occurs="ONEORMORE"/>
        <element href="bk:date" />
    </elementType>
</s:schema>
```

39.12 | XML-Specific Elements

39.12.1 *Attributes*

XML-Data schemas contain a number of facilities to match features of XML DTDs or to support certain characteristics of XML. The XML syntax allows that certain properties can be expressed in a form called "attributes." To support this, an elementType can contain attribute declarations, which are divided into attributes with enumerated or notation values, and all other kinds.

An attribute may be given a default value. Whether it is required or optional is signaled by *presence*. (Presence ordinarily defaults to IMPLIED, but if omitted and there is an explicit default, presence is set to the SPECI-FIED.) See the DTD at the end of this document for syntactic details.

Attributes with enumerated (and notation) values permit a values attribute, a space-separated list of legal values. The values attribute is required when the atttype is ENUMERATION or NOTATION, else it is forbidden. In these cases, if a default is specified, it must be one of the specified values.

```
<elementType id="Book">
    <element type="#title"/>
    <element type="#author" occurs="ONEORMORE"/>
    <attribute name="copyright" />
    <attribute name="ageGrp"
            atttype="ENUMERATION"
            values="child adult"
            default="adult" />
</elementType>
```

describes an instance such as

```
<book copyright="1922" ageGrp="adult">
    <title>My Life and Work</title>
    <author>
        <firstName>Henry</firstName>
        <lastName>Ford</lastName>
    </author>
</Book>
```

Attributes may also reference elementTypes, meaning that one may use the element type but with attribute syntax. This allows an attribute to explicitly have the same name and semantics even when used on different element types. There are of course some limits: The attribute can still occur only once in an instance, and it cannot contain other elements. However, this allows the semantics of the element type to be employed in attribute syntax.

```
<elementType id="Book">
    <attribute href="bk:title"/>
    <attribute href="bk:author"/>
    <attribute name="copyright" />
    <attribute name="ageGrp"
        type="ENUMERATION"
        values="children adult" default="adult" />
</elementType>
```

describes an instance such as

```
<book
    bk:author="Henry Ford"
    bk:title="My Life and Work"
    ageGrp="adult"/>
```

39.13 | Entity declaration element types

This and the next two declarations cover entities. Entities are a shorthand mechanism, similar to macros in a programming language.

```
<intEntityDcl name="LTG">
    Language Technology Group
</intEntityDcl>

<extEntityDcl name="dilbert" notation="#gif"
              systemId="http://www.ltg.ed.ac.uk/~ht/dilb.gif"/>
```

Here as elsewhere, following XML, systemId must be a URI, absolute or relative, and publicId, if present, must be a Public Identifier (as defined in ISO/IEC 9070:1991, Information technology – SGML support facilities – Registration procedures for public text owner identifiers). If a notation is given, it must be declared (see below) and the entity will be treated as binary, i.e., not substituted directly in place of references.

```
<notationDcl name="gif" systemId='http://who.knows.where/'/>
```

39.14 | External declarations element type

Although we allow an external entity with declarations to be included, we recommend a different declaration for schema modularization. The extDcls declaration gives a clean mechanism for importing (fragments of) other schemas. It replaces the common SGML idiom of declaring an external parameter entity and then immediately referring to it, and has the same import, namely, that the text referred to by the combination of systemId and publicId is included in the schema in place of the extDcls element, and that replacement text is then subject to the same validity constraints and interpretation as the rest of the schema.

Note that in many cases the desired effect may be better represented by referencing elements (and attributes) from the other schema or subclassing from them.

39.15 | Datatypes

A datatype indicates that the contents of an element can be interpreted as both a string and also, more specifically, as an object that can be interpreted more specifically as a number, date, etc. The datatype indicates that the elements contents can be parsed or interpreted to yeild an object more specific than a string.

That is, we distinguish the "type" of an element from its "datatype." The former gives the semantic meaning of an element, such as "birthday" indicating the date on which someone was born. The "datatype" represents the parser class needed to decode the element's contents into an object type more specific than "string." For example, "19541022" is the 22nd of October, 1954 in ISO 8601 date format. (That is, ISO 8601 parsing rules will decode "19541022" into a date, which can then be stored as a date rather than a string.

For example, we would like an XML author to be able to say that the contents of a "size" element is an integer, meaning that it should be parsed according to numeric parsing rules and that it can be stored in integer format. In some contexts an API can expose it as an integer rather than a string.

```
<item>
    <name>shirt</name>
    <size>8</size>
</item>
```

There are two main contexts for datatypes. First, when dealing with database APIs, such as ODBC, all elements with the same name typically contain the same type of contents. For example, all sizes contain integers or all birthdays contain dates. We will return to this case shortly.

Second, and by contrast, the type of the content may vary widely from instance to instance. The softer we make our software, the more often these flexible cases occur. For example, size could contain the integer 8, or the word "small" or even a formula for computing the size.

We expose the datatype of an element instance by use of a *dt:dt* attribute, where the value of the attribute is a URI giving the datatype. (The URI might be explicitly in URI format or might rely on the XML namespace facility for resolution.) For example, we might find a document containing something like:

```
<?namespace
        name="urn:uuid:C2F41010-65B3-11d1-A29F-00AA00C14882/"
        as="dt"?>
<?namespace name="http://zoosports.com/dt?" as="zoo"?>
<purchases>
  <item>
    <name>shirt</name>
    <size dt:dt="int">8</size>
  </item>
  <item>
```

```
   <name>shoes</name>
   <size>large</size>
 </item>
 <item>
   <name>suit</name>
   <size dt:dt="zoo:script">
      =(shirtsize*1.05) + 3
   </size>
 </item>
</purchases>
```

Clearly this technique works for the heterogeneous typing in the above example. It also works for the database case where all element's of the same type have the same datatype.

```
<item> <name>shirt</name> <size dt:dt="int">8</size>   </item>
<item> <name>shoes</name> <size dt:dt="int">6</size>   </item>
<item> <name>suit</name>  <size dt:dt="int">12</size>  </item>
```

As written above, this is inefficient. Fortunately, XML allows us in schemasto put attributes with default or fixed values, so we could say once that all *size* elements have a datatype with value "int". Having done so, our our instance just looks like:

```
<item> <name>shirt</name> <size>14</size>   </item>
<item> <name>shoes</name> <size>6</size>    </item>
<item> <name>suit</name>  <size>16</size>   </item>
```

In a DTD, we can set a *fixed* attribute value, so that all *size* elements have datatype "int" or we can set it as a *default* attribute value so that it is an integer except where explicitly noted otherwise.

```
<item> <name>shirt</name> <size>14</size>
       </item>
       <item> <name>shoes</name>
            <size dt:dt="string">large</size>
       </item>
       <item> <name>suit</name>  <size>16</size>
       </item>
```

XML DTDs today allow such attributes. For example, a DTD can say that all *shirt* elements have *integer datatype* by the following:

```
<!ELEMENT size PCDATA >
<!ATTLIST size   dt:dt "int" #FIXED >
```

XML-Data schemas allow the equivalent, though with specialized syntax:

```
<elementType id="size" >
   <datatype dt="int" />
</elementType>
```

Elements use *datatype* subelements to give the datatype so that an optional *presence* attribute of the datatype element can indicate whether the datatype is *fixed* or merely a *default*. Attributes can also have datatypes.

Because there is no possibility of their being anything other than a fixed type, the datatype of an attribute is signalled by a dt attribute:

```
<attribute id="size" dt="int" />
```

39.15.1 *How Typed Data is Exposed in the API*

Different APIs to typed data will use the datatype attribute differently. The basic XML parser API should expose all element contents as strings regardless of any datatype attribute. (It might also contain supplementary methods to read values as more specific types such as "integer," thereby getting more efficiency.) An ODBC interface could use the datatype attribute to expose each type of element as a column, with the column's datatype determined by the element type's datatype.

39.15.2 *Complex Data Types*

If a datatype requires a complex structure for storage, or an object-based storage, this is also handled by the dt:dt attribute, where the datatype's storage format can be a structure, Java class, COM++ class, etc. For example, if an application needed to have an element stored in a "ScheduleItem" structure and using some private format, it could note this like

```
<when dt:dt="zoo:ScheduleItem">M*D1W4B19971022;100</when>
```

The datatype does not require a private format. It could also use subelements and attributes such as

```
<when dt:dt="zoo:ScheduleItem2">
    <month>*</month>
    <day>1</day>
    <week>4</week>
    <begin>19971022</begin>
    <recurs>100</recurs>
</when>
```

In the case of the graph-oriented interfaces (e.g. XML/RDF) the mapping from the XML tree to a graph should add a *wrapping node* for each non-string data type. The datatype property gives the type of that node. For example, the following two are graphically equivalent:

```
<size dt:dt="int">8</size>
<size><dt:int>8</dt:int></size>
```

39.15.3 *Versioning of Instances*

Adding an attribute to an element does not change the other attributes or pose any special versioning problems. For example, an application written to expect an instance to contain "<birthday>19541022</birthday>" is not harmed if the schema reveals that this is ISO 8601 format. Versioning within datatypes should be handled by the author's making sure that that subtypes of datatypes retain all the characteristics of the supertype.

If a down-level application is given a datatype it cannot process, it should expose the element contents as a supertype of the indicated datatype. In practice, this will usually mean that unrecognized datatypes will be the same as "dt:string". However, there are cases in which a type will be promoted, for example exposing a boolean in a byte or word rather than a bit, exposing a floating point number in a language's native format, etc.

39.15.4 *The Datatypes Namespace*

The datatype attribute "dt" is defined in the namespace named "urn:uuid:C2F41010-65B3-11d1-A29F-00AA00C14882/". (See the XML Namespaces Note at the W3C site for details of namespaces.) The full URN of the attribute is "urn:uuid:C2F41010-65B3-11d1-A29F-00AA00C14882/dt".

You will have noticed that the value of the attribute, as used in the examples above, is not lexically a full URI. For example, it reads "int" or "string" etc. Datatype attribute values are abbreviated according to the following rule: If it does not contain a colon, it is a datatype defined in the datatypes namespace "urn:uuid:C2F41010-65B3-11d1-A29F-00AA00C14882/". If it contains a colon, it is to be expanded to a full URI according to the same rules used for other names, as defined by the XML Namespaces Note. For example

```
<?namespace
        name="urn:uuid:C2F41010-65B3-11d1-A29F-00AA00C14882/"
        as="dt"?>
<?namespace name="http://zoosports.com/dt?" as="zoo"?>
<item>
    <size dt:dt="int">8</size>
    <name dt:dt="zoo:clothing">shirt</name>
</item>
```

has two datatypes whose full names are "urn:uuid:C2F41010-65B3-11d1-A29F-00AA00C14882/integer" and "http://zoosports.com/dt?clothing".

39.15.5 *What a datatype's URI Means*

Datatypes are identified by URIs. The URI as simply a reference to a section of a document that defines the appropriate parser and storage format of the element. To make this broadly useful, this document defines a set of common data types including all common forms of dates, plus all basic datatypes commonly used in SQL, C, C++, Java and COM (including strings).

The best form of such a document is that it should itself be an XML-Data schema where each datatype is an element declaration. For this purpose we define a *<Syntax>* subelement which can be used in lieu of a content model. We also define an *<objecttype>* subelement. Each has a URI as its value. This integrates data types with element types in general.

```
<schema:elementType id="int">
<syntax href=
"urn:uuid:C2F41010-65B3-11d1-A29F-00AA00C14882/num_to_int"/>
<objectType href=
"urn:uuid:C2F41010-65B3-11d1-A29F-00AA00C14882/integer32"/>
</schema:elementType>

<schema:elementType id="date.iso8601">
<syntax  href=
"urn:uuid:C2F41010-65B3-...882/date.iso8601_to_int32"/>
<objecttype href="urn:uuid:C2F41010-65B3-...882/integer32" />
</schema:elementType>
```

The objecttype sub-element can reference a structure, Java class, COM++ coClass, etc. The syntax subelement identifies a parser which can decode the element's content (and/or attributes) into the object type given the storage type URI. Input to the parser is the element object exposing all its attributes and content tree (that is, the subtree of the grove beginning with the element containing the dt attribute). The objectType attribute in particular is assumed available to the parser so that a single parser can support several objecttypes.

Having said this, all *basic* data types should be built into the parsers for efficiency and in order to ground the process. For these, the datatype elements serve only to formally document the storage types and parsers, and to give higher-level systems (such as RDF) a more formal basis for datatypes.

I do not currently propose that we attempt to write any universal notation for parsing rules. Certain popular kinds of formats, particularly dates, are not easily expressed in anything but natural language or code, and the parsers must be custom written code. In other words, the URIs for the basic syntax and objecttype elements probably resolve only to text descriptions.

39.15.6 *Structured Data Type Attributes*

Attributes in cannot XML have structure. I will separately propose some techniques to avoid this problem, specifically that the XML API should contain a method that treats attributes and subelements indistinguishably, and also that the content which is an element's value can be syntactically separated from content which is an element's properties.

39.15.7 *Specific Datatypes*

This includes all highly-popular types and all the built-in types of popular database and programming languages and systems such as SQL, Visual Basic, C, C++ and Java(tm).

Name	Parse type	Storage type	Examples
string	pcdata	string (Unicode)	[Greek letters: see CD-ROM version]

number	A number, with no limit on digits, may potentially have a leading sign, fractional digits, and optionally an exponent. Punctuation as in US English.	string	15, 3.14, -123.456E+10
int	A number, with optional sign, no fractions, no exponent.	32-bit signed binary	1, 58502, -13
float	Same as for "number."	64-bit IEEE 488	.314159265358979E+1
fixed.14.4	Same as "number" but no more than 14 dights to the left of the decimal point, and no more than 4 to the right.	64-bit signed binary	12.0044
boolean	"1" or "0"	bit	0, 1 (1=="true")
dateTime.iso8601	A date in ISO 8601 format, with optional time and no optional zone. Fractional seconds may be as precise as nanoseconds.	Structure or object containing year, month, hour, minute, second, nanosecond.	19941105T08:15:00301

`dateTime.iso8601tz`	A date in ISO 8601 format, with optional time and optional zone. Fractional seconds may be as precise as nanoseconds.	Structure or object containing year, month, hour, minute, second, nanosecond, zone.	19941105T08:15:5+03
`date.iso8601`	A date in ISO 8601 format. (no time)	Structure or object containing year, month, day.	19541022
`time.iso8601`	A time in ISO 8601 format, with no date and no time zone.	Structure or object exposing day, hour, minute	
`time.iso8601.tz`	A time in ISO 8601 format, with no date but optional time zone.	Structure or object containing day, hour, minute, zonehours, zoneminutes.	08:15-05:00
`i1`	A number, with optional sign, no fractions, no exponent.	8-bit binary	1, 255
`i2`	"	16-bit binary	1, 703, -32768
`i4`	"	32-bit binary	
`i8`	"	64-bit binary	

ui1	A number, unsigned, no fractions, no exponent.	8-bit unsigned binary	1, 255
ui2	"	16-bit unsigned binary	1, 703, -32768
ui4	"	32-bit unsigned binary	
ui8	"	64-bit unsigned binary	
r4	Same as "number."	IEEE 488 4-byte float	
r8	"	IEEE 488 8-byte float	
float.IEEE.754.32	"	IEEE 754 4-byte float	
float.IEEE.754.64	"	IEEE 754 8-byte float	
uuid	Hexidecimal digits representing octets, optional embedded hyphens which should be ignored.	128-bytes Unix UUID structure	F04DA480-65B9-11d1-A29F-00AA00C14882

uri	Universal Resource Identifier	Per W3C spec	http:// www.ics.uci.edu/ pub/ietf/uri/ draft-fielding-uri-syntax-00.txt http:// www.ics.uci.edu/ pub/ietf/uri/ http:// www.ietf.org/ html.charters/ urn-charter.html
bin.hex	Hexidecimal digits representing octets	no specified size	
char	string	1 Unicode character (16 bits)	
string.ansi	string containing only ascii characters <= 0xFF.	Unicode or single-byte string.	This does not look Greek to me.

All of the dates and times above reading "iso8601.." actually use a restricted subset of the formats defined by ISO 8601. Years, if specified, must have four digits. Ordinal dates are not used. Of formats employing week numbers, only those that truncate year and month are allowed (5.2.3.3 d, e and f).

39.16 | Mapping between Schemas

Certain uses of data emphasize syntax, others "conceptual" relations. Syntactic schemas often have fewer elements compared to explicitly conceptual ones. Further, it is usually easier to design a schema that merely covers syntax rather than designing a well-thought-out conceptual data model. An effect of this is that many practical schemas will not contain all the elements that a conceptual schema would, either for reasons of economy or because the initial schema was simply syntactic. But is it useful to make the implicit explicit over time so that more generic processors can make use of data.

For example, the following schema is essentially syntax:

```
<elementType id="author">
    <string/>
</elementType>

<elementType id="title">
    <string/>
</elementType>

<elementType id="Book">
    <element type="#title"/>
    <element type="#author" occurs="ONEORMORE"/>
</elementType>
```

with instances looking like this

```
<Book>
    <title>Paradise Lost</title>
    <author>Milton</author>
</Book>
```

On the other hand, a conceptual schema could look like this:

```
<elementType id="name">
    <string/>
</elementType>

<elementType id="Person">
    <element type="#name/>
</elementType>

<elementType id="creator">
    <range type="#Person/>
</elementType>

<elementType id="title">
    <string/>
</elementType>

<elementType id="Book">
    <element type="#title"/>
    <element type="#creator" occurs="ONEORMORE"/>
</elementType>
```

If fully explicit, its instances would look something like this:

```
<Person id="thing1">
    <name>Milton</Person>
</Person>

<Book>
    <title>Paradise Lost</title>
    <creator>
        <Person>
            <name>Milton</name>
        </Person>
    </creator>
</Book>
```

In any case, what we want to express is a diagram such as this:

To do this, we will add mapping information into the syntactic schema which tells us how to interpolate the implied elements (and also to map *author* to *creator*) thereby creating a conceptual data model.

```
<?xml:namespace href="uri-to-the-conceptual-schema" as="c" ?>
<elementType id="author">
    <string/>
</elementType>

<elementType id="title">
    <string/>
</elementType>

<elementType id="Book">
    <mapsTo type="c:book"/>
    <element type="#title"> <mapsTo type="c:title"/> </element>
```

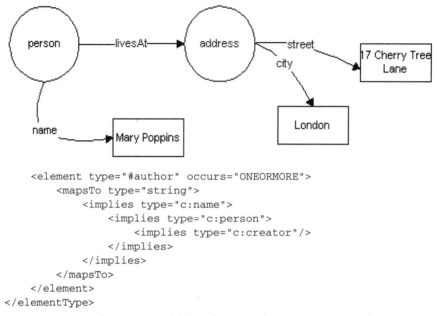

```
<element type="#author" occurs="ONEORMORE">
    <mapsTo type="string">
        <implies type="c:name">
            <implies type="c:person">
                <implies type="c:creator"/>
            </implies>
        </implies>
    </mapsTo>
</element>
</elementType>
```

A more complex case could involve needing to map several properties to have a common implied node. For example, suppose we wanted that a *street* element and *city* element should both imply the **same** *address* node.

```
<Person>
    <name>Mary Poppins</name>
    <street>17 Cherry Tree Lane</street>
    <city>London</city>
</Person>
```

That is, rather than creating two *address* nodes, we want to create only a single onc, and subordinate both the *street* and *city* to it. If the conceptual schema has elements *livesAt*, *address*, *street* and *city*, we could write a mapping thus:

```
...definitions of name, street and city...

<elementType id="Person">
    <mapsTo type="c:person"/>
    <element type="#name">
            <string/>
            <mapsTo type="c:name"/>
    </element>
    <element type="#street">
        <string/>
        <mapsTo type="c:street">
            <implies type="c::address" id="livesAtAddress">
                <implies type="c:livesAt"/>
```

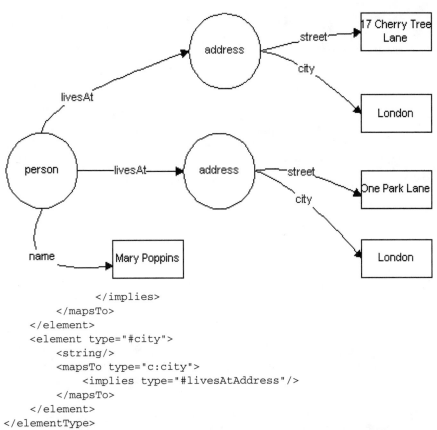

```
            </implies>
        </mapsTo>
    </element>
    <element type="#city">
        <string/>
        <mapsTo type="c:city">
            <implies type="#livesAtAddress"/>
        </mapsTo>
    </element>
</elementType>
```

Elements may be repeated, so mapping rules need to accommodate repetitions. Suppose that someone has two addresses in the grammatical syntax, this needs to map to two addresses in the graph while still keeping the structure correct.

```
<Person>
    <name>Mary Poppins</name>
    <street>17 Cherry Tree Lane</street>
    <city>London</city>
    <street>One Park Lane</street>
    <city>London</city>
</Person>
```

```
<elementType id="Person">
    <mapsTo type="c:person"/>
    <element type="#name">    <string/>
            <mapsTo type="c:name"/>
    </element>
    <group occurs="ZEROORMORE"/>
        <element type="#street">
            <string/>
            <mapsTo type="c:street">
                <implies type="c::address" id="livesAtAddress">
                    <implies type="c:livesAt"/>
                </implies>
            </mapsTo>
        </element>
        <element type="#city">
            <string/>
            <mapsTo type="c:city">
                <implies type="#livesAtAddress"/>
            </mapsTo>
        </element>
    </group>
</elementType>
```

Mappings within groups are handled together. Since *street* and *city* are in a single group, each occurrence of such a group results in one *address*.

Text markup can also be handled by mapping. Suppose that for some reason we choose to markup the number portion of a street address:

```
<Person>
    <name>Mary Poppins</name>
    <street>< streetNumber>17</ streetNumber >
    Cherry Tree Lane</street>
    <city>London</city>
</Person>
```

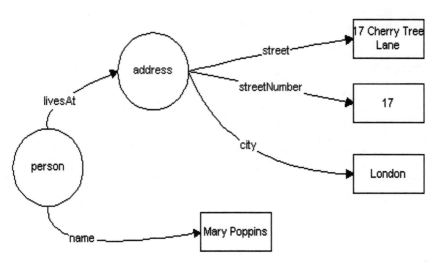

If this should be reflected in the graph,
We can do that with mapping such as:

```
<elementType id="streetNumber">
    <string/>
</elementType>

<elementType id="street>
    <mixed>
        <element type="# streetNumber">
            <mapsTo type="c: streetNumber">
                <implies type="#livesAtAddress"/>
            </mapsTo>
        </element>
    </mixed>
</elementType>

...Person defined as before...
```

39.17 | Appendix A: Examples

Some data:

```
<?xml:namespace name="http://company.com/schemas/books/" as="bk"/>
<?xml:namespace name="http://www.ecom.org/schemas/dc/" as="ecom" ?>

<bk:booksAndAuthors>
    <Person>
        <name>Henry Ford</name>
        <birthday>1863</birthday>
    </Person>

    <Person>
        <name>Harvey S. Firestone</name>
    </Person>

    <Person>
        <name>Samuel Crowther</name>
    </Person>

    <Book>
        <author>Henry Ford</author>
        <author>Samuel Crowther</author>
        <title>My Life and Work</title>
    </Book>

    <Book>
        <author>Harvey S. Firestone</author>
        <author>Samuel Crowther</author>
        <title>Men and Rubber</title>
        <ecom:price>23.95</ecom:price>
    </Book>
</bk:booksAndAuthors>
```

The schema for http://company.com/schemas/books:

```
<?xml:namespace
    name="urn:uuid:BDC6E3F0-6DA3-11d1-A2A3-00AA00C14882/"
    as="s"/?>
<?xml:namespace
    href="http://www.ecom.org/schemas/ecom/" as="ecom" ?>

<s:schema>

    <elementType id="name">
        <string/>
    </elementType>

    <elementType id="birthday">
        <string/>
        <dataType dt="date.ISO8601"/>
    </elementType>

    <elementType id="Person">
        <element type="#name" id="p1"/>
```

```
        <element type="#birthday" occurs="OPTIONAL">
         <min>1700-01-01</min><max>2100-01-01</max>
        </element>
        <key id="k1"><keyPart href="#p1" /></key>
    </elementType>

    <elementType id="author">
        <string/>
        <domain type="#Book"/>
        <foreignKey range="#Person" key="#k1"/>
    </elementType>

    <elementType id="writtenWork">
        <element type="#author" occurs="ONEORMORE"/>
    </elementType>

    <elementType id="Book" >
        <genus type="#writtenWork"/>
        <superType
          href="http://www.ecom.org/schemas/ecom/commercialItem"/>
        <superType
          href="http://www.ecom.org/schemas/ecom/inventoryItem"/>
        <group groupOrder="SEQ" occurs="OPTIONAL">
            <element type="#preface"/>
             <element type="#introduction"/>
        </group>
     <element href="http://www.ecom.org/schemas/ecom/price"/>
     <element href="ecom:quantityOnHand"/>
    </elementType>

    <elementTypeEquivalent id="livre" type="#Book"/>
    <elementTypeEquivalent id="auteur" type="#author"/>

</s:schema>
```

39.18 | Appendix B: An XML DTD for XML-Data schemas

```
<!ENTITY % nodeattrs 'id ID #IMPLIED'>

<!-- href is as per XML-LINK, but is not required unless
       there is no content -->

<!ENTITY % linkattrs
               'id ID #IMPLIED
               href CDATA #IMPLIED'>

<!ENTITY % typelinkattrs
               'id ID #IMPLIED
               type CDATA #IMPLIED'>

<!ENTITY % exattrs
               'name CDATA #IMPLIED
               content (OPEN|CLOSED) "OPEN" >

<!ENTITY % elementTypeElements1
               genus? correlative? superType*>

<!ENTITY % elementTypeElements2
               description,
               (min|minExclusive)?,
               (max | maxInclusive)?,
               domain*,
               key*,
               foreignKey*,
               (datatype | ( syntax?, objecttype+ ) )?
               mapsTo?>

<!ENTITY % elementConstraints
               'min? max? default?'>

<!ENTITY % elementAttrs
               'occurs
                  (REQUIRED|OPTIONAL|ONEORMORE|ZEROORMORE)
               "REQUIRED" '>

<!ENTITY % rangeAttribute
               'range CDATA #IMPLIED'  >

<!-- The top-level container -->
<!element schema       ((elementType|linkType|
                  extendType|
                  intEntityDcl|extEntityDcl|
```

```
                              notationDcl|extDcls)*)>
<!attlist schema %nodeattrs;>

<!-- Element Type Declarations -->

<!element elementType (%elementTypeElements1;,
                  ((element|group)*|empty|any|string|mixed)?,
                  attribute*
                  %elementTypeElements2 )>

<!attlist elementType %nodeattrs;
                      %exattrs >

<!-- Element types allowed in content model -->

<!-- Note this is just short for a model group with only
         one element in it -->
<!element element  (%elementConstraints;) >

<!-- The type is required -->
<!attlist element   %typelinkattrs;
                    %elementAttrs;
                    presence (FIXED) #IMPLIED >

<!-- A group in a content model: and, sequential
                        or disjunctive -->
<!element group      ((group|element)+)>
<!attlist group      %nodeattrs;
                     %elementattrs;
                     presence (FIXED) #IMPLIED
                     groupOrder (AND|SEQ|OR) 'SEQ'>

<!element any        EMPTY>
<!element empty      EMPTY>
<!element string     EMPTY>

<!-- mixed content is just a flat, non-empty
                          list of elements -->
<!-- We don't need to say anything about
                  <string/> (CDATA), it's implied -->

<!element mixed       (element+)>
<!attlist mixed       %nodeattrs;>

<!element superType  EMPTY>
<!attlist superType %linkattrs;>

<!element genus  EMPTY>
<!attlist genus %typelinkattrs;>
```

```
<!element description  MIXED>
<!attlist description %nodeattrs;>

<!element domain  EMPTY>
<!attlist domain %typelinkattrs;>

<!element default MIXED>
<!attlist default %nodeattrs;>

<!element min MIXED>
<!attlist min %nodeattrs; >

<!element max MIXED>
<!attlist max %nodeattrs; >

<!element maxInclusive MIXED>
<!attlist maxInclusive %nodeattrs; >

<!element minExclusive MIXED>
<!attlist minExclusive %nodeattrs; >

<!element key (keyPart+)>
<!attlist key %nodeattrs;>

<!element keyPart EMPTY>
<!attlist keyPart %linkattrs;>

<!element foreignKey foreignKeyPart* >
<!attlist foreignKey %nodeattrs;
                     %rangeAttribute;
                     key CDATA #IMPLIED >

<!element foreignKeyPart EMPTY>
<!attlist foreignKeyPart %linkattrs;>

<!-- Datatype support -->

<!element datatype (elementType?) >
<!attlist datatype %typelinkattrs;
       presence (IMPLIED|SPECIFIED|REQUIRED|FIXED) #IMPLIED >

<!element syntax >
<!attlist syntax %linkattrs; >

<!element objecttype >
<!attlist objecttype %linkattrs; >

<!-- Mapping support -->

<!element mapsTo (implies?)>
```

```
<!attlist mapsTo %typelinkattrs;>

<!element implies (implies?)>
<!attlist implies %typelinkattrs;>

<!-- Alias support -->

<!element elementTypeEquivalent EMPTY>
<!attlist elementTypeEquivalent %typelinkattrs; >

<!element correlative EMPTY>
<!attlist correlative %linkattrs;>

<! Subtype of ElementType that is explicitly a relation. -->

<!element relationType (%elementTypeElements1;,
                  ((element|group)*|empty|any|string|mixed)?,
                  attribute*
                  %elementTypeElements2)>
<!attlist relationType %nodeattrs;
                  %exattrs; >


<!-- Attributes -->
<!-- default value must be present if
                     presence is specified or fixed -->
<!-- presence defaults to specified if default
                     is present, else implied -->

<!element attribute  (%PropertyElements1,
                     %PropertyElements2,
                     %elementConstraints)>
<!attlist attribute  %typelinkattrs;
        name CDATA #IMPLIED
        %elementAttrs
        dt          CDATA #IMPLIED
        atttype     (URIREF|
                    ID|IDREF|IDREFS|ENTITY|ENTITIES|
                    NMTOKEN|NMTOKENS|
                    ENUMERATION|NOTATION|CDATA) CDATA
        %rangeAttribute;
        default CDATA #IMPLIED
        values NMTOKENS #IMPLIED
        presence (IMPLIED|SPECIFIED|REQUIRED|FIXED) #IMPLIED >

<!-- Notation and Entity Declarations -->
<!-- Note: as this is written, only external entities
     can have structure without escaping it -->
<!-- 'par' is TRUE iff parameter entity. -->
<!-- systemID and publicId (if present) must
                            have the required syntax -->
```

```
<!ENTITY % notationattrs '%nodeattrs
                          systemID CDATA #IMPLIED
                          publicID CDATA #IMPLIED'>

<!ENTITY % entityattrs   '%notationattrs
                          name CDATA #IMPLIED
                          par     (TRUE | FALSE) "FALSE">

<!-- Notation Declarations -->

<!element notationDcl       EMPTY>
<!attlist notationDcl       %notationattrs>

<!element intEntityDcl      PCDATA>
<!attlist intEntityDcl      %entityattrs; >

<!-- The entity will be treated as binary
                          if a notation is present -->
<!element extEntityDcl      EMPTY>
<!attlist extEntityDcl      %entityattrs;
                            notation CDATA #IMPLIED>

<!-- External entity with declarations to be included -->
<!element extDcls           EMPTY>
<!attlist extDcls           %entityattrs;>
```

The XML
SPECtacular

- International Standards
- W3C Recommendations
- XML applications
- ... and More!

For those of you who like to dig into the source material, our CD-ROM has plenty for you. Here's a full description.

Welcome to the XML SPECtacular, a collection of the relevant standards and specifications that you can browse, search, and print. This collection was compiled for The XML Handbook by Lars Marius Garshol.

For each document, we've included a link to a web site where you can learn more about the underlying project and obtain the latest version. Where copyright and production considerations allowed, we've also included a browseable copy on the CD-ROM.

All documents categorized as W3C recommendations or W3C work in process are subject to the W3C document use policy, which you can find on the CD-ROM and on the Web.

Not all specifications were available in HTML, so some of them are included as Adobe Portable Document Format (or PDF). A PDF viewer is available for free from Adobe for Mac, MS Windows, DOS, Unix and OS/2.

40.1 | Base standards

40.1.1 *International Standards*

40.1.1.1   Approved standards

SGML: Standard Generalized Markup Language

Charles F. Goldfarb
Information on web:
http://www.sil.org/sgml

This standard is really the ancestor of nearly all the other standards listed here. SGML is the mother tongue of most markup languages and the "big brother" of XML.

HyTime

Charles F. Goldfarb
Steven R. Newcomb
Eliot Kimber
Peter Newcomb
Information on web:
http://www.hytime.org/

HyTime is from the SGML family of International Standards. It describes many different things. There of the most important are architectural forms, hyperlinking, and structuring of time-based media like sound and film. Architectural forms is a technique for describing common semantics among different DTDs and is widely used. (The XLink standard uses something like it.)

DSSSL

Sharon Adler
Anders Berglund
Jon Bosak
James Clark

Information on web:
http://www.jclark.com/dsssl/

DSSSL is a powerful (and elegant!) style sheet language for SGML. DSSSL can be thought of as the "big brother" of XSL, but with a different syntax.

Unicode

Information on web:
http://www.unicode.org/

Unicode is an advanced and very complete character coding system. Using 16 bits (and various coding tricks), Unicode aims to encompass all human scripts, both those in use today as well as archaic ones. Unicode provides XML's character set.

40.1.2 W3C recommendations

40.1.2.1   Approved recommendations

Extensible Markup Language (XML)

Tim Bray
Jean Paoli
C.M. Sperberg-McQueen

Information on web:
http://www.w3.org/TR/REC-xml
Document included on CD-ROM:
./specs/w3c/rec-xml.html

Here it is: the XML standard itself. For a standard it is mercifully short and readable, and nicely unambiguous. This is definitely recommended reading!

Cascading Style Sheets (CSS2)

Håkon Wium Lie
Bert Bos

Information on web:
http://www.w3.org/Style/CSS/
Document included on CD-ROM:
./specs/w3c/pr-css2/index.html

CSS is the style sheet standard that is implemented in browsers today and can be used right now. It is simple, but effective and elegant.

40.1.2.2   Work in progress

XML Linking Language (XLink)

Steve DeRose
Eve Maler

Information on web:
http://www.w3.org/TR/WD-xlink
Document included on CD-ROM:
./specs/w3c/WD-xlink.html

XLink is a crucial part of the XML standards family as it describes hyperlinking in XML documents and takes major steps beyond the hyperlinking provided by HTML.

XML Pointer Language (XPointer)

Eve Maler
Steve DeRose

Information on web:
http://www.w3.org/TR/WD-xptr
Document included on CD-ROM:
./specs/w3c/WD-xptr.html

XPointer is a companion standard to XLink that describes mechanisms for addressing a particular part of a document.

Extensible Style Language (XSL)

Sharon Adler
Anders Berglund
James Clark
Istvan Cseri
Paul Grosso
Jonathan Marsh
Gavin Nicol
Jean Paoli
David Schach
Henry S. Thompson
Chris Wilson

Information on web:
http://www.w3.org/Style/XSL/
Document included on CD-ROM:
./specs/w3c/note-xsl-970910.html

XSL is what has been produced so far in phase 3 of the XML effort: a proposal for the style sheet language for XML. The document included here, though already implemented in products, is just a proposal, and it seems likely that it will undergo considerable changes before it becomes a recommendation.

Note that XSL incorporates Standard ECMA-262 ECMAScript: A general purpose, cross-platform programming language, which can be found below.

Document Object Model (DOM)

Lauren Wood
Jared Sorensen
Lauren Wood
Steve Byrne
Mike Champion
Rick Gessner
Scott Isaacs
Arnaud Le Hors
Gavin Nicol
Peter Sharpe
Jared Sorensen

Bob Sutor
Vidur Apparao
Bill Smith
Chris Wilson

Information on web:
http://www.w3.org/DOM/
Document included on CD-ROM:
./specs/w3c/wd-dom/cover.html
   The Document Object Model is a very important related standard. It is
to be the standard API for accessing and manipulating XML and HTML
documents in browser, editors and other applications.

Namespaces in XML

Tim Bray
Dave Holander
Andrew Layman

Information on web:
http://www.w3.org/TR/WD-xml-names
Document included on CD-ROM:
./specs/w3c/wd-xml-names.html
   This namespace proposal sketches a way to ensure that names used in
XML DTDs are unique, so that names from different DTDs can be combined in a single document when need be.

40.2 | XML applications

These are XML document types that have been designed for specific purposes.

40.2.1 *W3C recommendations*

40.2.1.1 Approved recommendations

Mathematical Markup Language (MathML)

Patrick Ion
Robert Miner
Stephen Buswell
Stan Devitt
Angel Diaz
Nico Poppelier
Bruce Smith
Neil Soiffer
Robert Sutor
Stephen Watt

Information on web:
http://www.w3.org/Math/
Document included on CD-ROM:
./specs/w3c/rec-mathml/index.html

MathML is the long-awaited solution to a problem many scientists and teachers have struggled with: how to publish mathematical formulae on the web.

40.2.1.2 Work in progress

Channel Definition Format (CDF)

Information on web:
http://www.w3.org/TR/NOTE-CDFsubmit.html
Document included on CD-ROM:
./specs/w3c/NOTE-CDFsubmit.html

CDF is a DTD proposed by Microsoft for describing push channels. One interesting aspect of this format is that it is already in use in MSIE 4.0, so millions of CDF files already reside on the hard disks of users all over the world.

Web Interface Definition Language (WIDL)

Information on web:
http://www.w3.org/TR/NOTE-widl
Document included on CD-ROM:
./specs/w3c/note-widl.html
   WIDL is a proposed metalanguage for descriptions of web service interfaces, from which client code can be generated automatically.

Resource Description Framework (RDF) Schemas

Information on web:
http://www.w3.org/TR/WD-rdf-schema
Document included on CD-ROM:
./specs/w3c/wd-rdf-schema/index.html
   RDF provides a standard framework for describing resource metadata and as such is very important for the future development of search engines and other web navigation applications.

XML-Data

Andrew Layman
Edward Jung
Eve Maler
Henry S. Thompson
Jean Paoli
John Tigue
Norbert H. Mikula
Steve De Rose

Information on web:
http://www.w3.org/TR/1998/NOTE-XML-data-0105
Document included on CD-ROM:
./specs/w3c/note-xml-data.html
   XML-Data is a proposal to use XML documents, rather than markup declarations, to describe DTDs. With XML-Data, the document type definitions can be augmented with additional properties, such as inheritance and datatypes.

Precision Graphics Markup Language (PGML)

Information on web:
http://www.w3.org/TR/1998/NOTE-PGML
Document included on CD-ROM:
./specs/w3c/note-pgml.html

PGML is a scalable vector graphics language based on the imaging model of PostScript and PDF, with hooks for animation and dynamic behavior.

Standard Multimedia Integration Language (SMIL)

Stephan Bugaj
Dick Bulterman
Bruce Butterfield
Wo Chang
Guy Fouquet
Christian Gran
Mark Hakkinen
Lynda Hardman
Peter Hoddie
Klaus Hofrichter
Philipp Hoschka
Jack Jansen
George Kerscher
Rob Lanphier
Nabil Layaïda
Stephanie Leif
Jonathan Marsh
Sjoerd Mullender
Didier Pillet
Anup Rao
Lloyd Rutledge
Patrick Soquet
Warner ten Kate
Jacco van Ossenbruggen
Michael Vernick
Jin Yu

Information on web:

http://www.w3.org/TR/1998/PR-smil-19980409/
Document included on CD-ROM:
./specs/w3c/pr-smil/index.html

SMIL is a language for describing multimedia presentations. It allows for the integration of independent multimedia objects into these presentations.

40.2.2 *Other initiatives*

40.2.2.1   Approved standards

ECMAScript (ECMA-262)

Information on web:
http://www.ecma.ch/stand/ecma-262.htm
Document included on CD-ROM:
./specs/e262-pdf.pdf

ECMAScript is a merger of JavaScript and JScript, standardized and described in detail. It is included here because it is the programming language used in XSL.

40.2.2.2   Work in progress

Simple API for XML (SAX)

David Megginson
A cast of thousands

Information on web:
http://www.microstar.com/XML/SAX/
Document included on CD-ROM:
./specs/sax.html

SAX is an event-based API for XML parsers written in object-oriented languages. Using SAX enables application programmers to switch XML parsers without changing their applications.

SAX is not presently being standardized by an official standards body. It is a defacto standard developed by the participants of the xml-dev mailing list. You should visit the web page, since SAX was due for an update when we went to press.

Guidelines for using XML for Electronic Data Interchange (XML-EDI)

Martin Bryan
Benoît Marchal
Norbert Mikula
Bruce Peat
David RR Webber

Information on web:
http://www.geocities.com/WallStreet/Floor/5815/xmlediindex.htm
Document included on CD-ROM:
./specs/edi/index.html

XML-EDI describes the use of XML in online commerce for exchanging transaction information. This isn't a complete specification, but more of a guideline to function as a precursor to a formal specification.

Index

LICENSE AGREEMENT AND LIMITED WARRANTY

READ THE FOLLOWING TERMS AND CONDITIONS CAREFULLY BEFORE OPENING THIS SOFTWARE MEDIA PACKAGE. THIS LEGAL DOCUMENT IS AN AGREEMENT BETWEEN YOU AND PRENTICE-HALL, INC. (THE "COMPANY"). BY OPENING THIS SEALED SOFTWARE MEDIA PACKAGE, YOU ARE AGREEING TO BE BOUND BY THESE TERMS AND CONDITIONS. IF YOU DO NOT AGREE WITH THESE TERMS AND CONDITIONS, DO NOT OPEN THE SOFTWARE MEDIA PACKAGE. PROMPTLY RETURN THE UNOPENED SOFTWARE MEDIA PACKAGE AND ALL ACCOMPANYING ITEMS TO THE PLACE YOU OBTAINED THEM FOR A FULL REFUND OF ANY SUMS YOU HAVE PAID.

1.**GRANT OF LICENSE:** In consideration of your payment of the license fee, which is part of the price you paid for this product, and your agreement to abide by the terms and conditions of this Agreement, the Company grants to you a nonexclusive right to use and display the copy of the enclosed software program (hereinafter the "SOFTWARE") on a single computer (i.e., with a single CPU) at a single location so long as you comply with the terms of this Agreement. The Company reserves all rights not expressly granted to you under this Agreement.

2.**OWNERSHIP OF SOFTWARE:** You own only the magnetic or physical media (the enclosed software media) on which the SOFTWARE is recorded or fixed, but the Company retains all the rights, title, and ownership to the SOFTWARE recorded on the original software media copy(ies) and all subsequent copies of the SOFTWARE, regardless of the form or media on which the original or other copies may exist. This license is not a sale of the original SOFTWARE or any copy to you.

3.**COPY RESTRICTIONS:** This SOFTWARE and the accompanying printed materials and user manual (the "Documentation") are the subject of copyright. You may not copy the Documentation or the SOFTWARE, except that you may make a single copy of the SOFTWARE for backup or archival purposes only. You may be held legally responsible for any copying or copyright infringement which is caused or encouraged by your failure to abide by the terms of this restriction.

4.**USE RESTRICTIONS:** You may not network the SOFTWARE or otherwise use it on more than one computer or computer terminal at the same time. You may physically transfer the SOFTWARE from one computer to another provided that the SOFTWARE is used on only one computer at a time. You may not distribute copies of the SOFTWARE or Documentation to others. You may not reverse engineer, disassemble, decompile, modify, adapt, translate, or create derivative works based on the SOFTWARE or the Documentation without the prior written consent of the Company.

5. **TRANSFER RESTRICTIONS:** The enclosed SOFTWARE is licensed only to you and may not be transferred to any one else without the prior written consent of the Company. Any unauthorized transfer of the SOFTWARE shall result in the immediate termination of this Agreement.

6. **TERMINATION:** This license is effective until terminated. This license will terminate automatically without notice from the Company and become null and void if you fail to comply with any provisions or limitations of this license. Upon termination, you shall destroy the Documentation and all copies of the SOFTWARE. All provisions of this Agreement as to warranties, limitation of liability, remedies or damages, and our ownership rights shall survive termination.

7. **MISCELLANEOUS:** This Agreement shall be construed in accordance with the laws of the United States of America and the State of New York and shall benefit the Company, its affiliates, and assignees.

8.**LIMITED WARRANTY AND DISCLAIMER OF WARRANTY:** The Company warrants that the SOFTWARE, when properly used in accordance with the Documentation, will operate in substantial conformity with the description of the SOFTWARE set forth in the Documentation. The Company does not warrant that the SOFTWARE will meet your requirements or that the operation of the SOFTWARE will be uninterrupted or error-free. The Company warrants that the media on which the SOFTWARE is delivered shall be free from defects in materials and workmanship under normal use for a period of thirty (30) days from the date of your purchase. Your only remedy and the Company's only obligation under these limited warranties is, at the Company's option, return of the warranted item for a refund of any amounts paid by you or replacement of the item. Any replacement of SOFTWARE or media under the warranties shall not extend the original warranty period. The limited warranty set forth above shall not apply to any SOFTWARE which the Company determines in good faith has been subject to misuse, neglect, improper installation, repair, alteration, or damage by you. EXCEPT FOR THE EXPRESSED WARRANTIES SET FORTH ABOVE, THE COMPANY DISCLAIMS ALL WARRANTIES, EXPRESS OR IMPLIED, INCLUDING WITHOUT LIMITATION, THE IMPLIED WARRANTIES OF MERCHANTABILITY AND FITNESS FOR A PARTICULAR PURPOSE. EXCEPT FOR THE EXPRESS WARRANTY SET FORTH ABOVE, THE COMPANY DOES NOT WARRANT, GUARANTEE, OR MAKE ANY REPRESENTATION REGARDING THE USE OR THE RESULTS OF THE USE OF THE SOFTWARE IN TERMS OF ITS CORRECTNESS, ACCURACY, RELIABILITY, CURRENTNESS, OR OTHERWISE.

IN NO EVENT, SHALL THE COMPANY OR ITS EMPLOYEES, AGENTS, SUPPLIERS, OR CONTRACTORS BE LIABLE FOR ANY INCIDENTAL, INDIRECT, SPECIAL, OR CONSEQUENTIAL DAMAGES ARISING OUT OF OR IN CONNECTION WITH THE LICENSE GRANTED UNDER THIS AGREEMENT, OR FOR LOSS OF USE, LOSS OF DATA, LOSS OF INCOME OR PROFIT, OR OTHER LOSSES, SUSTAINED AS A RESULT OF INJURY TO ANY PERSON, OR LOSS OF OR DAMAGE TO PROPERTY, OR CLAIMS OF THIRD PARTIES, EVEN IF THE COMPANY OR AN AUTHORIZED REPRESENTATIVE OF THE COMPANY HAS BEEN ADVISED OF THE POSSIBILITY OF SUCH DAMAGES. IN NO EVENT SHALL LIABILITY OF THE COMPANY FOR DAMAGES WITH RESPECT TO THE SOFTWARE EXCEED THE AMOUNTS ACTUALLY PAID BY YOU, IF ANY, FOR THE SOFTWARE.

SOME JURISDICTIONS DO NOT ALLOW THE LIMITATION OF IMPLIED WARRANTIES OR LIABILITY FOR INCIDENTAL, INDIRECT, SPECIAL, OR CONSEQUENTIAL DAMAGES, SO THE ABOVE LIMITATIONS MAY NOT ALWAYS APPLY. THE WARRANTIES IN THIS AGREEMENT GIVE YOU SPECIFIC LEGAL RIGHTS AND YOU MAY ALSO HAVE OTHER RIGHTS WHICH VARY IN ACCORDANCE WITH LOCAL LAW.

ACKNOWLEDGMENT

YOU ACKNOWLEDGE THAT YOU HAVE READ THIS AGREEMENT, UNDERSTAND IT, AND AGREE TO BE BOUND BY ITS TERMS AND CONDITIONS. YOU ALSO AGREE THAT THIS AGREEMENT IS THE COMPLETE AND EXCLUSIVE STATEMENT OF THE AGREEMENT BETWEEN YOU AND THE COMPANY AND SUPERSEDES ALL PROPOSALS OR PRIOR AGREEMENTS, ORAL, OR WRITTEN, AND ANY OTHER COMMUNICATIONS BETWEEN YOU AND THE COMPANY OR ANY REPRESENTATIVE OF THE COMPANY RELATING TO THE SUBJECT MATTER OF THIS AGREEMENT.

Should you have any questions concerning this Agreement or if you wish to contact the Company for any reason, please contact in writing at the address below.

Robin Short
Prentice Hall PTR
One Lake Street
Upper Saddle River, New Jersey 07458

About the CD-ROM

The CD-ROM is packed with useful XML tools and information. There are three main areas:

- A hand-picked collection of genuine, productive, no-time-limit XML free software. There are over 55 titles. A full description can be found in the *Free XML software* chapter.
- A showcase for leading XML software and service providers. It features in-depth product and service information, white papers, XML samples, live demos, and trialware.
- The XML SPECtacular, a collection of the relevant specifications that you can browse, search, and print.

How to Use the CD-ROM

The CD-ROM supports Windows 95, Windows NT, and UNIX systems. Simply load index.htm, located in the root directory of the CD-ROM, into your Web browser.

License Agreement

Use of *The XML Handbook*™ CD-ROM is subject to the terms of the License Agreement and Limited Warranty on the preceding pages.